American Protestantism and United States Indian Policy, 1869–82

Robert H. Keller, Jr.

American
Protestantism
and United States
Indian Policy,
1869–82

University of Nebraska Press

Lincoln and London

Publication of this book was aided by
grants from the United Presbyterian Church
in the United States of America and the
Episcopal Diocese of North Dakota.

Copyright 1983 by the University of Nebraska Press

Manufactured in the United States of America

The paper in this book meets the guidelines for
permanence and durability of the Committee
on Production Guidelines for Book Longevity of
the Council on Library Resources.

Library of Congress Cataloging in Publication Data

Keller, Robert H.
American Protestantism and United States Indian
Policy, 1869–82.

Bibliography.
Includes index.
1. Indians of North America — Government relations —
1869–1934.   2. Indians of North America — Missions.
3. Church and state — United States.   4. Protestant
churches — Missions — United States.   I. Title.
E93.K28   1983   973'.0497   82-8514
ISBN 0-8032-2706-X   AACR2

Contents

Illustrations and Maps

Preface

This account began as an inquiry into what at first seemed an isolated incident in the history of American Church-State relations: President Ulysses S. Grant's delivery of the Indian Office into the hands of Christian mission boards. My initial goal was to better understand religious history and to interpret the meaning of the First Amendment, but then, unexpectedly, the scope and content of the study grew to include a century of federal Indian policy and the long-standing conflict between two cultures in America. Although Grant's Peace Policy was unique in many aspects, his reform involved ideologies and dilemmas characteristic of all Indian-white relations.

The Peace Policy took place during the last violent decade of conflict between aboriginal people and the United States government. The period saw the end of armed resistance by tribes and a beginning of comprehensive forced assimilation into the dominant culture. As I watched these developments, I encountered remarkable individuals: William Welsh, Felix Reville Brunot, E. P. Smith, Enoch Hoag, Henry B. Whipple, John Miles, Francis Walker, John Lowrie, F. J. Critchlow, Ely S. Parker, John Johnson Emegebowh, Lawrie Tatum, Samuel Hinman, James Wilbur. Their thought and experiences changed my naïve perceptions of the 1870s.

Interpretations and conclusions obviously inform this book, and a few summary assumptions may prove useful to readers. I believe that land—its ownership, control, and use—was the single most persistent factor in Indian-white relations and in defining government policy. My inquiry began with a belief that European conquest of Indian land had been unjust, un-Christian, and inevitable. That belief was confirmed. During the struggle over a continent, myths about racial superiority and national expansion coexisted with Christian ideals of justice and human dignity. When unavoidable conflicts arose over control of land, as they did in the administration of the Peace Policy, ideals fell to the wayside. Material motives such as land ownership and the temptation of new, easy wealth proved more powerful than a desire for justice.

By the end of my study I came to concur with the judgment delivered by Ulysses S. Grant in his Farewell Address of 1877. Assessing his unfortunate presidency and his own motives, Grant concluded:

> It is impossible, where so many trusts are to be allotted, that the right parties should be chosen in every instance. History shows that no administration from the time of Washington to the present has been free from these mistakes. But I leave comparisons to history, claiming only that I have acted in every instance from a conscientious desire to do what was right, constitutional, within the law, and for the very best interests of the whole people.

When Grant and the reformers placed ideals into practice, events did not necessarily work out as planned. Examination of the Peace Policy dispels any easy notion that moral awareness and humane intentions during the 1870s could have ended America's "century of dishonor."

This study also rejects the concept of an absolute separation of Church and State. Such a motif finds little support in the history of federal Indian policy. Grant himself believed in a strict separation of religion and government, yet his pragmatic view of politics and his concern for Indians joined forces with an evangelical Protestant drive for social reform. The Peace Policy was a logical product in the long tradition of government-missionary cooperation. Grant offered evangelicals, Friends, philanthropists, and other Christians a bedrock experience to test their beliefs through performance. A Quaker committee of that time declared that "no such opportunity was ever before offered to demonstrate to the world, the practical and availing nature of the testimony for peace committed to the Church by Him who is declared to be the Prince of Peace." In Washington, D.C., and on the western frontier, Grant tested Christian willingness to sacrifice, to suffer, and even to die for religious conviction. Because churchmen were human and limited, they failed. Land rushes and railroads overwhelmed moral precepts and good faith.

On a happier note, a reward for any researcher is working with archivists, museum staff, librarians, and other persons who preserve historical evidence. Without exception I found them generous with their time and enthusiastic in their help. I especially wish to thank Jane K. Smith, Robert M. Kvasnicka, William B. Miller, Gerald B. McDonald, V. Nelle Bellamy, George Gardner, Arna Bontemps, Hazel Christiansen, Mary Avary, Colton Storm, Frederick Hall, Will Robinson, Mary Dempsey, Harvey Arnold, Gordon Collier, Mary Walker, Dorothy G. Harris, Marjorie F. Davis, Peter VandenBerge, Kathryn Johnson, and Hazel Mills for their assistance. Karen Daniels Petersen kindly allowed me to examine her family papers, and I am grateful to Clifford Samuelson and the Protestant Episcopal Church for a generous travel grant. The Bureau for Faculty Research at Western Washington University has provided prompt and enthusiastic support at various stages in the revision of manuscript copy.

I also wish to thank teachers, friends, and students, especially R. Pierce Beaver, who greatly enhanced my understanding of Christian missions, Sidney E. Mead, Bernard Weisberger, Martin E. Marty, Arthur Mann, Kathleen Keller, Vine Deloria, Jr., Stephanie Fox, Charles Bulger, Robin Richards, Rand F. Jack, Alvin M. Josephy, Jr., Patricia Karlberg, Francis Paul Prucha, Steven Brinn, and Florence Preder. To the extent to which they have persuaded me to maintain or change my ideas and have encouraged me to persist in writing, they share responsibility for this book.

American Protestantism and United States Indian Policy, 1869–82

Introduction

*I would not have the anni-
versaries of our victories
celebrated, nor those of our
defeats made fast days and
spent in humiliation and
prayer; but I would like to
see truthful history written.*

Ulysses S. Grant, *Memoirs*
(1885)

One Monday morning in July 1882, Dr. John M.
Reid, secretary of the Missionary Society of the
Methodist Church, wrote a lengthy letter to
Henry M. Teller, secretary of the interior. Reid
complained that he had not been consulted
about the hiring of two new agents by the
Bureau of Indian Affairs. Teller's reply arrived in
New York within a week. He informed Reid and
the Methodists that they no longer controlled
federal appointments, that they had no right to
nominate Indian agents, and that he had no idea
what Reid meant by a "peace policy" of the
government. Like Henry Teller of that time,
most Americans today would not know what
Reid meant by the United States' Indian Peace
Policy of 1869-82. People today would be even
more baffled to learn that the policy, the most
radical bureaucratic and ideological reform in the
history of United States Indian administration,
had been initiated by Ulysses S. Grant.

Grant's Peace Policy officially began with his
inaugural address in 1869, the same year that
John Wesley Powell began exploring the Grand
Canyon of the Colorado and the year that the
Union Pacific joined the Central Pacific at
Promontory Point, Utah. During the 1868 election campaign religious leaders, military officers,
and various congressmen had demanded reform
of abuses in the Indian Office. In reply, Grant
instituted changes in Indian administration that
effectively placed Indian reservations under

1

Church control. Assuming that churchmen were honest and capable of "elevating" Indian tribes, the president first gave the Society of Friends and then other denominations the right to nominate federal agents for more than seventy Indian reservations. In addition, Grant extended official sanction and financial support to Indian missions and Christian schools, and he created a Church-related advisory board of commissioners authorized to fight corruption within the Department of the Interior.

The Grant Peace Policy is the most extensive and prolonged attempt in United States history at cooperation between the churches and the federal government. Yet for a century historians and scholars seldom mentioned it in their discussions of social reform, Church-State relations, and American religious history. Even though it was an experiment that tested the vitality of religion in nineteenth-century America and hastened the destruction of Native American cultures, one rarely finds reference to the Peace Policy in history textbooks. Most Indian people, if they have heard of it at all, know few of the details. In the past ten years there have been several new accounts of the Peace Policy as part of various tribal histories or as studies of government policy and humanitarian reform. This book differs from those studies in that it is primarily a history of the Protestant Church's involvement.

To understand the adoption, failure, and meaning of the Peace Policy, its implications for Church-State relations, pacifism, moral reform, Indian-white relations, and the impact of culture on religious faith and mission, it is necessary to appreciate the place of established religion—"American civil religion"—and of American Indian tribes in our national life. Grant's experiment was radical but not unique, and it did not involve a significant departure from some imagined tradition of separation of Church and State. To the contrary, his policy followed logically from previous history in Indian affairs and was the natural result of cultural assumptions held by reformers, Indian missionaries, and government officials.

Evangelical American Protestants of Grant's day did not, to be sure, believe in creating a State Church, but they did believe in a State enlightened by the Christian Gospel and in a State cooperating with the churches to achieve common social goals. In the nineteenth century most Americans thought that school prayers, Christian morals, and the Bible were essential to education, white or Indian, public or private. They looked on local, state, and federal governments not as secular bodies, but as divinely created institutions obligated to assist Christianity in the moral and religious redemption of human beings. The protection and assimilation of Indian people likewise was a concern of nineteenth-century Protestants and Roman Catholics. More than any other reform groups, the churches sought and obtained government aid to educate Indians and to transform native cultures. Examination of the Peace Policy, then, can help destroy the myth that the American Church embraced our present notions of religious liberty as well as the separation of Church and State in the nineteenth century.

No one at the time considered Grant's Peace Policy as a radical departure from past practice, either in the sense of discovering a new Christian concern for Indians or of departing from some supposed tradition of separation of Church and State. Every one of Grant's "innovations" had historical precedent in principle and practice. The Peace Policy rested on the assumption that Christian missions had been successful, which in turn depended on two principles that Americans had accepted for at least a century: that Christianity alone could civilize the American Indians, and that Christianity needed and deserved the support of the federal government in doing so.

Advocates of the new policy of 1869 assumed that white Christians would become concerned about Indians, forget doctrinal differences, and make sacrifices of time and money to help the government. The reformers believed that Indians respected missionaries and that Indian missions had flourished prior to 1869. Unfortunately, most advocates of the Peace Policy knew little about missions or Indian history. They did not, or would not, recognize that most Protestant Indian missionaries before 1870 had experienced overwhelming discouragement and frequent failure. Had Grant and the reformers known more about the past, they would have found little to inspire their confidence that the Peace Policy could succeed. The factors that caused these past failures included the conditions on the frontier, the dynamics of American expansionism, racial attitudes, cultural differences, and conflicts within the churches themselves.[1] As the *Missionary Herald* observed in 1852, "The destiny of the red man has been a hard problem for the Christian." The factors that made this so had not significantly changed by 1869.

To an average Protestant American citizen of over a century ago the idea that Christian missions could consistently fail would have seemed much more startling than the idea that Church and State should assist each other. Today a program patterned on the Peace Policy, giving the Christian churches nominal control over an entire branch of the federal government, would be incomprehensible and constitutionally impossible. In 1870 such a policy drew little public attention because most Americans did not question cooperation between Church and State. Not until the mid-1860s did an evangelical Protestant nativist movement begin that by 1890 would produce the modern dogma of complete separation of religion and government. Grant's Indian policy, an expression of traditional beliefs that the United States was a Christian commonwealth and that government should aid religion in improving American society, largely escaped such criticism. The Peace Policy was an expansion of practices and traditions acquired over 250 years.

Throughout early American history Church and government had been joined officially in the French, Spanish, and English colonies. The First

Amendment to the Constitution did little to resolve that issue but only expressed the future terms of debate over Church-State relations in the new United States. Perry Miller has written that most Protestants never believed in religious liberty, but instead stumbled onto its practical value. Sidney E. Mead describes American Church-State relations as "practice searching for principles" while Americans trusted their democracy "to muddle through to truth, mercy, and justice regarding the problem of Church and State."[2] The American nation, which began with a vague constitutional statement about nonestablishment, proceeded in the nineteenth century to embrace both separation and cooperation in limited degrees at different times and in changing situations. No towering "wall of separation" appeared. Trial and error, conflicting precedents, and flexible interpretations slowly accumulated because American attitudes were pragmatic and most of the solutions political. The Peace Policy was an experiment following in this tradition, and neither a violation nor an implementation of doctrine.[3]

Most important in the "sympathetic relation" between the churches and government was public education and the belief that teaching the Bible provided the foundation stone for American society. This reasoning, which placed Christian teachings firmly in the public school curriculum, likewise inspired the federal government to finance missions and religious education for Indians. If the Christian faith seemed absolutely essential for a classroom in Detroit or New York, it was also indispensable to promote love of country among Indian children. An early-nineteenth-century missionary, Cyrus Kingsbury, explained to Choctaw chiefs why they were so weak: they lacked "the good book," the book that taught white men "to be industrious, to be sober, to educate their children, to obey the Great Spirit. The red people never had this book. . . . This is the reason why they have become few and feeble and poor. Their father the President, and the good people, have taken these things into consideration, and have sent the missionaries with the good book to instruct them."[4]

The common cause of Church and State in Indian missions produced both cooperation and conflict. Missionaries, being among the few educated, articulate white men and women living in or near Indian country, frequently found themselves to be the only critics of Indian agents, whose cooperation was crucial for the success of a mission. Churches therefore occasionally sought an agent's removal and endeavored to control agency appointments. And since missionaries knew native languages and usually had the confidence of a few tribesmen, the government often heeded the advice of clergy and sought their aid in negotiations. The War Department used a Moravian, John Heckewelder, and a delegation of Friends in an effort to pacify Indians before the Battle of Fallen Timbers in 1794. In 1820 the government directly assisted the Reverend Jedidiah Morse's survey of the Great Lakes tribes. The

Reverend John Schermerhorn helped negotiate the removal of the Miami, Potawatomi, Chickasaw, and Cherokee Indians between 1832 and 1837. The federal government considered Father Pierre De Smet a specialist in Indian treaty making and employed him as a federal negotiator at the Fort Laramie Council of 1851 and as an emissary to the Upper Missouri Sioux in 1864, 1867, and 1869.

In exchange for the government's use of ministers, missionaries, and priests in the Indian country, churches received moral support and money. As early as 1789 Secretary of War Henry Knox wrote to George Washington recommending that "missionaries, of excellent moral character, should be appointed to reside in their nations. . . . These men should be made the instruments to work on the Indians." Washington told the Moravians that his administration wished to cooperate with their mission, Thomas Jefferson sent government funds to Indian missions in 1802, and Cyrus Kingsbury of the American Board of Commissioners for Foreign Missions received an enthusiastic endorsement from James Madison, who promised to build mission schools and send supplies. James Monroe followed Madison's example when he visited Kingsbury's mission and instructed the Indian agent to build a chapel and to pay Kingsbury's expenses. A decade later President John Quincy Adams reminded Congress of its duty to convert Indians to "the doctrines of Christianity."[5] Both moral support, as when General Andrew Jackson introduced Kingsbury to the Cherokees on behalf of President Monroe, and financial aid proved extremely important in maintaining the tenuous mission stations. In 1840 missionary Isaac McCoy accused his own Baptist denomination of criminal neglect of Indian missions because for twelve years the church had given nothing: *"They have been sustained almost wholly by means obtained from the Government of the United States. This is a startling fact."*[6]

Thus long before the announcement of the Peace Policy, a pervasive identification of Church and State seemed a fact to the Indian tribes. Missionaries did little to discourage this misunderstanding because it provided official sanction and prestige for their work. Seneca Chief Red Jacket told his people that the government promised to send Christian teachers "for our own good."[7] In 1818 two missionaries informed another tribe that "the Good Spirit . . . has brought us to your nation . . . Brothers, the President of the United States and our Fathers . . . have sent us to teach your children and to preach the Gospel to you."[8] But such identification had its liabilities. When fur traders, the Indian Office, or the army mistreated the tribes, missionaries shared the blame. An unpopular Minnesota treaty turned Indians against American Board missionariees. Fond du Lac chiefs argued that the government had provisioned the mission and the president had sent the missionaries: "Those who sent you here want our Country. You are their forerunner. They

will come and ask for a little and then take a great deal."[9] Part of what
the missionaries themselves took were treaty funds intended to pay for
Indian land, a method the government used to support missions and a practice that some Indians resented and protested when they came to understand
it.[10]

Much government aid came to churches from erratic and unplanned administrative actions, but consistent funding resulted from federal legislation
that created the Civilization Fund. In 1818 a committee in the House of
Representatives reported on trade with Indians. It cited the success of missionaries in foreign lands as an example of what might be accomplished for
peoples living in "superstition, bigotry, and ignorance." Subsequent recommendations from this committee, together with lobbying by Thomas Mc-
Kenney, then superintendent of Indian trade, and Jedidiah Morse, and the
recognized inability of the churches to support Indian missions, led in 1819 to
a congressional appropriation of ten thousand dollars for Indian education
and civilization. The churches did not originate this plan; neither did they
question it. As the appropriation grew larger each year, and as the Civilization Fund came under attack, the churches quickly provided rationale to
silence critics. An 1822 church petition pleaded for the fund's continuation
in order to uphold the nation's honor, an honor that otherwise would be
blackened by the "cruel destiny which avarice stands ready to inflict" on Indian tribes. Two years later the American Board requested funds as "a proper
act of cooperation" between Church and State in bringing the Bible and the
skills of agriculture to Indians.[11] Even the fund's opponents did not raise
constitutional questions when Baptists, Moravians, Episcopalians, Presbyterians, Roman Catholics, the New York Missionary Society, and the Cumber-
land Missionary Society complied with regulations and accepted federal
money. Government financial support of missions reached sixty thousand
dollars annually and totaled a half-million dollars over a thirty-year period.[12]

By mid-century the Civilization Fund had improved Indian missions, but
had not stimulated the churches as much as originally expected. The commissioner of Indian affairs expressed disappointment in the program and
suggested that the government establish its own training schools that the
mission societies could operate. "By this measure . . . a far greater amount of
good will be accomplished than by the system heretofore pursued, of appor-
tioning the funds among different missionary societies to be expended as
they might deem best without any well defined and progressive plan, pre-
scribed by the Department; and by which it is feared comparatively little
good has been done, considering the amount expended."[13] But the churches
and mission boards, for their part, complained that they received no guidelines
or direction from the government as to how to spend the large sums of
money that they received.[14] After 1850 the Civilization Fund was gradually

discarded; its constitutionality was never challenged or tested in its fifty-year history.[15]

Presbyterians, Baptists, Methodists, Catholics, and the American Board received federal grants to support Indian missions for seventy-five years before the Peace Policy began. Indians were a foreign people and the principle of Church-State separation, such as it was, did not apply to red men as it did to white men, a sentiment succinctly expressed in a resolution passed by the Illinois Conference of the Methodist Episcopal Church in 1834: "*Resolved*: that it is inexpedient for any member of this Conference to hold any office of profit or honor in the government of our country, except in the case of Missions to Indian tribes."

In 1822 John C. Calhoun had told the House of Representatives that the government paid missionaries to demonstrate the virtues of sobriety, honesty, and hard work, to "impress on the minds of the Indian the friendly and benevolent views of the Government . . . as it may deem necessary for their civilization and happiness. . . . A contrary course of conduct [by missionaries] cannot fail to incur the displeasure of Government."[16] One might have expected such warnings and financial dependence to silence Christian criticism of the government, but they did not. Isaac McCoy unsparingly attacked the War Department for not stemming the flow of liquor onto reservations. Quakers rebuked the government for not protecting treaty rights and for laxity toward traders and squatters. Missionaries protested invasion of tribal lands, abuse of Indians by the army, harmful treaties, and misconduct by agents. Methodist William Goode said the United States had good theories, but in practice it abused Indians through its "blood-sucker" agents. Goode claimed that missionaries fought alone to halt "all this tide of corruption and debasement." In Minnesota, where missions relied heavily on military protection and aid, Mary Riggs publicly denounced the army as "a sink of iniquity, a school of vice." And in Kansas, Wisconsin, Michigan, Florida, and the Indian Territory, missionaries assumed that the welfare of Indians and of missions were identical, and they tried to force the firing of agents they considered indolent and evil. Some clergy and missionaries became so disgusted with the government that they accused their mission boards of compromising the Gospel by accepting federal largess. "The Church of Christ," wrote missionary Moses Adams from Lac Qui Parle in 1851, "has in all ages, not only independent of, but often in opposition to all the combined power of civil government, sustained herself."[17] Nowhere did missionaries find themselves in more difficult opposition to government policy than over the removal of eastern tribes to the West. The best-known but not the only example of missionary confrontation with state and federal government on behalf of the Indians was the American Board's defense of the Cherokees in the 1830s. Some missionaries assisted the government in removal programs, others resisted, but there is no evidence that federal money consistently determined what position a church would take.

In summary, Church and State in America had been intimately associated for 250 years before the Peace Policy. Cooperation between missions and government began during the colonial period and continued throughout the nineteenth century. Clergy and missionaries such as Samuel Kirkland, John Heckewelder, Jedidiah Morse, John Schermerhorn, James Finley, and Isaac McCoy aided the United States. The government in return provided employment, chapels, helpful agents, and dollars.[18] Indians viewed Church and State as one, a view that proved both a liability and an asset for the Church. Yet the dependence of the Church on the State did not silence Christian criticism. Few Americans spoke for Indians, but many of those who did were missionaries and churchmen. For those who remained silent on the most difficult Indian question of the early century, Indian removal from the East, the reason was not fear of the government but a pietistic, apolitical religion. Evan Jones, a Baptist, understood his responsibility for the suffering and oppressed Cherokees to be "administering consolation to dying saints, pointing awakened sinners to the Lamb of God, as the only ground of hope." The American Board believed that more was necessary, but neither Jones nor the Board were intimidated by government. Whether pietistic or activist, the churches had been long involved with government and Indians. The Peace Policy did not surprise anyone familiar with the history of Indian-white relations.

Cooperation with the government was not sufficient to ensure the success of Protestant Indian missions. To the contrary, by 1869 most of those missions had failed or only barely existed. How, then, can one explain the government again turning to the churches and the missionary societies as the solution to the "Indian question" of the 1870s? That can only be answered through understanding developments in the decade immediately prior to the Peace Policy and through recognizing that certain religious myths were powerful enough to override actual failure.

The 1860s constitute one of the most pivotal decades in American history, a period in which the nation began its rapid shift from a rural agrarian society to an urban industrial social order.[19] The disruption caused by the Civil War, religious revivals, reform interest in other causes, Social Darwinism, a dilution of Christian faith through conformity with American culture, fascination with foreign lands, and the harsh life on reservations had caused Indian missions to founder. Therefore the government did not turn to the churches for help in 1869 and 1870 because missions were strong and vigorous. Instead, a period of desperate violence in Indian-white relations and then the Peace Policy itself were required to reawaken a limited Christian concern for Indians.

The 1860s, which saw the completion of the first transcontinental railroad, also saw frontier violence between Indian and white reach a peak. After twenty years of increasingly hostile contact with wagons on the overland trails, there came the Colorado, Idaho, and Montana gold rushes; the decimation of the bison herds; Indian conflict with western businessmen and traders; and the fresh influx of settlers on railroads. The results were the Sioux uprising of 1862, the Sand Creek Massacre of 1864, the Navajos' long forced walk to Bosque Redondo, Fetterman's defeat in 1866, the closing of the Bozeman Trail by the Sioux at mid-decade, all of which produced a series of congressional investigations and reports. Some reports blamed the Indians, others blamed the white invasion, and all agreed that the status quo was intolerable.

The plains Indians' violent resistance could be interpreted as aggression and savagery requiring forced repression, or it could be blamed on the federal government and on the Indian Office in particular. The last course was taken by two influential reports late in the decade, one by a joint congressional committee, the so-called Doolittle Committee, and the other from a group of distinguished citizens appointed to form the Peace Commission. Sneered at on the frontier, the Congress's *Report on the Condition of the Indian Tribes* (1867) and the study by the Peace Commissioners (1868) became important documents that helped to arouse the nation to the cause of the Indian reform.[20]

The two reports contended that Indians were perishing in "the irrepressible conflict between a superior and an inferior race"; the reasons given for the conflict left doubts about exactly who was superior. Liquor, loss of game, disease, starvation, lack of shelter, political corruption, "lawless white men," and constant warfare were destroying the tribes. The joint committee opposed returning Indians to the War Department, which had supervised them until 1849. Not soldiers, but teachers, missionaries, and honest men were needed. Businessmen who contracted to supply annuity goods had been guilty of "the most outrageous and systematic *swindling* and *robbery*." Government agents purchased sheet-iron shovels, shoes with paper soles, blankets made of "shoddy and glue," iron spoons, mirrors, jew's harps, "useless gewgaws," and hair oil at prices 100 percent above the market value. One tribe acquired a thousand elastic garters. During the Lincoln administration, Indian agents on annual salaries of $1,500 somehow could save $50,000 in three years. An Indian recalled an agent: "When he come he bring everything in a little bag, when he leave it take two steamboats to carry away his things." The agent at the Tulalip reserve on Puget Sound had used government funds to hire loggers to cut Indian timber for the agent's profit. On the Oregon coast, an agent had sold stolen whiskey, rifles, and ammunition to Indians. William Welsh, an independent Episcopal investigator, reported frauds on the Sioux reserve that netted white entrepreneurs a profit of $250,000 in one summer. He discovered that the government had paid $3.50 for sacks of flour worth $2.00, and that it had purchased steers nearly three hundred pounds short of their reported weight. The congressional committee discovered agents who awarded contracts to the highest bidders, who "lost" funds, whose account books strangely disappeared, and who reportedly forced Indians to eat horse feed, dead mules, and poisoned wolves. Until the Indian Office was released from its "political thralldom," Welsh, the congressmen, and the Peace Commissioners all agreed, its wards were "doomed to perpetual beggary at a fearful cost to the nation."[21]

Caught between Indians, the Indian Office, speculators, and the reformers, the federal Indian agent on the reservation rightly or wrongly became the scapegoat for corruption and violence in the system. Earlier duties of agents had been to protect the rights of Indians and enforce trade regulations, but as Indian reservations grew in number after 1840 and as the government assumed responsibility for feeding, clothing, and teaching the tribes, the agent was expected to serve as a military liaison officer, a policeman, an educator, a purchaser and distributor of huge amounts of food, and a banker who dispensed treaty annuity funds. In a period of administrative turmoil and inefficiency, and with much political power directly dependent on patronage, an agency assignment became a ripe plum in the spoils system.[22] For the weak and dishonest it was a wide-open opportunity for quick wealth; for the honest man, it was an impossible job. Before the Jackson administration, being an Indian agent could be a career position for a man of respected competence, yet even Lawrence Taliaferro and Henry Rowe Schoolcraft, who spent twenty years in the government service, could make errors and poor judgments, and they could experience failure and personal bitterness over their jobs.[23] After appointments fell under the patronage system, the public reputation of the service declined until it joined the myth of the existence of an Indian Ring as one of the ready explanations for problems in Indian administration. In certain cases there was ample basis for the public skepticism, as at the Wichita agency, where a succession of seven almost totally incompetent agents in a twelve-year period contributed to a story of disaster, violence, and corruption.[24] Nevertheless, even for a man whom many considered an ideal agent and "model Christian warrior," such as General James Carleton at Bosque Redondo, life at an agency could be destructive and brutal. Although Carleton met all the requirements considered necessary for an honest agent, his administration of the Navajos suffered accusations of fraud, was denounced by local whites, lacked minimal equipment and funds, and failed in its agricultural program.[25]

Indian agents absorbed much Church criticism, both from the denominational headquarters in the East and from missionaries on the western reservations. Baptists, Methodists, Episcopalians, and Presbyterians accused unfriendly agents of lacking "talent, industry, energy or the proper spirit" and agents in retaliation reported that the "inactive, dronish" habits of missionaries set a poor example for Indians. Episcopal bishop Henry Whipple described agents as generally "a disgrace to a Christian nation; whiskey-sellers, bar-room loungers, debauchers." Convinced that good agents were essential to reform, Whipple advised Lincoln that the president must select men of "purity, temperance, industry, and unquestioned integrity . . . men who love their work. They must be something better than so many drudges fed at the public crib."[26]

Whipple's harsh condemnation of agents as a class was unfair and extreme. Not every agent proved incompetent, most were underpaid and abused, and many resisted incredible temptations. An Indian agent enjoyed a maximum of temptation and a minimum of restraint. He usually lacked any experience or training and came to a reservation totally ignorant of Indian life and languages, conditions that also plagued missionaries. From the day of their appointment until their replacement, Indian agents had to endure the slander of rival job-hunters and the whims of politicians. Whatever trust and understanding of Indians an agent managed to acquire was lost when the spoils system evicted him from office. To cite an example, between 1854 and 1867 New Mexico's four Indian agencies operated under eleven superintendents and thirty-eight agents. Contributing to rapid turnover were low salaries, chaotic administrative rules, and miserable living conditions. Retiring agents often stripped the agency of all supplies, leaving the new appointee destitute and empty-handed.[27] Not until 1875 did Congress require strict inventories and accounting of agency finances.

To blame the "savage" Indian or the "corrupt" Indian agent of the federal government is to reduce human history to single causes and individual culprits, and the extent to which any reform would be based on such a concept meant that the reform would be too simple. Although the federal government did fail to implement many policies, it was not as inconsistent or inept as its critics and reformers seemed to think. Regard for Indian rights, control of the Indian trade, and other elements in a just and humane policy had evolved by 1830 and in fact remained federal policy for a century. The problem was, before and after 1869, that the government of the United States had committed itself to three contradictory ends: protecting Indian rights, promoting westward expansion, and protecting American citizens. The Indian Bureau and its agents were never intended to serve mainly as an Indian rights association. Government practice, regardless of policy, depended on white society, promoted white expansion, reflected white values, and protected white frontiersmen. The government ultimately was committed to its own citizens, to settlers, to white taxpayers and voters. In reality, all effective

Indian policy was destined to succeed or fail in relation to local communities in the West, not in relation to official thinking in Washington, D.C. Indian affairs were but a small impediment to the powerfully expanding nation of the 1860s.[28]

The 1860s were also a decade of evangelical revival in the northeast. With revival came the usual impulse to set society as a whole on the correct moral course.[29] This course included the end of violence in Indian affairs and the belief that a Christian commonwealth could accomplish that goal despite its failures in the past. Such a belief was encouraged by the churches' success in hiding the failures of missions and by the popularity of two ideas: the legend of Marcus Whitman and the myth about William Penn.

The Whitman legend contended that, despite the destruction of the famous Oregon mission by the Cayuse Indians in 1847, the enterprise had nevertheless achieved success. Developed and propagated by Henry Harmon Spalding, himself a survivor of the massacre, the legend glossed over Whitman's shortcomings as a missionary and instead emphasized his service to the United States, especially his imagined "saving" of the Pacific Northwest from the British Empire. The result was the spread of the idea of the missionary as a powerful, effective, and patriotic hero.

The Penn myth was even more persuasive. Basically it held that William Penn through his 1682 treaty with the Delaware Indians secured peace in Pennsylvania. The honest dealings of Penn and the Quakers were a model for Europeans to follow that would prevent war and secure peace on the frontier. The subsequent history of frontier Pennsylvania and the fate of Indians in that colony made little difference as the myth was enthusiastically promoted by the Society of Friends and other humanitarians who insisted on alternatives to violence. Artists Benjamin West and Edward Hicks romanticized Penn negotiating with Indians beneath a giant elm on the banks of the Schuykill River: "The leopard with the harmless kid laid down / And not one savage beast was seen to frown." In its various forms this veneration of William Penn and the folklore of the Holy Experiment asserted that Indians had never shed a drop of Quaker blood, that Quakers of all men especially cared for and understood Indians, that Indians never broke a treaty, and that any dispute over land could be settled peacefully if only Penn's example of negotiation was followed. Throughout the 1860s and '70s few other ideas about Indian relations were repeated so often by humanitarians on behalf of Indian reform.

The story of American Christianity and the Indians contains failure, dishonor, and tragedy. It can also qualify the meaning that historians such as Peter Mode, Frederick Jackson Turner, and William Warren Sweet assigned to the frontier—progress, optimism, endless success, heroism. John Finerty, an Irish immigrant and correspondent for the *Chicago Times*, found the West barren of historical events, lacking in significance, and boring. In the Powder River country of 1876 Finerty saw only "sad desolate old hills, that have no history," and for him the Big Horn Mountains were "mere heaps of rock, sand and clay, destitute of . . . the magic lights and shades of antique story."[30] Such declarations about the United States, the virgin land, confirm speculations that many of its people have little sense of the past and are innocent of their history. Reinhold Niebuhr, for example, censured Americans for their careless confidence, their shallow optimism, and their persistent failure to perceive the "grand and tragic outlines" of human history. C. Vann Woodward argues that the South's experience contradicts the nation's stereotypes: the majority celebrated victory and success while the South knew frustration and defeat; the nation boasted freedom and wealth while the South experienced bondage and poverty.[31] We are not limited to the South for conditions that undercut national pretensions. In the history of Indian people since white contact, and in the painful story of the Peace Policy in particular, "infant illusions of innocence and virtue" disappeared as white men and Indians alike experienced humiliation and failure.

There were no easy programs for dispossessing ten million original inhabitants on the North American continent. Repeatedly men and women experienced moral failures and dilemmas, even to the extent of admitting that the treatment of Indians was one subject about which Americans did not boast in Europe. Instead, on this issue, one writer remarked, "We are constrained to confess something like failure to accomplish the purposes of our national destiny."[32] But most confessions were too restrained to please European critics or American humanitarians to whom the nation's westward expansion seemed to destroy Indians without compunction. Yet when humanitarian authors condemned white Americans as hypocritical or, at best, shameless, their literature characteristically failed to describe the complexity of the Indian problem. There were, to be sure, frontier demands for extermination; there were also demands from people who believed that Indians must be treated fairly. Philanthropists, missionaries, and peacemakers constantly reminded the nation of its injustice to Indian tribes.

The humanitarians' approach to Indian affairs acknowledged the guilt of white people and helped to break down national delusions of innocence and virtue. Yet, often smug, shortsighted, and self-righteous, the Indian reformers, too, frequently wrapped themselves in cloaks of innocence and virtue. In a study devoted to Indian reform, it is well to remind ourselves at the outset that suffering and social injustice in the United States have not been limited to Indians. Indian reformers and missionaries often were obsessed with their cause, making it easy for them to overlook the widespread disillusionment and despair among whites and blacks and thereby magnify the suffering of Indians out of proportion. They forgot the conflict of white men in the Civil

War—a blood bath that dwarfed the Indian wars—and the hatred of privileged whites toward "crackers" and "white trash." They overlooked the pitched battles over placer mines, land claims, and railroad rights. White contempt for "riffraff" and for blacks was as vicious as any hatred directed toward Indians. Indians on reservations were less abused than blacks in southern prisons and no more neglected than immigrants in Massachusetts, where, in the 1870s, there were droves "of poverty-stricken children, often girls, clad only in one or two ragged and dirty garments, down on their hands and knees in the gutters, greedily picking out of the mud and dirt and eating the bits of spoiled and decaying fruit which had been thrown away."[33] Along the overland trails of the West and under the searing July skies of Nebraska, Wyoming, and Montana the destruction and starvation of white settlers as well as Indians ground history into the soil. Often misled by propaganda and primed with false hopes, emigrants struggled with ague, death, and starvation. In 1846 Francis Parkman observed the discarded furniture and shallow graves of children dug by emigrants on the Oregon Trail, "abundant and melancholy traces of their progress." He found carved on a plank "standing upright on the summit of a grassy hill: 'MARY ELLIS, Died May 7th, 1845, Aged Two Months.' Such tokens were of common occurrence." Far from recreating the heroic pioneer character imagined by nostalgic historians like Mode and Turner, Parkman described the western emigrants as wistful, angry, melancholy, afraid, "divided between regrets for the home they had left and fear of the deserts and savages before them."[34] On the plains men and women met a new environment as immense and overpowering as the sea, filling them with a "nauseating loneliness," inflicting suffering in a land extreme in summer droughts and winter blizzards. Some suffered, surrendered, and turned east: "In God we trusted / In Kansas we busted."

The American West was not a garden and not without tragedy, whether red, white, or black. If wandering Omahas and Pawnees knew dispossession, death, and hunger, so did the many Irish, German, and English families who marched onto their vacated lands. If Indians felt racial hatred, so did black soldiers and the Chinese. To read Indian-white relations as a morality play in which the actors are greedy settlers, corrupt Indian agents, ecologically minded Indians, martyred chiefs, drunken fur traders, and noble missionaries, all conforming to a plot of the white man's "consistent injustice and insensitivity" and "almost unrelieved record of destruction of Indian social cultural integrity,"[35] is an oversimplification, an ideological and not a historical conclusion. Such a view assumes that an ethical answer to the Indian problem was possible and that the answer was deliberately rejected by the United States. In melodrama, the tragedy, pathos, and irony of American Indian history is lost, the diversity of good and evil forgotten. Indian-white history is tragic not because Colorado militia shot Indian children for rifle practice, not because whites valued gold more than solemn promises, not because starving people were evicted from their homelands, but because these events took place in spite of humane policies, in spite of genuine commitment to reform, and in spite of devoted efforts by good people to prevent evil from happening.

Relations between Indians and whites were not tragic because people failed to ask ethical questions about how to treat Indians. Some men and women asked that question again and again. The correct answer was often given: "We should treat them as humans." Yet good intentions create few new realities when moral principles are pressured by events beyond human control. In 1763 the British proclaimed that the crest of the Appalachians should be the limit to western American growth; next, the Continental Congress in 1783 and 1788 forbade settlements in the Ohio Valley; and in 1873 the Grant administration officially excluded miners and settlers from the Black Hills. Accident, chance, the limits of human knowledge, the objects of human desire—fur, gold, guns, rum—rendered royal proclamations and peace policies impractical and seemingly irrelevant. Some historical forces were impersonal and technological: railroads, telegraphs, repeating rifles. Some forces were weaknesses in the Indian cultures: racial pride, whiskey, susceptibility to disease, inability to cooperate in the common defense. Some were white vices: racial pride, brutality, greed. And some were white virtues: courage, the creation of a powerful material culture, the desire for security and homesteads. No single historical factor explains the settlement of the American West or the treatment of the Indians; no motive or circumstance by itself is sufficient to bless, curse, or excuse history.

Unmoved by prayers and proclamations, history rushed past reformers and Indians alike. A Minnesota missionary wrote that Americans in 1864 were "living *centuries in years* . . . God is opening a continent before us, and we are every month losing golden opportunities." After the collapse of the Peace Policy, reformers complained that the policy simply had not been allowed time to prove itself. The United States grew too swiftly.

The foregoing comments begin to place a narrow subject in its historical context. Just as United States history too often is written omitting Indians, Indian history can be written as if it were central to America's past. It was not. The Peace Policy lasted less than a dozen years and was a minor factor in the history of the 1870s. Yet in itself it is a vast and complex subject. It involved thirteen religious bodies and their various boards, more than seventy Indian reservations, four presidential administrations (Grant, Hayes, Garfield, Arthur), and four divisions of the federal government (the army, Department of the Interior, Bureau of Indian Affairs, and Board of Indian Commissioners). To study the consequences of Grant's policy for one church or on a particular reservation are book-length topics in themselves, and to attempt an overall assessment of the relationship between the government, the churches, and the Indian agencies, as here, creates problems of organization and emphasis. The themes, institutions, and personalities interact throughout the years 1869–82.

The campaign of 1868 gave no indication that, if elected, Ulysses S. Grant would introduce a Quaker Indian policy. Republicans at Chicago's Crosby Opera House unanimously nominated Grant on the first ballot and adopted a platform that did not mention Indians. Neither the Republican party nor its candidate made any public promises, although William Tecumseh Sherman confided to his brother that a Grant victory would mean the end of "that old Indian system." Grant went on to defeat Horatio Seymour in an electoral landslide on November 3. Between the election and March 4, 1868, he met with several Quaker delegations and promised to help the Indians.

In his inaugural address on March 4 the new president said he needed to study the problem further. He committed himself to "any course . . . which tends to [Indian] civilization and ultimate citizenship." The president mentioned no new policy, but Grant's words inspired the nation's most aggressive Indian reformer, William Welsh, to call Quakers and philanthropists to Philadelphia for an emergency meeting. One month later a surprised *Nation* described Grant as "smitten" with the Quakers. The president was about to initiate a new holy experiment, a policy built on a myth, a reform that to Quakers seemed a vindication of the ideals they had brought to America "when the great PENN his famous treaty made, with Indian Chiefs beneath the elm-tree's shade." For other Christians, it would eventually test their entire religion, too. An Episcopal bishop from New York later predicted that if Christian love could win "the painted Dakota and the murderous Modoc" it could win the world; if it failed here, Christianity was finished. "No defense of documents, antiquity, logic, or ritual can save it . . . [for] Christianity deals in general principles. . . . But each of its great principles comes to its proof on some rugged, barbarous outpost. The Red Man's barbarity is a particular outpost where American Christianity is tried once more."[36]

1. Launching a Reform: The "Quaker Policy"

I wish the Good Father Quaker, William Penn, would rise from his grave.

Ke-wa-ze-zhig (Boston, 1861)

President Grant's new policy descended like a howitzer shell among the Indians' friends and foes alike in 1869. What it did, who did it, and what it meant confused everyone. Indians probably viewed the Peace Policy, or "Quaker Policy," as a continuation of previous practice; Indian reformers and humanitarians praised it as the best Indian opportunity of the century; frontiersmen called it mawkish sentimentality; and to congressmen, *Peace Policy* became a synonym for treaties, or abolition of treaties, or pacifism, or religious agents, or handouts, or protecting reservations, or abolishing reservations, or the Board of Indian Commissioners, or any combination of these.[1] While recognizing that a dozen or more different definitions of the Peace Policy came into use during the 1870s, we will limit the definition here to Grant's radical innovations in 1869 and 1870: (1) the appointment of Ely S. Parker as commissioner of Indian affairs, (2) church control of agents on reservations, (3) the creation of the Board of Indian Commissioners, and (4) a greatly expanded and intensified program of federal aid to Indian education and missions.[2]

Grant first startled Congress and the public by appointing an Indian as commissioner of Indian affairs for the first time in American history. A full-blood Seneca educated at the Baptist Tonawanda mission, forty-year-old Ely S. Parker (Ha-sa-no-an-da, "the Reader") had studied law

17

for three years, only to be refused entry into the New York Bar Association on racial grounds. He then trained himself to be a civil engineer and first met Grant in 1857 after moving to Galena, Illinois, to build a federal customs house. During the Civil War, Parker remained beside Grant from Vicksburg to Appomattox, rising to the rank of brigadier general. After the war, Parker advised Grant that fraud riddled the Indian system and that only a return to army control could end corruption.[3] His appointment as commissioner in 1869 fulfilled Parker's lifelong ambition to directly help his people, but for reformers the appointment inspired fear of military control of Indian affairs.

Grant next removed all Indian agents and in their place appointed army officers and Quakers. Hicksite (Liberal) Friends were asked to select and supervise agents on the Omaha, Winnebago, Pawnee, Oto, and Santee reservations of the Northern Superintendency (Nebraska), whereas Orthodox Quakers were given jurisdiction over the Kaw, Kickapoo, Shawnee, Kiowa-Comanche, and Cheyenne-Arapaho reserves in the Central Superintendency (Kansas and the Indian Territory). Grant assigned all other appointments to the army and on May 7, 1869, sixty-eight officers reported for duty to the commissioner of Indian affairs. When Congress eventually prohibited military appointments in July of 1870, Grant retaliated by offering other denominations the right to nominate agents, giving these churches the same responsibility he had already given the Quakers.

Grant next created a Board of Indian Commissioners (BIC). More than a mere review or advisory commission, the BIC was intended to be a group of wealthy, independent citizens armed with authority equal to that of the secretary of the interior to oversee and correct abuses in that department and its Indian Office. BIC members were to be Christians.

Last, the president promised the churches that his administration would do everything in its power to support Indian missions morally and financially. Church and State would cooperate in a determined effort to civilize Native Americans and finally bring them into the mainstream of American life. Belief in education was the major underlying assumption in his entire program, a program seeking to end frontier warfare and relieve the oppression of Indian tribes.[4]

Grant's motives and inspiration for his Peace Policy seemed mysterious to many of the president's associates. Military appointments could be easily explained by 1868 congressional legislation cutting back the Union Army by twenty regiments, which in turn meant the release of six hundred officers. But the religious agents and the BIC puzzled his friends, and the puzzle was further complicated by preinauguration rumors that Grant planned to place the Indian Bureau entirely within the War Department. Transferring the Indian Office from the Interior back to the War Department (where it remained from its establishment until 1849) to humanitarians would have symbolized a national policy of violence and extermination.

The day after Christmas 1868, lame-duck Secretary of the Interior O. H. Browning begged Episcopal Bishop of Minnesota Henry Whipple to come to Washington as soon as possible to fight an army transfer bill already passed by the House. More than any other person, including Grant, Henry B. Whipple must be considered the major architect and defender of the Peace Policy. By 1869 Whipple had struggled against apathy and opposition in his own church for a decade as he watched Episcopal Indian missions, weak before the Civil War, become almost nonexistent. Whipple had risked his life to protect innocent Sioux after the 1862 uprising in Minnesota. He also converted William Welsh to the Indian cause, and throughout the sixties Whipple often was asked to represent both the government and the church in Indian affairs. Now, two days after Browning's letter, another friend told Whipple that the Peace Commissioner's *Report* had definitely moved the Congress to favor reform, adding, "My only fear is that Gen. Grant seems to approve this surrender of the whole bureau into military hands." Whipple immediately wrote to the president-elect and then rushed to Washington, where, on one occasion, he apparently angered Grant. As late as January 7 both the Society of Friends and Whipple anticipated a Grant policy of army control over reservations and had received no hint of anything different forthcoming.[5]

For several years delegations of Quakers had met with Grant when he was secretary of war under Andrew Johnson. They came to discuss government policy in the Far West, and although he had disagreed with their pacifism, the Friends found Grant cordial and open-minded. As the Society lobbied for reform prior to 1869, its members discussed the Quaker calling to serve the Indians; in 1867 the *Friends' Intelligencer* reported that unnamed politicians were predicting "a wide door for useful labor . . . will soon be open to us." That hope had dwindled with Grant's election; nevertheless, on January 25, 1869, a group of Baltimore Friends hoping to forestall transfer of the bureau to army control met privately with Grant. He supposedly told them: "Gentlemen, your advice is good, I accept it. Now give me the names of some Friends for Indian agents and I will appoint them. If you can make Quakers out of the Indians it will take the fight out of them. Let us have peace."[6] Shaken and stunned by this totally unanticipated challenge, the Friends requested time before answering. On February 16 Benjamin Hallowell received the first formal announcement of the new policy from Parker:

> Gen. Grant, the President elect, desirous of inaugurating some policy to protect the Indians in their just rights, and enforce integrity in the Administration of their affairs . . . and appreciating fully the friendship and interest which your society has ever maintained in their behalf, *directs me*

*to request that you will send him a list of names, members of your So-
ciety, whom your Society will endorse,* as suitable persons for Indian
agents.

Also, to assure you, that any attempt which may or can be made by
your Society, for the improvement, education, and Christianization of the
Indians, under such Agencies, will receive . . . all the encouragement and
protection which the laws of the United States will warrant him in giving.[7]

The Society postponed answering Parker's letter until after a Quaker convention in Philadelphia. Certain Friends whose sympathy for Indians was "far
in advance" of others told Hallowell that they had to decline a job that meant
exposing their families to danger on the frontier. The general response, however, was encouraging and on April 19 the Society officially expressed its
pleasure in Grant's "sagacity, wisdom, and peaceful tenor" as it formally
accepted responsibility for nominating agents. The new policy, it was observed, promised to bring Indian affairs to a "speedy and happy issue," since
the Society of Friends would supply agents who were *"really representative
men,* free from sectarian prejudice, and such as recognize the Fatherhood of
God, and the *Brotherhood of all men,* and are deeply impressed with the
filial and fraternal obligations which this recognition imposes."[8] By mid-
June both the Orthodox and Hicksite Friends had appointed superintendents
and agents. Each group had organized a special committee on Indian affairs.[9]
By the end of 1869 nearly forty Quakers labored at Indian agencies, trusting
in Grant's "good omen" and believing that the federal government now
intended to follow Christianity's "fixed principle" of loving one's enemy.
The test had begun whether "cordial cooperation" between Church and
State could bring the Indian problem to a speedy solution and, although few
Quakers recognized it in 1869, whether Friends under pressure could steadily
adhere to their "fixed principles."

While Quaker officials searched for men willing to jeopardize their wives
and children in the West, their Episcopal friend William Welsh busily tried
to create what he considered an essential element in Indian reform—a watchdog committee to oversee government bureaucracy. Mindful that Whipple
had earlier created a Board of Christian Visitors on the Chippewa reservations and using the example of the Civil War Christian Commission, Welsh
set to work on Grant.

The concept of a review board—the Board of Indian Commissioners—had
many sources. Following the Sioux uprising of 1862, Henry Whipple had advised the government to establish a "council of appointment" to curb the
spoils system and to locate agents of high character; its unpaid members
would hold office ex officio. Whipple's concept of high-minded, disinterested
citizens aiding the government was not unique. Thomas McKenney's New

York Indian Board of 1829 had not offered advice so much as political help to the Jackson administration; nevertheless, it conveyed the idea that prestigious Christians could join together and speak out on Indian affairs. A Minnesota minister, Edward Duffield Neill, made a proposal similar to Whipple's to Senator James Doolittle in 1863, and in 1861 the Society of Friends had appointed a board of supervision for the Kansas Indian agency.[10] Four treaties with the Chippewas bore Whipple's imprint by providing for boards of visitors nominated by Catholics, Episcopalians, Methodists, and Congregationalists.[11] Beginning in 1866, Whipple, William Welsh, and the Quakers lobbied for legislation to create a national board of inspectors. A variety of existing organizations served as models, one of which was the Freedman's Bureau created by Congress in 1865. A more important precedent for voluntary cooperation between Church and State was the United States Christian Commission (1861-65), organized by the YMCA to provide religious literature and worship services for Union soldiers. Financed by the government, it worked closely with civilian and military officials. In the minds of Grant and his first secretary of the interior, Jacob D. Cox, this was the prototype for their Board of Indian Commissioners.[12] Also a precedent was Peter Cooper's Indian Commission in New York. A Unitarian philanthropist, Cooper had lobbied, sent petitions to Congress ("pipings of benevolent preachers," according to the army), and tried in various ways to educate the public about Indians. On May 18, 1868, he founded the U.S. Indian Commission with a membership that included John Beeson, Henry Ward Beecher, Vincent Colyer, and William Dodge. All but Beecher became participants in the Peace Policy; the Commission itself remained active through 1870, publishing *A Specific Plan for the Treatment of the Indian Question*, which was similar to Grant's program.

An 1867 congressional report likewise suggested a review board. Its plan differed in detail from Grant's BIC but the principle was the same. The congressmen proposed five inspection districts with supervising boards empowered to hold hearings, investigate treaty violations, examine agency accounts, and recommend the suspension of agents. To avoid patronage control, the Indian Office, the War Department, and the churches would name three members of each board, thereby rendering it "impossible to [appoint] any other than a man of high character and great ability."[13] Still another precedent for the BIC was contained in an 1867 letter to Grant from Ely S. Parker. Parker suggested a permanent ten-member commission of Indians and whites that would visit the tribes and inspire confidence in the government.

Late in February 1869, William Welsh left his Philadelphia home and stayed in Washington for two weeks while lobbying for Indian appropriations. After ratification of a Sioux treaty, but with the Congress still deadlocked over other Indian funds, Welsh sensed an opportunity for change. Congressmen, weary of wars and treaties, listened carefully to his plans. He returned to Philadelphia, where, on March 18, he called a meeting of six influential citizens.[14] Encouraged by Grant's inaugural address, Welsh's committee visited the president and the new secretary of the interior, Jacob Cox, on Friday, March 24, to propose a Sioux advisory board. Grant's administration, Welsh told the president, needed help in its struggle against corruption in the Indian service. A five-man commission to supervise the Indian Office's relations with the Sioux, if successful, could be expanded to oversee other tribes. Such a commission, Welsh advised Cox, would liberate his department from the thralldom of patronage and from "thievish party politicians," and would enable Cox to enlist the aid of philanthropists and Christians. Welsh realized that his request was presumptuous and fully expected Cox to reject it. To his astonishment, both Grant and Cox agreed that there should be such a board for all tribes. "This interview was altogether memorable," George Stuart, a wealthy Philadelphia dry goods merchant and evangelical activist, reminisced years later, "and one never to be forgotten." Welsh left the meeting ecstatic. On Sunday he wrote to Whipple that Jacob Cox was "a noble fellow after your own heart"; he apologized to the bishop for missing church: "I have Indians on the Brain so violently that I could not have collected my thoughts in church today. . . . Congressmen of every grade are now crying Stop thief! Stop thief! and seem to have lost their relish for Indian spoilations."[15] Aided by a Philadelphia politician, Welsh pushed his BIC bill through Congress on April 10.

Assuming that the basic outlines of the Peace Policy were suggested to Grant by Whipple, Welsh, and the Hallowell delegation, this still does not explain why the president so readily adopted the reform.[16] One might argue that Grant planned to transfer the Indian Office to the War Department and was using the Quakers and philanthropists to soften the blow, but there is little firm evidence to support that conjecture, which has the further problem of conflicting with what we do know of Grant's character.[17]

William Tecumseh Sherman speculated that warfare had made Grant oversensitive to suffering. Although a victorious general, Grant was not a traditional military man like Sherman. Grant abhorred violence and bloodshed, opposed dueling, and detested bull fighting—"I could not see how human beings could enjoy the suffering of beasts, and often of men." He felt that the Mexican War and the Civil War were "unholy" conflicts, but he believed men must obey their governments even if the cause were unjust.[18] Grant also enjoyed the infrequent luxury in American history of gaining the presidency while remaining free from political commitment. Others came to him. He campaigned indifferently, made no promises, owed no debts to the Republican party or to politicians. Before the election Grant expressed few opinions other than his belief that a president should follow the will of the people by leaving policy to Congress. He was convinced that actively seeking the office of president rendered a man unfit to hold it. Both the religious and secular press celebrated his election and lauded the "universal confidence" of Americans in his ability to solve the era's problems. *Harper's Weekly* rejoiced that Grant's wisdom, persistence, and honesty guaranteed a long rule for Republicans as he assumed his place beside Washington and Lincoln, "a man so true and tried, so sagacious and modest . . . the prayers of all good men attend him . . . the hearts of the poor and oppressed everywhere bless him. . . . The national confidence is unbounded, but it will not be betrayed."[19] Political victory did not change Grant's characteristic silence; his plans remained a mystery. Cabinet appointments baffled politicians. He refused to answer letters from men who claimed that party allegiance guaranteed government jobs. Thus one of the most notorious administrations in American history began with honor, trust, and good intentions. Four years later Grant would finally concede that it was impossible to escape the party leaders and job seekers: "Office-seeking in this country . . . is getting to be one of the industries of the age," he wrote to his daughter; "it gives me no peace."[20]

The sources of Grant's sympathy for Indians are difficult to locate. Before 1865 he had had little to say about Indian affairs. At West Point when he was nineteen Grant read James Fenimore Cooper and completed a class assignment by painting a scene, "Indians Bargaining."[21] His few comments about Indians during his service in Mexico were detached and objective. While stationed in the Pacific Northwest at Fort Vancouver (1852-53) Grant again painted Indian scenes. He admired the Hudson's Bay Company and felt the company, compared to American traders, brought out the best in the Indians' character.[22] On March 19, 1853, he answered his wife, Julia, who had warned him to be cautious about Indian ambushes: "Those about here," he explained, "are the most harmless people you ever saw. It is really my opinion that the whole race would be harmless and peaceable if they were not put upon by the whites."[23] Four months later Grant informed Major Osborn Cross that only a few harmless Klickitats resided near the fort, "and even this poor remnant of a once powerful tribe is fast wasting away before those blessings of civilization 'whiskey and smallpox.'"[24] Later and during his presidency Grant would occasionally repeat his observation that the basic cause of the Indian problem was the white man, but immediately after the 1869 election he journeyed across the plains, praising the white man's progress on the frontier and saying nothing about Indians.[25]

An intensive education in the complexities of Indian policy began for Grant after the Civil War, when he was appointed secretary of war (1866-68), a position with responsibility for military operations in the Far West. During this period he was influenced by William Tecumseh Sherman and John Pope. The attitudes of both generals were far from consistent. Sherman, who became Grant's secretary of war, shifted between understanding and sympathy for the tribes on the one hand, and calls for their "punishment" and extermination on the other. Grant apparently agreed with Sherman that any Indians who blocked the westward path of civilization must be eliminated and he once recommended to Andrew Johnson the complete suppression or extermination of the Apaches.[26] Grant, like many other army regulars, had unromantic notions of western settlers and traders, despite his belief in Manifest Destiny, and his ideas were based partly on his experiences at Fort Vancouver and partly on Sherman and Pope's dislike of frontier whites. Grant, as secretary of war, understood and acted on the need to protect Indians from white men.[27]

Two other military leaders whom Grant respected were George Crook and James Carleton. As president, he would jump ranks in promoting Crook from lieutenant colonel to brigadier general for service against the Apaches in Arizona.[28] As secretary of war, Grant had supported Carleton's extreme and hard-line forced acculturation of the Navajos at Bosque Redondo. In letters to Carleton in New Mexico, Grant deplored "utterly worthless" civilian agents, traders, and contractors while he praised the controversial Carleton for his success in rapidly forcing the Navajos to give up their native culture for that of European civilization, a conclusion in which Grant was largely mistaken. Carleton, an evangelical Christian, very likely represented a model of the ideal Indian agent to Grant.[29] During his years in the Johnson cabinet, Grant, like practically everyone else in the army, favored transfer of the Bureau of Indian Affairs to his department, but he never used his position to undercut the bureau, even as he directly experienced the corruption in the government's patronage and purchasing systems.[30]

There is no evidence that Grant's religion inspired the Peace Policy, although some writers have speculated that Grant possessed a dynamic quality of religious leadership and charisma that mysteriously inspired others to follow him with exceptional trust.[31] Raised in a Methodist home and associated with Methodism throughout his life, he never joined the church and remained unconverted until the last days of his life. He often was critical of organized religion, including Methodism, and he still remains America's most outspoken president in favor of repeal of church tax exemptions and removal of religion from public schools. As a West Point cadet, Grant resented the compulsory Episcopal chapel services and once was punished for refusing to attend.[32] Even though he personally disliked Catholicism and Mormonism, he resisted the bigotries of his age when he resigned from a reactionary anti-Catholic Know-Nothing party in the 1850s and when he defended the Mormons in the 1870s.[33] His annual messages and religious proclamations contained customary references to the "Supreme Author from whom blessings flow" and asked for the public's "fervent prayers" to the "bountiful Father of all Mercies." In another expression of popular religion, after two years of indecision and delay, Grant and his cabinet designed what is probably the most religious Indian peace medal in American history. On one side of the medal, used to honor Indian chiefs, was placed a profile of Grant surrounded by the words LET US HAVE PEACE LIBERTY JUSTICE AND EQUALITY; on the other side was an open Bible placed over a rake, a plow, an axe, a shovel, and other farm implements, with the caption: ON EARTH PEACE GOOD WILL TOWARD MEN 1871.[34] In 1876 Grant set aside a special centennial day for thanking "Almighty God for the protection and bounties which He has vouchsafed to our beloved country." Grant's other official declarations often mentioned religious liberty and just as often omitted any reference to God. His second inaugural address contained one of his few public statements of faith: "I believe that our Great Maker is preparing the world, in His own good time, to become one nation, speaking one language, and when armies and navies will be no longer required."[35]

Grant had been careless about church attendance before his election. Once in the White House, the president's wife, her friends, and his relatives constantly tried to persuade him to attend Dwight L. Moody revivals and the Evangelical Alliance meetings, but Grant usually found demands that took him elsewhere. He thought that most Christians failed to practice their professed beliefs, and one suspects that his personal view of religion was similar to that of his friend Mark Twain. When asked if he prayed, Grant replied, yes, "mentally, but briefly." While he was dying, Grant tolerated praying on his behalf, but his son Fred told Twain that although his father "was a good man, and indeed as good as any man, Christian or otherwise, he was *not* a praying man."[36] Grant once advised his brother-in-law that he did not care to talk much about religion, but that he thought about it often. His piety was practical. He supported foreign missionaries because, in addition to preaching, they helped men and women by teaching agriculture. His religion permitted no tolerance for racism: "I do not believe our Creator ever placed the different races of men on this earth with a view of having the stronger exert all his energies in exterminating the weaker."[37] He was also convinced that the God who ruled human events had ordained human labor and strict obedience to one's superiors. Grant considered atheism illogical and envied his sister's deep faith in Christ.[38] Before his agonizing death in 1885, Grant's religious friends and relatives urged a Methodist minister to warn the cancer-stricken former president that without Christ "he is a poor lost sinner, that His blood alone can save him." Grant refused communion and refused to confess a faith in Christ. Only as he lay delirious and semiconscious did a contrived baptism accomplish his formal conversion to the Christian faith.[39]

The military historian J. F. C. Fuller wrote that Grant, like Oliver Cromwell, was an inscrutable, simple man. To explain his ideas and his Peace Policy we need not uncover hidden loyalties to the Church, analyze his theology, or search for Methodist ministers lurking in his Kitchen Cabinet. Despite his criticism of Christians, Grant probably idealized pious men. His first message to Congress cited the "well-known fact" that William Penn and the Friends had brought peace to Pennsylvania whereas churches elsewhere were constantly fighting Indians. The former general hoped that Quaker pacifism and integrity could halt Indian conflict in 1869 as he thought they had after 1683. As criticism grew in the 1870s, Grant stood firmly behind the Friends and he never weakened in his resolve to pursue the Peace Policy. "If any change is made," he wrote to George Stuart of the Universal Peace Union, "it must be on the side of the Civilization and Christianization of the Indian."[40] His annual messages and second inaugural address clearly reaffirmed his intent and revealed his motives: the Peace Policy cost less than war, it protected settlers better than war, it eased railroads through Indian country without conflict, it stopped extermination, and it was just.[41]

Ullysses S. Grant deserves more praise than he has been given or perhaps gave himself for his Indian policy. He never revealed many of his inner thoughts. J. F. C. Fuller concluded that, "Enigma he lived and enigma he died, and . . . enigma he remains." Since Grant seldom spoke or wrote directly about his Peace Policy, historians are tempted to accord him little credit. The typical Grant stereotype, a cigar-smoking alcoholic, the second or third worst president in American history, can blind us to his humanity in Indian affairs. What historians too often overlook is the high esteem in which he was held by his contemporaries and by almost everyone who has carefully studied his life. His virtues of fortitude, intelligence, trust, innocence, patience, loyalty, resolution, self control, kindness, in some ways became liabilities in a politician. "The unmilitary general was also an unpolitical president."[42] War, and not politics, brought out the best in Grant, "as did his wife and family and horses."[43] Lincoln admired him, and Mark Twain respected him as a writer, as a person of courage and power, and as "a very great man and superlatively good."[44] Henry Adams made a telling criticism of Grant in observing that "when in action he was superb and safe to follow; only when torpid was he dangerous." Edmund Wilson would later expand this insight into an assessment of Grant's presidency, an office that to him demanded passivity:

Whenever, as President, he did anything wise, it had the look of a happy accident. In the field, as commanding general, he could be patient, farseeing, considerate, adroit at handling complicated situations. But in Washington he had no idea of what it meant to be President. . . . One can hardly even say that Grant was President except in the sense that he presided at the White House, where the business men and financiers were extremely happy to have him, since he never knew what they were up to. . . . Grant was the incurable sucker. He easily fell victim to trickery and allowed [others] to betray him into compromising his office because he could not believe that such [dishonest] people existed.[45]

Grant was not, however, gullible and naïve when it came to Indian policy. He never assumed that religious agents and the Board of Indian Commissioners were sufficient by themselves. He knew that military force would be necessary to move tribes onto reservations where, unless they organized their own state, Indians must be assimilated into white culture. Grant's ineptness as an administrator and his unquestioning loyalty to those friends who surrounded him compounded these complexities in his Peace Policy, a policy that neither reformers nor generals ever fully understood.

His policy employed Quakers and soldiers, olive branches and swords. Most Americans never realized that Grant first of all advocated the removal of unyielding Indians from the white man's path. Whether it required fighting, teaching, starving, or feeding, Indians could not be allowed to block the nation's progress. If this seemed contradictory, it also was practical. One of Grant's commissioners of Indian affairs, Francis Walker, understood the ambiguity and tragedy of the 1870s: to the white man "freedom of expansion is of incalculable value. To the Indian it is of incalculable cost. . . . We are richer by hundreds of millions; the Indian is poorer by a large part of the little that he has. This growth is bringing imperial greatness to the nation; to the Indian it brings wretchedness, destitution, beggary."[46] Grant, like Walker, rejected simple solutions and believed that violence as well as education and goodwill was necessary in national policy. For coercion, he relied on the army; for education, he turned to the churches.

The responsibility of Quakers and other Christians who joined the Peace Policy did not end with the nomination of agents. The mission boards were obligated to convert and teach Indians, thereby halting frontier wars and eradicating differences in culture. Although it was unrecognized or avoided by several denominations, the responsibility for turning the Indian Bureau into a missionary enterprise was clearly stated by Grant at the beginning of the Peace Policy.[47] Subsequent policy statements by the federal government and by the Board of Indian Commissioners made the churches' missionary obligations even more inescapable. In 1872 the BIC's secretary, Thomas Cree, sent a religious questionnaire to every denomination. Cree pointed out that church appointment of seventy agents gave mission societies control of nine hundred other government employees, a vast opportunity opened "at little or no expense to [church] treasuries, as the Government pays all these men and women fair wages." Presbyterians entered the Peace

Policy only after being assured that they could control all employees "so as to make each Agency a unit in purpose and Spirit." Francis Walker justified Grant's "somewhat anomalous order of appointment" as a system that provided better agents and promoted harmony between government employees and missionaries. In 1873, Secretary of the Interior Columbus Delano complained that certain denominations had failed to build churches, had not organized Sunday schools, and had appointed men who neglected their religious duties. He requested the removal of any agents who did not cooperate with "the missionary branch of the present policy of the Government."[48]

Most churches had understood their obligations very early. Quaker officials wrote to Jacob Cox that their agents were coworkers with missionaries; the Society acknowledged that the government, through the Peace Policy, held out its hand to American Christians, and it told applicants that an agent must combine frugality, industry, and mildness with trust in God and a prayerful heart.[49] The Episcopal Church committed its agents to the moral improvement of tribes, and the Presbyterian Board of Missions informed employees that both the national government and the church expected everyone to be "servants of our blessed Lord and Redeemer": "The Agents nominated for appointment by the [church] should be men in full sympathy with its missionary and education work for the Indians, and also, that all the employees on the Agency . . . be men of correct morals and also men willing to promote the object of the board."[50]

Despite flimsy protests from certain denominations that they had no responsibilities other than selecting Indian agents, the Grant Peace Policy obviously was a mission policy.[51] Few in the government or the Church questioned that Indian education required the Christian religion. Conversion, they thought, always brought fast acculturation and guaranteed assimilation. "The religion of our blessed Saviour," the Board of Indian Commissioners maintained in 1869, "is believed to be the most effective agent for the civilization of any people." William Welsh assured his friends that the Peace Policy enjoyed "a power that God has placed in the hands of Christians which is everywhere and under all circumstances irresistible, for the Holy Spirit works in it and through it." In 1871 a special agent to the Upper Missouri reservations summed up the philosophy and goals of the new reform. Missions, he reflected, "are the handmaids of the Peace Policy" and essential for presenting "ideas of civilization in the most attractive forms. . . . with the great work of these missionaries, co-operating with the just and benevolent policy of the Government, these reservations will soon become self-supporting and shields to frontier settlements, and will effectually protect white settlers from the savage sorties of the wild prairie Indians."[52]

William Welsh, the Episcopal investigator, realized that something more than trust in the Holy Spirit and Quaker piety was needed to overcome temptation.

He knew from experience that many problems at the agencies actually began in Washington, D.C. "Practically there is no responsibility whatever in the Indian Department," Colonel John Gibbon once protested to Henry Whipple, "and no reform will take place until the corrective is applied there." Welsh's corrective was a powerful review board to oversee operations of the Department of the Interior and its Indian Office.

Passage of a bill to create the Board of Indian Commissioners remained doubtful until April 8, 1869. Opposition came not only from the "Spoilsmen & Plunders" whom the board was supposed to eliminate, but from Quakers whom it was intended to help. Hicksite Friends like Samuel Janney feared that it would be a tool of Episcopalians, evangelicals, and "their self-constituted com^{er} [Welsh]." Other Friends wrote to Benjamin Hallowell that "Grant had better keep the money out of the hands where sectarian influence may produce unhappy results."[53] Joseph Wharton of the Camden Nickel Works asked his senator to vote against the bill because Quakers wished to remain subservient to the administration and he thought the new plan would make the Society seem eager for political power. Wharton protested that Welsh's delegation to Washington in support of the legislation was not a Quaker group: "The scheme which they advocated is totally different from that enunciated by Grant, and would if adopted entirely destroy the original plan of Grant." An independent, irresponsible review board, Wharton predicted, would "precipitately overthrow [the government] to give place to a scheme hitherto unheard of." He bluntly charged that Congress had to block the "very sharp piece of juggling" by William Welsh and the evangelicals. The next week Wharton and Hallowell traveled to Washington to call on Grant. On April 8 the president assured both men that the Society of Friends would retain full control over its agencies and that they could appoint Quakers to the Board.[54]

The bill establishing the Board of Indian Commissioners was passed on April 10.

And be it further enacted . . . for the purpose of enabling the President to execute the powers conferred by this act he is hereby authorized, at his discretion, to organize a board of commissioners, to consist of not more than ten persons, to be selected by him from men eminent for their intelligence and philanthropy, to serve without pecuniary compensation, who may, under his direction, exercise joint control with the Secretary of the Interior over the disbursement of the appropriations made by this act or any part thereof that the President may designate; and to pay the necessary expenses of transportation, subsistence, and clerk hire of said commissioners while actually engaged in said service, there is hereby appropriated, . . . the sum of twenty-five thousand dollars, or so much thereof as may be necessary.[55]

During the spring of 1869 Friends arrived at their new posts and saw the Kiowas, Kickapoos, Pawnees, and Comanches for the first time. By summer, the Board of Indian Commissioners had been organized and its first chairman, William Welsh, was, Samuel Janney conceded, certainly "the right man in the right place."

2. Allocation of the Agencies: 1870

No such opportunity was ever before offered to demonstrate to the world, the practical and availing nature of the testimony for peace committed to the Church by Him who is declared to be "the Prince of Peace."

Orthodox Friends, *Annual Report* (1870)

As new settlers in Montana slowly edged onto Piegan tribal lands during the summer of 1869, several Indians killed two white men. In retaliation, white cattlemen killed four Piegans, including a boy and an old man. With threats of war and revenge spreading across the territory, General Phillip Sheridan ordered reprisals against Indians in northern Montana. On January 23, 1870, a detachment under Colonel E. M. Baker attacked and killed 173 Piegan while losing only one of its own men. Reactions to the fight varied. The Board of Indian Commissioners' secretary, Vincent Colyer, accused Baker of murdering 140 women and children, whereas Baker reported that 53 noncombatants and 120 braves had died in battle. Reformers in the East used the "Piegan Massacre" to demonstrate the army's inability to civilize Indians and to halt a nearly successful drive aimed at transferring the Indian Bureau from the Interior to the War Department. The BIC sent Colyer to testify against Sheridan and William Tecumseh Sherman. The resulting exchange of accusations destroyed any possibility of cooperation between the Board and the army.[1]

Although Grant, Indian Commissioner Parker, and the *Nation* defended Baker and Sheridan, the humanitarian protest against the Baker affair grew more and more strident. *Harper's Weekly* accused the army of genocide and called for a new approach to Indian affairs. "War has plainly

31

failed. Let us try a policy of peace." Artist George Catlin remembered the Piegans as a kind, trustworthy tribe—"my heart sickens at the fate they have met at the hands of an artful, designing, & wicked enemy." After comparing the "cowardly" Baker with Chivington of Sand Creek, Catlin exclaimed that Sheridan had been duped by Montana land speculators into annihilating "a naked and defenseless people." An editor of the *Baptist Watchman*, who reported a "chill of horror" as he read the story, requested that army "assassins" be "cooly and deliberately hanged."[2] Indian apologists in Congress denounced advocates of army control as bloodthirsty. Montana's territorial delegate, Jim Cavanaugh, responded with the frontier maxim that Indian women and children were nothing but "nits, and will become lice, and it is better to kill them in their chrysalis state." His colleague, Representative Daniel Voorhees of Indiana, deemed it a contradiction for Grant to welcome with one hand "Indian agents in their peaceful garments and broad brims . . . missionaries of a gospel of peace" and with the other hand to welcome Sheridan, a man "stained with the blood of the innocent, a man who strikes in mid-winter at sick and dying women and children."[3] Whatever the reason, whether it was this "anomalous piece of conduct" by the president or perhaps a cynical legislative attempt to wrest patronage away from army control, in mid-July of 1870 the U.S. Congress prohibited the appointment of any military men to civilian posts. Congress thereby removed all federal Indian agents except the Quakers.

An indefatigable worker, first secretary of the BIC, and critic of the army, Vincent Colyer (1825–88) symbolized to the military and the frontier the typical eastern Indian reformer. He was intensely mistrusted and disliked by both the army and most settlers west of the 100th meridian. Colyer, who was also a painter, Episcopalian, and vice-president of the New York YMCA, had been appointed secretary of the Cooper Union, an intellectual reform organization, in 1865. During the first spring of the Peace Policy, 1869, the BIC's new secretary toured the Southwest, where he preached to soldiers and was fascinated with Indians. Colyer concluded that transcontinental railroads and land speculation would bring violence, injustice, and misery to the plains Indians, and he believed that the Peace Policy could help prevent that from happening.[4]

Other reformers and humanitarians had reacted with mixed emotions to Grant's appointment of army officers in 1869. Surprisingly, the Friends were relieved because it made them appear less specially favored, and William Welsh admitted that the military agents of the years 1869–70 did a relatively good job. But Vincent Colyer was convinced that any policy that employed Quakers and soldiers had to be inconsistent. After the Quaker Policy survived its first Senate debate in June 1870, he and Secretary of the Interior Jacob

Cox grew anxious as they contemplated Congress removing the army agents, a move that they feared would mean a return to patronage control. To prevent this and to expand the Peace Policy, Colyer conceived of allowing other denominations to nominate agents.

On Monday, June 6, Colyer wrote to various mission boards on behalf of the BIC. Although discouraged by a slow response, he told Cox and Grant of his new plan and gained the president's approval. When John Lowrie accepted the offer for the Presbyterians on June 22, Colyer immediately wrote again to the churches. Using denominational rivalry as an incentive, he said he had found Mormons, Presbyterians, and Roman Catholics eager to accept a "glorious opportunity for doing a great work for our dear Redeemer . . . whoever comes to the poor Indian with goods and food and protection, to him will he turn and listen." A month later Colyer rejoiced when Congress removed army officers from the agencies and Grant in turn formally approved the plan with the churches.[5]

In the Senate debate on June 4, 1870, John Thayer of Nebraska had accused Grant of making an invidious distinction by selecting Quakers for agents, and Senator George Edmunds of Vermont amused his colleagues when he answered that the president could not use every sect: "He could not make a commission composed of one Catholic, one Episcopalian, one Presbyterian, one Congregationalist, one Quaker, and so on, going through all the thirty or forty different kinds of religions; if he did, I think we should see a pow-wow when they got together over points of doctrine instead of seeing [goods] delivered to the Indians. [Laughter]"[6] As far as the Peace Policy was concerned, the problem was not humorous. Much turmoil resulted from failure to define denominational participation clearly: how should agencies be apportioned among the denominations? how binding on the Indian Office were church nominations? who, church or government, possessed the power to remove agents? did control of a reservation include the right to exclude other denominations? In trying to answer these questions, Grant supplied only a vague set of principles. Different churches, the president told Congress, had been given the right to select agents subject to executive approval, and the cooperating denominations were ones that had "heretofore established missionaries among the Indians," or who agreed to assume responsibility "on the same terms—i.e., as a missionary work." The new program, the president predicted, would convert Indians to Christianity and assimilate them into individual homes and into the churches within a few years.[7] The distribution of agencies seemed a simple task based on simple principles, but, as Senator Edmunds had predicted, it rapidly became a problem that set the churches brawling over their assignments.

After cursory research, Colyer sent Secretary Cox a color-coded map and a list of denominational assignments. This allocation gave the Minnesota,

Wisconsin, and Michigan agencies to the American Missionary Association, the Dakota reserves to the Episcopal Church, the Pacific Northwest to the Methodists, and the Southwest to the Northern Presbyterians. Unitarians picked up an agency in the Colorado Rockies, the Dutch Reformed were assigned to the Pima and Colorado River agencies, and Baptists gained control of Utah, Idaho, and the Indian Territory. The American Board of Commissioners for Foreign Missions received assignments in the Indian Territory (Oklahoma). Roman Catholics were not mentioned, though Cox told Felix Brunot that they eventually would be included.[8] In compiling his list, Colyer had relied on his own inaccurate knowledge of Indian missions and on Grant's vague principle of "heretofore established missionaries." But who was a missionary—itinerate priests, local preachers, native converts? What constituted a valid mission—a chapel, a church, a school? And what happened when an agency had more than one mission—clearly the case in Michigan, Dakota, New Mexico, and Washington Territory. Colyer's preliminary division made no sense in terms of any single principle; he bypassed large denominations and, as Southern Presbyterians would later complain, he ignored ecclesiastical and regional facts of life.[9]

The proliferation of churches and religious bodies in North America (Presbyterians north and south, Methodists north and south, the American Board and the American Missionary Association, the Presbyterian Home Board and the Presbyterian Foreign Board, Dutch Reformed and German Reformed, Anglo-Catholic Episcopalians and evangelical Episcopalians) was sufficient to confuse any layman. Colyer justified his list by saying he had given the Indian Territory to churches that had "the *larger part of the mission work*" and that, in some instances, he decided to use railroad routes as division lines.[10] Government and denominational officials later developed a half-dozen conflicting, unresolved theories to explain agency allocation:

1. A religious denomination had the right to a reservation if, regardless of success or failure, it had established the first mission; the American Board used this argument against Episcopalians in Dakota, and the same principle rationalized the transfer of Nez Perce Indians from Catholic to Presbyterian control.
2. Roman Catholics insisted that Grant had promised to assign agencies to churches with missionaries active in 1870; when there was more than one mission on a reservation, the church that had founded the first mission gained preference. The purpose of the Peace Policy, according to the Catholics, was to support existing missions and establish new ones, not to reclaim abandoned missions. According to Roman Catholic calculations, this entitled their church to seventy-five out of one hundred agencies.[11]
3. Catholic officials also argued that Indians should be allowed to determine which church had charge of a reservation.

4. Nathan Bishop, a Baptist member of the BIC, proposed allocation relative to denominational size. Neglecting to mention the Roman Catholic Church, he argued that his church with its low number of agencies had been cheated because there were a million Baptists, a million Presbyterians, and only three hundred thousand Episcopalians in the United States.[12]

5. The Board of Indian Commissioners at times felt forced to deny all principles of assignment and to say that no right to any agency existed other than the federal government's right to change apportionment whenever conflicting claims, lack of "rapid improvement," or "presumptive evidence" warranted such change. In defending itself against Catholic criticism, the BIC claimed that the welfare of Indians, and not the benefit of any particular church, was the only consideration.[13]

6. Another approach permitted the churches to settle differences by themselves. In 1872 the Methodists surprised the government by unofficially trading the Grand Ronde agency to the Catholics in exchange for Fort Hall and Klamath. The American Board in 1873 gave its Fort Berthold and Sisseton agencies to the American Missionary Association, which also received Lake Traverse from the Episcopalians. The American Missionary Association then surrendered Leech Lake to an "excellent body of Christians," the Free Will Baptists, and the Episcopalians offered Devil's Lake to the Catholics. Such voluntary redistribution, "denominationalism by geography," had been common mission practice elsewhere in the world for half a century.[14]

Confusion in policy and a paucity of reliable information hampered government administrators who apportioned the agencies. Early in 1871 territorial delegate R. C. McCormick of Arizona asked Ely Parker to shift the Pima from Dutch Reformed control to Roman Catholic because, McCormick reported, the Pima had a Catholic mission and desired priests. The Indian Office then told the Reformed Church that the Pimas had become Catholic property and that the Reformed agent would be transferred to a newly created agency, a decision that brought an immediate protest. Within two days after hearing that only Methodists and Presbyterians had worked with the Pima, that Catholic claims perverted the truth, and that McCormick courted Catholic votes, the Department of the Interior revoked its previous ruling and transferred the Pima tribe back to the Dutch Reformed.[15]

Even after the modification of Colyer's original 1870 plan, agency assignments remained disproportionate. Of seventy-one agencies assigned in 1871, Hicksite and Orthodox Friends already controlled a total of sixteen; Methodists received fourteen; Presbyterians, nine; Episcopalians, eight; Roman Catholics, seven; Baptists, five; Dutch Reformed, five; Congregationalists

(American Missionary Association), three; the American Board, one; Unitarians, two; and Lutherans, one. Of these, the American Missionary Association, Lutherans, Unitarians, and Dutch Reformed at the time had no Indian missions. The Methodists could only claim Father Wilbur among the Yakima—and he already was a federal agent. Episcopalians were concerned about the Sioux, but had sent only a few missionaries to the Dakota territory. The Roman Catholics alone were making a vigorous effort in 1869, and even their work was not as universal, successful, or harmonious as they later claimed.[16]

Changes in apportionment continued throughout the Peace Policy for reasons of comity, prejudice, and politics.[17] To appease unhappy politicians in Washington Territory, the government abruptly shifted the Skokomish agency from Methodist to Congregational control in 1872. Similar changes elsewhere appeased no one. Catholics, Moravians, and Southern Methodists felt cheated; Universalists, who had had no missions anywhere in the world, asked why the government had given them no Indians. In 1880, the Disciples of Christ claimed that they had been ignored when in fact they had declined an offer in 1872 because they lacked supporting funds. A Lutheran warned the federal government that it was imprudent to ignore the four hundred thousand members of that denomination. Receiving the Warm Springs agency in Oregon calmed anxious United Presbyterians. Secretary of the Interior Jacob Cox refused to reassign the Choctaw and Chickasaw reservations to Southern Presbyterians who sympathized with the "rebel feelings" of ex-slaveholding Indians. There was no logical reason for omitting the Mormons who had Indian missions in Utah and Arizona, but one has only to read the anti-Mormon literature of the 1870s to learn the reason for this oversight by eastern humanitarians. Moravians, who had a long and honorable record, were totally excluded, as was Judaism, which had no such record. A. B. Meacham and others would later point to allocation mistakes and blame the "grotesque blunders" of Colyer and the BIC for the Peace Policy's failure. But the most serious problems arising from Peace Policy apportionment did not come from excluded Jews, Moravians, and Mormons. The real problems involved Methodists, Catholics, Presbyterians, Episcopalians, and Congregationalists securely entrenched in the program.

The Methodist Church had virtually no Indian missions in 1870. After early activity in Illinois, Wisconsin, Minnesota, Kansas, and Oregon, and after almost all of its Indian missions fell under the jurisdiction of the southern churches as a result of the 1844 schism, the Northern Methodist Missionary Society entrusted its few Indian missions to local conferences. These bodies expressed little concern for the tribes. Yet in 1870 the Northern Methodists were assigned almost 20 percent of all agencies, and later they secured even more. To suspicious Catholics and other Protestants, Grant's Methodist associations provided a ready explanation—the president had replaced political patronage with religious favoritism. A. C. Barstow retired from the Board of Indian Commissioners in 1881 and declared that the BIC had been nothing but a Methodist Kitchen Cabinet. Much earlier Catholics had charged that in allotting agencies, Grant was duped as a "tool in the exaltation and propagandism of the Methodist Church."[18]

Although no direct evidence supports the specific charges against it, the Methodist Church did enjoy unusual power in Washington during the 1870s. Grant himself once remarked that there were three political parties in the United States: the Republicans, the Democrats, and the Methodists. The *Independent* wondered about the denomination's political goals when a Methodist bishop instructed two thousand Boston laymen and clergy to pray for Grant's third term. There were rumors, the paper reported, of Methodists eager to rival "the political aspirations and conquests of the Roman Catholic Church."[19] Grant's awkward attempts to nominate Methodist clergyman Frank Hass for a consulate in Jerusalem had proved futile, but observers noted his successful appointment of evangelist William Pike to a consulate in Brazil; his appointment of his own brother-in-law, M. J. Cramer, a Methodist minister, to Copenhagen; and his assignment of his wife's friend, the Reverend John P. Newman, to a world consulate-inspection tour. Adam Badeau, the president's secretary, considered Newman to be Grant's most intimate clerical friend. Newman, who was pastor of the Metropolitan Memorial Methodist Church in Washington, D.C., escorted the Grants to seances and allegedly had an untoward influence with women in the White House family. The *Nation* linked "that notorious intriguer, Dr. Newman of Washington," with yet another Methodist minister, Senator James Harlan. According to the *Nation*, Harlan, a former secretary of the interior, controlled the Indian Ring. Much of this was sheer rumor. Despite his friendship with Newman, Grant had gruffly told the family minister to go through proper channels when Newman requested a navy chaplaincy for a friend. At the end of his life Grant was much closer to Mark Twain than to Newman or to any other minister.[20]

Another Methodist seeking Grant's favor was Bishop Matthew Simpson. A Radical Republican and an acclaimed, highly paid, patriotic evangelical who once declared that "God cannot afford to do without America," Simpson had long been active in Washington politics as a personal advisor to Abraham Lincoln. His invocation had opened the 1868 Chicago Convention and later Grant would appoint him to the Santo Domingo Commission. After the 1872 election, Methodist letters flooded into Simpson's office urging him to present "our wishes and claims as a church." Men seeking Indian agencies in New Mexico, Arizona, and elsewhere begged the bishop to exert his religious authority—"worth more than Political"—with Grant. Simpson made requests but, as with Newman, Grant coldly ignored them.[21]

A different explanation of agency apportionment, namely anti-Catholic prejudice, can be more easily proved. Vincent Colyer and the Indian Office paid little attention to the 1867 *Report on the Condition of the Indian Tribes* in which non-Catholics praised the effectiveness of Roman Catholic missions and told of Indian requests for priests. Generals James Carleton and Alfred Sully recommended that Catholics be given exclusive care of Indian tribes. Agent P. P. Elder at Neosho, Kansas, surmised that because Indian religion was based on error, "the Catholic religion more readily commends itself to their benighted minds."[22] Elder obviously did not like Catholics, a prejudice that was common at a time when the *Syllabus of Errors* (1864) and the Vatican Council (1870) intensified traditional American distrust of the "Romish" hierarchy and priesthood.[23] Many Protestant missionaries classified "Papists" with Moslems, Jews, Orientals, and other "heathen"; some thought unconverted Indians less dangerous than Catholic Christians. J. J. Smith's *Impending Crisis* (1871) warned that Roman Catholicism planned to subvert American civil liberties, destroy American public schools, and reduce the United States to the condition of sixteenth-century Spain. Between 1870 and 1874 the *Missionary Herald* printed numerous stories illustrating the "low wiles and intrigues" of Catholics overseas and told how priest-driven mobs reportedly mutilated and lynched Protestants in Mexico. The president of Knox College in Illinois (1870) warned of deceit, fraud, and falsehood used by a "semi-pagan" Roman Church. A writer in the *Baptist Quarterly* insisted that Jesuit "puerility and crookedness" be tolerated no longer in America. Articles and editorials in the *Baptist Watchman* consistently reflected the widespread anti-Catholicism of the period. Although the Peace Policy did inspire some instances of cooperation between Catholics and Protestants, more frequently it increased animosity and distrust. To suppress the "grasping power" of Rome was a mission goal for many Protestants. A large number of evangelicals would have agreed with Nez Perce agent John Monteith and with Methodist secretary John Reid, both of whom preferred Indians to remain unconverted rather than join the Roman Catholic Church.[24]

Early apportionment problems arose when Methodists, Presbyterians, and Catholics clashed in the Southwest and on the Pacific Coast. The Roman Catholics claimed every agency assigned to the Methodist Church and several given to the Presbyterians. This protest in turn stimulated a Methodist reaction. During the early shifting of agency allotments, the Methodists lost three assignments: the Warm Springs reservation to the United Presbyterians, the lower Puget Sound agencies to the Presbyterian Church U.S.A., and the Skokomish agency to the American Missionary Association. The Methodists gladly accepted these changes, perhaps because the BIC had warned that prompt appointments were required "on acct. of the Catholic Influence."[25] Yet Methodists desperately and successfully fought to gain and then keep the Yakima agency, to which Catholics had an equal if not better claim, and Methodists insisted on obtaining Fort Peck, Fort Hall, Klamath, and Grand Ronde, to which their church had no legitimate claim of any kind. Methodist agents were sent to the Blackfeet whom the Jesuit Pierre DeSmet had visited in the 1840s and among whom a Presbyterian mission had failed in the 1850s. A Catholic priest who had worked in northern Montana since 1859 declared that in 1870 there was not a single Methodist among the Blackfeet.[26] The shift of Grand Ronde from Methodist to Catholic control in 1872 involved congressional intervention and brought bitter, illiterate protests from Oregon Methodists who slandered the new agent, Patrick Sinnot, as an Irish whiskey-drinking Catholic who could only be a "christian such as *Catholic* Church would admit: But not such as our Church would send as *Missionaries.* . . . What can the Government expect to do with such men as agents . . . it would be much better to leave them alone, und[er] the old civil policy. There is another thing about an Indian they do not like the *Irish*. They well know that most of them are *Democrats*."[27]

Violence eventually broke out between agents and priests at a number of Methodist agencies during the Peace Policy, but these conflicts pale beside the bitter fights that flared up over the Nez Perce agency in Idaho. Henry Harmon Spalding, driven from the Lapwai mission and perhaps deranged by his ordeal during the Whitman massacre in 1847, resented the Catholic missionaries who later occupied this region. He longed to return and expel the priests, a goal underlying his zeal in making Marcus Whitman a legendary figure and in telling tales of Catholic treachery. Even before the Nez Perce agency was assigned to the Roman Catholics, Spalding sensed a conspiracy to restrain him from reaching the Indians. The aged missionary believed that priests seeking control of the entire Pacific Coast had duped frightened Protestants into believing that Spalding and Whitman were scoundrels. Little hope remained, he wrote to a friend:

Grant & the Government are inexorable. They are determined that Protestants shall not be allowed among the Indians, but only Romanish [illegible] . . . & this is the first Protestant missionary West of Rocky Mountains. Have Catholics in our place. How long will you submit to be robbed of your missions, your churches & your farms, homes & schools yet suffer that infamous band of [illegible] . . . publish that Pres. Grant & heads of departments wants honest agents & have benevolent designs toward the Indians. . . . Grant intends no such thing. He intends to do just what he has done drive Protestants Church of God . . . & probably out of United States & to establish the Catholic church. This was the design of Johnson, Lincoln, Buchanan before him.[28]

The allocation of the Nez Perces to the Catholic Church soon confirmed Spalding's suspicions. He immediately left for the East, stopping in Chicago to help the editor of *Advance* write an editorial on "St. Bartholomew's Day in Oregon," then continuing on to Boston and Washington where he met with the American Board, the BIC, and financier Jay Cooke. In January of 1871 Spalding persuaded a Senate committee to print a scurrilous account that accused Catholics of plotting Whitman's murder and of allowing Indians to rape white women.

Vincent Colyer meanwhile had requested that the Nez Perce reservation be reassigned to the Presbyterians in exchange for the Umatilla agency, which, he confessed, rightfully belonged to the Catholics. Officially, the Indians themselves requested the transfer but Spalding had a different explanation of this Protestant victory. It was his "long & expensive labors" that alarmed Grant and forced the change.[29] Spalding, returning from the East with an appointment as the government teacher at Lapwai, now agreed that it was a glorious idea when the Presbyterian General Assembly endorsed the Peace Policy. If the Presbyterians rejoiced over capturing an agency in their war against "Popish tyranny and priest-craft," they soon would discover that controlling Henry Harmon Spalding would be even more difficult. At the same time, they turned to help the Board of Indian Commissioners repel Catholic challenges in the Southwest.

After his tour of the Southwest in 1869, Vincent Colyer returned with an impression that the region's Indians needed Protestant missions. The next spring he allocated the Navajo agency to the Presbyterians. Recalling frequent mission troubles with Navajo agents in the past, Secretary John Lowrie accepted the agency for the denomination's Board of Foreign Missions. Colyer next offered the Moqui and Pueblo agencies to the Presbyterians, assuring a worried Lowrie that these were docile tribes. Then, when the American Board refused to help in the Southwest, Colyer asked Lowrie to take responsibility for the Mescaleros and Southern Apaches.[30]

If Lowrie and the Presbyterians wanted docile Indians, the Apaches of Mangas Coloradoas, Victorio, and Nana were not their people. Information available in the Indian Office described the Mimbreños, Mescaleros, and Chiricahua as "the most savage, barbarous, and unprincipled Indians on this continent. Their . . . thirst for rapine and blood seem unquenchable . . . murder, robberies, and torture are unparalleled. . . . They have robbed mails, burned stage coaches and stage passengers." If either Colyer or the Presbyterians had read these reports they might have realized that some Apaches did respect Roman Catholic priests and that former agents in the Southwest had encouraged the government to support Catholic missions.[31] Determined to give as many agencies as possible to Protestants, Colyer ignored such information. He also ignored outcries from the frontier press and petitions from

Catholic bishops. Years later, their missions ruined and their agents crippled by dissension and corruption, the Presbyterians would deny ever wanting the agencies, blaming what they called the "varnish of Romanism" for their failures.[32]

While Catholics and Protestants clashed in the Northwest and Southwest, an apportionment struggle on the Upper Missouri threatened to further weaken the Peace Policy. In the 1830s Stephen Riggs and Thomas Williamson of the American Board had become Minnesota's first Protestant missionaries. Defeated in the Cherokee removal controversy, the board had gradually lost interest in Indians but allowed the Minnesota missionaries to remain with the Sioux and then to faithfully follow their exiled Indians onto the desolate western prairies after the 1862 uprisings. At that time Bishop Whipple, William Welsh, and an Episcopal missionary named Samuel Hinman began to compete for Sioux loyalty. In 1869 both the American Board missionaries and the Episcopalians watched enviously as the Friends assumed control of the Santee agency. When the government assigned Yankton, Sisseton, and Cheyenne River to the Episcopalians in 1870, Stephen Riggs protested. Secretary of the Interior Cox asked Whipple to surrender Yankton as a compromise. William Welsh, with his characteristic energy, held Cox to the original assignment. Welsh almost succeeded in taking the Santee agency from the Quakers, a move that alienated the Society of Friends and further alarmed the American Board. Unable to find signs of corruption at Santee, Welsh told Cox that the Indians wanted an Episcopal agent, that the Episcopal Church had been there first, and that the Quakers had neglected their mission work. Welsh threatened the secretary, saying that if the government denied his request, the Episcopal Church would withdraw entirely from the Peace Policy. The Friends, supported by Riggs, answered Welsh's charges and retained the agency. The American Board, knowing that a single defeat never discouraged Welsh, turned to fight the Episcopalians on another front.[33]

Bishop Henry Whipple had appointed Dr. Jared Daniels as Sisseton agent in 1868 and, to Whipple's satisfaction, the physician proved highly effective with the Sioux.[34] Daniels continued at his post after the Episcopal Church was assigned the reservation in 1870. American Board missionaries, however, wanted to nominate the Sisseton agent and early in 1871 a former missionary, Moses Adams, urged the board to seek Daniels' removal. Adams argued that at the Devil's Lake reservation the government employed a Roman Catholic agent who resisted Protestantism and degraded the Sioux, while at Sisseton, Adams marveled, the Indian Office tolerated the "High Church Propagandism" of Episcopalians. The American Board's secretary, S. B. Treat, agreed but was reluctant to oppose Welsh and the Episcopal Church again. Informed by Stephen Riggs of a scandal at the Ponca agency (Episcopal), Treat confidentially asked the Presbyterians to attack the Ponca agent. This was necessary, he advised, to break the "inside track" whereby Whipple and Welsh had gained control of the Dakota agencies. Treat went to the new secretary of the interior, Columbus Delano, and pressed Delano on the board's right to Sisseton. Treat declined to attack Daniels, except to vaguely hint that the doctor had somehow harmed the Indians. Alerted by Delano, who was an Episcopalian, William Welsh declared that Riggs had fabricated charges against the Ponca agent. Bishop Whipple reminded the secretary that the appointment of Daniels in 1868 actually began the Peace Policy, and General H. H. Sibley wrote from St. Paul that Daniels was irreplaceable. In May, Delano made his decision: Sisseton went to the American Board. The new agent was Moses Adams.[35]

Jared Daniels was convinced that in trying to turn the Sioux against him Riggs had only succeeded in making the Indians angry. The physician warned Whipple to prepare for trouble:

> The excitement is much greater than I expected. It is not safe to tamper with them by changing into that mission for I am satisfied trouble will surely come. . . . Among the reliable men the feeling is very strong against Mr. Riggs & Gabriel say[s] it will not be less for he will soon preach to empty houses. When I drove up the agency on my return he Mr. Riggs skulked away in the opposite [sic] as though he was guilty of a bad act. . . . What a Gentleman![36]

Riggs believed that a majority of the Sioux were overjoyed with Daniels's removal; he gloated that the doctor was in tears on leaving the agency. Adams, whose intolerance even Riggs later admitted "has become *too over-bearing*," had nothing but trouble and was discharged in 1872.[37] Throughout the Peace Policy the Sisseton agency remained a hotbed of factionalism and strife. Riggs claimed that Daniels and Gabriel Renville, who was part Sioux, tried to turn all the Indians against Adams by giving away a year's rations and by leaving the agency six thousand dollars in debt. Thus the American Board, which decided to withdraw from the Peace Policy a year later, gained a Sioux agency. The Congregational-Episcopal quarrel at Sisseton lasted until 1879, when the American Missionary Association appointed an agent named Charles Crissey—an Episcopalian who attended the Congregational Church.

Animosity between the two denominations broke out elsewhere in 1872. After the success at Sisseton, the American Board registered a claim to the Cheyenne River agency by telling Delano that his predecessor, Jacob Cox, had been mistaken and that Congregationalists had priority at all Sioux agencies. In June, Stephen Riggs's son Thomas reported that Episcopalians at Cheyenne River tried to expel him from his mission, but that he had gained the upper hand. On June 4 Thomas Riggs encountered William Welsh at Fort

Sully on the Missouri River. At first both men refused to speak; then Welsh began to present the Episcopal arguments. Riggs turned his back. Welsh, he later said, was "the most presuming man I know . . . and my opinion of him as a gentleman and a christian is, to say the least, not increased. . . . Words waxed warm. I had to work hard to control myself. Mr. W. lost all bearings." When Welsh insulted Riggs's father and brother and threatened to expel the entire American Board mission, Riggs glared and told Welsh to shut up:

> [Welsh] fired up wildly and said he would talk as he chose. I said "then you will excuse me from listening Sir." I believe he said "well clear out then" . . . and I turned and left . . . if I were not a good deal changed from what I have been Mr. W. would have been knocked down several times for threatening to have me removed from the reserve. One of the items demanded was that I endorse the activities of their appointed agents and not oppose efforts of their Church here. I told him that the Am Board would *promise* no such thing and that moreover we never should ask their permission to work in a field ours by birthright and past effort.[38]

According to Riggs, his speech "floored" Welsh and made the Episcopalian appear ridiculous, but his father, Stephen Riggs, also knew that "it will be war to the knife and he will leave no stone unturned to have us driven out."

The next day a man was shot at the agency and Thomas Riggs wrote that this frightened Welsh badly. "I rather enjoyed it. Mr. W. knows so much about Indians that it is a sad pity that he cannot have a closer view of them." Welsh saw matters differently. He was willing to surrender the dangerous Missouri River agencies, but detested leaving the Sioux under the Riggs family. "I left the young Mr. Riggs at Fort Sully healthfully exercising in fox hunting with the officers, intending, as he said, to go over the river and preach to the Indians."[39] The Episcopalians retained the agencies and for a time the Congregationalists brooded over their mistreatment: "The Lord is wiser than we are—and he permits Welch [sic] to rule." But with the western Sioux continuing to pose serious problems, the American Board decided that it was unwise to risk responsibility for such agencies. The board's Prudential Committee, over strong protests from the Riggs family, severed all formal ties with the federal government and its Peace Policy in March of 1873. They ceded the Sisseton and Fort Berthold agencies to the American Missionary Association. For a number of years they nevertheless continued to snipe at Episcopalians for having "more than their share."

The Congregationalist-Episcopalian problem demonstrated the difficulty of agency apportionment under the Peace Policy. Even if the government had clearly defined principles of allotment, and even if someone had bothered to evaluate historic church claims to territory fairly, differences in theology, mission theory, and personality would have caused conflict between the churches. Sisseton, Yankton, and Cheyenne River were new fronts in a world-wide jurisdictional battle over missions. In the 1870s the American Board protested Anglican violations of "Christ-taught comity" in the Near East and India, and warned that the Saviour would notice those "ritualists" who used methods from which "Christian courtesy instinctively shrinks."[40] Threatened by the prospect of an Episcopal mission at Sisseton, the board reminded the government that throughout the world all major denominations agreed that "there shall be no *intrusion* into each other's fields." By intruding and using devious methods in Dakota, the Episcopalians stood to reap the Congregationalists's harvest. Episcopalians made the American Board feel it had lost face when Episcopal missionaries instructed Sioux converts to request salaries and housing, offered "illegitimate inducements" to Indians, and raided eastern Congregational churches for mission funds. Episcopal bishops, according to the board, controlled government policy and their missionaries had appropriated Riggs's Sioux dictionary and hymnal:

> It is a grief to think that Christian men—men who proclaim the gospel of the Son of God to the perishing—are willing to enter, uninvited, into fields which others are cultivating, and participate in their harvest, when extensive regions, a little beyond, are open and ready for their occupation, unmolested. It is a grief [to] be more anxious to build their own church than see God's kingdom advanced by another. . . . It is a grief [to] press in and occupy a field, already occupied by other missionaries in violation of the principles of comity which are recognized by the leading missionary societies of the world.[41]

Episcopalians, for their part, resented the "very elegant and costly" chapels that the American Board, like Methodists and Catholics elsewhere, built in the Dakotas. Nor were Congregationalists beyond using inducements themselves. Congregationalist Charles Lemon Hall at Fort Berthold defied Sioux parents and evangelized their children by offering food, candy, and Christmas presents.[42]

Besides these conflicts over mission method and violations of comity, Christians differed in their attitudes toward Indian culture. Neither side admitted that Indian opposition to missions made any difference, but Episcopalians generally were more understanding of Indian ways than were Congregationalists. The American Board denounced Episcopalians as overtolerant because they temporized on polygamy and native games. The board had first requested Daniels's removal from Sisseton because the physician allowed Sioux to celebrate the Fourth of July by dancing, racing, and playing ball.

Daniels thought that Congregationalists too hastily accused Indians of sinfulness and weakness, he believed that they too often encouraged bigotry in native converts toward non-Christian Indians, and he learned to his dismay that Moses Adams imprisoned Indians who opposed the agent's attempt to halt polygamy. While later serving as a government inspector, Daniels concluded that "among all the agencies I have visited, I have found the missionaries of the A.B.C.F.M. the most intolerant toward Indians. They seem to be living in the fifteenth century and do not comprehend the present."[43]

To nineteenth-century Congregationalists the Anglicans seemed "full of superstition . . . tied up by certain ecclesiastical notions and rubrics that violate democratic ideas," and even before the Peace Policy began, William Welsh and Stephen Riggs had rebuked each other for proselytizing, stealing lexicons, and indulging in "sectarian bigotry." Their emotions grew increasingly hostile after 1870. Alfred Riggs eventually attacked his own American Board for "fraternizing" with Episcopalians; the board's "Ideal catholicity" might work well in the East, he declared, but it sickened him to watch Welsh and Felix Brunot "promise big & lie & strut." Missionaries in the West "ruled by the stern logic of facts must fight the Episcopalians as any other children of the Evil One. Whatever truce is had at the East *no truce is possible here.*"[44] William Welsh, never at a loss for words, told Bishop Whipple that the Riggs family was insane, but should be tolerated "like bed bugs, to promote cleanliness and we must try to improve their bitings." Later Welsh wrote to the secretary of the interior about the Indian belief that different tribes inherit animal characteristics: "This is certainly true of the Riggs who have the porcupine's propensities. The father has been shooting off his quills . . . at Bishop Whipple for several years."[45]

Such intolerance boded ill for an experiment based on altruism, brotherly love, and the Golden Rule. The government failed to adopt clear principles of agency apportionment based on accurate mission history and it discriminated against Catholics, Jews, Mormons, and southern churches while favoring Methodists, Episcopalians, and the northern denominations.[46] Catholics suspected a Protestant Establishment and Henry Spalding insisted that the Catholics conspired to become the official state religion. Congregationalists feared an Episcopal State Church while other Protestants grumbled about Grant and the Methodists. Even if Christians had trusted each other, ignored doctrinal differences, and forgotten personal jealousies, Grant's Peace Policy faced perhaps insurmountable challenges. But with Christians calling each other "bed bugs" and "porcupines" and "children of the Devil," the Peace Policy lurched forward precariously from the beginning.

3. The Protestant Response

President Grant, William Welsh, Bishop Whipple, Jacob Cox, Felix Brunot, and other founders of the Peace Policy assumed that the American churches, given an opportunity and financial encouragement by the federal government, would answer the Indian Question by providing money of their own to support devoted teachers, dedicated missionaries, and honest agents. The immediate response of the Protestant churches proved unenthusiastic. Baptists disliked starting new missions in desolate Utah. Unitarians virtually ignored Colorado. Although some Methodists claimed that the Peace Policy "deeply awakened" them to the Indians' plight, other Methodists apologized for poor performances and confessed that they had entered the program against their better judgment. Presbyterians haltingly turned to help the Apache, "the worst set of Indians to manage on the continent," then offered these agencies to three other denominations, none of which accepted the offer. An embarrassed American Missionary Association invoked the principle of comity to excuse a weak response, and Episcopalians balked at taking agencies where they had no prior missions. Even the Quakers became discouraged over the difficulties in recruiting men and raising the funds necessary for participation.

It was an inauspicious beginning for a policy that demanded lay talent, extraordinary administrative skills, and a willingness to spend money.

46

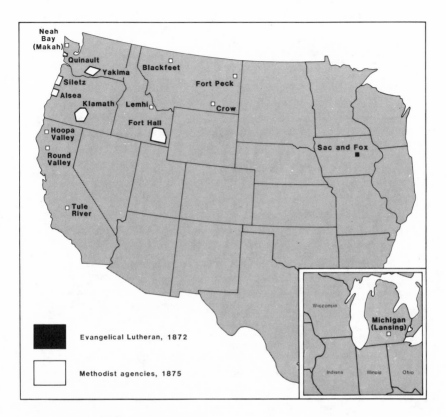

Neah
Bay
(Makah)
Quinault
Yakima   Blackfeet
Siletz   Fort Peck
Alsea
Klamath   Lemhi   Crow
Fort Hall
Hoopa
Valley
Round   Sac and Fox
Valley

Tule
River

Wisconsin

Michigan
(Lansing)

Indiana   Illinois   Ohio

Evangelical Lutheran, 1872

Methodist agencies, 1875

Evangelical Lutheran and Methodist

Dutch Reformed and American Missionary

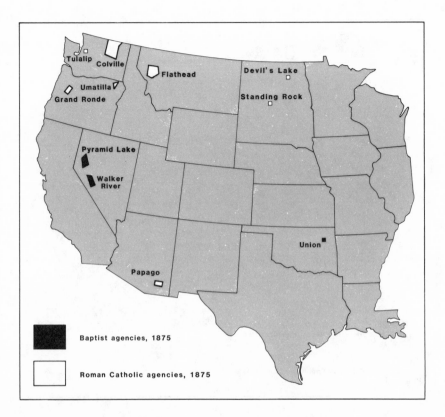

Tulalip
Colville
Umatilla
Grand Ronde
Flathead
Devil's Lake
Standing Rock
Pyramid Lake
Walker
River
Union
Papago

Baptist agencies, 1875

Roman Catholic agencies, 1875

Baptist and Roman Catholic

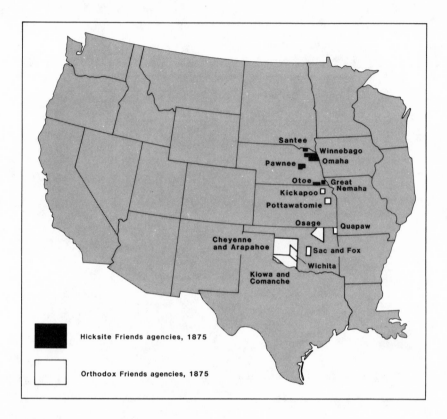

Hicksite and Orthodox Friends

Unitarian and United Presbyterian

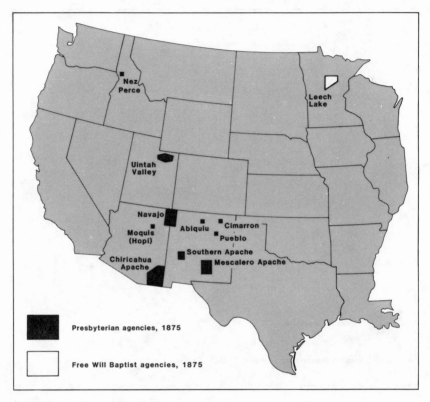

Presbyterian and Free Will Baptist

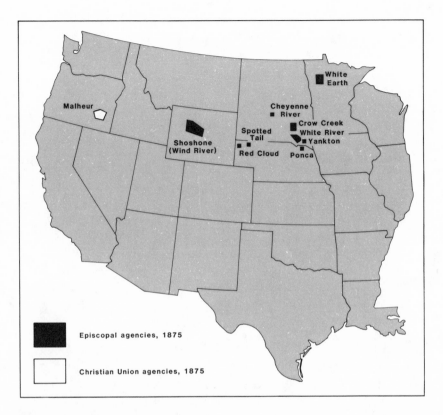

White
Earth

Cheyenne
River

Crow Creek

Malheur

Spotted
Tail

White River

Shoshone
(Wind River)

Yankton

Red Cloud

Ponca

◼ Episcopal agencies, 1875

☐ Christian Union agencies, 1875

Episcopal and Christian Union

The Quakers and Episcopalians, who helped initiate the Peace Policy, met the demands most effectively; their response was nearly matched by the Roman Catholics, who felt persecuted by the Policy. The church most favored by the government, the Methodists, did the least.

A Quaker in the 1870s belonged to a small sect in which an acute sense of religious and biblical identity, of belonging to a peculiar people, compensated for relatively low membership. Slowly breaking away from their traditional forms of language and dress, the Society of Friends first of all sought "the beauty and joy and peace" of immediate religious experience. From an Inner Light came vocation, the divine selection of a person by God for the "concerns" of the world.[1] A pressing concern in 1869 was the destiny of American Indians.

The Quaker concept of lay vocation explained why the Friends supplied so few missionaries for the Peace Policy. The Society emphasized that Indian agents, agency employees, physicians, and teachers could succeed when sent "not only by a clear sense of the call of the Lord . . . but by the pointing of the Divine finger to this particular field." Quaker clerks, agents, and doctors *were* missionaries. Their official duties included distributing rations and annuities, settling tribal disputes, teaching agricultural methods, reconciling Indians with local whites, establishing schools, and hiring teachers. Quaker agents always counted the hogs raised, the bushels harvested, and the teachers employed because secular accomplishments, not chapels built or Indian converts enumerated, were signs that showed progress away from native culture.

No other group in the Peace Policy organized more carefully or more rapidly to meet its new obligations. Hicksite Friends appointed the venerable Samuel Janney as federal superintendent of Nebraska. They assigned one agency to each yearly meeting in the East; these groups frequently sent delegations west to check on the progress and needs of agents. The Orthodox Quakers were even more organized. Superintendent Enoch Hoag of the Central Superintendency (Kansas and Oklahoma) had support from an associated executive committee of Friends, which hired a full-time general agent and a clerk specifically to address the Peace Policy. The committee, composed of two members from each of nine yearly meetings, met annually in Lawrence and in Philadelphia and had five subcommittees, one of which lobbied in Washington. Its auxiliary branches included the Indian Aid Association (founded in April 1869) and the Female Indian Aid Association (founded in December 1870). The executive committee nominated Orthodox agents, men whom it screened with great care. It supervised agents and teachers and supplemented inadequate government salaries.[2]

Officially, the Quaker effort seemed highly successful in the years between 1869 and 1872. Schools, pupils, and farmland in the Central Superintendency tripled. Native ownership of horses grew from eighteen thousand to forty-three thousand. Indian production of potatoes and hogs increased tenfold in four years. Missionary teacher Thomas Battey went west to live and travel with the Kiowas. Slow progress in religious faith, however, worried some Orthodox Friends who instructed their agents and government employees to tell Indians that "Jesus Christ died to redeem us, that He is the only Savior and only Mediator between God and man, and that His Spirit must be allowed to rule and reign in our hearts to make us happy here and hereafter." Children on the Kaw reservation were "stored with hymns" and at the Quapaw agency an awakening marked the "good fruits of religious labor." Another agent reported that many Indian souls were born into the Redeemer's Kingdom after witnessing the calm, placid death of a Quaker child firm in the Christian faith. With such government workers, Orthodox Friends needed few missionaries.[3]

Hicksite Friends followed a similar pattern. They employed only Christian teachers and they hired only Friends for all agency work until they could hire capable Indians. All of their agents opened Sunday schools and offered manual labor instruction. Eastern Quakers back home sent bundles of clothing and supplies to provide reservation children with "citizen's dress." Hicksite Friends, like the Orthodox, carefully counted every yard of fence erected, every bushel of produce harvested, and every hog and sheep raised.

Nevertheless, frontier conditions took a greater toll among the Friends and their tribes than official reports indicated. Difficulties and conflicts, internal and external, engulfed even the more peaceful Quaker agencies from the beginning; at many agencies, Quaker pacifism would be tested to its breaking point.

In the relatively peaceful Northern Superintendency the acculturation of Indians proceeded slowly or not at all because Quaker administrators could not consistently overcome the physical problems of disease, mosquitos, grasshoppers, drought, soil exhaustion, and error in farming techniques. Nor could they reverse Indian attitudes opposed to schooling and to an agrarian way of life.[4] Tribal populations and vitality continued to decline despite earnest efforts and hopeful reports by the Friends. At the Omaha agency, Indians soon became dissatisfied and even angry with their new agents. Quakers from the East, for their part, felt little sympathy for native culture. In addition, some Friends expressed dissatisfaction with others as disharmony and quarrels over money and nepotism broke out almost immediately after their arrival in Nebraska.[5]

Friends also clashed with non-Quakers. A Quaker physician described Omaha agent Edward Painter as a "crazy man" when Painter collided with Presbyterian missionary William Hamilton. Hamilton accused Painter of closing a Presbyterian school in order to raise money "by *his own pet scheme*."

Hamilton, who was henceforth unrelenting in his opposition to Quaker agents, caustically continued: "So they love power & money less than others?"[6] When Painter refused to release previous employees to make room for Friends, he was reprimanded by Superintendent Samuel Janney. Painter did not sound like a gentle Friend when he responded to Janney's "officious intermeddling . . . bitter taunts and sarcasms" and "the great unkindness and injustice by some I have had about me who were *called* Friends."[7]

By 1877 Nebraska agents had experienced trouble with other whites who sold liquor to Indians and with Indians who illegally sold timber to whites. Kansas's governor had verbally attacked Superintendent Hoag, and various Quaker agents reported stealing, adultery, and failing pupils among the tribes. The Quaker claims that they never selected dishonest agents and that Friends never quarreled were patently untrue. At the Otoe agency a nonprofit general store operated by the Friends angered white merchants, and at the Santee agency the Quakers's opposition to using the vernacular infuriated American Board missionaries. A more curious circumstance was the reluctance of Orthodox Friends to accept Indians as Christians; when Jeremiah Hubbard finally did so late in the 1870s, the Society considered it a revolution in Quaker polity.[8]

Quaker enthusiasm for the Peace Policy had waned by 1873. The Society's leaders pleaded for renewed conviction by Friends to counter the growing depression and disillusionment caused by Comanches who did not turn the other cheek, and by Indians and government officials who ignored the example of William Penn. An 1877 government report cautiously noted that Friends had been successful at some agencies, unsuccessful at others, and misunderstood and misrepresented in many places on the frontier. The Society acknowledged that tribes such as the Osage and Quapaw had been thoroughly demoralized by whites and they also found the diseased and declining population of the Kaws distressing. Such embarrassing, negative results of the Peace Policy were rationalized by Friends as "largely ascribable to certain evil social customs" of the Indians.[9]

The Quaker Policy as administered by Quakers produced indifferent results. It failed to realize the vision of 1869 when Friends were confident that control of agencies would allow them to "teach by example the pure effectiveness of God's law of universal love, not as a fancied Utopia but as a policy practically vindicated in the past and in the present and slowly but surely winning its way to the confidence of all."[10]

The Episcopal Church contributed more leadership to the Peace Policy than the Society of Friends did. Bishop Whipple, William Welsh, Felix Brunot, Samuel Hinman, Vincent Colyer, Bishop William Hare, Jared Daniels, Columbus Delano, and Edward Kemble enthusiastically promoted the Indian cause and engaged in most of the decade's great controversies. Much Episcopal concern was of recent origin and was stimulated by Grant's policy. Although the Church of England had first baptized Indians in 1585, sent a missionary to the Six Nations in 1701, and supported an 1844 delegation to investigate the possibility of missions to the Indian Territory, prior to 1870 Episcopalians possessed a weak, ill-supported mission program. During the summer of 1870, after Grant made his offer to the churches, it appeared as if the Episcopal Church might entirely neglect the reform for which its bishop in Minnesota had worked so long.

Whipple, Welsh, and Brunot had contended against Episcopal social conservatism and moral quietism in the 1860s. Laymen, priests, and bishops alike seemed uninterested in raising funds for Indian missions. In 1868 the church provided only seven hundred dollars for Indian work, and E. A. Washburn sadly informed Whipple that he saw little hope in "that most Christian, & conservative lumber wagon," the General Convention.[11] In 1869 the Episcopal Church for the first time contributed to its Santee station, which previously had been supported solely by missionary Samuel Hinman. Then William Welsh praised the Quaker Policy in the *Spirit of Missions*, urging attention to the Episcopal mission program. His pleas went unheeded, and in 1870 evangelical Episcopalians such as Welsh feared that their apathetic church would refuse to nominate agents. Only slowly did denominational officials accept new commitments and even then, as they admitted, "with great hesitation and reluctance."[12]

Late in the summer of 1870 Episcopalians sent William Welsh to visit agencies proposed for their care. His report was enthusiastic but alarming, for the opportunities were immense and the dangers great. In early October, Welsh appeared before the Episcopal Board of Missions and persuaded it to accept the Dakota agencies. The board resolved to awaken the church and to nominate agents "with the express stipulation that the Agents so appointed are to be wholly free from the control of interference of politicians." The Board of Missions told Episcopalians they must now attend to Indian missions, where "the present enormous wastage of sublime opportunities" evidenced a "culpably feeble faith." There was some protest. Bishop Charles Robertson did not oppose the government program but he told board members to remember that prosaic home missions were as important as "the more poetical" Indian work and that one dollar spent on white men produced more results than two spent on Indians. Welsh shot back that Robertson's so-called poetry had attracted neither men nor dollars. Another resolution created a lay Indian Commission despite objections that this introduced a new element into the church hierarchy and improperly gave ecclesiastical authority to some "unknown and irresponsible party." Welsh replied that the Indian Commission could only supervise and would be under the control of the Domestic Committee of the Board of Missions. Finally convinced that the government had offered a novel opportunity, the Episcopal Church voted to officially enter the Peace Policy.[13]

Admittedly "dragged into it," Episcopalians responded enthusiastically once committed to the Peace Policy.[14] Bishops prayed for Indians and preached about saving the church from "lasting shame and reproach." Bishop J. B. Kerfoot of Pittsburgh said God's love in Christ meant that only sinful Christians, caring only for themselves, would ignore the Great Command to go into all the world and preach "an historic, unbroken Church, an historic, uncorrupted, entire creed, a worship and liturgy unstained by error."[15] Such appeals proved effective as interest in missions increased steadily after 1870. The *Spirit of Missions* told its readers that the Peace Policy was an Episcopal innovation and a special responsibility through which God had unmistakenly spoken directly to them. In 1872 William Welsh jubilantly boasted that he had "stirred our Church up pretty thoroughly."[16]

The Peace Policy forced Episcopal reorganization. Arrangements were made to assign certain agencies to the American Church Missionary Society. Women's auxiliaries and parish societies for Indian work were founded in 1872 and 1873.[17] Equally important was the appointment of William Hobart Hare as the first missionary bishop to Indian tribes. The ambiguous ministry to whites and Indians on the frontier previously had caused problems, as bishops Whipple (Minnesota), George Randall (Colorado), Daniel Tuttle (Montana), and Robert Clarkson (Nebraska) knew. With this in mind, Clarkson suggested the creation of a special Indian jurisdiction. The new practice of sending a bishop to a racial group began in 1873 with the consecration of thirty-four-year-old Hare.[18] Delivering a bishop to tribes in advance of missionaries not only solved the problem of divided white loyalties on the frontier but also provided Indians with an exceptional spokesman in Hare, and it allowed Episcopalians to effectively plan, organize, and control their work. Indeed, through his ties with the Indian Office and with Episcopal merchants in Yankton, his control of agencies, and the church's influence in the territorial Republican party, Hare helped to build an Episcopal oligarchy that would control the political economy of Dakota Territory throughout the 1870s.[19]

The church had selected an ideal man for the first bishop of Niobrara. Hare previously had observed the Ottawa, Chippewa, and Winnebago in Michigan and Minnesota, finding nothing in the Indian problem that, as he put it, called for either quackery or despair. Solid, practical work by church and government could end the reservation system and achieve complete Indian assimilation into American life. To accomplish this, Hare believed that Indian children should be separated from their parents as early as possible and placed in boarding schools. Under his administration, the Yankton agency became a showcase of progress by 1876 with its four chapels, five schools, and effective scholarship program. By the end of the Peace Policy, Hare could count seven Episcopal missions in Dakota, several native pastors, eleven Indian catechists, and nine native church workers.[20]

In contrast to these achievements, Hare and his church also experienced reverses and difficulties. By 1875 William Welsh's incessant prying into the Indian Office had alienated most government officials. The Episcopalians' Shoshone agency still had no school or chapel. Among the Sioux, Indians at the Red Cloud and Spotted Tail agencies were requesting Black Robes (Catholics) to replace White Robes (Episcopalians) and there was a national scandal involving the Red Cloud agency. Matters worsened steadily. Money from the East became scarce after the Panic of 1873. By the end of the decade, missionary Hinman and Bishop Hare were exchanging charges in the courts. Many missionaries had lost their zeal and imagination: "Work here," reflected Yankton's Joseph Cook, "appears to go on in such a humdrum, routine sort of way that there is nothing special to record . . . the heroic and romantic days of the Missions here long ago passed away, and we have settled down into the ordinary course of affairs."[21] By 1880, a general decline in interest, together with other problems, made the Episcopal Church eager to retire from all cooperation with the government.

Especially somber and depressing for Episcopalians was the controversy at White Earth, an agency not originally allotted to their denomination and one most vigorously sought by the Roman Catholics. After Episcopalians did gain control of the agency in 1875, their first agent, Lewis Stowe, promptly accused the governor of Minnesota of undermining the federal government. Stowe also battled with the Catholics and drove the agency deeply into debt. Bishop Whipple, before and after Stowe's arrival, poured men and money into White Earth in an effort to build a church and hospital. Reports in the Episcopal *Spirit of Missions* glowed with this example of the Gospel's effectiveness in Minnesota, repeatedly praising missionary Joseph Gilfillan and the model Indian convert, "our faithful Enmegahbowh." As early as 1873 the Peace Policy had been judged so effective at White Earth that whiskey, profanity, and theft supposedly had disappeared from a reservation where Chippewa, "more tenderhearted . . . than most white people," dutifully observed every Sabbath. That, at least, was the enthusiastic news in official reports. Private correspondence from White Earth indicated that life was more complicated. After the Catholics petitioned for the agency in 1875, Whipple and the Congregational agent denounced a priest who told Indians that all Protestants went to Hell and that their "devil's church" was cursed by God. A sympathetic government investigation vindicated the Protestants.[22] Not all troubles could be blamed on Catholicism, and even so benevolent a project as the Bishop Whipple Hospital at White Earth created grave problems for the church. Early in 1875 Joseph Gilfillan confided to Whipple that the hospital had had an unhappy influence on the reservation because the Indians refused to use it. This embarrassing situation was caused by the temper of an Episcopal nurse, Sister Maria, who in one instance distributed eight thousand dollars worth of clothing to Indians by flinging it in their faces. Sick Chippewa soon left the hospital, Gilfillan said, cursing her, the clothing, and everyone else: "[her] spirit of hate shines through the thin varnish of politeness and makes itself plain to [the Indians] . . . at a time when we are passing through a furnace of trial with the Romanists."[23] Sister Maria's letters to the bishop contained sour denunciations of Gilfillan and the Episcopal agent. The turmoil soon included an agency physician who was dismissed and replaced by another doctor who was considered a Christian.

Peace seldom lasted long at White Earth. George Johnson was the son of the Reverend John Johnson (Enmegahbowh) and an Episcopal convert. On his wedding day a young Indian woman—who was not the bride—accused George Johnson of having had sexual relations with her during the last sugarmaking. After confessing, Johnson proceeded to beat the young woman and her mother on Thursday and Friday nights and then to sleep with her on Saturday night. Gilfillan concluded that the beatings and cohabitation "does not seem to show that [George] is repenting."[24] When Gilfillan refused to let Johnson preach, the Indian complained to agent Stowe that the missionary was racially prejudiced. "It seems," Stowe lamented, "the Devil is trying to do his worst just now." Other Indians harassed the agent during the next year and even "our faithful Enmegahbowh" fought with Gilfillan, complaining to Whipple that "everything is going down."[25]

Problems also arose within the Episcopal hierarchy. Lack of men and money crippled the denomination of the Astors, Duponts, and Morgans. Episcopalian officials found it increasingly difficult to locate agents and Indian missionaries at a time when the church did not have enough ministers to serve the white settlers on the frontier. "What am I do do," wrote one Episcopalian official from the Pacific Northwest, "with this Vast *Empire* on my hands to which so few *good* men are willing to come? Bishop Tuttle writes me that he has recently called *26* men to vacant places in his field & that 23 said 'No I thank you' . . . Such is the Missionary Spirit (?) of our Clergy & people."[26]

In 1870 the Episcopal Indian Commission had issued an ultimatum to the churches: either produce more missionaries and raise an extra fifty thousand dollars each year, or consign the Indians to destruction. By 1875 the commission not only was ten thousand dollars in debt, but found itself under increasing attack from within the church. When the Board of Missions tried unsuccessfully to liquidate the commission, William Welsh submitted his resignation, only to retract it two weeks later. In 1877, with the commission now fifteen thousand dollars in debt, Bishop George Bedell of Ohio openly called for its termination and charged it with being an administratively unsound anomaly that violated the Church's constitution.[27] Bedell's comments irked commission secretary Robert Rogers, who published a sharply worded rebuttal. Rogers feared that his opponents would demand his resignation and that Indian work would be the "little ewe lamb" sacrificed to save dollars. "Did it ever occur to you," he wrote to a friend, "that the Methodist system is a sort of 'missing link' between the spontaneous outcome of liberal giving, according to ability on the part of the Disciples in the Apostolic day, and the non-giving of lots of so-called Churchmen? Mind you, I don't propose to turn Methodist or Romanist. . . . But they do manage to reach and secure contributions."[28] The board of managers reluctantly agreed to provide onefourth of the commission's budget and Rogers retained his job amid "a good deal of friction & of feeling (I suppose I mustn't say bad blood)."[29]

Robert Rogers despaired for the Episcopal Indian Commission as it again sunk into debt and when William Welsh, his greatest ally, died in 1878. On January 14, 1879, the Board of Missions officially resolved: "That the present Committee for Indian Missions be discharged and the administration of these Missions be confined to the Domestic Committee." This effectively ended Episcopal participation in the Peace Policy. Ten days later, with no signs of bad blood, the *Churchman* calmly reported that the mission board had reduced church expenses by eliminating an organization that no longer filled a useful function because "the Church will do her duty in the matter without constant urging."[30]

Robert Rogers was deceived if he thought the Methodist Church easily recruited men and money for the Peace Policy. They did not, one reason being that they made little effort to do so.

In 1882 John Reid of the Methodist Missionary Society informed the secretary of the interior that Methodists entered the Peace Policy with "extreme reluctance" and only after the president of the United States had pressed them to cooperate. The church nominated agents because it was "glad to bear the burden" for the Indians, but making nominations, Reid maintained, was his only responsibility. When questioned by the Board of Indian Commissioners several years earlier, Reid had admitted that his church should do more and had offered the same excuses: Methodists were cajoled into the Peace Policy, they could not support Indian missions because of their peculiar episcopal system, and the system made it impossible for the mission board in New York to control agents, many of whom were not Methodist.[31]

Reid correctly remembered the reluctance with which Methodists responded in 1870. It is also true that they were assured that their responsibilities ended with the nomination of agents. By 1873 Reid had recognized the poor performance of his church. He offered to surrender several agencies and apologized that only a permanently established Peace Policy could gain wholehearted Methodist cooperation.[32] Reid was also correct in blaming Methodist polity for the failure. Instead of creating a special committee, the Methodist Missionary Society assumed that frontier churches would be sympathetic to Indians and it therefore gave local conferences the duty of nominating agents and supervising missions. This procedure not only resulted in the appointment of unemployed ministers as agents but also guaranteed an apathetic Methodist performance. Most Methodist agents reported no missionary effort and no schools on their reservations. When local conferences attempted to do more than name agents, the results were meager. At Klamath the agent and his employees offered to donate money for half the salary of a missionary, but the Oregon Conference was unable to pay the balance or to find a candidate. The Missionary Society in New York seldom sent funds to agencies, rarely communicated with the government, and quite blissfully ignored the Indian problem.

Methodists spent little on either secular or religious education. Except for sustained mission efforts at the Michigan and Round Valley agencies, teaching was left to government employees and local preachers. More than any other church under the Peace Policy, Methodists allowed the federal government to sustain their entire Indian mission program.[33] The commissioner of Indian affairs reported in 1875 that Methodists used their authority under the Peace Policy "for the promotion of Church interests rather than for . . . Indians."[34] In 1873 Inspector Edward Kemble castigated the Methodists when he urged his fellow Episcopalians to apply for the Pacific Coast agencies:

If you had seen as I have the spiritual destitution, the utter starvation, yea worse, the total perversion of gracious means to secular and unholy ends, in the administration of affairs at some of the Agencies on this coast, you would not think me over zealous. The Peace Policy is in great danger of overthrow from the corrupting influences which have crept in under the name of religious teaching out here. The Washington agencies, with one or two exceptions, are in lamentable state . . . on Puget's Sound there is a Methodist elder allied to a clique or ring of politicians, and speculators, who is endeavoring to "run the Superintendency" in his own interest. . . . The denomination having charge here, are not, in one single instance, carrying on a religious work separate from the Govt. The Methodists are not able to carry on the Agencies they have grasped here.[35]

One exception to Kemble's indictment was the Yakima agency, where "Father" James Wilbur, a deep-voiced, egotistical, three-hundred-pound giant, established a benevolent and iron-fisted despotism. Wilbur had migrated from

New York to Oregon in 1847 and was hired at Yakima in Washington Territory as a government teacher in 1860. After intolerance for non-Methodists and quarrels with his superior led to his suspension in 1862, Wilbur went to Washington, D.C., and spoke with Lincoln, who appointed him Yakima agent. In 1869 Wilbur was replaced by an army officer under Grant's new policy, but he returned to the post the next year after much dissension and name-calling, destined to become, in Carl Schurz's words, "the most successful agent in the service." Wilbur declared his intentions to the Washington superintendent in 1871: "I do not propose to spend my time in talking, or *writing,* the wrongs done to the Indians formerly, or recently, but in taking hold of the work, according to the ability given me, to make what you desire, a *'Model Reservation.'*"[36] A model reservation it became, especially in Methodist propaganda. While boasting about its model agency in Washington Territory, the Methodist Church somehow forgot its failures and negligence in Montana, Idaho, Oregon, and California.

Even Yakima, moreover, was a far from perfect model. Methodist spokesmen neglected to mention that Wilbur failed to provide sufficient schools, that he was an autocrat (although he treated Indians no more harshly than he did whites who trespassed on his reservation), and that he was fanatical in his hatred of Roman Catholic priests and converts. Wilbur was exceptionally successful in promoting white culture, but factors other than his Methodist faith help to explain this success. Blessed with good land, ample water, and seemingly inexhaustible timber, the Yakimas were an energetic and self-sufficient tribe. The Methodists sent more church money to Yakima than to any other reservation. For James Wilbur, brotherly love included tyranny and forced starvation as incentives to make Indians labor. Nor was there a happy ending. During the blizzard of 1880-81 the model agency lost nearly all its livestock and was reduced to desperation. The following year the service's most successful agent retired.[37]

If the Methodist Church expressed determination in Washington Territory, in Montana it showed none; if at Yakima it scored its single success, at the Fort Hall, Crow, Blackfeet, and Milk River agencies it recorded its most miserable failures. In northern Montana, Methodists might have shared the Quaker, Episcopal, and Presbyterian experiences with Indian warfare and violence, except that the Blackfeet, the most bellicose tribe under the church's jurisdiction, had suffered a smallpox epidemic in 1869-70 that devastated tribal population, morale, and ability to resist white encroachments. The painful story of Methodist and government neglect of Blackfeet poverty, starvation, and cultural disintegration during the 1870s extinguishes any image of humanitarian glamour from the Peace Policy.[38] Agents appointed by the Rocky Mountain Conference criticized their church for neglect and for the church's indifference to its obligations. When the conference finally did send a missionary to the Shoshone in Idaho, it did not provide a salary and the agent was forced to hire the new missionary as a teacher. John Reid explained that if his denomination had not done as well in Montana as on the Pacific Coast, it was because of the low character of Montana whites and the church's "constant fight with the basest immorality." In 1874 Montana's governor complained that the Peace Policy was a total failure in his territory.[39]

It also remains a mystery why four agencies were assigned to a church that had no missions and almost no white congregations in Montana and Idaho.[40] The Peace Policy was not mentioned at the Rocky Mountain annual conferences until 1874, when a newly formed Indian committee confessed that little had been done and admitted that several agents did not even belong to the church. The committee reported that success at a mission and boarding school operated by a Reverend Mr. Bird at the Crow agency might convince skeptical Montana Methodists that "Indians can learn." The Rocky Mountain Conference then endorsed the Peace Policy and passed a resolution which said that the Gospel was mightier than the sword. They had second thoughts two years later. A month after Custer's debacle on the Little Big Horn, Montana Methodists sent a resolution to Congress: "WHEREAS Present indications betoken an Indian War, and as our people and territory are constantly exposed to these bloodthirsty savages; therefore, be it *Resolved,* That . . . the General Government should at once take prompt and efficient means to reinforce our heroic army and drive the various tribes to their reservations inflicting severe punishment on every Indian."[41] Montana Methodism's uncertain commitment to the Peace Policy ended in 1879, when the special Indian committee was dissolved.[42]

Back in the East a writer for the *Methodist Quarterly* (1877) praised Grant. The president had turned the Indian service "into a field for missionary enterprise" and, the writer concluded, "the Indian problem . . . has been solved." Episcopalians thought otherwise. They were astounded that of six hundred thousand dollars spent for Methodist missions for 1879, only seven hundred dollars were spent on American Indians. A writer for the *Churchman,* an Episcopalian journal, calculated that this averaged fifty dollars an agency and that if Methodists continued to spend "$15 on a Brahmin [and] fifteen cents on a Blackfoot" the North American Indians could be evangelized by the year 17,865 A.D. Methodists, the writer observed, spent fifty dollars and obtained a job worth fifteen hundred dollars: "their neglect of this field [is] not only a breach of trust, but a colossal blunder." A later editorial suggested that uninterested churches should gracefully retire from the Peace Policy.[43] Episcopal criticism was harsher than that of the new Quinault agent, Oliver Woods, who discovered that the Methodist Church in Montesano, Washington Territory, was guilty of extorting money from agency employees. Woods said that forcing Indians to aid the church instead of the church aiding the Indians "has been a reversal of the object intended by the government."[44]

Presbyterians, like Episcopalians and Methodists, hesitated to join the Peace Policy. They complained that they had been given the most difficult agencies in the nation, and they feared that the Peace Policy might violate Presbyterian scruples about separation of Church and State. But after a year's experience the denomination concluded that the Board of Indian Commissioners and church nomination of agents were "two things full of good." Presbyterian leaders were likewise confident that goodness would eventually prevail in the Southwest. They told their members that the entire church was morally responsible for Indian agents, that the Peace Policy was a boon to evangelism, and that the Presbyterian Church had an obligation to create missions at all assigned agencies. With doubts laid to rest, the Presbyterian Church quickly and enthusiastically moved into the work—and into unexpected hardships.

Unlike the Friends and Episcopalians, Presbyterians developed no special body to administer the Peace Policy. Unlike the Methodists, they did not trust local churches to appoint agents and so they gave that duty to their Board of Foreign Missions and its secretary, John Lowrie. Supervision of agents, however, was left to local presbyteries, which were not required to report to the board but which through a so-called circle of sympathy informed the church of an agent's morals. This plan might have worked well if Presbyterians in New Mexico and Arizona had been honest and interested in Indians.

Less than a year into the program the Presbyterian Church in the Southwest was racked by a controversy between ministers, missionaries, and Indian agents. On February 23, 1872, Jicarilla Apache agent W. D. Crothers wrote to John Lowrie that a drunken Presbyterian minister in Albuquerque had disgraced himself and the church by shooting his wife. The accused man, the Reverend Patrick MacElroy, then replied that these charges were a scheme to libel him because he opposed the efforts of Crothers and Navajo missionary James Roberts to defraud the Presbyterian Church by planning a fake university in Santa Fe. Two Indian agents, one a minister and the other an elder in the church, had told MacElroy of the swindle. If Lowrie refused to expose the guilty parties, MacElroy threatened to go to the civil courts in order to convict "men [who] are nothing more than unscrupulous henchmen, wire pullers, twisters."

After Crothers and Navajo agent William Arny, who was also under attack, were supported by two ministers, the Presbyterian Home Missions Board recalled MacElroy. At this point Alex Irvine, soon to succeed Arny as Navajo agent, came to former Catholic MacElroy's defense, and the latter again castigated the Home Board for its ignorance: "A poor Missionary who had enough experience of *priestly tyranny* in another Church certainly did not expect to find a greater and a more unatural [*sic*] one practiced in his Church of adoption. . . . I cannot reconcile it with the multitudinous expression of *liberty*, etc., allowed in your Church."[45] Rumors from Crothers that Episcopalians had lured MacElroy into their fold, and that Navajo missionary Roberts should be removed, further complicated the affair. Disgusted with the Home Board, MacElroy implored Lowrie to rescue him from "diabolical torture" by Presbyterian ministers and agents whose actions "must proceed from hearts as black as the clerical coats they wear." He threatened to expose conditions in New Mexico so that "when the public once sees individuals & Boards unmasked, then I feel your *Boards* . . . shall go down before the blast of honest indignation . . . and suffer as well merited a fate as Tammany."[46]

With the MacElroy affair revealing internal weaknesses, Lowrie soon realized that helping the Indians in New Mexico and Arizona would not be easy. Frequent resignations and release of agents at the Jicarilla, Navajo, Cimarron, Mescalero, and Southern Apache agencies, the church's failure to support the Navajo mission, endless acrimony over Navajo agent W. F. M. Arny, and back-stabbing between agents and clergy all verified the judgment of Catholic bishop Lamy of Santa Fe: Presbyterian efforts were "merely nominal missions without any result."[47] In 1873 the Presbyterians offered their southwestern agencies to three other Protestant denominations, but not to Roman Catholics. When no one accepted, the Presbyterians held on.

In the Pacific Northwest similar problems arose. Henry Harmon Spalding, who had been an Indian agent in 1850, seethed with anger when the Nez Perce nomination, recently allotted to the Presbyterians, went to John Monteith. By the end of 1871 Spalding resolved to protect the honor of the Presbyterian Church and the Board of Indian Commissioners by forcing Monteith's removal. Using the agent's own stationery and enlisting the cooperation of an agency physician, Spalding cataloged Monteith's sins in a letter to Vincent Colyer. They were considerable in number and magnitude: (1) Monteith was not a Presbyterian—"an honest, honorable man," but not a Presbyterian; (2) "the strong smell of his breath" revealed that the agent was an alcoholic; (3) he had consumed a ten-gallon keg of whiskey in a short time; (4) Monteith banned the Bible and prayer; (5) only one other employee at the Lapwai agency was a Christian; (6) the agent did not attend Spalding's "deeply interesting" revival meetings; (7) he prohibited Indians from attending Spalding's meetings; and (8) he had hired an interpreter, Perin B. Whitman, who was immoral, a Sabbath breaker, and a patron of grog shops and dance halls. Two missionaries and Colyer firmly endorsed Spalding's accusations, whereas two other missionaries rallied behind the agent. The Presbyterians conducted a full investigation, finding the charges false on each count. After a stunned Spalding was released as a government teacher, the struggle did not end. Bitterness at Lapwai continued unabated, missionary against missionary, mission wives and daughters against mission wives and daughters, missionary against agent, Catholic against Protestant.[48]

Despite the strong leadership and participation of Foreign Board secretary John Lowrie in the Peace Policy,[49] the overall Presbyterian performance was weak. The denomination remained confused for three years about its responsibilities and relation to the government beyond the nomination of agents. Only reluctantly did it support reservation schools; at no time did Presbyterian Indian mission expenditures exceed 5 percent of its total mission budget, and only a small fraction of the 5 percent went to the Peace Policy agencies.[50] Opposed to the nomination of clergy as agents, Lowrie had trouble finding suitable volunteers. Almost all of his agents were dedicated laymen, married and middle-aged. Only a few had had any contact with Indians; more than a third volunteered for reasons of health. The fruits of the Peace Policy, in terms of Presbyterian conversions and acculturation of Indians, proved most disappointing to Lowrie and his Board.[51] Their participation closed with yet another internecine struggle, this time not between missionaries in the West, but between denominational officials in the East. The conflict involved differences in mission theory, had deep historic roots, and included a fight to control financial contributions from church women.

The merger of Old School and New School Presbyterian missions had created the new Board of Home Missions in 1870. This had been preceded by the formation of the Ladies Board of Missions to serve both groups, but when the new Home Board refused to send money to frontier schools, both Sheldon Jackson, the Home Board's outstanding missionary to Alaska, and the Foreign Board turned to the women for help in the Indian country. At the same time there was discussion of transferring Indian missions from the Foreign to the Home Board. The debate continued until 1877, when the General Assembly confirmed the transfer. At the Board of Indian Commissioners' annual meeting in 1878 the Home Board, the Foreign Board, and the Southern Presbyterians were represented. The conflict that followed was not over the right to nominate agents, which Lowrie's Foreign Board retained but did not want, or over the control of Indian missions, which were divided between the Home Board and the Southern Presbyterians. Instead, the question concerned who had the right to accept money from the Ladies Board of Missions.

In January of 1878 the Foreign Board sent the Women's Foreign Missionary Society (organized in 1871) a circular that claimed that Sheldon Jackson wanted their money and sought to control all American missions. The women were informed that Jackson had badly distorted his Indian program. There were "but a few points among our Indians where judicious school work can be done" and this limitation resulted in a disproportionate spending on Indian education, "a lavish waste of funds in unpromising Home fields taken up in mere rivalry." Jackson's success in obtaining money, the circular warned, would cause jealousy and confusion, push the Foreign Board out of the West, and create a selfish ingrown spirit "bottled up in Arizona or frozen up in Alaska." The Home Board, confident that a backlash against the circular would injure its rival, simply answered that such talk was "clap-trap."[52] For the next three years the two Presbyterian bodies refused to cooperate. In 1880 they fought over who should send teachers to the long-neglected Uintah agency and the next year a missionary in Oklahoma reported that his Indians were aware of the jealousy between Presbyterians, a fact that embarrassed him and which he felt helped southern Methodists and Baptists to surge ahead in recruiting members. A Presbyterian official described the situation as a "fearful mess."[53]

Ulysses S. Grant had begun his Peace Policy because he believed Indian affairs were in a fearful mess; he had not guessed that Christians would come to condemn Indian missions as a lavish waste. Perhaps Grant made this error because he believed the type of propaganda that churches habitually publish about themselves. In 1936, when Arthur Judson Brown wrote *One Hundred Years*, a history of Presbyterian foreign missions, he did not mention any conflicts or jealousies. Rather, Brown said that the idea of transferring all Indians to the Home Board grew slowly until 1893, when a mandate from the General Assembly placed all Indian missions under Home control. The Foreign Board found itself "cheerfully acquiescing in this order." With such concord and cheerful acquiescence within the Presbyterian Church, who could have doubted the success of ventures such as the Peace Policy or the triumph of Christianity?

The Quakers, Episcopalians, Methodists, and Presbyterians were awarded almost two-thirds of all agencies; the four denominations controlled the largest and most important of the seventy-one reservations that existed in 1870. The remaining agencies were assigned to the Congregational, Baptist, Unitarian, Roman Catholic,[54] and Dutch Reformed churches.

Antipathy toward Catholics was the main reason why Vincent Colyer and the Board of Indian Commissioners pushed the Dutch Reformed into the Peace Policy. The Reformed went flinchingly into their difficult Arizona agencies, contributing as little as possible. Only after being lectured and scolded by General O. O. Howard did the suspicious "birthright Democrats" of New York and New Jersey find any merit in Grant's Republican policies. When told in 1871 that they had been awarded an Apache agency, they had at first declined. After one agent died enroute to Arizona and the attempt to recruit a replacement from seminary classes failed, the Reformed admitted "we overcalculated, not the ability, but the disposition of the church to cooperate."

For several years the Dutch Reformed simply rubber-stamped nominations made by Vincent Colyer. Not until 1873 did they send a man of their own choice and then only when assisted by the German Reformed Church. Reformed agents included a Methodist, Congregationalist, and three Presbyterians. The church explained that those denominations had better men on the frontier, but such ecumenicity did not allow the church to escape scandals and controversy. As with other denominations that performed poorly in the Peace Policy, the Dutch Reformed entrusted their work to an already existing foreign mission board and created no special Indian committee; their only supervision was reading an agent's report. The Ladies Union Missionary Association did send supplies "from a melodeon to a primer" to the Pimas, but many agents in Arizona complained about a lack of interest in New York. The outstanding Reformed agent was John Clum at San Carlos; the only effective mission was at the Pima agency where an immigrant Methodist, J. H. Cook, taught the Indians to speak English with a German accent. This success notwithstanding, in 1880 Reformed officials realized that their church had failed and they requested that the Apache and Pima be assigned to other churches.[55] This confirmed what one of their members had predicted in 1871—the Arizona frontier was no place for New Yorkers:

> I was very much gratified to learn that you [Colyer] had appointed an agent for the Pima and Maricopa Indians—and that he is a Methodist. Methodists are our Pioneers . . . we must cooperate with them. The Dutch church is an *excellent* church to belong to—it is *slow* and *sure*, but advances slowly. In doctrine it is the true standard of Christian faith and practice; but in a grand army, we need *skirmishers*, as well as a solid column and impenetrable lines.[56]

Colyer must have shaken his head over the assertion that true Christian faith left one unfit for Indian agencies.

The Dutch Reformed proved to be graceful losers; Congregationalists were not. In 1870, before the Peace Policy expanded beyond the Society of Friends, the American Board of Commissioners for Foreign Missions was in the process of transferring their Ondanah, Yankton, and Flandreau missions to the Presbyterian Church. Though it quickly endorsed the expansion of Grant's Policy, the board offered little support. Despite frequent pleas from the Riggs brothers, Indian missions were seldom mentioned in the board's *Missionary Herald.* The Dakota fight over agency control was obviously initiated by the Riggs family and not by Boston. The board's weak response was due in part to financial problems: during 1875, donations and bequests to the board decreased by thirty thousand dollars; after another twenty-five-thousand-dollar drop in 1877, the board secretary despaired that "we know not whither we are going."[57]

When one of its committees told the board in 1875 that the Peace Policy merited more attention, the commissioners responded by making a special plea for "the Occupation of Fort Berthold." In May of that year Charles Lemon Hall traveled up the Missouri River with "some forty rough 'Black Hillers,' most of them gamblers or worse." He disembarked at Fort Berthold, where he began his labors to save the Sioux from the negative forces of white civilization. During Hall's five years he suffered through death and sacrifice in his family; there was little to reward and much to discourage a man outnumbered by miners, gamblers, and traders. In 1881 he recorded the fruits of his work: "Four of the nearest and dearest to me have gone home. Two of the influential young men in whom I put much hope have gone, and others whom we had hope have gone, but God is our portion still."[58] As the plains winter approached that year, a woman teacher at Forth Berthold wrote to Boston: "Sometimes when I have thought how the American Board takes pains to select the *very choicest* women to be found & then sends them to such a place as Berthold, to be overworked and underfed and to suffer from cold, and to have their intellects starved, because of the *sheer ignorant-stupidity* of those at the head of things, my *whole soul has* risen to an indignant protest against the *cruel wrong*."[59]

In 1873 the American Board had transferred its agency responsibilities to the American Missionary Association and, except for reopening the Choctaw mission in 1872, Fort Berthold was the board's only attempt to expand its Indian work during the decade. Yet the board's impact on the Peace Policy was much greater than these few missions indicate, Congregationalism's contributions being in the East, not the West. At least three board members served on the Board of Indian Commissioners and several others were influential congressmen. Actual discouragements in the field contrasted starkly with the American Board's praise of the Peace Policy: "The missionaries of this Board wrought out the solution of the 'Indian Question' of this country. They have applied the gospel faithfully, and nothing but the gospel to this problem, and the gospel has solved it."[60] The problem solved, the board transferred all Indian missions to the American Missionary Association in 1883, thus ending what it officially called "a bright page in history."

The American Missionary Association had been founded in 1846 in protest of the American Board's toleration of slavery. After the Civil War the association concentrated on the freed slaves and had no American Indian program. Embarrassed by its assignment to four agencies, the association nevertheless accepted the Peace Policy with determined optimism as it carefully selected agents, supplemented their government salaries, and widely publicized the new reform. The association's ardor cooled after 1873, perhaps the result of a bitter clash between William Welsh and Edward P. Smith, the commissioner of Indian affairs (1873–75) and an association leader. Lacking money and devoted to its work for the freedmen at Fisk University and Hampton Institute, the association doubted if Indians could overcome the barriers placed in their road to redemption. By the mid-1870s it had surrendered the Minnesota agencies to the Episcopal and Free-Will Baptist churches and tried to rid itself of commitments in Dakota.

In 1873 Stephen Riggs had convinced the American Missionary Association that it should support him against the Episcopalians. If it would do so, he promised to secure control of the American Board agencies in Dakota for the association with the understanding that the board would continue to support its missions there. Riggs confided to the American Board that this would be an ideal arrangement because *"none of us covet* the responsibility [for] . . . Indian agents."* By 1875 Riggs had grown disillusioned with the missionary association and urged the American Board to accept agencies that the association now wished to abandon. *Advance* magazine, a Congregational publication, called for the American Board to relieve the missionary association, and its editor chastised both groups by pointing to Episcopal accomplishments. In 1877 the association again tried to drop the agencies, but transfer in Dakota still did not occur despite frantic lobbying efforts by the Riggs family in Washington and Boston. In 1881 the American Board urged the continuation of church nomination of agents, which led the missionary association to answer that the board had always carefully avoided assuming such responsibility. When the board finally did give its entire Indian program to the association two years later, the question of agent nomination was academic.[61]

The American Missionary Association used reasons of comity to excuse its own failings under the Peace Policy. Aside from importing a few Comanches and Sioux to Hampton and maintaining the Eells family (who had been part of the original Whitman mission group) at Skokomish, the association's missions were negligible. Its contribution came through men who served the government directly: A. C. Barstow, Edward Tobey, Clinton B. Fisk, and Eliphalet Whittlesey of the Board of Indian Commissioners; General O. O. Howard; Vice President Henry Wilson; and Indian Commissioner Edward Smith.

If Congregationalists shirked responsibility, most Baptists and Unitarians probably were unaware that they had any obligations at all. The Baptists resented Quakers in Indian Territory and claimed that reservations should be allocated to churches whose missionaries spoke the native language.[62] Baptists did little more than recruit agents, finding even this difficult. The Nevada agent in 1880 summarized mission work among the Paiute and Shoshone: "The Baptists, whose missionary hand so faithfully extended to others all over the land . . . had never reached these benighted souls. Here is an abounding harvest waiting to be garnered, but an absolute dearth of reapers and sickles."[63]

Baptist hesitation could not be excused because of scruples about church and state. The church enthusiastically endorsed Grant's Peace Policy. Between 1878 and 1881 its Home Missionary Society expressed strong aversion to any change in the "only humane and Christian" policy toward Indians. When Grant retired, the society for the first time mentioned that Indians had been neglected by the church and spoke of a need to awaken Baptists to this "too much overlooked" and "feebly prosecuted" topic.[64] As the Peace Policy drew to a close, the home society blessed it with unqualified approval and lamented its demise.

Baptists cared too little too late. A denominational publication, the *Watchman*, had earlier shown interest in Indians only when Baptists were alarmed about Catholics in Oklahoma and Mormons in Utah. In 1873, A. S. Patton, editor of the *Baptist Weekly*, grumbled that the vexing Indian problem would remain unresolved and should be "laid on the table indefinitely, while discussing the newer question [of Chinese labor]." Judging from Patton's dislike of Chinese, Indians were fortunate to escape his attention.[65] Baptists left the Indian question on the table, indefinitely.

Unitarians, responding as feebly in Colorado as Baptists did in Nevada, at least enjoyed two distinctions in supplying the agencies at Los Pinos and White River: They sent out the most unusual agent, the Reverend Jebez Neversink Trask, and they were the only Protestant body to officially appoint a Roman Catholic, Charles Adams. Actually, Adams secured the post when Colorado governor Edward M. McCook, a close friend of Grant's, misrepresented him as a Unitarian. Adams proved to be a most capable agent for the Utes. Trask, on the other hand, was an authentic Unitarian. He walked the three hundred miles from Denver to Los Pinos agency, where he served as an honest if abnormal Indian agent. Trask was not insane, as rumored in Denver, though one government inspector confirmed that there was "a certain eccentricity in the manners and oddity in appearance peculiar to Mr. Trask." Marshall Sprague has written that Trask with "his enormous green goggles and buckthorn stick frightened the [Ute] children . . . he waddled around glowering at everybody in his navy blue swallow tail coat with brass buttons, his skin-tight pants flaring funnel-shaped at the ankles, his ancient broad-brimmed Puritan hat."[66] After the Utes forced the Unitarian agent to ride a rail, Jebez Neversink Trask resigned, commenting, "My relations with the Indians have been peculiar."

In 1870 the Unitarians had one mission to the black freedmen and another in India, but none to American Indians. Denominational officials hoped, in vain, that cooperation with the Indian Office would stimulate Unitarian concern. Jabez Trask's attempt to enforce Sabbath observance at Los Pinos was the extent of Unitarian evangelism. Like the Methodists, Unitarians frequently appointed ministers and counted Indian agents as missionaries. Agents received the "hearty sympathy of many brethren" but little else. The *Unitarian Review* (1874) noted the apathy of the denomination toward Indian reform, and the American Unitarian Association (1876) chastised Unitarians for failing to do what the government expected.[67] Although Unitarians asserted that their agents tried to subdue the "fleshly lusts" of the Utes and to instruct them in a righteous, godly life, their church came under attack for not providing capable agents and for not building schools. Three months before the White River massacre of 1879, the church was condemned as the most negligent in the Peace Policy. After the murder of the White River agent, the denomination excused itself by saying that the high altitude of the Rockies made work difficult and that Utes "were not up to the mark" in farming.[68]

Unitarians had demonstrated that they were not up to government expectations in missions. Nevertheless an editor of the *Unitarian Review*, thinking that his church still controlled the Ute appointments when the Peace Policy ended in 1882, commented that the government needed help: "Surely, it is for us to send to them a missionary."[69]

Critics of the Peace Policy have often assumed that the reform failed because of church pettiness and denominational rivalry, a charge that is only partly true. The Friends, chosen for their tolerance and ability to cooperate with others, antagonized Congregationalists, Presbyterians, Baptists, and Episcopalians. The Presbyterians closed their Omaha and Winnebago missions and ended years of cooperation with the government after Quaker Samuel Janney blocked public funds previously sent to missionaries and after he refused to allow Presbyterian clergy to use agency sawmills. Quakers also denounced missionaries who taught in the vernacular, and in the East, Hicksite and Orthodox Friends refused to speak to each other about Indian affairs.

Still more pervasive was hostility between Catholics and Protestants. The Methodists, though they wasted considerable time disputing with each other,[70] acted most vigorously when they expected Catholic action. Episcopalians and Catholics clashed at the Spotted Tail agency and Bishop Whipple tried to expel Catholics from White Earth. Congregationalists resented the success of priests and nuns at Devil's Lake. At Skokomish, the Eells family considered Catholic converts as being "captured" by the opposition. Presbyterians opposed Catholics at LaPointe, Wisconsin, and threatened to close all their New Mexico schools when a Catholic agent was appointed in 1882. In the Pacific Northwest, W. H. Gray published an abusive tract against "the papal sect," in which Gray urged the total removal of Catholics from the Peace Policy because they supposedly had incited the Cayuses to kill Marcus Whitman and had caused the Nez Perce and Bannock wars. The *Unitarian Review* described Catholics as slaves of tyrannical and despotic priests. Catholics themselves were not immune from prejudice against Protestants or from intrachurch acrimony and discord.[71]

Given the competition and distrust, it is easy to overlook efforts toward ecumenical cooperation and understanding in the 1870s. The *Independent* spoke out for fair treatment of Catholics, publishing articles by priests and bishops. The editor of *Advance* chastised Protestants who used the government in order to attack Catholicism.[72] Felix Brunot, though often irritated by Roman Catholics, sent a statue of the Blessed Virgin to Tulalip, a Catholic agency. On a visit to that Puget Sound reservation, Brunot praised Father Chirouse and the Sisters of Charity, telling assembled Indians that all white men believed in one God and in redemption through Jesus Christ: "If you all want to go to Seattle, some would go around one side of the island, some would go by the other; you would all meet there, and you would know that some had only taken a little different way in which to go. We are all going to the same God and the same heaven, and if in earnest we will all meet there at last."[73] Methodist Robert Milroy also praised Chirouse and requested higher salaries for the priest and his staff. Episcopalians William Welsh and Jared Daniels commended the St. Ignatius school for the Flathead tribe in Montana. Welsh also praised Catholic work at Devil's Lake, and Protestant agent I. L. Mahan reported that Roman Catholic schools in Wisconsin were completely satisfactory. A. B. Meacham, another Protestant official, lauded Catholic endeavors on the Pacific Coast.[74]

One can find a considerable number of instances of cooperation and comity among Protestants. Evangelicals such as Brunot and Welsh had long worked for Church union because they believed that closing ranks among denominations was a scriptural command. Welsh often praised the Quakers and, despite loathing the Riggs clan, he reported that Presbyterian Thomas Williamson in Dakota worked well with Episcopalian Samuel Hinman. In an address to the Episcopal General Convention of 1871, Episcopal bishop Daniel Tuttle thanked God for the cooperation of Presbyterians, Baptists, and Methodists. In 1878 the Baptist *Home Mission Monthly* republished the entire annual report of the Episcopal Indian Commission. Congregationalist Charles Lemon Hall could preach in Methodist churches, attend Episcopal and Roman Catholic services, and have his children baptized in Fargo's Presbyterian church. Oregon Methodists invited Lutherans, Disciples, Baptists, United Brethren, and Evangelicals to their annual conferences. California Methodists asked Presbyterians to lead worship at their agencies. In the Indian

Territory, Baptist appointee G. W. Ingalls insisted that as agent he tried to act fairly toward all denominations, and Quakers in the same region encouraged a Mennonite to spread the "gospel net" over Cheyennes and Arapahos. Presbyterian agent William Arny asked for Methodist teachers in 1872, and by 1875 his employees included an Episcopalian, a Presbyterian minister, and a Baptist minister. The American Missionary Association's Green Bay schools were taught by an Episcopalian, a Methodist, a Presbyterian, a Catholic, and three Congregationalists.[75]

Two important examples of Protestant cooperation were the Board of Indian Commissioners and the work of Bishop Henry Whipple. Members of the Board belonged to a variety of denominations except the Roman Catholic; their meetings and annual conferences, which always included officials from the mission societies, never produced sectarian quarrels. Infrequent communication and inadequate sharing of common problems did hinder the churches but, in the East, they remained outwardly cordial.

Bishop Whipple especially was a symbol of Christian unity and cooperation. Despite his distrust of Catholics and his conflict with the Riggses in Dakota notwithstanding, Whipple worked well with other denominations and negotiated comity agreements among missionaries. He instructed Episcopal missionaries "never to say a word against any of our Protestant brethren, nor for that matter, against the Roman Catholics." In 1870 he protested Yankton's transfer to the American Board and wanted Episcopal control at Santee and White Earth, but at the same time he warned that "the poor heathen are going to death & we must not wrangle." All missions must work together, he told a friend, and although Whipple cherished the Nicene Creed, Apostolic Succession, and the Anglican Church, he loved all Christians: "I hear from any lips that Christ is preached. The days in which we live are full of meaning and many a prophecy is being fulfilled. It is 'the Eventide'—we must waste no hours in strife and learn to take the things wherein we differ to that Savior who alone can help us to be of one mind."[76] The feeling was mutual. The American Missionary Association, which had good reason to dislike Episcopalians after clashes with William Welsh, continued to print essays by Whipple on behalf of Indians. After the death of Presbyterian Thomas Williamson, the missionary's son wrote to the bishop:

> In his family father very often spoke of you . . . always in terms of the highest commendation, and rejoiced in what you accomplished a little less but not less truly and sincerely than if accomplished by himself and others of his own loved denomination. . . . he was thoroughly presbyterian in his views concerning a liturgy as in other things, yet as a presentation of divine truth and as devotional reading, he prized your prayer book very highly. . . . I think he loved no other more if as much as he loved you.[77]

At the beginning of the Peace Policy, a Unitarian writer praised the denominations joining together "in a spirit of entire harmony, and of readiness to associate in this common work." At the end of the Peace Policy, Ely Parker concluded that Grant had tried to find virtuous men, but that "religious bigotry, intolerance, and jealousies by various Christian bodies at home and between the agents in the West robbed all the efforts of their benevolent and humane character."[78] The truth lay somewhere between perfect harmony and arrant bigotry. Any claim that denominational jealousy killed the Peace Policy, or conversely, that Christians always labored together in love, ignores the complexity in religious emotions. Overemphasis on either enmity or cooperation is mistaken. Agent Isaiah Lightner, although he believed that the different denominations at Santee had sincerely tried to work together, struck a reasonable balance when he remarked, "Yet we have our difficulties and contentions to meet and overcome. Our success depends on our being able to overcome the difficulties as they arise."[79]

The maze of cooperation and conflict in the Peace Policy demonstrates how misleading simple generalizations concerning church performance can be. In 1882 Herbert Welsh of the Indian Rights Association said that news about Indian wars and massacres had made headlines, whereas the public knew little about "the beautiful though unnoticed triumphs of the Church, the schoolhouse, and the farm." It is difficult to evaluate the "beautiful though unnoticed" in history. Does one test the success of religious missions by the number of souls saved? by the eating habits and dress of converts? by hogs and potatoes raised? by chapels built and schools constructed? by the number of native preachers? Ecclesiastical magazines and reports tended to measure accomplishment by reporting revivals, temperance meetings, the "Happy Death of an Indian Girl" or the "Dying Medicine Man Seeking Christ." The churches also glossed over their failures. Ely Parker complained that the denominations responded slowly in 1870, and Secretary of the Interior Jacob Cox agreed that few religious bodies had conscientiously assumed their moral and religious obligations under the Peace Policy.

Yet the Christian churches did respond, in many different ways. Except for the Quakers, who were enthusiastic, and the Catholics, who were antagonistic, the churches at first were reluctant and cautious. Then, accepting the challenge, many religious leaders participated with excessive optimism, confidence, and self-congratulation. This in turn exposed them to sharp disappointments. The American Missionary Association, for example, in 1872 predicted the ultimate if not immediate success of the Peace Policy and then one year later became dejected by the "powerful barriers" of corruption and "border ruffians" contributing to the apparent extinction of the Indians. At Warm Springs, disappointed agent John Smith obtained a transfer from

Methodist to United Presbyterian control, but no aid came from that church either, and in 1875 Smith told the government that "for all the tangible evidence that exists here, there might as well be no such things as missionary societies."[80]

Internal administrative structures were crucial for church success. Dutch Reformed, Unitarians, Methodists, Presbyterians, and Congregationalists performed poorly partly because they established no committees to work with the Indian Office or to supervise agents and missions. Quakers, Episcopalians, and Catholics who created special committees and bureaus performed more effectively. Catholics and Episcopalians especially excelled in improving existing mission programs. The Baptists, Methodists, Dutch Reformed, and Unitarians, on the other hand, established no schools or mission stations. Episcopalians consistently spent large sums to finance the Peace Policy; only Friends and Presbyterians made comparable sacrifices. Methodists and Baptists spent the least.[81] Using Yakima as the contemporary ideal for Peace Policy success, by 1880 the Policy had done very well on about one-third of the reservations, had sound results at another sixth, was only moderately successful at a fifth of the agencies, and proved poor or dismal at the remainder. Using the existence of missions, schools, farming, and cultural assimilation as norms, the Catholics performed best, followed by the American Missionary Association and Quakers. Unitarians, Baptists, Methodists, and Dutch Reformed did the least.[82]

In July of 1880 an *Independent* editorial on "The Escaping Opportunity" praised the Peace Policy and observed that most churches had performed well. The editor then said that Unitarians, Dutch Reformed, and Methodists merited the scorn of Christians. Unitarians had contributed neither money nor men, having withdrawn in 1877: "The question might be properly raised whether on the Day of Judgment it [will be] better to be a Ute or a Unitarian." The Dutch Reformed admitted they had done nothing; to refute the excuse that they lacked money, the editor pointed to three pastors serving the Collegiate Church in New York City. But Methodists were more reprehensible than the Reformed because the latter "confess and lament their failure. . . . Methodist authorities defend their neglect." Methodists boasted about "Father" Wilbur, whom they did not appoint; they used circuit riders to collect money from Indians; they discouraged their agents; and they sent no missionaries. According to the *Independent,* only fear of Catholics had motivated the Methodist Missionary Society to do anything.[83]

The editor of the *Independent* hoped his exposé would stimulate the lazy churches. It did stimulate the Methodists. The *Pittsburgh Christian Advocate* acknowledged the charges and asked its Missionary Society if they were true. If they were, the *Advocate* editor said, "a little less self-laudation for the next twelve or fifteen years will be quite becoming." The *Northern Christian*

Advocate denounced the *Independent* for sensationalism, claiming that Methodists had been very successful despite frequent insults from the Indian Office. In response, the *Independent* published a statistical table with a list of ciphers reported by Methodist agents. The *California Christian Advocate* then accused the *Independent* of lying, blamed the government for appointing evil agents, and denounced Indians as being "utterly impossible." The debate lasted for six more months, during which time B. R. Cowen, a former assistant secretary of the interior, charged western Methodist churches with segregating Indians and stealing their land. Methodists finally conceded that their work flowed at low ebb.[84]

Fresh from its triumph in religious journalism, the *Independent* next aimed harsh words at all denominations, especially the Presbyterians and Baptists. By 1880, it concluded, the Peace Policy had "fallen far short of accomplishing what it might have done had the Churches appreciated the opportunity offered and the responsibility laid upon them. . . . A rarer opportunity was never given, and the time may come when the Churches will realize how half-heartedly it has been improved."[85] The editor overstated the case. The Christian Church by itself could not make the Peace Policy effective. The tenacity of Indian culture, conditions on the western frontier, the needs of eastern investors, and political pressures caused the Policy's failure. The churches had not been assigned the job of changing the American economic system. Nor were they assigned the task of eliminating politics and corruption in Indian affairs. The last was the duty of the Board of Indian Commissioners.

4. Overseers of Reform: The Board of Indian Commissioners and William Welsh

In April of 1869 the forty-first Congress of the United States created the Board of Indian Commissioners. Members of the new board would be men "eminent for their intelligence and philanthropy," serving without pay as consultants to the commissioner of Indian affairs and, under the president's direction, exercising joint control with the secretary of the interior over the use of Indian funds.[1]

On June 3, President Grant announced his first appointments to the board. All were wealthy men. Episcopalian Felix R. Brunot, "the finest flowering of American gentility," was a partner in a Pittsburgh steel mill; William Welsh, also an Episcopalian, was a Philadelphia merchant. Robert Campbell, a Presbyterian, was a partner in Sublette and Campbell of St. Louis, real estate broker, dry goods merchant, and president of two banks.[2] William Dodge, also a Presbyterian, had mining and railroad interests and was a partner in Phelps, Dodge and Company. Another Presbyterian member of the board, George Stuart, was a dry goods merchant, the sole agent for Stuart's Celebrated Soft Enameled Spool Cotton.[3] John V. Farwell, a Methodist, owned a large dry goods firm in Chicago;[4] another Methodist, Henry Lane, was a former governor and U.S. senator from Indiana. Edward S. Tobey, a Boston Congregationalist, was a member of the Massachusetts Senate and the director of the Union Steamship Company

72

and the United States Insurance Company. Nathan Bishop, a Baptist, had been a superintendent of the Boston public schools. John Lang, a former Quaker preacher, had accumulated a fortune manufacturing blankets.[5] At its first meeting on May 26, 1869, the Board of Indian Commissioners elected Welsh as chairman. Vincent Colyer was hired as secretary.

The rationale for selection of the original board remains unclear. George Stuart later asserted that Grant had requested him to name the ten men in 1869 on the basis of denominational affiliation and geographical location.[6] After the first board resigned en masse in 1874, the secretary of the interior apparently called a meeting of six denominations, each of which made nominations but left the actual selection to the president.[7] Only a few statements can be made with certainty about the selection of the board members and their relationship to the churches: the Department of the Interior tried to control appointments long before 1874; after 1874 Interior directly influenced board membership and at times made the actual selections even though the department was eager for the churches to endorse board members; in no sense were BIC members official representatives of the Protestant denominations—they represented American Protestantism, but not particular denominations. Roman Catholics were not welcome on the board.[8]

On June 3, 1869, Grant announced the rules governing what he called the board's "joint supervision" over the Office of Indian Affairs. Charged with helping Indians to change their way of life, the board was empowered to organize itself and employ a staff. It would enjoy free access to any records in the Indian Office, and it had the right to inspect agencies and all goods purchased for tribes. Expenses of board members who visited agencies, attended councils, and witnessed treaty negotiations would be paid by the federal government. All government officials, Grant directed, must heed the board's advice "within the limits of such officers' positive instructions from their superiors."[9]

In his 1869 outline Grant stipulated that the board's recommendations must pass through the Indian Office to the Interior Department. All board recommendations involving public money were subject to approval by the secretary of the interior and the president. Whereas Congress in April had used the words "joint control," Grant in June now spoke of "joint supervision." The difference between control and supervision resulted in the almost immediate resignation of the board's first chairman, William Welsh.

For sixty years William Welsh had led a vigorous and varied life. He was born in Philadelphia in 1807; sixteen years later he left school to work as a longshoreman on the city's wharves. There he developed the physical strength and energy that impressed both friend and foe throughout his life. Following a heart attack in 1861, profits from the S. & W. Welsh Company's West

Indian sugar imports enabled him to devote almost all of his time to civic and Church reform. A Republican, director of Girard College, owner of the *North American* and the *Philadelphia Gazette,* uncle of Herbert Welsh of the Indian Rights Association, and author of books on home missions and laymen in the Episcopal Church,[10] Welsh founded several Episcopal churches and a hospital in Philadelphia. He generously contributed his money to these and other projects.

Assessments of William Welsh's personality and method varied. To his friends he seemed quick, frank, strong-willed, principled, unsentimental—a "plain blunt man" who had little regard for the opinions of others and whose confident, evangelical faith permeated all he did. To others he seemed a cross, nervous, intolerant, and often pompous bully. Ely S. Parker described Welsh as a presumptuous person who would use any pretext to gain private ends. Welsh's greatest weakness was a nagging suspicion of conspiracies, a trigger judgment that anyone who disagreed with him on Indian affairs was a member of the Indian Ring. Although he was overly optimistic about the ability of Christian missions to bring white civilization to Indians, at the same time he was skeptical of other white men's intentions, including churchmen. Though accused of sectarianism, Welsh was often critical of his own church. He also strove for cooperation with other denominations, believing that all Christians must share in the burden of white guilt. He did not hesitate to end his treasured friendship with Henry Whipple when he concluded that the bishop had erred in Minnesota. Welsh's Christian commitment was rooted in an evangelical theology of lay responsibility for the world. The Church, he felt, had erred for centuries by discouraging the laity from social action when it should have provided the base for individual spiritual welfare and for assaults on social injustice. The wealthy were especially called to service and stewardship: "Education, social position, and money are all trusts involving a fearful personal responsibility."[11]

Beginning in 1862, a new responsibility for Welsh was the American Indian. For a while Indian tribes occupied only a portion of his attention; then he turned to them with all his energy and passion in 1869. "How providential," remarked an Episcopal official, that Welsh decided to work for Indian reform in the government and through the church: "I do not see how we should get along without him. He has the love of God in his heart and has no fear of man or devil. And then he is ready to show his faith by his works. Who but Mr. Welsh would take so much pains, do so much unpleasant work, and expend so much money, when for a time at least he will receive more curses than thanks."[12] The official was correct about the ratio of curses to thanks. Welsh as the arch Indian reformer eventually alienated not only the American Board of Commissioners for Foreign Missions and the Riggs family, but he lost the friendship of Whipple, Grant, Cox, Delano, Brunot, and many

Quakers. The *Nation* said in 1875 that the Interior Department considered Welsh "a thorough scoundrel and falsifier, engaged in a damnable conspiracy."[13] To frontiersmen, he was a "religiously washed thief," a do-good easterner, a hypocrite who disbursed "a large share of the religious stealings and patronage." The Episcopal missionary Samuel Hinman, however, considered Welsh a man of strength, wisdom, and character. Many members of Congress admired and supported his efforts and declared that he knew more about Indians than anyone else in the United States, but James Garfield, in negotiating the Flathead land cession, resented Welsh's encouragement of tribal resistance.[14] Falling out of favor with Grant, Welsh was back at the White House in 1877 to act as an intermediary between Sioux chief Red Cloud and the new president, Rutherford B. Hayes.[15]

After Welsh died suddenly at a meeting of the Philadelphia Board of Trusts in 1879, the tributes were profuse. Bishop William Hare exclaimed, "Verily a mighty man has fallen!" The bishop described how Welsh's integrity drove him to solitary stands, a severe model for every layman: "Earnest and determined, he sometimes differed from his dearest friends as to the methods which should be pursued and the persons who should be attacked. Their consciences required that they should part company with him and stand aloof. His conscience required that he should stand alone. But warm as the differences of opinion occasionally were, bitter as the pain on each side was, he manfully pressed his pursuit."[16] The *Churchman* recognized Welsh's ability as a preacher when designating him the foremost layman of the Episcopal Church. The Episcopal Indian Commission eulogized him as "this most earnest and devoted of fellow laborers, this ablest of administrators, this most versatile of counselors, this noblest of givers, and this firmest of friends." Carl Schurz considered Welsh one of the most important and capable friends of the American Indian.[17]

In 1882 Senator Thomas Francis Bayard remembered Welsh as a good man "who did great public service in a quiet way." Welsh did much for Indians and perhaps for the public, but seldom in a quiet way. He believed that Indians must become white men and women, and he felt, at best, pity for their culture and religion. In Indian country he traveled unarmed and refused military escorts because such behavior revealed lack of trust. Chippewas called him Big Heart and Dakotas named him *Wapaha hota,* Grey Hat. In 1871 the Dakotas reportedly said that they trusted only the Christian clergy, "of whom they reckon Mr. William Welsh the great High Chief." Ten years later the Sioux would present his nephew Herbert Welsh with gifts in his memory.

Welsh compelled the Episcopal Church into the Peace Policy, and his vision dominated its Indian Commission. He traveled to seminaries to recruit missionaries and he donated personal funds to missions. Early in the Peace

Policy, Welsh bought out a Missouri River whiskey-seller for twelve hundred dollars. He fed starving Poncas and pledged to pay their annuity if the government failed to honor its treaty with them. When a cyclone flattened the Santee agency, Welsh rebuilt it.[18]

William Welsh was convinced that the tide of westward migration in the United States made it imperative for the federal government to confine Indians to reservations and grant permanent land title. This required the suppression of all considerations of political gain. The patronage system, "the claims for party spoils by political victors [that] render every attempt to civilize the wild Indians utterly abortive," he said, had to be eliminated. That task, and the exposure of fraud, were the solemn duties of his Board of Indian Commissioners: "To strangle the political vampire that has hitherto sucked out much of the life-blood of the Indian."[19]

In March of 1869 William Welsh declared that he would not serve on the Board of Indian Commissioners unless he approved of the other members. On April 15, Secretary of the Interior Jacob Cox asked Welsh to join the board. He accepted, but personally resolved to secure veto power over Interior decisions. Welsh realized that his own bill in Congress, which gave the board full control over Indian funds, contracts, and treaties, and allowed it to inspect agents or superintendents, had been opposed by Cox. The final legislation provided joint control over expenditures only. Grant's executive message of June 3 withdrew even this, leaving the board, in Welsh's words, "emasculated . . . a mere council of advice." Such a state of affairs, he felt, left no choice but to resign. He rejected responsibility without power because he believed that the Indian Ring, that "deep-seated malady of the Indian Office," would persist despite Grant's good intentions. Welsh immediately set about to vindicate his judgment by single-handedly exposing fraud.[20]

Welsh's critics at the time insisted that Welsh resigned because he was power-hungry and sought appointment as Commissioner of Indian Affairs or Secretary of the Interior. His later attacks on these officials seemed to support this view, but in 1869 Welsh could explain his resignation with convincing bluntness: Congress had given the board joint control and the president had withdrawn it. "No control of any kind, over any part of the special or general appropriation was entrusted to them, they were powerless to remedy wrongs for which both Congress and the community would naturally consider them responsible. The law had virtually become inoperative." Welsh explained that Grant's fame and aloofness from politics had allowed the president to launch the reform in 1869, but by 1872 the pressure of party and spoils would be strong once again despite Grant, and therefore a firm, effective system had to be established quickly. Privately, Welsh was disappointed with the men whom Grant appointed to the board and he hoped that the Supreme Court would be asked to make new appointments. The president and Secretary Cox, he thought, lacked experience and had been influenced by emotions.

Permanent, independent control exercised by the board was a fundamental issue and, for Welsh, supervision did not mean control. Secretary Cox declared that yielding direct authority to the board would accomplish nothing; Welsh contended that the board could do nothing without such authority. Six months later Welsh noticed that certain commissioners had taken their wives with them on official western tours, causing the secretary to conclude that they were not serious and to ignore their recommendations about new reservations. "Unless someone has power this must go on. I have the kindest personal feelings to the Secy & the Commissioner [Parker] & my late collegues [sic] but I could not act the part of a man if I allowed myself to be emasculated."[21] After resigning in June, Welsh became a self-appointed investigator. He considered the board a useful tool and did not wish its termination. Instead he urged the others to continue. Succeeding him as chairman was a man whom Welsh knew possessed "sterling and valuable qualities," Felix Brunot.

Dismayed by Welsh's impulsive resignation, neither the new chairman nor other members of the board thought that Grant's decree of June 3 had emasculated them. Jacob Cox implored them to continue, insisting that he and Grant shared the sincerest disappointment over Welsh and that Welsh had misunderstood Grant. The president at no time had intended to give the board direct control over government spending. Grant, according to Cox, wanted advice and supervision from disinterested men who could not touch a cent, thereby assuring a system of control beyond criticism. Acceptance of Welsh's demands, Secretary Cox persuasively argued, would have produced two Indian Bureaus, "a double headed organization from which nothing but confusion could come."[22]

Felix Reville Brunot, like Welsh, believed that government and politics must involve the Church. To this concern he had devoted half of his life. Brunot (1820-98), the son of a wealthy army officer and Pittsburgh industrialist, and the nephew of an Episcopal priest, left the Midwest in 1847, invested his savings in a Pittsburgh steel mill, moved to a mansion on the Monongahela River, and began a philanthropic career.[23] Although he was an abolitionist, Brunot refused a generalship during the Civil War, preferring to work in hospitals and with Confederate prisoners. In doing so he met government officials, including Grant. Often mistaken for a clergyman, he was a Sunday school superintendent, a trustee of the Philadelphia Divinity School, and a strong supporter of the Evangelical Alliance. He promoted temperance and Sabbath legislation and advocated a Christian amendment to the U.S. Constitution. Following his board appointment, Brunot devoted almost full time and attention to Indian affairs. He spent five consecutive summers in the Far West to negotiate removal and right-of-way treaties.

Brunot was a complex man who did not accept responsibility in the Peace Policy with blind idealism.[24] He was fully aware of the pitfalls in government and Indian reform. On the surface, he praised the Indian Office and Grant's administration. Among friends he admitted that he distrusted Parker and Cox, that the reform's accomplishments were minor; "The difficulties in the way are so many and so complicated as to make me almost despair."[25] His most onerous task as board chairman was negotiating Sioux, Flathead, Crow, and Ute treaties that he knew would destroy tribal rights. In the summer of 1870 he conducted a treaty council with the Sioux that left him outreasoned, outnegotiated, and outclassed by the Dakota chief Red Cloud. In 1872, while bargaining very hard-headedly to remove the Flatheads from the route of the Northern Pacific through the Bitterroot Valley in Montana, Brunot realized the injustice of his actions: "Having done all I could to prevent the unjust removal of the Flat Heads, my heart sickens with the new evidence every day coming up that after all there is no justice for the Indian where he stands in the path of the greedy white man."[26] Later he successfully convinced a reluctant Crow tribe to cede the Yellowstone Valley and he was congratulated by Montana governor Potts for his labor in forcing the peaceful surrender of one of the richest valleys in the northern Rockies.[27] Brunot realized that the railroad invasion of the Montana grasslands, a refuge of the Sioux, violated treaties of the mid-60s and would mean Indian war. He strove to block passage of the railroad bills in Congress but, unlike William Welsh, Brunot believed that open opposition to powerful interests was futile. He warned the board secretary, "Please be careful not to let the Railroaders find that *we* are interfering with their schemes."[28]

Although Brunot's friendship with Welsh continued after 1869, the two men had dissimilar ideas about politics and reform: Welsh was the absolutist and purist; Brunot the prudent practitioner of compromise. Felix Brunot understood that the board had limited power and he wanted the Indian Office removed from politics, but he felt the Board of Indian Commissioners must be quiet and courteous if it wished to accomplish its goals. Yet Brunot, too, after five frustrating and painful years, would reach a breaking point.[29]

When under attack in later years, the board reminded Congress that the commissioners had no real authority over the Indian Office, although they did initially. Between 1869 and 1874 Congress had gradually curtailed any illusions of power. In 1869-70 the board was a clearing house for agent nominations. It gradually lost this function and eventually the Indian Office insisted that the board should have no voice whatsoever in agent selection. In 1870 Congress had instructed the commissioner of Indian affairs to consult with the board whenever he purchased annuity goods. In 1871 Congress affirmed that all contracts for supplies must obtain the board's approval before payment, but with the condition that if the board disapproved of a contract, the vouchers must be sent to the secretary of the interior, who could act on the board's findings. For a short time after 1871 the board retained the right to investigate accounts, though its approval was not required for payment. Then in 1873 Congress asked board members to pay their own expenses. Reform was becoming nominal.[30]

The Board of Indian Commissioners worked indefatigably between 1869 and 1874 and they did manage to secure significant changes in Indian administration. During the first three years its members traveled more than 256,000 miles to negotiate treaties and evaluate policy, to check on contractors and supplies, to inspect reservations and missions, and to listen to Indians, army officers, missionaries, and settlers. The board met with Grant and his cabinet, the president asking it to nominate a new commissioner of Indian affairs in 1871. The board requested and obtained major changes in federal policy, abolition of the superintendencies, the creation of an inspection system, and the reduction of Indian lands.[31] The two most important functions of the board, however, were investigating the financial accounts of the Indian Office and serving as a liaison between the government and the churches.

The law of 1871 required the board to audit Indian Office records, a task it described as "very onerous but cheerfully undertaken." Four members served as a purchasing subcommittee that inspected annuity goods before shipment and then checked the records of the freighters and receiving clerks. The purchasing committee rented a warehouse in New York City, where it examined, among other things, flour, coffee, sugar, beans, blankets, bolts, nuts, nails, mirrors, suspenders, fishhooks, thimbles, brandy, wine, whiskey ("hospital stores" in thirty-two-ounce bottles), awls, anvils, stomach pumps, and vaginal syringes. Another subcommittee examined bids and invoices from suppliers. In 1871 this group reviewed eleven hundred vouchers, rejected forty as fraudulent, and declared a five-hundred-thousand-dollar saving for the treasury. In 1873 they audited 250 bids, seventeen hundred vouchers, and changed the bid system. Previously merchants had bid on entire classes of goods with the right to increase or decrease various items in each class. This meant a bidder could list expensive and inexpensive merchandise and win on a low total price. The merchant then would supply just a few of the low-profit items and all of the high-profit merchandise. When board member George Stuart realized what was happening, he insisted that suppliers submit bids on each item. Commissioner of Indian Affairs Ely Parker protested but finally yielded to the board's new system. The results were large savings and an increase in the number of bidders, from ten to one hundred.[32]

Such reforms saved money and brought superior goods to the Indians. The price of flour at Milk River, for instance, dropped from $11.20 to $4.70 per sack. Yet, despite the board's careful inspection, fraud remained. Some agents complained that their flour was worthless while others reported inferior knives and axes, worthless pants and coats. Board member John V. Farwell cabled from Chicago in 1872: "The Ring is still *in*. Would suggest that our chairman appoint some one to go *on every cargo* of goods that go up the Missouri *without* fail."[33] Gradually, as the board's early control weakened and as confusion grew concerning the relative authority of the executive and legislative branches, the board was increasingly bypassed and eventually ignored.[34]

The same pattern emerged in the board's liaison role between the federal government and the churches. Its members were selected because they were prominent Christians—Vincent Colyer declared that the board itself was ordained by God and that service on it was a divine calling. On January 13, 1871, the board called a meeting with the several mission boards, the secretary of the interior, and the commissioner of Indian affairs. The conference became an annual session to discuss agent nomination, school construction, mission programs, and the general health of the Peace Policy. Congressmen at times visited the January meetings, which were meant to serve as catalysts for reform. Even though John Lowrie complained that the sessions were "somewhat like a Methodist experience-meeting where everyone may give his own narrative," there was healthy self-criticism during the early years. Unfortunately, by 1874 attendance began to lag and the discussions lost their spirit and earnestness.

On February 26, 1870, from his office in Pittsburgh, Felix Brunot sent a note to a friend. Distressed, Brunot carefully crossed out the words *Department of the Interior* on the letterhead, leaving only *Board of Indian Commissioners*. It had taken six months for him to learn that the board, as William Welsh predicted, could achieve few reforms if the department and the Indian Office did not approve. Brunot felt that Secretary of the Interior Cox had deliberately ignored the board, a situation that worsened in November of 1870, when Grant appointed Columbus Delano to replace Cox. The board members disagreed on how to treat high government officials. Mild, naïve John Lang thought that men like Cox and Delano must be trusted, but John Farwell called for secret board investigations of federal corruption in Dakota.[35] When Brunot deleted references to Grant's wisdom and "cordial cooperation" from the 1870 *Annual Report* of the board, Nathan Bishop suggested that whenever possible the commissioners should pamper administration officials: "As human nature has an inborn desire for a certain amount of "soft soap" I advise the *lather* in the latter part of this manuscript be rubbed onto the faces of the parties named. . . . It will not do us any harm & may make them & others treat us a little respectfully henceforth."[36]

After 1871 the cool relations between the board and other government officials became a cold war. The Department of the Interior refused to honor board travel vouchers, neglected to forward the board's mail, and often snubbed the commissioners. In 1874 the Treasury Department picked at the board's budget by questioning such items as a twelve-dollar copyist charge, ten dollars for the *Congressional Record*, and one dollar spent on a telegram.[37] As it suffered such indignities, the board grew increasingly distrustful and resentful of the Interior Department, while the department, irritated by the board's secretary, Vincent Colyer, grew more jealous of the Interior's traditional prerogatives.

William Welsh's sudden resignation from the Board of Indian Commissioners in 1869 hardly represented his retirement from reform. To the contrary, it ensured the freedom necessary for his crusades. Welsh became his own board. Enjoying full access to the files of the board, the Indian Bureau, and the Department of the Interior, Welsh referred to himself as an honorary member of the BIC and boasted of his connections with the "inner sanctum of the political arena." He became the most troublesome figure to confront government officials and the most sustained critic of the Office of Indian Affairs in its fifty-year existence. His letters to Bishop Whipple reveal Welsh swirling in activity and immersed in his own egotism. In January of 1870 he declared that Congress, by requiring board approval of vouchers, had unanimously "passed a verdict in [Welsh's] favor." In February he boasted that he needed only three days with Senators Morrill, Harlan, and Dawes to "smooth down Indian affairs." In April he wrote that Nevada's Senator Stewart had attacked "his" bill on agency inspection, but he knew who would triumph: "Five times have I gone to Washington in Seven weeks, gaining Strength in the Senate and House at each visit. I am ferreting out the thieves, knowing that the President and Secretary Cox will aid me. If I am successful we will have it all our own way, that is, God's way, in which we will certainly acquiesce."[38] Not everyone in Washington agreed. By 1871 Welsh had lost his influence with the Interior and with his major ally, the president. Ely Parker informed Felix Brunot that he was tired of Episcopal agents claiming that they were responsible only to William Welsh. White settlers in Dakota Territory also complained that Welsh had excessive power. Brunot expressed disbelief, yet warned his friend to be cautious.[39] Meanwhile, Welsh planned on trapping Parker in order to prove that the entire Indian system, from top to bottom, festered with corruption.

When Grant appointed Parker, a few churchmen worried about the drinking habits of the new commissioner of Indian affairs. An elderly missionary, Asher Wright, had predicted that Parker would be tempted yet prove "as good as *gold*." Though the missionary knew that any Indian must overcome prejudice against his race, and though Wright regretted not having a "truly christian man" as commissioner, he considered Parker an "unconverted believer in christianity" who would support Protestant missions.[40] Contrary to Wright's opinion, Parker had no enthusiasm for Christianity or for the role of the churches in the Peace Policy. His first report to Secretary Cox acknowledged the churches but warned of well-intentioned, ignorant humanitarians who saw Indian history exclusively from a Christian viewpoint and who did more harm than good by convincing recalcitrant tribes that they had a legal right to resist the government.[41]

Both Parker's race and religion soon came under attack. During a Senate debate in 1870 Joseph Fowler of Tennessee asserted that the Peace Policy had failed because Grant had placed the Bureau of Indian Affairs under "not one of the highest, but the lowest types of humanity." Although he admitted that Parker was educated, Fowler declared that the commissioner was a barbarian and that Christians should not expect barbarians to convert other barbarians. History proved that no Indian "has yet ascended to the atmosphere of the Christian religion":

> It is from such a fountain as [Parker] that there is to flow a stream of morals and spiritual light that is to illuminate the wild hordes that wander amid the vast plains of the distant West. As well might you hope for the noonday splendors of the sun from the earth. Who gives out light . . . must have it. It is vain to hope from such a source to illuminate the heathen and the Christian world. It is ridiculous in itself.[42]

Senator George Edmunds of Vermont rebuked Fowler for racist slander and reminded the Senate that the Constitution guaranteed the commissioner the right to hold whatever religious opinions he chose. In later years Parker would grow even more caustic toward whites and missionaries. He recognized that a mission education was responsible for his own position in life, yet he believed that Christian missions generally had caused much agony and bloodshed. He described himself as an "uncivilized, unchristian, benighted savage" who had little use or need for philanthropists. Such whites thought they knew more about Indians than Indians did, passing resolutions "high sounding and perhaps tickling to the churchman's ear. . . . I have little or no faith in the American christian civilization methods of treating the Indians. . . . It has not been honest, pure or sincere. Black deception, damnable frauds and persistent oppression has been its characteristics, and its religion today is, that the only good Indian is a dead one."[43]

William Welsh soon decided that Parker's appointment was a mistake. He reportedly told a cattle contractor that he intended to discredit Parker, the "representative of a race only one generation from barbarism." Convinced that the commissioner had an inferior business mind, drank too much, and would succumb easily to temptation, Welsh was further irked by the Indian Bureau's opposition to board investigations.[44] Grant would not dare retain Parker, Welsh confided to Whipple, after the Philadelphia merchant "by God's help" cleansed the Indian Bureau. Not sharing the board's reticence to offend Grant or Cox, Welsh steadily built a case against the "neglectful, incompetent, and lawless Commissioner," gaining information from sources within and without the Indian Office.[45]

Welsh visited the Missouri River agencies during the autumn of 1870. He considered the trip a blessing because it allowed him "to throw so large a bomb shell into the Indian Office . . . as to drive out all the vermin." He learned that Parker had approached the agents and tried to force them to accept inferior cattle. He also discovered that in Sioux City, Parker, suspecting what Welsh was up to, had searched for testimony to discredit the Philadelphian. Vexed with the "great Indian commissioner" and convinced that Parker had violated the law, Welsh wrote to Vincent Colyer: "I do not think I have any unkind feelings to the poor fellow & if I knew how to bring him to repentence . . . I would like to do it. Please keep your eyes & ears open for if I am an innocent kitten I am sure you do not want to burn me to a crisp."[46] Returning to Washington on December 9, Welsh laid his evidence before Grant and Cox, both of whom pledged their support and then refused to act. Rebuffed at the White House, Welsh persuaded the House of Representatives' appropriations committee to investigate Parker.[47]

Acting as an unofficial prosecutor, Welsh presented the charges: (1) Parker had purchased surplus cattle and flour without advertising for bids; (2) he did so prior to congressional appropriations; (3) he paid exorbitant prices for beef and freight; (4) he did not consult with the board; and (5) he had shipped inferior blankets to the Osages. Parker's attorney, N. P. Chipman, denied the charges and assailed Welsh's case. Under cross-examination Welsh produced little concrete evidence and Felix Brunot faltered badly. Parker, contended Chipman, had not made one penny from government contracts as Welsh's own investigation of the commissioner's bank account had shown. Welsh, on the other hand, had purchased his evidence. Chipman admitted that Parker had been careless and made hasty contracts, but only when dire emergencies existed. True, the commissioner had neglected advertising procedures and made a trifling mistake in oversupplying the Whetstone agency, but Parker was not responsible for the government's poor accounting system. If the charges were valid, Chipman asked, why had Welsh made them instead of the board? As for the Osage blankets, Chipman ridiculed agent Isaac Gibson's complaint as petty and inquired why Gibson wrote to William Dodge of the board instead of contacting Parker. Actually, the blankets were part of a scheme to trap his client, a "delicious morsel for the *coup de etat*" planned by Colyer and Welsh. Vincent Colyer's actions, Chipman concluded, were "indelicate and improper" ploys hidden behind a Christian facade; Welsh's accusations had no foundation "except in his own fertile brain."[48]

The House committee judged Parker incompetent, negligent, ignorant of the law, but not dishonest. They did not demand his resignation. Colyer and the board, stung by Chipman's needling, hoped that the commissioner would quickly retire. Parker was exasperated but determined to remain in office.[49]

The investigation left William Welsh even more determined to eliminate Parker. He advised the board to use the 1871 purchases to expose the commissioner. The opportunity to do so came in May, when Parker again failed to publish bids, refused to forward vouchers to the board, and awarded a questionable teamster contract. The board was outraged. An astonished George Stuart considered the procedures insulting, Robert Campbell wrote from St. Louis that the future of the board depended on forcing Grant to dismiss Parker, and cautious John Lang prayed that Grant's enemies would not learn of the scandal and that all wounds would be healed. Somewhere in the barrens between Cheyenne and Fort Laramie, Felix Brunot scribbled on a piece of torn paper that Parker was obviously guilty and a liar. Vincent Colyer replied that Secretary Columbus Delano mysteriously had left Washington and that "every day develops some new phase of the collusion of the department with the Indian ring." Delano returned in early July to order all vouchers sent to the board. A week later Ely S. Parker resigned.[50]

Friends of the Peace Policy greeted the resignation jubilantly. The president's infatuation with his Seneca friend had been broken by sheer power, exclaimed William Welsh; "I think we may consider the victory in the Indian Office complete. . . . We have strangled the Wild Beast but the little foxes are nibbling still."[51] The *Nation* and the *American Missionary* declared that a vast revolution in Indian affairs had resulted in the "complete overthrow of a most gigantic system of wrong, robbery, hypocrisy, greed, and cruelty, and in the triumph of right, of official integrity, of administrative economy, and of the principles of a Christian civilization." Creation of the board had been the first blow against the Ring, the *Nation* declared, but when the Indian Ring gained control of the commissioner it nullified reform until the board exposed and ousted Parker. Warning that the "snake has been scotched, but we are afraid not yet killed," the *Nation* asked Brunot to accept Parker's position and crush the Ring completely.[52] Though William Welsh would have welcomed the office for himself, he knew his appointment as commissioner of Indian affairs was impossible, so he joined other board members in "praying hard" that Brunot would accept the offer and forever break the Indian Ring. Brunot declined the position when Grant offered it.

In the summer of 1871 the overseers of reform had won the first round. There remained more than little foxes to battle and enemies of the Peace

Policy would do more than nibble. Forced to remove Parker, the Department of the Interior would strike back by pressing for the resignation of the board's secretary, Vincent Colyer.

On an April afternoon in 1871 a group of Mexicans, Papago Indians, and white men rode northeast from Tucson, Arizona. That night they swept down on Apaches at the Camp Grant reserve; of 118 Apaches killed in the raid, only eight were adult men. After Grant ordered the Arizona territorial government to indict all the participants, a mock trial acquitted everyone. This event, and the threat of a general Indian uprising, prompted Vincent Colyer, strongly supported by Grant, to tour the Southwest once again. "I am going among the 'beasts of Ephesus,'" he wrote to Felix Brunot, "but the same dear Saviour that guided Paul will take care of me." The beasts from whom Colyer needed divine protection were not Indians, but resentful whites in the U.S. army and on the Arizona frontier. They had not forgotten his earlier remarks about them in 1869 and this time they were prepared. At public meetings he was rudely heckled and harassed by frontiersmen who referred to the Apaches as "Mr. Vincent Colyer's Lambs." Only two newspapers in the West, the *Sacramento Union* and the *Santa Barbara Press*, deplored the abuse directed at Colyer. Arizona and New Mexico papers reported his progress through the Indian country: "Mr. Vincent Colyer went among them with honeyed words and lavish presents, and also, be it noted, a formidable escort. . . . in his very track his lambs were murdering and plundering and scalping."[53] The *Arizona Miner* told citizens of Prescott that Colyer was a "cold-blooded scoundrel" and a "red-handed assassin": "Colyer will soon be here. . . . We ought to dump the old devil into the shaft of a mine, and pile rocks upon it until he is dead. A rascal who comes here to thwart the efforts of military and citizens to conquer a peace from our savage foe, deserves to be stoned to death like the treacherous, black-hearted dog that he is."[54] A year later Nevada's *Tri-Weekly Ely Record* remembered that the "red devils" began to murder and rape just as "Peace Commissioner Collyer [*sic*] superseded Gen. Crook in command."[55]

Returning to Washington, Colyer wrote a detailed account that placed the blame for the Camp Grant massacre squarely on Arizona whites. The article prompted Secretary of the Interior Columbus Delano to demand Colyer's resignation "for the welfare and prosperity of [our] part of the public service." Delano wrote that he had Grant's support. Board chairman Brunot refused to inform Colyer of Delano's request and merely asked the secretary to resign. Informed of the facts by another board member, Colyer demanded to see Delano's letter and asked to have it placed in the board's files, but Brunot replied that the letter was not relevant. After exposing Brunot's coverup to the board, Colyer decided that the welfare of the Peace

Policy required his departure, and on a Monday evening in February 1872, he submitted his resignation. The Interior Department, acting on the advice of John Lang, dispatched General O. O. Howard to study conditions in the Southwest. Howard's investigation revealed friendlier whites, deadlier Apaches, and a long-suffering army.[56]

Eighteen seventy-four was a dismal year for the churches. In newspapers and religious periodicals Henry Ward Beecher's adultery overshadowed the charges of corruption and scandal under the Peace Policy. Yet the Reverend Mr. Beecher's extramarital problems must have seemed small to the men and women who faced discouragement, trials, and embarrassments with the Indian program. In Dakota, Nebraska, and Kansas, grasshoppers and chinch bugs devastated the crops of Pawnees, Poncas, Otoes, Osages, and Santees. Quakers could not preserve Pawnee and Ponca crops in Nebraska; they could not stop Sioux raids into Nebraska, and neither could the Friends stop Kiowas and Comanches from attacking settlers in Texas. With the renewal of Sioux war, with charges of fraud at scattered Episcopal agencies, with William Welsh attacking Indian Commissioner E. P. Smith, and with the army seeking full control of Indians, the dazed Board of Indian Commissioners ran into an unsympathetic Congress. William Dodge, a board member for five years, spoke of a dangerous Indian Ring but under congressional cross-examination he could not name a single guilty person or even describe the Ring's activities. The Office of Indian Affairs, protected by the Interior and enjoying increased support from Congress, acted independently of the BIC. Bishop Whipple noted mounting pressure in the churches against reform, and Felix Brunot reported attacks from many quarters.

In December of 1873 Welsh had learned that Delano approved three hundred thousand dollars worth of vouchers deemed fraudulent by the board. Welsh then urged the Board of Commissioners to resign in protest, which they declined to do. At a House committee hearing in April of 1874 the board members appeared confused. Robert Campbell and Nathan Bishop testified that all was well between the board and the Interior, but Thomas Cree, Colyer's replacement as the board's secretary, said that he was disgusted by Delano's contract awards, though he could prove nothing. A House debate ensued, during which democratic representative James Burnie Beck of Kentucky accused Republicans of crippling their own watchdog and thus aiding in the theft of millions. When James Garfield answered that the board could never be given actual administrative powers, Beck called for abolition of the board.[57]

At the height of all the controversy, Bishop Whipple believed that if the Peace Policy could somehow endure another four years, it would become permanent; Felix Brunot realized that, unless immediate changes were achieved, it was already doomed. Brunot advocated separating the Indian Office from the Interior and giving it status as an autonomous department. His recommendation ignored, Brunot did what he had criticized William Welsh for doing five years earlier. He resigned and this time, unlike in 1869, the entire board followed suit.

The causes of the mass resignation of the Board of Indian Commissioners in May of 1874 went beyond the apparent reasons. Grant had told Brunot that both he and Delano were eager to separate the Indian Office from Interior, but that the change had to wait until after Congress passed its annual appropriations.[58] Despite this assurance, ten days later the commissioners sent Grant a joint letter announcing their tentative resignations. They regretted that Delano did not want a separate department and they suggested that certain conditions made it impossible for them to work with the secretary.[59] Though the board members did not say so, they were convinced that the entire Department of the Interior, from Delano on down, was a maze of corruption.[60] Grant read the letter and repeated that he and Delano favored a separate Indian Department. On June 8, the resignations became official.

Whatever the reasons for the resignation of Brunot and the original board, the results were obvious. If the board had been weak, it became weaker, and the idealism of the first members was replaced by cynicism. The secretary of the interior chose new members for the board and, although the churches were consulted, congressmen also submitted names. The board henceforth would be entirely bypassed in the nomination of agents. After 1874, attendance of board members at treaty councils dwindled and their direct inspection of supplies virtually ceased. Rutherford B. Hayes's election in 1876 seemed to momentarily invigorate some members, but a scandal in 1880 involving the board itself sapped their energy and destroyed whatever trace of effectiveness still remained.[61]

Even more important than its lack of activity were shifts in the board's attitude. Defeatism replaced the zeal of Welsh and Stuart; distrust of the Peace Policy replaced concern for Indians. In 1877, when certain board members complained of difficulties in inspecting beef, new members not only argued that it was impossible to expose the Indian Ring, that "mysterious organization . . . ubiquitous and strategic," but they also warned that any attempt to do so conflicted with the profit motive: "Contractors would be more or less than human if . . . they did not enter into combinations or preconcerted plans whereby they could obtain the best possible prices for their commodities. Such has ever been the case and such ever will be."[62] The post-1874 board endorsed the government's blundering treatment of the Poncas. After the Ute War they insisted that the Ute's claim to Colorado land, guaranteed to the tribe by Brunot in 1873, was feeble and inconsequential. Using an argument that Indians had heard for two hundred years, the board in 1879 said that tribes only had a right to land that they actually cultivated. So-called wild tribes must disappear:

> No 12,000,000 acres of the public domain whose hills are full of ores, and whose valleys are waiting for diligent hands to "dress and keep them" in obedience to the divine command, can long be kept simply as a park, in which wild beasts are hunted by wilder men. The Anglo-Saxon race will not allow the car of civilization to stop long at any line of latitude or longitude on our broad domain. If the Indian in wilderness plants himself on the track, he must inevitably be crushed by it.[63]

By 1880 many congressmen echoed what Representative Samuel Jackson Randall of Pennsylvania said in 1875—the Board of Indian Commissioners had become "utterly useless." When James Throckmorton of Texas moved to terminate all funds for the "entirely superfluous" board in 1877, his motion failed, 38–47. In 1879 board chairman Clinton Fisk berated his organization for its inaction and called it a bump on a log. Three years later he protested that the board had "nothing but existence." Congress, voicing suspicion of men who donned the "robes of philanthropy" without pay, voted in 1882 to appropriate no more funds for the board.[64] From then until its complete termination in 1934 the Board of Indian Commissioners continued to meet annually, but only as a humanitarian vestige of the Grant administration.

In 1869 Congressman James Garfield declared that he would vote for no further Indian appropriations until the money stopped flowing "through that filthy channel" of the Indian Office. The Board of Indian Commissioners was created to clean the channel and, from the beginning, had been stripped of the tools needed to accomplish its task. In the early 1870s the board served as a dedicated, hard-working, efficient sentinel for the president. After 1874 it became, at best, a sergeant-at-arms.

The board made many mistakes, including the denial of a position to Roman Catholics. But Welsh's replacement in 1869 by the mild, trusting, and naïve John Lang symbolized its major weakness. Welsh refused to accept what he called emasculated responsibility; in 1874 Felix Brunot and the rest of the board implicitly conceded that the fiery Philadelphian had been correct. Audits that could be arbitrarily overruled were of no consequence and a board without authority was, they realized, a "comparatively useless appendage to the service." They also were correct when they admitted that an independent board with actual authority and power could never coexist with the Interior.[65]

With little left to do in 1881, the BIC turned to rewriting history. It somehow concluded that the Peace Policy had been the board's own creation. Even more misleading was the assertion that the Policy failed because churches had nominated poor agents. It was obviously true that the denominations and the board itself contributed to the demise of the Peace Policy, but much more fatal was the general ineptitude of Grant's administration and the powerful political and economic forces that worked to undo his idealistic reform.

5. A Faltering Reform

The resignation of the Board of Indian Commissioners was not a spiteful act by men who
had some trivial disagreement with the president. The board's problem represented only one
aspect of the pervasive distrust within and
without the Grant administration. Republican
reformers had grown disillusioned with the chief
executive long before May of 1874 and near the
end of Grant's first term the liberal Republicans
attempted to prevent his return to office. Indian
reformers, however, rejected the anti-Grant
insurgents and remained loyal to the president. A
week before the election they obtained his
promise that the Peace Policy would continue
and that any changes would favor the humanitarian cause.[1]

Most of the religious press supported Grant
in 1872. The *American Missionary* did so because of the Peace Policy; the *Religious Magazine* said that he had been "self-forgetting, single-
eyed, silent under imputations and slanders, and
subordinating everything to his country's salvation." Unperturbed by the liberal defection,
Grant coasted to victory in November by carrying twenty-nine of thirty-five states, including
all those directly affected by the Peace Policy
except Texas. A month later he announced
that his Policy, "as successful as its most ardent
friends anticipated," would continue without
change.

The problems of the Peace Policy were symptomatic of Grant's administration and, to understand the difficulties that continued to plague this supposedly successful Indian reform, one must examine Grant and his conception of the presidency.

After Grant's death in 1885 the Board of Indian Commissioners praised his wisdom, modesty, and self-reliance as president—"his devotion to duty, his firm defense of national honor, his . . . administrative abilities rarely equaled, never surpassed."[2] Most of Grant's contemporaries were less kind, especially while he held office. In 1872 Father Pierre DeSmet complained that all the forces of corruption supported Grant, a "cipher in himself." Four years later an equally unsympathetic writer alleged that "a more corrupt government could not be found from China to Constantinople."[3]

When Grant accepted the Republican nomination in 1868 he announced that he had no policies contrary to the will of the people, believing that the chief executive should lead quietly if at all. A military hero, he was far from being the "Kaiser Ulysses" about whom Democrats raged. Henry Adams described Grant's concept of the presidency "as that of the commander of an army in time of peace . . . to obey the civil authority without question." This concept resulted in fragmentation and confusion among those elected to support him in Congress and those appointed to serve on his cabinet. His cabinet selections in 1869 delighted the nation, though it became a cabinet from which twenty-five men resigned or were dismissed. Secretary of State Hamilton Fish observed that the cabinet, on which Fish served for eight years, gradually disintegrated because it lacked any identity and unity.

Grant, however, remained a popular hero who in 1876 and 1880 could speculate about a third term.[4] His most determined opponents hesitated to attack him personally and he seemed imperturbable, immune, and aloof from politics. In reality, Grant was stubborn and confused, witty and moody, friendly and irritable, his actions so unpredictable that those close to him at the time and those who wrote of him later spoke of a Kitchen Cabinet and the mysterious influence of White House cronies. Defective in even rudimentary knowledge of American law, finance, and foreign policy, Grant made no pretense at studying and learning. He committed monumental blunders, made illegal appointments, and soon yielded to demands of the professional spoilsmen whom he had vowed to eliminate from the federal government. By the end of Grant's second term there not only was moral and administrative chaos, but a need to restore presidential controls usurped by Congress; not only was there corruption at many levels, but paralysis froze the federal bureaucracy. Allan Nevins has written that 1876 was the only year that American government completely broke down. For this, as well as for the failure of the Peace Policy, Grant's laxity and negligence were partly responsible.[5]

Other conditions combined with Grant's weaknesses to cause his failure as president. He led a radical party that was becoming conservative. Supported by banks and railroads, the Republicans came to advocate social change less often than they defended special interests and the status quo. To this Grant brought his own suspicion of reformers and his personal loyalty to friends, including the friends who scandalized his administration. Many reformers eventually learned what William Welsh discovered in 1870, when he alerted the president to frauds on the Teton Sioux and Grand River reservations. Grant was slow to investigate "owing to implicit confidence in his friends . . . [and was] blind to their wrong-doings."[6] Humiliated when he tried to annex Santo Domingo and irked by bolting Liberals in 1872, Grant retreated and sought refuge with regular Republicans. Such men as Benjamin Butler and Zachariah Chandler became more influential than Carl Schurz, Elihu Washburne, and Jacob Cox. During Grant's second campaign for the presidency William Tecumseh Sherman gave perhaps the fairest explanation of what had happened to his friend:

> I feel for General Grant in his sad position. When he entered his present office I believe he intended what he said—to administer his office according to his own best judgment—but he soon found that he reckoned without his host, that Congress and individual senators controlled all the details of Government and that if he did not concede to senators and representatives, the appointing power, they would Johnsonize him. In trying to compromise . . . he was more and more departed from his true course and now a few designing senators and members surround him and he cannot see beyond them. . . . influence and money—a crowd of flatterers surround him and he cannot know the whole truth.[7]

In 1878 Grant bitterly remarked to Hamilton Fish that Rutherford Hayes appeared influenced by "two great humbugs . . . reform and reformers."

President Andrew Johnson's secretary of the interior told Bishop Henry Whipple in 1869 that although he had wanted to appoint honest agents, he was powerless to remove the men already in office.[8] Grant resolutely decided to change this condition. Perhaps unaware of his impact, Grant actually surprised the spoilsmen and politicians with his Peace Policy. In the summer of 1869 the *Boston Commonwealth* warned that shocked western congressmen and land speculators were determined to eliminate Grant's meddling Quakers.[9] It required four years for the "political vampires," as William Welsh labeled them, to move part way out of this trap. Even though Grant's original goals became badly compromised, the patronage brokers never again recaptured the pervasive control that they had enjoyed under Lincoln and Johnson.

During the Peace Policy there were frequent illegitimate efforts by many persons, including the president himself, the Board of Indian Commissioners, and church officials, to influence agent appointments and to compromise the authority given to mission boards. Ultimately the Department of the Interior determined who received agencies, and therefore the resignation of Jacob Cox in 1872, a man highly respected by reformers, was a severe blow for the new system. Cox's resignation, like that of Rockwood Hoar as attorney general, harmed the administration and alarmed liberals. The *Nation* complained that Grant had forfeited a brilliant man and had lost heart in his fight against corruption.[10]

Columbus Delano, an Ohio attorney who had gained a poor reputation as head of the Bureau of Internal Revenue, replaced Cox. Under Delano the Interior was racked with one scandal after another until he was forced to resign in 1875. Zachariah Chandler's subsequent appointment as secretary ended any lingering respect that reformers held for Grant.[11] Under Delano and Chandler the confused department sank further into malfunction and corruption. In a period of growing Democratic power, patronage had become imperative for Republicans.[12]

Delano's relation to the churches became apparent soon after he replaced Cox. He offered Episcopalians the Shoshone agency in Wyoming if they would appoint a non-Episcopalian, James Wham, at Red Cloud. The church protested that it did not want the new agency and that it should not have to nominate men at the department's whim, but, satisfied that Wham was a good man, they agreed. Two weeks later they were asked to appoint another unknown person as Shoshone agent. Vincent Colyer grumbled that the church at least had been asked to approve the Shoshone nomination before it became final.[13] Other religious bodies later reported the same relationship with the department. According to Dr. John Reid of the Methodist Missionary Society, names of prospective agents came from Washington "under such circumstances as led us to believe that we had better accept, and we did."[14] A religious rubber stamp meant that politicians in the Interior could select the agents and the churches would be officially responsible. At Delano's initial meeting with the Board of Indian Commissioners and mission representatives he laid out the rules: mission boards would continue to name agents and have complete control over them—unless Delano deemed a man unworthy. He reserved, Delano said, "the right to chop off the political heads of your friends whenever occasion may require it, and you must not complain of this."[15] In effect, the denominations had lost their right of appointment and retained only the privilege of nomination after 1871.

The Department of the Interior was not the only source of patronage attacks on the Peace Policy. Grant's personal secretary privately requested Methodists to endorse nominations, and Grant himself was directly attacked for securing his brother's trade monopoly on the Fort Peck and Fort Belknap reserves. In 1870 Grant had interfered with the church nomination process when he supported the rejection of the Methodist appointee at the Mackinac agency and had personally appointed a man nominated by Zachariah Chandler, then a Michigan senator. The president's weakness for friends was obvious in the rigging of the sham Denver agency by Colorado governor Edward McCook, a land speculator who had been involved in making fraudulent beef contracts for the Utes. In 1873 Grant was forced to remove McCook from office for defrauding Indians, yet he reappointed McCook a year later.[16] A similar story surrounded the suspension of Washington Territory's Indian Superintendent R. H. Milroy in 1873. Milroy, a close friend of Vice-President Colfax, was soon reinstated by Grant. The Board of Indian Commissioners, too, occasionally engaged in favoritism and even Felix Brunot used his and the board's influence with Grant to gain a general's appointment to an agency in Indian Territory.[17]

Favors sought by Grant and Brunot seem insignificant compared to pressures exerted by Congress. In 1876 Senator William Boyd Allison of Iowa proclaimed in Congress that the president had withdrawn all party influence over Indian agents and that the "absolute control" of the denominations meant that all fraud in the Indian service was the responsibility of the Christian Church, not the Republican party. Since 1870, Allison said, "no person except connected with those religious associations has ever recommended an Indian agent, nor has an Indian agent, to my knowledge, been appointed except upon the recommendation of the religious societies."[18] So starkly does this statement contrast with the record that it seems impossible that any senator, much less a member of the Senate Indian committee like Allison, could have ignored the actual situation. Army officers, state legislators, and congressmen simply had never accepted the practice of denominational selection of agents or agency employees. Agents and superintendents from the beginning were deluged with letters requesting the appointment of old friends, unemployed politicians, destitute doctors, former agents, and crippled Civil War veterans.[19]

A deliberate congressional effort to subvert the Peace Policy began as early as April of 1869, with an attempt to block Grant's first Quaker appointments. Unaccustomed to political infighting, Friends such as Benjamin Hallowell were startled to learn that anyone questioned their recommendations or would try to discredit the Society. The 1869 nominations were eventually accepted, but in 1871 Senator James Harlan of Iowa, a former secretary of the interior, sought to secure the Orthodox Friends' Quapaw agency for his brother-in-law. Quakers feared that Harlan had "an influence which seems to have exceeded that of the President's Indian Commission," and though they admitted that their Society was too timid, they decided not to contest

Harlan for fear of retribution in the future. The diffident approach worked at Quapaw, but not elsewhere. In 1876 the renomination of agents Mahlon Stubbs and Isaac Gibson was rejected by the Senate Indian Affairs committee, acting on the advice of a Kansas senator. Finding politics distasteful, the Friends took comfort in being right: "The Politicians of Nebraska are disposed to give thee trouble," a Friend reassured Barclay White, "but thou hast justice on thy side."[20]

Another early patronage crisis in Congress occurred during September of 1870. The American Missionary Association had nominated Major Selden Clark as agent for the Lake Superior Chippewas. As soon as Clark's name was submitted, the Senate, aided by one of Grant's personal secretaries, tried to block the nomination in order to retain the former agent. Alerted by a senator from Minnesota, Cox journeyed to Philadelphia and spent the weekend conferring with William Welsh. Welsh was impressed. The secretary was "a noble Christian man, and the more I see of him the more I love him." After spending Sunday in prayer and Bible classes, the two men hurried back to Washington and asked Hamilton Fish to intervene with Grant. Fish demurred, so Welsh himself called at the White House late one evening and talked for an hour with Grant and his wife. The president promised to meet privately with Welsh before a cabinet meeting the next morning. "You ought to be assured," Welsh reported to Whipple,

> the President gave me the strongest assurances of his fixed determination not to yield an inch to Political or personal considerations in producing the most thorough and radical reform in the Indian Department. He authorized me to say to my colleagues that they would be sustained to the full extent of his power in all proper efforts to civilize and Christianize the Indian. I put him to some stronger practical tests than I ever applied to anybody else, but he never flinched, and in each case gave order that the thing should be, although in one prominent case he knew that it would be most offensive to a Senator whom he desires to please as much as any other man in the country.
>
> Surely we may thank God and take courage. I made some revelations of the machinations and combinations of the Indian ring and of honest dupes who have been put forward by it. The President was amazed at the snares that have been set for him, even by men of his own household.[21]

Welsh sent the same message to Cox. There had been a "terrific fight" and though he feared some Christians and church leaders would grow fainthearted, Welsh assured Cox that Grant had "counted the cost and . . . [would] not swerve from this holy purpose."[22]

After Grant sent word that the American Missionary Association had the right to appoint agents, the Senate confirmed Clark's nomination and the Peace Policy survived an initial patronage crisis. In the process a more serious setback occurred. On October 3, Jacob Cox had asked Bishop Whipple to write to Grant on behalf of the Indian policy. "I do not know how we shall come out," the secretary insisted, "but you may be assured that I shall administer no other." On October 5, Cox resigned. Cox had come to feel that Grant would not support civil service reform and he had disagreed with the president over the role of the churches in Indian affairs. When Cox thought that Grant was pulling away from the denominations and giving in to the patronage and spoils system, he publically criticized his superior, an act of disloyalty that hurt and angered the president. Grant gladly accepted the secretary's resignation.[23]

Cox's successor, Columbus Delano, faced the same pressures to name Indian agents for the Republican party, but Delano proved to be more open to patronage demands than Cox had been. In 1871 a group of western senators refused to confirm the Baptist nomination for the Paiute agency. Delano asked the politicians for the name of "a good Christian man residing in Nevada" and then persuaded the Baptists to accept the person named. The agent, Charles F. Powell, proved something less than a good Christian. When Nevada settlers protested that Powell drank and gambled, the Baptists tried to remove him and politicians struggled to keep him. "We cannot loose [sic] the services of Major Powell as Indian Agent," one local politician pleaded with Delano; "we are commencing the most important political fight in the State and his services and position are of great importance to us as Republicans."[24]

Political pressures took many other forms. Republicans requested that Senate page boys "needing open air exercise" be sent west to solicit funds for the party on the western trips of the Board of Indian Commissioners. To block church nominations, the Senate Indian Committee delayed confirmation for months or confirmed men for agencies other than those for which they were nominated, meanwhile filling the first agency with a favorite. Senator Allison refused to confirm agents in 1875 because mission boards did not submit evidence of fitness, an excuse that undercut the churches' role in the Peace Policy. A ruse often employed by Congress was to reject men who did not live in the same state as the agency. When Ely Parker told the Dutch Reformed that only western men could be accepted, church officials complained that this automatically eliminated the Reformed from the Peace Policy. Secretary Delano answered that western residence was no sine qua non for appointment, but that westerners were preferred. The same method was used in 1876 in an attempt to remove the Quakers from Nebraska. Churchmen were further confused by instructions from Indian Commissioner

John Q. Smith, who told them not to nominate anyone from west of the Mississippi. At various times the government protested against naming ministers as agents.[25]

Little evidence justified Senator Allison's cynical assertion that the Christian Church enjoyed absolute control over Indian agents, yet the churches themselves were not beyond reproach in the practice of patronage. Seeking desperately to secure the Yakima agency, "Father" James Wilbur asked the Board of Indian Commissioners to "say what is necessary in the proper ears at Washington." Bishop Matthew Simpson was frequently under pressure to obtain appointments for Methodists. One man offered to pay Simpson's expenses in Washington and to contribute a large percentage to the Methodist Church as a "double benefit" if the bishop would help him become an agency inspector. Another person wanted the same position because he needed several years' rest and travel; he told Simpson that his clerical friends had already visited government officials and he hoped that the bishop could speak with Delano.[26] The Methodist Missionary Society later admitted that between 1870 and 1872 politicians and government officials had asked them for agency appointments and that the church had indeed named men on blind faith. When several of these appointments embarrassed the denomination, the Missionary Society resolved to name men "in the interest of religion and humanity alone."[27]

Other denominations ran into similar perils. Bishop Henry Whipple experienced the same pressures in Minnesota as Simpson did in Washington. Father DeSmet complained that Catholic agents had to favor Grant's reelection or lose their jobs, yet the Roman Church could shrewdly employ its political connections within the administration to its benefit.[28] In New Mexico unhappy Presbyterians faced a welter of charges and countercharges over who should receive agencies. One minister urged John Lowrie to dismiss a Methodist at the Presbyterian Pueblo agency because the agent had been nominated by a government official who was a friend of the agent's father in Ohio. When Navajo agent William Arny was accused of being profane, he defended himself by saying that jealous contractors and politicians had contrived to defame and remove him. P. D. MacElroy wrote from Cimarron that the Republican election committee asked all agents to donate to the party: "Hence it is that everything in and around an Indian Agency savors of politics, and hardly one employee gets to be so, except by political influences."[29]

The Peace Policy's naïve assumption about the churches' ability to accomplish civil service reform in the Indian Office proved unsound. As Herman Melville wrote in 1845, churchmen, as well as congressmen and cabinet members, were "but human and, like everyone else, subject to errors and abuses."

Opinion of the Peace Policy: 1869-73

Between 1869 and 1873 there were few attacks on the Peace Policy in the East. Democratic and liberal Republican writers trying to flatter Catholics and gain immigrant votes denounced the "evil genius of General Grant" and excoriated the president as a venal hypocrite, drunkard, and liar. But they seldom mentioned Indians. Even Charles Sumner, who proclaimed that Grant had established a military despotism that destroyed the Constitution, overlooked the Peace Policy. Some felt that the Policy cost too much, and a few former agents remarked that religion was no substitute for experience. The *Cleveland Herald* argued that Grant had put the cart before the horse by trying to civilize Indians before giving them property rights. In the same paper, Colonel Charles Whittlesey said that missions had failed for 250 years and that Indians obviously were doomed, but he praised Grant for having original ideas on the subject.[30] Before the election of 1872 the *New York Herald* was the only major eastern publication opposed to the Peace Policy. It advocated transferring troops from the South to the West and applying "Sheridan's cure" to the "squalid savages and privileged murderers" on reservations. The *Herald* described Christians as sitting at a safe distance, supplying Indians with guns and ammunition, and locking up vacant mineral and agricultural lands: "While the Quaker agents are quietly filling their pockets the Indians are plundering and murdering without hindrance or opposition. The Department turns a deaf ear to the cry of our perishing frontier population, or dispatches the pious General Howard. . . . And so the mingled farce and tragedy continues, while the night sky is red with the flames of the frontiersman's cabin."[31]

The *Nation, Philadelphia Inquirer, Chicago Tribune,* and *Boston Commonwealth* supported the reform. *Harper's Weekly* endorsed Grant, printed almost nothing about the Indian Bureau, and ignored the Peace Policy. A writer in *Harper's Monthly* said that no other administration had covered itself with so much honor as had Grant's. The Maine legislature passed a resolution praising the Peace Policy. A huge rally at Cooper Union in New York convinced the Board of Indian Commissioners that the public supported Grant. During the election of 1872 the board dutifully reported, as it did every year, that patronage had ended, that the Indians were pleased and progressing, and that reform of the Bureau was an accepted fact.[32]

Western citizens were more aware of the Peace Policy and much more opposed to it than were people in the East, although there was confusion in the West over the Policy's exact definition and opposition was far from unanimous. The *Junction City Union* greeted the new program by calling Vincent Colyer a liar and by advocating Indian extermination as the final solution. After Colyer's second trip to the Southwest, General O. O. Howard found almost universal opposition to Grant's reform. Grant himself received emotional letters in opposition. From Texas, a Charles Sanard spoke for the "bleeding and ravished frontier . . . a feeble voice for the suffering hundreds whose mouths [were] mute," and he begged the president to end "this . . . insane Pseudo humanitarian policy: Called the 'Quaker Indian Peace Policy!'" Sanard's letter continued: "How many oh, Mr. President, of our best men and women must be immolated in order to satiate this ungodly fanaticism. I am told that there is an "Indian Ring"; that our people are but chased, burned, Ravished and Robbed, That such ring may grow opulent with the *Blood Money*, Can this Oh! my God, be possible?"[33] Equally vehement was Virginia City's booster sheet, the *Montanian*. An 1871 editorial declared that the Grant administration had convinced Indians that white men were a "lot of squaws" who would do anything rather than fight and such a policy encouraged the Sioux to block the Northern Pacific's route along the Yellowstone. Any conciliation, the editor reasoned, was based on false history and on the erroneous assumption that kindness to Indians begat kindness.[34] To the contrary, Indians only responded to kindness and generosity with cruelty: "They have murdered our people, they burn our frontiers, they steal our stock, they slaughter, imprison, violate and mutilate our women and children, and carry desolation and destruction into every locality." In place of missionaries and government gifts, extermination was the only answer:

> Territories driven to desperation, rise in their might, burry [*sic*] conciliation with humanity and the calumet of peace, dig up the hatchet and annihilate them, bucks, squaws and papooses, all, we are opposed to making any distinction, in sex or age. They are as much the enemy of the *human* race as the serpent, and should be destroyed when opportunity offers. . . . There possibly has been some pretty good Indians; but they died very young—likely before they got their eyes open.[35]

Two weeks later the same editor warned Virginia City not to depend on the army and he advised settlers to arm themselves, advice they were bound to heed "as Quakers are scarce in the mountains."

Many frontiersmen protested that if only Baker and Sheridan could pay the Indians more "missionary visits," all tribes would soon emulate the Piegans who had become peaceful farmers after Baker's raid, but the government would never allow this because "some poor red-skinned pet of the Government, with its Quaker policy would get hurt, and tender-hearted philanthropists in the east would be thrown into convulsions of grief."[36] The same frontier spirit excited the *Bismarck Tribune* when Custer marched up the Yellowstone valley in 1873 and the headlines read "WHOOP! Custer's Cavalry Turned Loose on the Sioux. The Indians Are Most Woefully Thrashed. . . . THE HATCHET BURNED WHERE IT WILL DO MOST GOOD FORTY OF THE RED HEATHEN GONE TO KINGDOM COME AND THERE IS MORE OF THE SAME LEFT WHEN WANTED THEIR NOBLE FORMS ARE CLOTHED IN ANNUITY BLANKETS."[37] Nevertheless it is a mistake to assume that these attitudes characterized the entire West. Many people had genuinely mixed feelings. Republicans from western states were divided over the Peace Policy while most but not all Democrats opposed it.[38] During the Modoc War a writer in San Francisco said that most whites accepted the Peace Policy, though many also favored General George Crook's methods over the "sugar plum treatment" for resisting tribes.[39] Columbus Crocket, a poet claiming to be a "simon pure American," a "plain, rough, honest backwoodsman" who spoke only the truth, thought that all brutes must be suppressed with brute force, yet he believed Indians, brutes though they be, were more sinned against than sinning and that the white race owed the tribes a huge debt on the "balance sheet of heaven." This debt Grant sought to repay:

> There's one act, *Gen'l Grant*
> One splendid chapter in your life, —
> That must survive the gloom of death,
> And light your path beyond the grave.
> You've proved the *Red Man's truest friend*,
> And striven hard to lift him up
> To take his place 'mong Christian whites
> And be an honor to our land.

White men should be thankful for the Peace Policy because it would allow them to pass through the Pearly Gates and "find the name of *U. S. Grant /* High up on the 'Rolls' of Heaven."[40]

There were a variety of responses in the West. The *Montanian* printed letters from readers favoring Indian rights and opposing its own editorials. The governors of Montana and Wyoming, while admitting that their constituents opposed the Peace Policy, attributed this opposition to ignorance. The *Omaha Daily Herald* endorsed the Policy as "A Universal Verdict" and predicted that Grant would end frontier bloodshed. In Denver the *Daily News* had little use for "rose water" views of Indians but complimented the Board of Indian Commissioners for its hard work. The *Sacramento Union* and *Grand Rapids Eagle* had nothing but praise for the board, and the *Cheyenne Daily Leader* was a strong defender of Grant's policies. William Welsh reported that the Minnesota press had changed radically since 1862, and from Washington Territory Thomas McKenney wrote that although new agents were bitterly assailed by a few "designing knaves," the Peace Policy was accepted. New Mexico and Arizona Presbyterians reported that local women's missionary societies soon took a fresh interest in helping Indians.[41]

The religious press represented Christians east and west, and church periodicals between 1869 and 1873 overwhelmingly supported the Peace Policy. The *Independent*, an avowed Republican religious journal, praised the president and declared that it had long urged such reform. The editor expected Grant to retreat on civil service reform, but he felt that by remaining true to the Indians and resisting political efforts to "peel and plunder" them, the president could bring eternal glory to his administration. During the election of 1872 the *Independent* continued to laud Grant for his persistent good will in Indian affairs.[42] Among churches with large frontier memberships, both the Methodist and Baptist publications endorsed the Peace Policy. In 1869 the *Baptist Watchman* described Grant as "a rock in the midst of heaving and restless tides," citing his inaugural address as the first time a president had ever spoken wisely about Indians. A year later the same editor praised the Peace Policy as the brightest light in the government and, though he predicted that white civilization would eventually crush the tribes, he felt that the Peace Policy would make Indians comfortable in the process. The *Baptist Watchman* called for all Christians to support Grant and the Policy in 1872, while the Unitarian *Old and New* sarcastically attacked every denomination including its own for failing to help a president harassed by a "horde of hucksters." The *Congregationalist* praised Grant, Cox, and "that large-hearted man," William Welsh, but after Cox resigned it concluded that Grant's reforms were "a mournful failure . . . backed down and caved in . . . wheedled, or scared, or worn out." In the West, the *Pacific Churchman* praised Grant for the Peace Policy and the *Presbyterian Banner* defended the Board of Indian Commissioners against the more scurrilous western press.[43]

There were obvious exceptions to the general optimism of the churches. Roman Catholics continued to attack the Peace Policy as turning Indian reservations into training camps "for the friends of *State-Churchism.*" The Riggs family sullenly objected as the American Board in Boston blandly ignored their advice to fight the Policy. Presbyterian missionary Thomas Williamson warned that the Indian problem, "like Banquo's ghost," would always return and he criticized the churches for their poor response; in 1873 he decided that the Peace Policy had failed to provide honest agents and had sparked no new mission work. The *Christian Union* echoed Williamson's remarks and predicted extinction for the Indian race. Jebez Neversink Trask delighted in caustically attacking everyone. He wrote in 1873 that the government mistakenly sought to extinguish the Ute title in Colorado, "where the government ought first to have extinguished the miners and squatters." Trask admonished the churches that Indians did want bread and wine but not as sacraments, and he sharply rebuked the Board of Indian Commissioners for being quaint, foggy-minded, and too fond of printing extravagant missionary reports. Neversink Trask said that proponents of the Policy only reported delusions when they peered through "something like magnifying and multiplying glasses" to count their good deeds and Christian Indians.[44] A similar criticism from a different theological perspective came from Quaker John Lang of the board. Lang asked his fellow board members to be more humble because

> it is not in the power of man to direct his steps aright, and God is jealous of His own honor. . . . The Votaries of the President's "peace policy" have been favored with a large measure of success since its inauguration, and I have feared that there has been too much elation of poor finite self, as having been the cause of success, and an unhallowed feeling engendered that it was mine own hands that hath "gotten me the victory."[45]

As Lang observed, supporters of the Peace Policy seemed inclined toward self-congratulation. William Welsh in 1870 exclaimed that God had miraculously removed all obstacles to peace, broken the Indian Ring, and ended the spoils system. In 1872 Welsh was more cautious, yet he still believed great inroads had been made against patronage and corruption, and he pledged his full support for Grant's reelection.[46] In 1869 Henry Whipple had told Jacob Cox that he wept like a child because God had answered his prayers. Four years later the bishop realized there was even more of a silver lining in the dark cloud of American's inhumanity to Indians: "My wildest dream of what might be done for the Indians has been accomplished." The Episcopal Board of Missions exulted that Grant had eliminated spoilsmen: "Never was a grander act performed by any ruler . . . All honor be to our President." Nebraska's Bishop Robert Clarkson said that Grant's courage in fighting the speculators equaled his courage at Vicksburg. The Reformed and Presbyterians agreed, and the Minnesota Congregational Conference "hailed with joy" the advent of the reform. The American Missionary Association saw an opportunity sent by God and it pledged to support the government with the Gospel.[47] Hicksite Friends, warned early by Ely Parker that they must expect opposition, girded themselves and overcame, in their opinion, "mountains of difficulty" to reach summits of success. After two years, Benjamin Hallowell called for a celebration of God's victory over evil forces: "The dark cloud which, for many years impended so ominously over the western Indians . . . seems now to be rapidly passing away . . . I have never known their cause and condition as favourable as at present. The world is manifestly improving."[48]

The United States Congress was more representative of public opinion than were Quaker officials, church leaders, or the religious press. For a year members of both the House and Senate remained discreetly silent about the president's new experiment to deprive them of patronage. Almost no debate accompanied the passage of the Board of Indian Commissioners legislation or the 1869 assignment of Quaker agents. Congress welcomed the reform as a means of reducing Indian appropriations. George Julian of Indiana expressed a common sentiment when he thanked God for Grant and his policy. The influential John Sherman of Ohio favored anything that prevented Indian wars, and Representative Charles Eldredge of Wisconsin felt confident that Christian kindness and charity by the government would solve all problems. In February of 1870, when Edward Degener of Texas warned that force alone, not schools, teachers, or the New Testament, could civilize the "savage fiends" of his state, other westerners from California, Kansas, and Nevada endorsed the Peace Policy and praised the Quakers as the most generous and wise Indian agents in American history.[49] At the close of its first year, the Peace Policy had avoided congressional debate. The initial test arose in the spring of 1870.

On the morning of June 4, the Reverend J. G. Butler opened the Senate with a brief prayer. Following a short discussion of the census, a senator moved to appropriate thirty thousand dollars requested by the Hicksite Friends. John Thayer of Nebraska objected, thereby opening a debate over the Peace Policy.

Thayer began by saying that the Quakers, although honest, had been no better than previous Nebraska agents. The Indians remained unchanged; whatever Quakers might accomplish with extra money could be done equally well by others. Cornelius Cole of California agreed and termed the request "ridiculous . . . a pretty severe comment upon this case by the Friends Society." Speaking for the Quakers, Oliver Morton of Indiana praised their benevolence, praised William Penn, and pointed out that the Society had spent much of its own money. To this, Nebraska's Thomas Tipton replied that Quakers, like other Indian agents, practiced patronage and nepotism in agency hiring. They had a special talent, Tipton insisted, for protecting their own financial interests and, much to his feigned astonishment, the Friends had proved as frail as other men. The only solution was to stop feeding lazy, indolent, slothful Indians: "[They who] slaughter and brain our defenseless children, who ravish the women upon the plains . . . one portion of the people of this country work and work and work and toil, in order that your agents may go and feed and feed and feed . . . the system is rotten; the system is false; the system can no longer be maintained or endured." Tipton requested the complete removal of the Pawnees, Poncas, Otoes, and Sioux from Nebraska, and Thayer added that murders in Nebraska had multiplied since the Quakers' arrival because the tribes no longer feared punishment. When Morrill of Maine accused Thayer and Tipton of seeking to remove all Indians from their state, Thayer challenged him to locate Maine's original inhabitants. Senators shouted further objections back and forth, but only George Williams of Oregon thought to ask why the federal government favored Quakers over other Christians. Williams asserted that anyone who believed Quakers more qualified or pious than Methodists or Presbyterians was guilty of a "good deal of humbuggery." Thayer then called for the Senate vote. The bill passed thirty-three to twelve, with the East strongly in favor of aiding the Peace Policy and the West divided.[50]

Opposition to the Indian policy smoldered in Congress for the remainder of Grant's first term with few politicians daring to attack the president directly. In the House, James Garfield, Aaron Sargent, Henry Dawes, and James Burnie Beck led an able, intelligent defense. Their opponents accused them of partisan and sectional blindness and of wanting to depopulate the West. John Connor of Texas declared that Henry Dawes had lived so long in New England isolation that he was totally ignorant of frontier life. In these debates, defenders of the Peace Policy usually appealed to ethics, economics, logic, and the Christian religion. Opponents spoke emotionally about frightening experiences on the frontier. Westerners gleefully pointed out how New England and the South had earlier disposed of their Indians.

A favorite target for congressional attack was the ideal of philanthropy. Representative Michael Kerr of Indiana argued that sentimentality harmed both whites and Indians by creating a kid-glove government that might rule saints but not men: "I have been filled with disgust, I have been inspired almost with detestation, for that abominable sort of policy. . . . Some call it humanitarian, others the policy of peace, love, and generosity; but it seems to me to be none of these. It is the policy of weakness, of mere unmanly time-serving, of maudlin sentimentality."[51]

An effective reproach was ridicule. Degener of Texas boasted that men in his state knew that Indians were "savage beasts of the forest" and that Texans despised any "Quaker policy of forbearance and humanity which, with Bible in hand, tries to bear conviction to the minds of the Indians that their habit of cutting off other men's hair is so very wicked." Delegate Thomas Fitch from Nevada agreed that good Indians were dead ones, an insight that inspired him to comic heights in describing preachers assigned to agencies. Fitch had heard that the Baptists were assigned to Nevada, and if indeed this were true, it provided an excellent reason to cancel all Indian funds, the Baptists being the worst possible sect for his territory: "Such a selection would necessitate the taking there of materials for boring artesian wells; for, unless like Moses, the agent could obtain water by smiting the rocks, or unless he should inaugurate a sect of dry Baptists, his agency would fail of usefulness . . . there is not water enough to enable him to run the agency. [Laughter]"[52] Speaking for Ohio, Allen Thurman denounced "phrase-mongering philanthropists" who praised an overrated Indian policy "singing hosannas to the Almighty and to Grant." In the Senate, Nebraska's Thayer inquired whether Christians were more honest or truthful than other men, or whether Christian agents "manifest just as strong a desire to make the dollar as their predecessors?"[53]

The notion that Christians were devoted to brotherhood, that they were less greedy and more honest than other men, had been the foundation of the Peace Policy. More than the rhetoric in Congress, an examination of agency life and conduct will shed light on the validity of these assumptions.

6. The Test of Temptation

It would corrupt the angel Gabriel to be an Indian agent.

James Henry Randolph,
House of Representatives
(1877)

In 1875, two years after Grant's second inauguration, an editor of the *Independent* expressed fear that Congress would abolish the Board of Indian Commissioners and thereby terminate the Peace Policy. If this happened, he warned, the system that had provided the most honest Indian agents in American history would end and the nation would witness a return to the corruption of the 1860s. Three years later Presbyterian E. M. Kingsley, a member of the Board of Indian Commissioners, told a Senate committee that nothing justified the wholesale abuse heaped on Christian agents whose integrity had excelled that of most businessmen.[1] Others disagreed with these optimistic assessments. The Chippewa chief Wabonoquet in Minnesota was quoted as declaring that the Policy had added religious hypocrisy to white greed and corruption:

> When our Great Father found he could not obtain proper men for our agents, he made up his mind to try religious societies. You cannot imagine what feelings of surprise it caused us that after a clergyman was appointed our agent, we found our property being taken away away without even our consent being asked. . . . Will you blame me if I had the thought that a minister should be above fraud. Here stands the minister of God, says he comes here to take care of the Indians. Who is his God? Is he a greenback?[2]

106

The problem of evaluating the performance, honesty, and integrity of church-selected agents has remained as difficult for historians as it was for contemporaries between 1870 and 1882. In studying the period we learn that few men escaped accusation, most were ardently defended by their church, and virtually none admitted any guilt.[3] The Peace Policy's founders assumed that honest agents could eliminate Indian wars and agency corruption, they assumed that churches and mission boards could select honest men and that honest men would remain honest, and they assumed that dedicated Christians were willing to serve as agents.

The new system produced a considerable increase in pious language in the Indian agents' reports, not only those of clergy-agents, but laymen such as I. L. Mahan at LaPointe, who annually informed the government that God the Father had sent timber, land, and fish to Indians. Mahan also requested missionaries to lead Indians to a "loving Saviour's arms." At White Earth, Lewis Stowe reported, "God in his great mercy has been pleased to bless this reservation," and agent J. H. Fairchild at Siletz observed that Christianity effectively civilized Oregon Indians. A Catholic agent reported to the Indian Office that Umatillas needed "charity which falleth like the gentle dew from heaven, blessing him that giveth." C. A. Huntington at Neah Bay described Indian children as kneeling at his church's altar morning and night and saying grace at meals. At Pyramid Lake, A. J. Barnes convinced Indians not to work or play on the Sabbath, and Quaker John D. Miles in the Indian Territory knew that sins of Cheyenne and Arapaho fathers brought venereal disease to their third and fourth generations, an observation that he carefully reported to the commissioner. Agent John Smith cautioned that Warm Springs Indians were "babes in Christ," unprepared for civilization. For Smith, religion was the most important element of Indian education and of an agent's duties because "Bible Truths and Bible teachings carry with them a power that none can gainsay nor resist."[4]

Yet unless one believed that verbal piety insured honesty and dedication, realization of the Peace Policy's major assumptions and goals was open to doubt. Many temptations that had brought agents to despair and dishonesty before 1869 continued during Grant's administration. An irresponsible Congress, neglectful churches, daily conditions of life in the Far West, and the fact that even pious men are human, worked to counteract the professions of faith.

Neither the critics nor the supporters of the Peace Policy gave sufficient attention to conditions of agency life, conditions that often led men to leave their posts soon after arrival or to succumb to temptation. A federal Indian agent had to be bonded, he could not leave the reservation without permission from his superior, and he was personally responsible for all agency property and employees.[5] He might live and work in ramshackle buildings in a semianarchic environment, amid antagonistic Indians surrounded by lawless whites. An agent was obligated to maintain order and educate young Indians while at the same time protecting the reservation from white and Indian desperados, regulating trade with whites, receiving and distributing food and annuity funds. He had to be a bookkeeper and was required to report at least monthly to Washington. An agent's relationship with Washington was often chaotic, especially in regard to money. The agent usually had little extra money, and whenever Congress delayed appropriation bills, which was often, he could find himself with no funds at all or with having to purchase agency supplies out of his pocket. Nor did any uniform accounting exist until halfway through the Peace Policy. The Board of Indian Commissioners urged that agents be compelled to follow elementary bookkeeping procedures, a suggestion that the government finally adopted in 1876, when it required quarterly audits and tightened regulations on the purchase of beef and flour. This fiscal reform and the adoption of a new inspection system implied that even church-agents had to be regulated. The opportunity for financial windfalls in adjusting claims for Indian depredations off the resevation also afforded nearly irresistible temptations, but the government refused to abolish or reform that system. The problems of crime, jurisdiction, law enforcement, justice, contracting, and poor accounting ruined more than one agent.[6]

Besides their struggle against legal anarchy, a number of Indian agents lived in wretched physical conditions and were subjected every day to terror, squalor, and disease. Bishop William Hare, whose own health broke after three years at Yankton, complained that life in the West consisted of hot sun, swarms of mosquitoes, and filthy ranches. Many agencies were located on the Great Plains, where temperatures could rise to over one hundred degrees on summer days and drop to forty degrees below zero during winter blizzards. Agents in Nebraska reported digging out from under fifty-foot snow drifts in 1881. Agents to the north that same year said ice on the Missouri was four feet thick. During the winter months many agencies were isolated, and even in the summer exasperatingly slow communication with Washington hindered understanding and prompt action at both ends. Summers also brought polluted water, quicksand, prairie fires, potato bugs, grasshoppers, and drought.[7]

The average agent faced these conditions while using houses and schools that were barely habitable. In 1878 all but six agents attributed failure in education to poor facilities, and throughout the 1870s church-appointees refused to subject their own families to frontier conditions. Presbyterian Henry Breiner found no quarters fit for his wife and daughters when he and his family arrived in Indian Territory. Breiner patched together a shed that served as the agency building and there they shivered through the winter of 1871, but he vowed to leave and never return. Inspector Jared Daniels could not even find a shed at the Southern Apache site where an agent and his wife lived in a tent. Conditions at the Hopi agency drove that agent and his family to remove to and remain at the already overcrowded Navajo headquarters at Fort Defiance. From the Presbyterian Moqui Pueblo school, teacher Edward Walsh wrote: "I am discouraged out here a hundred miles from any white persons, my family sick and one child died last week—great difficulties in procuring provisions, etc. I have therefor concluded to resign and remove to Santa Fe."[8] A Cimarron agent told of the Episcopal missionary-priest who left in disgust after two weeks. The agent added that he was leaving also:

I think sometimes that if the Government had tried to make Ind. Agts. dishonest they could not have adopted a better policy. . . . It is utterly impossible for you to form an idea of the fearfull state of society here. Most Americans . . . sink right down into licentiousness, drunkenness, gambling & murder. Many of them shoot at a man quicker than at a dog . . . there is not a virtuous mexican woman who has arrived at the age of womanhood. They live with Americans in miserable sin & shame as long as either is pleased. The Maxwell Land Grant & Railway Co. are for Northern New Mexico what Jim Fisk was for New York with the addition of perjury, arson & murder.[9]

A Baptist farmer working for the government at Pyramid Lake likewise found his work "incompatible with [his] high calling as a minister of Jesus Christ," or as Presbyterian William Defrees succinctly explained when he left his station: "It is the duty & it is required that the Agent live among his Indians. I cannot consent to take my wife back to that place; hence, I resign."[10] At Fort Berthold the agent, his family, and employees lived in dilapidated, vermin-infested log buildings erected and vacated decades earlier by the American Fur Company. Here, next to the Missouri River, typhoid and cholera struck down women teachers who lived amid "the foul dust and almost constant din of drum and dance . . . a shame to our Government and a disgrace to Christian culture." Conditions were similar at Uintah Valley and Los Pinos. John Critchlow concluded that he had been deluded by eastern novelists and confessed that he would never have accepted the Uintah appointment had he known how miserable living conditions were.[11] Life was even worse at Cheyenne River, where a flood swept away the entire agency in 1877. That natural catastrophe actually may have been a blessing if an Episcopal agent's earlier report was correct:

The engine, saw and grist mills, shingle-machine, etc., were down and scattered in different directions. . . . The mowing-machine was worn out and worthless. . . . The wagons were broken and out of repair. . . . Tools of various kinds scanty and nearly worn out. The beef-cattle were on the opposite side of the river and could not be crossed. . . . The subsistence stores were at a low ebb and soon gave out. . . . The location presents many discouraging features. That of the greatest magnitude is the encroachment of the river upon its bank, rendering it necessary at certain times to remove the buildings . . . the buildings are few in number, of the roughest and cheapest description, faulty in construction, and bad in condition. They are inconvenient, uncomfortable, and unsightly. They harbor thousands of vermin, the ravages of which upon the subsistence stores are immense.[12]

When Charles Hudson replaced John Stout at the Pima agency in May of 1876 Hudson found a building but no furniture. When he protested that his small salary and lack of job security would not permit him to purchase the "necessaries and decencies of life," the Indian Office asked the Treasury Department if it could authorize purchase of such items. The official answer was negative: "Hudson's case is hard but no worse than a score of others. It would be but naked justice to permit the purchase of some permanent articles of a bulky character not easily *confiscated* by retiring agents—such as Bedsteads, chairs, tables, stoves, &c. . . . Such purchases have been uniformally disallowed but if you can provide a safe way out of the difficulty I am with you with all my heart."[13] Evidently a loophole was never found. Hudson resigned in September.

A salary that did not permit agents to enjoy the "necessaries and decencies" of life was a constant problem for churches seeking to recruit solid, dependable agents. The federal legislation of 1834 establishing the Indian Office had set an agent's annual salary at fifteen hundred dollars—and there it remained for thirty-five years. The adequacy of the fifteen hundred dollars depended on factors that varied greatly from reservation to reservation: if the agent had to rent his home, purchase his food, fuel, and clothing, and pay long-distance transportation costs, then the pay was clearly insufficient; but if the government provided a comfortable house, as at Yakima, and if the agent took government rations or if local prices were low, the salary was more than adequate. Southwestern agents could purchase their personal supplies from government contractors, but even so, as General O. O. Howard noticed, the high prices forced one agent to exhaust his entire salary on food. At Uintah Valley, John Critchlow and his employees ate from agency supplies until an Indian Office directive instructed all agents to secure their own groceries, which for Critchlow meant sending orders to Salt Lake City, several hundred miles to the west. Critchlow complied with the order, but his best men left the service.[14]

Another expense was a fifty-thousand-dollar bond. The Society of Friends at first posted the bond for its agents, but later this became the responsibility of each agent. Some men had difficulty securing bonds; the government rejected others. In New Mexico, where few persons had fifty thousand dollars in collateral, a Navajo agent complained that he had no choice but to take the bond from two men who planned to acquire Indian lands. They later hinted that the agent should cooperate with them and "delicately reminded him that *they went on his bond when no one else would do this.*"[15] In Wisconsin, a Presbyterian missionary reported that bondsmen controlled agents Clark and Mahan, who made "absurd purchases, both as to place & price, simply at the beck of these men."[16]

Throughout the Peace Policy many churchmen and agents protested that a fifteen-hundred-dollar salary was insufficient, incommensurate with an agent's responsibilities, and created a temptation if not an invitation to cheat in order to survive. William Welsh admitted that the churches had difficulty finding qualified men because of poor salaries, and Bishop Henry Whipple argued that low pay was a critical problem facing the Peace Policy when he called for churches to supplement federal payrolls. The American Missionary Association did so, and Quakers, who admitted that Society members were "as a rule comfortably established," added five hundred dollars to government wages at four agencies. Friend Benjamin Tatham considered fifteen hundred dollars "very niggardly and utterly disgraceful," whereas Dr. John Ferris of the Reformed Church argued that the penny-wise, pound-foolish practice should be replaced by a thirty-five-hundred-dollar salary. Baptists agreed that their men in Nevada had to cheat and steal to survive on an agent's salary; the church promised to send additional funds. Only a few churchmen disagreed with these complaints. Unitarians felt that salaries were adequate, while Presbyterian John Lowrie objected that so much complaining about money was not becoming to Christians. Lowrie reasoned that the only purpose of salary was subsistence; higher pay would make men desire the positions, which was unwise because Indian agents, like missionaries, should be motivated by a disinterested spirit.[17]

In the minority among religious leaders, Lowrie had much company in a Congress that rebuffed every pay increase for agents. On February 22, 1871, a Senate appropriations amendment was introduced that would have raised salaries to two thousand dollars. John Sherman of Ohio objected on several grounds. He expressed surprise that ministers would expect a 40 percent raise after one year's service, especially when the government provided them with homes, gardens, and Indian servants. No Indian, he continued, received fifteen hundred dollars and there was no place on a reservation to spend such money. Furthermore, the missionary societies themselves did not pay that much and, finally, honest men elsewhere worked for fifteen hundred dollars or less. A wild, irrational debate followed. Sherman withdrew his objections, but Senator Thayer of Nebraska argued that the agents had accepted the salary level when they took the jobs and, in any event, Christians should labor "for the love of the human race . . . if they have enough to live upon, to eat, drink, and wear, they are satisfied." It was therefore a sign of bad grace, Thayer said, for churches to request more money. The amendment failed, thirty-three to eleven.[18]

Senators Thayer and Sherman appeared rather stingy to denominational officials who knew that a senator's salary was five thousand dollars, that Senate clerks earned twenty-five hundred dollars, and that pages drew from thirteen hundred to eighteen hundred dollars. The assistant keeper of the stationery in the Senate received eighteen hundred dollars and the acting assistant doorkeeper was paid twenty-six hundred dollars. Some businessmen argued that the skills required for a good Indian agent were worth at least five thousand dollars a year. Yet whether or not the federal government actually underpaid its agents depended on the location, size, and facilities of the agency. In relation to wages of skilled workmen in the East, many agents were well paid and did better in the service than they would have in private business or in the churches.[19]

A practice often justified by low pay, and one for which Grant himself set an example, was nepotism. Whether agents could hire anyone they wished, and whether their employees could use agency flour, sugar, and coffee appropriated for Indians, were issues debated throughout the '70s. Bishop Whipple cautioned that the churches must help agents employ men of high character for agency jobs. Quaker William Nicholson observed that finding such men on the frontier was almost impossible. The low pay, scarcity of good men, and concern for the morale and conduct of all agency employees induced some agents to hire relatives. In 1870 the government allowed each Indian agent to hire all of his teachers and other workers, with the government paying each person's transportation to the reservation. By 1874, every employee had to be approved by the Indian Office and the government would no longer provide travel expenses for employees or for an agent's family. A number of agents had hired their wives and children, a practice that under the Hayes administration brought quick dismissal. Indian Commissioner Ezra Hayt (1877–81) exposed this procedure when he accused certain Quakers of employing as many as four or five relatives. The Commissioner cited a Friend who had hired his wife and seventeen-year-old son at one thousand dollars each and a younger son at nine hundred dollars. Hayt insisted on having absolute control over agency employees, a power he would use to help destroy the Peace Policy.[20]

It cannot be proved that low pay alone tempted some men to fraud and drove others to nepotism, and that higher salaries would have eliminated these vices. A contemporary assessment was given by one of the Peace Policy's critics. Lieutenant Colonel Elwell Otis argued in 1878 that higher pay for agents was essential because "a great government should not be conducted upon the theory that its citizens will serve it from a sense of moral or religious obligation and without receiving adequate pecuniary reward."[21] Otis was probably correct, but rejecting disinterested moral and religious idealism meant rejecting a cornerstone of the Peace Policy.

If the government failed to adequately support agents, the churches too fell short of their responsibilities whenever they neglected to supervise their appointees and whenever they nominated inept or unknown men. Advertising in the *New York Observer* for volunteers, the Presbyterians received applications from exceptional men like John Critchlow and also from many preachers and church elders who had absolutely no qualifications for the work. One Presbyterian recommended John Clum in 1872 because he hoped Clum would enter the ministry; an agency would provide time for Clum to study and "replenish his purse." The Reverend George Ainslie requested an agency because the northern climate hurt his lungs and, "God adding his blessing," a move to Arizona could restore his health. Ainslie added, *"I voted for both Lincoln and Grant,"* but was rejected with "health will not do" marked across his application. Nevertheless other ailing Presbyterians were appointed.[22]

Indian Commissioner E. P. Smith, himself a former minister-agent, warned the Board of Indian Commissioners in 1874 of a tendency in the churches to use the nominating authority unwisely: "It is one of the onerous things of these political times that such a power can be given to the church." Smith reiterated that federal Indian agencies were not homes for retired clergy or refuges for those who failed in the ministry. He admonished the churches to send their best men and then support them with prayer and money, but, as he probably realized, many churches groped in the dark to find agents and often based their choices on recommendations from unknown persons. Methodist applications, for instance, required only the endorsement of a bishop and a local clergyman, whereas Presbyterians appointed a special board to sift applications. The American Missionary Association, as conscientious as any group in selecting agents, discovered that the task involved endless perplexities. Because it found most letters of recommendation untrustworthy, the association spent considerable time and money searching for competent nominees. Association officials must have been startled to find one of their own missionaries hesitant to recommend anyone. LaPointe missionary Isaac Baird declined to comment about a Presbyterian because "Mr. C. might make a very good Agt. but then, you know, he *might* fail, and where would your missionary be if he had recommended him warmly! I much prefer to keep my fingers out of such pies, for they sometimes get unaccountably hot."[23]

The churches were uncertain about their obligations to an agent after his appointment. Episcopalians and Quakers assumed they were accountable for an agent's conduct and therefore supervised his work closely. Presbyterians and Dutch Reformed insisted that once a man was appointed, they retained no further responsibility. Methodists denied any responsibility and did nothing to check on their agents—or to support them. These denominational abnegations of duty were challenged at the first January conference between the Board of Indian Commissioners and the churches in 1871, where ecclesiastical representatives fully discussed government policy and then passed a resolution making each denomination morally responsible for its nominees. At one time or another, all Protestant churches would request removal of agents. Yet the mission boards could not help but be confused by contradictory statements from the Department of the Interior. Columbus Delano told the 1871 conference, "The agents sent to the Indians are your own, and we intend that they shall be emphatically your own. The only right we reserve is the right of instantaneous dismissal where they are unworthy." Six months later the Indian Office told A. B. Meacham that churches had no official relationship to the Peace Policy, that only the Office appointed and removed agents, and that Indian agents were solely responsible to the government. Delano apparently changed federal policy again the next year when he remarked to the Dutch Reformed that he wanted their full cooperation in supervising agents.[24]

The confusion was compounded even further by Congress. Long after mission boards had lost control of appointments, congressmen insisted that the churches still supervised the Indian Office and owned the Indians body and soul. As late as 1879, a House committee reported that Grant and his successor, Rutherford B. Hayes, not only were under obligation to appoint religious nominees but that they uniformly did so. The inaccuracy of these charges is revealed by a Methodist confession in 1873 that at one of their Montana agencies an "odious and disgraceful" man had been appointed, perhaps by the Methodist Church, but the Missionary Society of the Methodist Episcopal Church in New York did not know when or how this was done or who he was. Methodists admitted that they received no reports from their agents, that they had accidentally named non-Methodists, and that they did not understand the Peace Policy.[25]

Confusion and poor performance by the churches may have led Congress to employ special inspectors to supervise and report on agents. To some members of the Board of Indian Commissioners and Congress the initiation of the Indian inspection system signified the failure of the Peace Policy, but Senator Stewart of Nevada, who introduced the bill in 1873, correctly argued that the board itself had recommended inspectors and added that the churches could nominate persons for the positions. Indian inspectors, Stewart said, would be young, active men able to assist the elderly board members who only took short pleasure trips into the West. Stewart thought the denominations had done a satisfactory job in selecting agents for four years, but he added, "a great many men join the churches and become very religious when it is profitable." A suggestion that inspectors should be army officers occasioned an outburst of religious sarcasm from the eloquent James Nye. The senator from Carson City compared the appointment of such inspectors to the Lord's placing a sentinel over Joshua:

> Indian policy has been changing like every view of a kaleidoscope ever since I have been in public life . . . till in the end we are brought upon the Christian rock; and after beating about the bush for several years, we are told now that we have struck the last resting-place of the Christian hope, the Church of Christ. . . . My colleague, it seems to me, is guilty of almost infidelity, in desiring to set a guardian angel, armed with a sword, watching the Church, for fear they will steal. [Laughter] . . . And so, under the amendment of my colleagues, the ears of the clergy are to be greeted by the rattle of the dashing warrior's spurs. . . . in the dead hour of the night, or in the more sacred hour, that of prayer. [Laughter] . . . . Sir, that will not do. Set no armed guards over the clergy.[26]

After more debate in the House, the bill passed easily. It abolished four of the eight superintendencies and created five inspectorships, setting forth sentinels to watch over Joshua.

The inspection bill, though it implied church ineffectiveness, had been advocated by Episcopalians since 1866 and by the board since 1870. The original bill specified that churches could name the inspectors, but it is not clear if the mission societies were to exercise authority after appointment. Creation of the new posts, each with an annual salary of three thousand dollars, prompted a deluge of applications from politicians, soldiers, Indian agents, and church members. Seminole agent Henry Breiner asked Lowrie for an inspectorship to allow him to recoup financial losses suffered as an agent and because it was "a position where I can serve the Master to the best advantage without doing an injustice to my family." Although Episcopalians Edward Kemble and Jared Daniels were selected, there is no evidence that the Episcopal Indian Commission nominated them. In 1877 the commission made a point of saying it had no voice in the matter; by then the secretary of the interior had secured firm control of the appointments.[27] But the use of inspectors did little to solve the problems of fraud and incompetent Indian agents. Inspection reports were sometimes unfair and inaccurate, only adding more pieces to the bewildering kaleidoscope of Indian administration.

Even before the creation of an inspection system, no church involved in the Peace Policy escaped scandal, both real and fabricated, in appointing agents. Almost nothing that happened in the Bureau of Indian Affairs during those years remained immune from public scrutiny. The resulting controversies often deeply embarrassed the Protestant churches, for the sins of their Indian agents included incompetence, sexual misconduct, fraud, theft, and abuse of power. Methodists and the Dutch Reformed compiled the worst overall records, but even Quaker, Presbyterian, and Episcopalian mission boards that took their responsibility quite seriously appointed agents and teachers who morally faltered and failed. There is not room here for the stories of these men and women. That is unfortunate, for their varied experiences with temptation and failure can only be appreciated and understood within the actual circumstances of their daily life at Santee, Fort Berthold, White Earth, Fort Defiance, and Red Cloud. And, of course, one must understand not only the agent under attack, but the accusers as well. Out of the many agency scandals and controversies, one in particular must be related in some detail. It had the most significance because it involved a commissioner of Indian affairs and because it eventually destroyed the friendship of the Peace Policy's two most powerful founders, William Welsh and Henry Benjamin Whipple.

In the early 1870s William Welsh, in one of his many campaigns against the Indian Office and the Department of the Interior, brought charges against a Red Cloud agent named J. J. Saville. When Saville refused to spy and report on other government officials, Welsh encouraged public attacks against the Sioux agent.[28] But Welsh became distracted from the Red Cloud agency when he attempted to indict Commissioner of Indian Affairs Edward Smith, a Congregational minister and former agent at White Earth in Minnesota. The Welsh-Smith conflict grew into the most bitter of the many Indian Office scandals in Wisconsin and Minnesota and probably did more to discourage proponents of the Peace Policy than any other controversy of the seventies. Here the issue was not pork, flour, or beef, as it was at Red Cloud, but another commodity: pine trees.

When the Christian agents first arrived in the Old Northwest they perceived that northern pinelands could provide a vast source of profit to the tribes—and a great potential resource for whites. The American Missionary Association's William Richardson at Green Bay was the first to encounter trouble.

An experienced Episcopal missionary warned Richardson of schemes to rob Indians of their pine; the logs recently had doubled in value and many speculators were eager to enter the reserves. The new agent taught the Menominees and Oneidas how to reduce timber waste and to cut the trees themselves. In 1872, with the approval of Indian Commissioner Francis Walker, Richardson supervised a tribal sale of two million board feet through which the tribe netted sixty-two thousand dollars, five times its usual profit. When Richardson discovered that Wisconsin representative Philetus Sawyer previously had purchased twenty thousand dollars worth of timber for four thousand dollars, he demanded that Sawyer compensate the Indians with an additional six thousand dollars. Sawyer and Wisconsin senator Timothy Howe then requested Richardson's dismissal. Despite the Missionary Association's refusal to remove Richardson "unless absolutely required to do so," and unless the reasons were openly stated, the Indian Office acquiesced in the political demands. The association later had to resist another attack on a Wisconsin agent, and through the course of the Peace Policy other association agents reported threats and extortions over the pine question. Although one inspector reported in 1879 that Congregational agents had stolen Wisconsin pine and were a "stench in the nostrils of good people," government investigations officially cleared all of the Missionary Association appointees in Wisconsin.[29]

E. P. Smith faced similar problems in Minnesota. Smith (1827-76) had been ordained into the Congregational ministry after graduating from Yale and Andover. During the Civil War he served as superintendent of the Christian Commission's western division. Smith later recorded some of his observations and experiences as superintendent in *Incidents of the U.S. Christian Commission,* which contained five hundred vignettes of piety, conversion, and personal salvation on the battlefield. When the American Missionary Association hired Smith, first as its general secretary in 1866 and then as missionary to the White Earth Agency in 1870, they had selected an agent highly regarded as a man of exceptional character and ability.

The pine question at White Earth troubled Smith. He blocked attempts by lumbermen to hastily remove 200 million board feet of timber from the reserve, even though he realized fires might destroy much of the pine. In 1871 he assured the Indian Office that the Chippewa and Pillager tribes would approve sale of their pine as soon as they understood that the "Great Father is exercising his right of guardianship for their good."[30] The next year Smith became even more convinced that the government should sell six townships on the reservation because the Indians did not need the land and because the railroad wanted white pioneers near its route. In the summer of 1872 Smith traveled from White Earth to tour the Southwest with his friend O. O. Howard. He returned to discover that the Indian Office had placed the Pillagers in danger of starving by diverting more than half of the fifty-seven thousand dollars that Congress had appropriated for the tribe. Believing that timber sales could quickly bring both food and peace, Smith proposed selling pine stands near the Mississippi River, Red Lake, and Leech Lake. After he accepted bids and rebuked lumberman Charles Ruffee for trying to bribe him, Smith signed two contracts. He knew that the pine was worth considerably more than he obtained, but he felt immediate action was necessary to protect the Indians during the coming winter. Although Smith became a target for Minnesota lumbermen, several losing bidders regarded him as an honest and sincere man. Bishop Whipple heard from another disappointed logger that Ruffee had vowed to ruin the agent for selling so high. Whipple himself opposed the pine sales on conservationist principles and he thought that Smith had not sufficiently advertised for bids, yet Whipple defended the agent's integrity against such detractors as the *St. Paul Pioneer,* an anti-Grant paper which charged that Smith had hidden his ads in an obscure corner of the *Minneapolis Tribune.* The *Pioneer* expressed curiosity about how an agent "of GRANT'S favorite christian commission breed can get from under such a weight of suspicious circumstances . . . if the very Reverend SMITH can do it, [it] will be immediately fatal."[31]

The Pillagers and Chippewas were momentarily forgotten in January of 1873 as Washington speculated about who would replace retiring Commissioner of Indian Affairs Francis Walker. Although William Welsh longed to obtain the position, Secretary of the Interior Delano appointed E. P. Smith. The Board of Indian Commissioners, who had officially endorsed Welsh, were privately very pleased with Smith and when Welsh tried to block Smith's confirmation, board members testified before the Senate that rumors against Smith were being circulated by men whom the agent had displeased in Minnesota.[32] Smith was confirmed and his controversy with William Welsh began.

Smith first met Welsh in 1870, when the Philadelphian sought to remove Ely Parker. At the time Welsh impressed Smith as a busybody and egotist who planned to control the Indian Office. Though he agreed with Welsh on the removal of Parker, Smith was surprised that one man could muster enough political power to eliminate a high government official. During his tenure as White Earth agent, Smith confided in Welsh and requested help in protecting the Chippewa lands. This impressed Welsh and he considered the agent completely trustworthy, though it irritated him when Smith left his post in Minnesota to travel with Howard in 1872. Such neglect of White Earth was, to Welsh, a sign of weakness and poor judgment. Even after he failed to block Smith's confirmation as commissioner, Welsh apparently believed that the new leader of the Indian Office could cause no harm. He told Henry Whipple at the time that four years earlier "all was dark dark dark but now the cause of the Indian is bright indeed." But Welsh changed his mind and became convinced that Smith was dishonest. By September of 1873 he suspected that the Indian Ring's A. H. Wilder controlled the commissioner and that there had been gross malfeasance in the Minnesota pine sales. Welsh secretly warned Bishop Whipple to open his eyes and ears and to be prepared for rough action because "the so-called Christian appointments are likely to disgrace Christianity." Later during the same month the *St. Paul Dispatch* and the *Minneapolis Tribune* condemned Smith. The fuse was lit.[33]

Subsequent investigation convinced Welsh that inspectors O'Connor and Daniels belonged to the Ring and, furthermore, that Wisconsin pineland had been stolen:

> Wilder has the control of Smith & has used him shamefully. . . . We must be true to God & the Indians suffer who may, and we must not let the stigma fall on the Church. What my duty may be I know not but God will open the way. I will by His help try to work in it. Clergy & laity when pushed out beyond holy influences seem alike self-reliant & frail. . . . I believe there has been a deep game at Washington and some parties fooled us so shamefully that it will make me too wary hereafter.[34]

Felix Brunot and the Board of Indian Commissioners confessed themselves "befogged" by Welsh's ventures in the northern woods, and they feared explosive new controversy might destroy both E. P. Smith and the board. In November, Welsh uncovered documents that proved to his satisfaction that Smith was guilty. He determined to void the Wilder contracts: "Peaceably if possible, forcibly if I must." Delano invited Welsh to Washington and publicly called for an investigation, but he privately told the Philadelphia merchant to present some facts or be quiet. After a visit with Grant, Welsh almost conceded Smith's innocence. Then he discovered vouchers that persuaded him that Wilder actually did control Smith and that the entire western branch of the American Missionary Association was corrupt. Without consulting Grant or Delano, he made the charges public: Smith had illegally sold land, failed to advertise, and rejected high bids; he cheated the Indians and government by consorting with the Reverend Edward Williams, General Charles Howard, and agent Selden Clark to steal Lac du Flambeau pinelands.[35] When an investigating committee tried to meet with him, Welsh informed the delegation that his own duties outweighed theirs, refused to talk, and accused the committee of whitewashing Smith. After Smith denied him access to government files, Welsh directed Bishop Whipple to attack the Indian commissioner. Whipple declined and thereby ended a long friendship.[36]

Whipple had remained a quiet supporter of Smith until Welsh's publications forced him into public support of the commissioner. Although Whipple had opposed the pine sales and disagreed with Smith's assertion that the Leech Lake Pillagers could be saved in no other way, he never doubted Smith's honesty. For Whipple the issue was not Smith's character but the Indians' future and the conservation of their resources. He believed that the government, and in this instance, Smith, had no right to recklessly dispose of timber for immediate tribal benefits. Smith, in the bishop's estimation, was overzealous in raising money for the Indians and had sold their valuable pineries for low prices—too low to include graft. Whipple told Smith so at the time. In the bishop's eyes, Wilder was an honest, hard-driving capitalist who simply bought as cheaply as possible from anyone. Now, as charges and pressure mounted, Whipple described Smith as the best Chippewa agent he had known and praised his wife as a saintly woman.[37]

Despite difficult opposition from Whipple and the Episcopal Indian Commission, Welsh pursued his prey. Two tracts added more charges: as commissioner, Smith had submitted false expense accounts, mismanaged his office, ignored the Board of Indian Commissioners, and sold pine at one-fourth its true value. Welsh's accusations subjected Smith to five investigations between 1873 and 1875: one by the board, another by the Department of the Interior, two by the House of Representatives, and one by the Red Cloud Commission. During the Interior's investigation in May of 1874 the White Earth chiefs presented their grievances to inspector Jared Daniels. Expressing their disappointment in Grant, the Peace Policy, and Smith, Wabonoquet spoke for the tribe:

> We heard that the timber was sold we were keeping for our children. I alluded to our Great Father stripping us, our children. . . . We are not pleased to have it sold without permission. We want to keep it as a fund for our young men. . . .
>
> Pity [the Leech Lake bands] if they leave their reservation and get into trouble. They cannot subsist without game, and there is no game on their reservation. . . . We are all sinking, and dwindling away. From the time of the first cession dates the loss of our chieftainship. Then wasted from our hands all power. We ask not for pity . . . [agents] have been made rich by collusion and measures of dishonesty. From many getting rich on the mere pittance of $1500 a year, we have been led to believe that we have been tampered with, and that unmercifully.[38]

The board investigation of Smith occurred when a bureau clerk, Samuel Walker, tried to link Smith at White Earth with agent Saville's alleged misconduct at Red Cloud by showing that A. H. Wilder was involved at both places. Congress's Red Cloud Commission vindicated Smith on all counts and found William Welsh and Minnesota senator Henry M. Rice (Welsh's main informant) guilty of character assassination, irresponsible accusations, "reckless aspersions and false insinuations." This investigation, however, did confirm Welsh's suspicion that the American Missionary Association was deeply and illicitly involved in northern pine and that the association's Chicago office served as a clearing house for timber sales in Wisconsin and Minnesota.[39]

The congressional investigations arrived at the same conclusions that the board did and also cleared the commissioner. Congressmen listened to clerks, traders, and lumbermen who testified against Smith, but cross-examination weakened their contradictory testimony and, in one case, uncovered a plot to blackmail Smith. William Welsh failed to provide any evidence, prompting one congressman to comment, "Mr. Welsh finds it one thing to write in the quiet seclusion of his sumptuous residence . . . and quite another thing to meet the man whom he has maligned face to face upon the witness stand."[40] The Red Cloud Commission with typical committee jargon absolved Smith of dishonesty but condemned him as more guilty than Saville of "a want of due diligence . . . vigilance, astuteness, and decision of character."[41]

Smith fared even less well in the press. The *Nation* announced that he had fallen from grace and the *New York Tribune* accused Smith of participating in one of the most gigantic Indian swindles of all time. The *Washington Chronicle* and a St. Paul paper supported the commissioner, but Philadelphia editors endorsed Welsh. *Advance* saw Smith as a victim of Democrats, and the *Independent* hoped that a libel suit by A. H. Wilder would end the "Welsh nonsense." The *American Missionary* (the American Missionary Association's publication) at first remained silent, then supported Smith, and next said that though Smith was honest, the temptations had been great and the charges came from unquestioned sources. The *American Missionary* finally theologized that even if Smith were found guilty it would simply confirm the Christian doctrine of original sin.[42] All this controversy proved to be too much for Grant. Before the end of 1875, even though he still officially supported Smith, the president decided that public opinion demanded a new commissioner of Indian affairs.[43]

E. P. Smith may have been, as Bishop Whipple thought, too eager to sell Chippewa timber. He may have been, as the Red Cloud Commission concluded, a poor businessman, an agent easily "deceived and imposed upon by cunning and unprincipled men." But, except for incidents of favoritism to his friends in the ministry, there is little evidence against him proving deliberate fraud.[44] Smith's generally poor judgment was evident when a medical quack pressured him into buying five thousand bottles of Dr. Dart's Sanitary Specific, a potion made from "sweet oil and musk," which cost a dollar a vial and was guaranteed to protect anyone against syphilis and gonorrhea for a year. Anson Dart promoted it as the "only salvation" for American Indians, causing congressmen to wonder how an intelligent clergyman like Smith could be so stupid. But Smith confessed his mistake, admitted that Dart's drugs were not worth a nickel, and saved some face by showing that the Board of Indian Commissioners had also approved purchase of the nostrum.[45]

More unfortunate than money wasted on patent medicine was the rupture between Welsh and Whipple. The Smith affair ended a partnership of nearly twenty years. The two friends had worked closely together on an Episcopal mission to Cuba, and it was Whipple's "trumpet tones" that awakened the Philadelphia merchant to the Indian cause in the 1860s. In 1870 Welsh wrote, "My heart clave to Bishop Whipple as Jonathan's heart clave to David." But Welsh's rash attack on Smith and then on Whipple himself were more than the bishop could endure. In 1874, like David and Jonathan, they parted. In May, Bishop Hare had written from Philadelphia to confirm Whipple's fears: "Mr Welsh has worked on precipitately of late & made shipwreck of his influence in Indian Affairs. Our investigations have not sustained his operations. Unfortunately he *suspects* all who differ with him. I feel sad enough about it."[46] In July, Welsh returned a letter from Whipple, sarcastically thanking the bishop for his advice and implying that Wilder's donation to an Episcopal school had influenced the prelate. Whipple was so angered that he ended their correspondence. He resented anyone who thought that his love for Indians was for sale. In his last letter to Welsh, Whipple wrote, "Had a man of the world written me I could not have answered that letter. You are very dear to me, & whatever you may think or say of me, will ever be dear. . . . It cost me more than you will ever know to speak clear ringing words when my whole diocese were against me, when even those who knew I was right said it is hopeless. I am not conscious of ever having failed to do my duty."[47]

Whipple remained convinced that Smith was a devoted Christian and an honest public servant. Twenty-five years later the bishop recalled Smith's desperate plea to the American Missionary Association's secretary in 1875: "They have assailed my character and robbed me of the dearest thing in life. Give me any work, however hard, and I will do it."[48] After his removal from the Indian Office, Smith was named president of Howard University and then, in February of 1876, the American Missionary Association sent him to Africa. Four months later a telegram arrived in their New York office. "E. P. Smith is dead." He had died delirious with fever aboard the steamer *Ambring*, near the Isle of Fernando Po in the Gulf of Guinea. The fifty-year-old minister was buried June 16, 1876, at a Presbyterian mission station in West Africa. In the United States, the author of an obituary noted that "the merciless opposition which he met from designing men who so sought to profit at the expense of the Indians, exhibits one of the saddest phases of our republicanism."

Writing in 1845, Herman Melville commented in *Typee* that "an unwarranted confidence in the sanctity of its apostles—a proneness to regard them as incapable of guile—and an impatience with the least suspicion as to their rectitude as men or Christians, have ever been prevailing faults in the Church."

Melville could have made the same observation about Christian participation in Grant's Peace Policy. William Welsh died in Philadelphia two years after Smith's death. His eulogists recalled that he had been a generous, untiring churchman, beloved by all. Welsh's death, the Episcopal church announced, was a "most afflictive dispensation" for the cause of missions. The church neglected to mention that Welsh himself had been an afflictive dispensation in the lives of Ely Parker, J. J. Saville, E. P. Smith, and eventually Henry Whipple. Yet if the Church was unwilling to confess the faults and follies of its members, other men stood ready to do so. Thus Richard Dodge wrote in 1882 that Indian agents had always been bad men, "but . . . the leaving of that selection to the Christian churches . . . [was a] fitting climax to the preposterous acts which for a century have stultified the governmental control and management of Indians."[49]

The Christian Church had an uneven record in selecting honest agents for Grant's Peace Policy. No amount of faith and piety allowed the Church to escape distressing problems that had aggravated the federal government for nearly a century.[50] Christian agents were denounced, just as agents before them were denounced. To be fair in judging their innocence or guilt proved as difficult as it had been when agents were selected under the patronage system. An easy evaluation was to say that some men had performed well, others poorly, and church nominations made no difference. The Board of Indian Commissioners, for example, asserted in 1873 that most agents were honest, a few inept, and a number ruined by the frontier. This says little or nothing, and it ignores a basic question about the Peace Policy: could the Church provide men more capable and honest than those selected by politicians?[51] Perhaps a definitive answer is impossible.[52] What is certain is that most churches found Indian agents a burdensome, distasteful responsibility.

Episcopalians, Friends, Presbyterians, and the American Missionary Association tried to select agents with care. All but the Friends failed to inspect the agencies regularly and defend their men when necessary. At Red Cloud, personal loyalty to Jared Daniels and J. J. Saville at first blinded Episcopalians to the agency's problems. As attacks continued, the church increasingly became concerned about its own reputation. At a hearing of the Red Cloud Commission, Bishop Hare protested that he had been tricked into self-incriminating statements; he squirmed in his chair, lost his temper, and contradicted himself while trying to defend Saville. Finally the commission drove the bishop into William Welsh's habitual error of presuming guilt. The desperate Hare abandoned Saville because "the Episcopal Church should no longer be responsible in any way for an agent regarding whose character so many questions have been raised."[53]

David Halberstam once remarked that the Congo in the early 1960s and Vietnam in the late sixties were places that destroyed good men of good intentions. The same can be said of Indian reservations in the nineteenth century. Poor housing and food, insufficient salaries, and threats of violence often made an agent's life extremely unpleasant. A miserly Congress endorsed these conditions again and again when it defeated appropriations or delayed Indian funding until the last hour, a practice that made competitive bidding impossible and left the Indian Office in a turmoil. Congressional policy, Senator Preston Plumb observed, was to "save at the spigot and lose at the bung." Agents found themselves faced with the choice of closing reservation schools or borrowing from other allocations until the annual appropriation passed. This solution was dangerous because if Congress defeated or delayed the legislation, then borrowed funds would be missing in the government's confused accounting system. When reformers found such irregularities, they broadcast them not as error but as iniquity.

Peace Policy agents were watched more closely than any agents before them. Local politicians, agency clerks, army officers, Indians, William Welsh, and the Board of Indian Commissioners were eager to discover fraud. The agents struggled with tribes who could not speak English, with local whites who hated Indians, with long reports and depredation claims required by Washington officials, and with an endless flow of new regulations and orders from the bureaucracy.[54] In return they received the salary of a third-class clerk in Washington, D.C. If they employed son or wife, someone protested about nepotism. There was, James McLaughlin concluded in 1878, no good reason for a man to remain at an agency: "The hardest-worked, poorest paid, and worst abused officers now in the public service . . . it has became almost a disgrace to be known in public as an Indian agent." A half-century later matters had changed little. In 1928 the Meriam report on the Indian service listed the major problems among Bureau of Indian Affairs personnel as being poor salary, insufficient training, lack of job security, and poor living conditions.

Church officials often attributed the downfall of their agents to such conditions. William Welsh suspected Jared Daniels of mischief and lamented to Bishop Whipple, "Living in the frontier without the ordinary means of Grace seems to draw mere men down." Yet errors and vice were not limited to the West and the agencies. One might paraphrase Melville to say that Welsh's own prevailing fault was an unwarranted distrust of everyone but himself. Nor were Indian agents the only men dragged down on the frontier. Mission boards experienced similar misfortunes with missionaries as religious programs suffered from lack of funds, confused financial reports, rancor over policy and appointments, misinformation, and other human foibles. An unsavory example of how vice and pride clogged spiritual channels was a vicious dispute that erupted in Dakota between two of the most widely respected Episcopal churchmen in Indian affairs, Bishop Hare and the missionary Samuel Hinman.[55] For a weary Henry Whipple, who first defended Hinman and then switched to support his fellow bishop, it was one more perplexing trial in his effort to redeem American Indians and lead them along the white man's path. The humiliating scandal within his church substantiated Whipple's conviction that the Christian doctrine of human depravity applied not only to heathens, government officials, and Indian agents, but to trusted missionaries as well—to close friends with or without the ordinary means of Grace.

7. The Ordeal of Battle

A pure and successful peace
policy necessitates a total
abnegation of military support and of personal carnel
protection.

Alfred H. Love, Universal
Peace Union (1873)

No man is a philanthropist
on the prairie.

Francis Parkman,
The Oregon Trail (1849)

In August of 1869 the *Omaha Daily Herald* expressed the opinion that all unbiased men considered the Peace Policy a success: "Under the
Quaker administration . . . we shall have no war.
Peace will reign throughout all the frontiers. Our
settlements will uninterruptedly progress. No
more massacres and murders. Guards will not be
required along our great railways. The Indians
will gradually acquire the arts of peaceful industry."[1] New York's *Weekly Tribune* agreed:
"Quakers who do not fight, can conquer where
our fighters fail." And General R. B. Marcy
asserted that the "eminently wise philanthropic
disciples of William Penn" would do well and
prove to be outstanding Indian agents. Several
months later President Grant justified his selection of Friends by saying that they were opposed
to all violence and war and that they had achieved
a record of peace in colonial Pennsylvania. To
the Quakers themselves, Grant's Peace Policy
seemed an unexcelled opportunity to verify the
wisdom of Christian pacifism.[2]

In view of these pronouncements and in light
of the humanitarian assumption that, if treated
with understanding and kindness, Indian tribes
were amenable to white civilization, it is not
surprising that the Peace Policy frequently and
mistakenly was characterized as an adoption
of doctrinaire pacifism and nonviolence. Indian Commissioner Francis Walker's careful
explanation to the contrary did little to enlighten

126

skeptics. Furthermore, a momentary cessation of warfare during the Policy's early years led its supporters to claim too much—to claim that they had indeed resolved the problems that led to Indian-white violence. Therefore when the Modocs in California were driven onto the warpath in 1872, the Peace Policy faced a severe and unfair test.

The Modoc War began after white men attempted to push the tribe from its lands in northern California. The Indians resisted with force, retreated to their lava bed fortress near the Oregon border, and for months repulsed a siege by the army. In April of 1873 the Modocs violated a truce and murdered two negotiators, General E. R. Canby and the Reverend Eleasar Thomas. They badly wounded another negotiator, A. B. Meacham. This treachery confirmed the beliefs of men such as William Tecumseh Sherman, who responded by ordering the total extinction of the tribe. The Board of Indian Commissioners heard reports that many Christians had become disgusted with Indians and were advocating the closure of all missions. Bishop Hare later recalled that even calm, rational men and women called for revenge and denounced the Peace Policy as demonstrating the weakness of pacifism. The board apprehensively disclaimed any responsibility and asserted that the Modocs did not come under their jurisdiction. The board, like Grant, advised severe punishment for the tribe. The commissioners also moralized that had the Peace Policy been followed in California, war and bloodshed could have been averted.[3]

As the board feared, newspapers like the *New York Herald* leaped at the opportunity to attack the entire Peace Policy and to call for military control of the Indian Service. The *Herald* announced that "the Peace Policy Party was buried out of sight as soon as the news of the massacre flashed over the wire." Dishonest agents plus corruption to the core in Washington, the *Herald* declared, were the basic causes of the Modoc War. The *Baptist Watchman* shifted from favoring the Modocs to calling for punishment "even to the extent of vindictiveness. . . . Rose-water is not the equivalent of blood, and should not be taken in exchange for it." Another Baptist writer argued that all Indians lacked moral character, and a publication called the *Evangelist* demanded relentless destruction of the Modocs. At the other extreme, pacifists such as Alfred Love advocated sending peace medals to the Indians. Love asserted, "William Penn's treatment of the Indians, and the course of Friends and others in the present, prove that a thorough radical peace policy is possible and will succeed." The *Friend's Intelligencer* agreed, telling its readers that pacifism never failed when practiced by true believers. The Modocs, according to the *Intelligencer*, had resisted only after the United States used force and, in any event, the federal government's role in California was "certainly somewhat different from the peace policy as managed by Wm. Penn when he was Governor of Pennsylvania."[4]

Most public opinion fell between these extremes. The *New York Times* argued that one incident could not invalidate a policy that ultimately would be the crowning glory of Grant's administration. *Harper's Weekly* pitied the Modocs and asked for mercy on all Indians who were "swiftly fading away, like vegetation of some extinct geological era." Contempt for the Peace Policy on the basis of one incident, the *Nation* editorialized, was absurd. The *Cheyenne Daily Leader* described all criticisms of the reform as ridiculous and irrational. Most religious publications, including those on the Pacific Coast, called for punishment of the guilty Indians but advised against mass extermination. The *Oregon Churchman* denounced critics of the Policy, and *Advance* blamed the old Indian system. While urging execution of the Modocs without mercy and without trial, the *Congregationalist* recommended that a Christian nation must be just and not kill all Indians everywhere. Even the *Baptist Watchman* still favored the Peace Policy and cautioned against extermination. The army's attack on a defenseless Kickapoo village at Remolino in Mexico the next year tended to give credence to the extreme pacifist position and to fears of military extermination, thereby counteracting the effect of the Modoc War.[5]

Statements by such pacifists as Alfred Love[6] naturally inclined uncritical persons to think that all humanitarians favored Quaker doctrines of nonviolence. Actually the Society of Friends was almost alone in its beliefs. The great majority of clergy and laymen in the Peace Policy accepted Bishop Hare's theology of necessary force: "Hand [Indians] over to the Church alone?" he asked a large gathering at the New York Academy of Music in 1874.

> No, not to the Church alone, because many of them are too wild, too barbarous, too savage, too cruel. I do not want Christian people in this part of the world to think that a mere sentiment about Indians is ever going to solve this Indian problem. All that was ever published in the newspapers about wild Indians is true in substance. . . . There is no barbarity so great they will not practice it. . . . You must have somthing more than moral suasion. . . . What we want is, brethren, all three; the military, as the arm of the divinely ordained power put forth to maintain the right; civilization, as a gentler training still; and the Church, as the pitying Mother of their souls, who shall take them to her bosom.[7]

Hare's theories in New York accorded with his actions in Dakota. He knew that the army protected Indians, missionaries, and white settlers, and he knew that Indian agents would be "toys and tools of lawless savages" unless supported by force. Whenever he represented the government in Indian country, Hare armed himself.

Other Episcopalians certainly shared Hare's sentiments. Henry Whipple had close, friendly relations with the army, and Edward Kemble was an outspoken critic of Quaker pacifism in the Northern and Central superintendencies. One Episcopal missionary favored military rather than civil control of the Sioux, and at the Red Cloud agency, Episcopal agent Jared Daniels became convinced that the Indians would never appreciate leniency. Daniels contended that as long as the federal government and the eastern humanitarians slumbered "in the belief that their savages' prejudices [were] to be overcome by generous acts, fatherly care, and kindness," there would continue to be massacres and bloodshed in the Far West.[8]

When Robert Patterson wrote in the *Overland Monthly* that Quaker nonviolence was heretical because it violated St. Paul's demand for obedience to the state, he expressed the dominant view of nineteenth-century Christians. From the president down through the ranks of the Indian service under the Peace Policy, no officials except the Quakers believed in pacifism, much less tried to practice it. Although Grant wanted peace, he ordered the use of force when necessary and he advised army officers that defense of white settlements was their first duty: "It is not proposed that all the protection shall be to the Indians."[9] This understanding was accepted by the Board of Indian Commissioners, the Indian Office, informed congressmen, all agents except Quakers and all churches except the Society of Friends.

In the Senate debate of June 4, 1870, Jacob Howard of Michigan asked whether the Quakers could actually control the "humanized wolves" on reservations. Would not the Indian "steal the broad brim of his benefactor and carry it off and sell it?"[10] Quakers, too, wondered what effect a frontier environment might have on pacifists. The Society's leaders warned their agents not to forsake peace principles whatever the provocation: "We must go . . . in the peaceful guise of William Penn . . . one that neither uses the Sword or relies upon it." In theory this meant renouncing not only the army and any police, but all coercion. Some Friends insisted that Indian children must not be compelled to attend school because teachers must depend on love instead of arbitrary authority.[11] A Hicksite agent's first obligation was to rely entirely on God and His wisdom, not on men or arms. Quaker officials realized that this might at times seem impossible, yet by faith, they believed,

> every offering of self-sacrifice to the demand of Eternal Love must bring the return of Peace. How wisely, how beautifully the eye of faith is enabled to . . . behold conditions of people that human reasoning will not, cannot, by its limited sight of the Love of God . . . but as we are lifted by the power of Faith, and our spiritual vision is cleansed from the mists of

self, and expanded beyond the atmosphere of Earth, we get at least some faint conception of the great truth, that it is God's way.[12]

The Peace Policy was a divine opportunity to demonstrate to the world that the Quaker vision of truth and compassion was not utterly impractical.

On most of the upper midwestern reservations in Nebraska and Kansas the Friends did well in adapting self-sacrifice and spiritual vision to the requirements of operating an Indian agency. But even here the world presented difficulties and demanded compromises. Maintaining law and order was a serious problem on Omaha, Winnebago, Shawnee, and Osage reserves, where traditional cultural controls and authority had been shattered by white civilization. One solution was to create an Indian police force. Asa Janney at Santee organized one of the first Indian police forces in the nation in October of 1869, and other Quakers in Nebraska used both the army and native policemen during their first year, when Omaha and Pawnee Indians had killed local whites. Yet even this limited use of force against murders brought complaints from the eastern Yearly Meetings. Another problem was motivating Indians to assimilate white culture. Some Quaker agents and teachers appeared to make rapid progress, whereas others found the Indians apathetic and lethargic. Teaching Indians, a teacher among the Winnebago learned, was "similar to raising good fruit on a wild stock . . . a great and difficult work." Friends might deplore physical violence in teaching, but coercion crept into their daily practice and their example. Taylor Bradley, the Winnebago agent, compelled Indians to work by withholding annuity funds, and Thomas Battey, recognizing that the Kiowa with whom he lived truly enjoyed killing people, did not hestiate to use force in disciplining Kiowa children.[13]

Quakers were also committed to the inviolability of Indian reservations, which created the problem of expelling white squatters. Seeking to persuade frontiersmen to respect Indian rights, Quaker Sidney Averill learned that there were white men who had no scruples and who acknowledged no law. Enoch Hoag vainly called for the observance of justice when railroads, land speculators, and the booster press in Kansas brought a horde of hostile whites onto Indian lands. When settlers overran the Neosho reserve, the only suggestion by eastern Friends was to remove the Indians.[14]

The problem of white incursions became most serious on Osage lands in Kansas and Indian Territory. Osage agent Isaac Gibson felt he had proved the truth of Quaker methods when he and Jonathan Richards of the Wichita agency prevented a war between their respective tribes in 1873. Gibson experienced less success with white men. When most of the Osages left Kansas in 1870, a few decided to remain on their land and establish homesteads, a right provided by the removal treaty. Kansas whites then began to terrorize Osages who stayed behind. Joseph Mosher, who was part Indian, and his family were chased from their burning home in the middle of a winter night, stripped and pistol-whipped; two other Osage families suffered the same fate. In the East, John Lang learned of Mosher's death and prayed that it would awaken white men "to do justice & love mercy." Out on the reservation, an exasperated Isaac Gibson realized that something more was needed.[15] He pressed for police protection, an action that upset the eastern Quakers. The Orthodox Friends did ask Grant to keep whites out of the Indian Territory. When the president responded by ordering Sheridan to remove squatters, Superintendent Enoch Hoag ignored the army and refused to cooperate.[16]

Gibson discovered another limitation of peaceful methods in 1874, when the Medicine Lodge Massacre occurred. After a group of white men had murdered and scalped four unarmed Osage and robbed twenty-five others, the Kansas governor enrolled the same men in the state militia, thereby legalizing the murders. When Gibson visited border towns and protested that his Indians were peaceful, he was laughed at and called a liar. The Osage agent finally conceded to himself that some force was required to restrain both Indians and whites.[17]

In Nebraska the most serious Quaker problem was on the Pawnee reservation. Four months after arriving, agent Jacob Troth happily reported that the Pawnee, traditional fighters and excellent army scouts, no longer needed rifles, pistols, or knives. Instead they requested plows, wagons, and cattle. Pawnee disarmament, whether it came through the Indians' own choice or through Quaker coercion, exposed the tribe to attacks from their traditional northern enemies, the Sioux. Troth asked the army to protect Pawnees from the Brules and Oglalas and to force his own tribe to surrender stolen ponies. Continuing Sioux raids so retarded progress that the Friends finally recommended removal, a recourse that delighted Nebraska settlers. With removal imminent, troops were again called by the agent "as a last resort" to protect tribal timber from the whites. Even after removal of most of the Pawnees to Indian Territory by April of 1875, it was deemed expedient by the Quaker agent to request a company of soldiers to protect the few Indians still in Nebraska.[18]

Although other Hicksite agents depended on the military, this seemed to place no visible strain on Quaker principles. Senator John Thayer of Nebraska and others felt that the Friends very prudently had selected reservations where major conflict had ended ten years earlier: "They ought to have selected the warlike tribes who are creating the difficulties on the frontier."[19] Thayer apparently did not realize that as he spoke, Kiowas and Comanches in Indian Territory were pushing Quaker pacifism past the breaking point.

The Orthodox Friends had been assigned three agencies at the far western end of Indian Territory, 150 miles east of the Staked Plain of the Texas

Panhandle. The agencies were located every thirty miles along a northeasterly line: Fort Sill (Kiowa-Comanche) to the south, Wichita in the middle, and Upper Arkansas (Cheyenne-Arapaho) to the north. Once the land had supported enormous herds of buffalo, but by the end of the 1870s only the coyote, hawk, turkey buzzard, and prairie dog remained. The Indians who occupied this flat, semiarid expanse of buffalo grass, mesquite, and dwarfed oak were among the best warriors in the West. Their new agencies were the result of their reluctant consent to the Medicine Lodge Treaty of 1867. Most volatile of the three groups were the Kiowas and Quahada Comanches. Seemingly wild, vicious, and incorrigible, these southern plains tribes had bedeviled and bewildered previous agents. Led by their warriors—Big Tree, Kicking Bird, Stone Calf, White Horse, Lone Wolf, Satanta (whom even Felix Brunot would wish dead)—they had murdered agency employees and stolen government livestock. Periodically they kidnapped and killed Texas ranchers and white families who had settled on tribal lands to the south. The protracted violence between the Comanches and the Texans dated back to the 1830s, when the first whites had moved into west Texas. Ely Parker was convinced that only severe military repression could tame the Kiowas and Comanches and stop their raids south across the Red River. Patience and meekness, white men said, only encouraged more brutal attacks. Once again, the Peace Policy inherited the troubles of the past when the Quakers walked into forty years of bitter warfare.[20]

The Kiowa Indian agency was located one mile southeast of the army post at Fort Sill. An addition to the agency office, a corral and a few rough sheds were scattered about the landscape. Snow and sand seeped through the building's cottonwood walls, and at times rain poured through its cracked roof. The summer winds baked the earth along a reddish-brown rutted path connecting the agency's two main buildings with the army's commissary. The path lay between torpid swamps that collected the effluent draining from Fort Sill into Cache Creek. Although officers at the fort commended their men for practicing "remarkable chastity," the proximity of the garrison to the agency gave soldiers easy access to Indian women.[21] Surrounding the agency was a reservation of 3.5 million acres, containing nearly five thousand Indians speaking nine languages. In the summer of 1869 Lawrie Tatum, an Iowa farmer, Orthodox Friend, and Indian agent, arrived here to test his ideals in a very real world.[22]

At Fort Sill, Tatum fortunately found an officer in command who was a friend of Felix Brunot and of the Peace Policy. Benjamin Grierson, for whom Tatum gained great respect, later defended the Quaker agent to the point of endangering his own position. "Friend Tatum," he once told the agent, "I too, must be considered *too much* of a *Quaker myself* or *peace man* to be left

here. . . . If I had launched out and killed a few Indians . . . I would no doubt
have been considered successful . . . you may rest assured that I will pursue
such a course to control the Indians & prevent depredations without loosing
[*sic*] sight of the object contemplated by the phylanthropic [*sic*] and good
people of the land—*without bringing on a war for the purpose of gaining an
opportunity of killing off Indians*—let those who may wish it done either on
account of material interests or *personal advancement grumble as they
may.*"[23] Grierson convinced Tatum that he would use force only in extreme
emergencies, but Tatum had difficulties from the start. When the Kiowas
and Comanches ignored him as he enclosed agency land and began to plow
the earth, Tatum remained confident that food and fair treatment would
pacify the tribes.[24] A delegation from the Board of Indian Commissioners
eventually arrived to lecture the Kiowas. When Felix Brunot warned the
chiefs that their Texas forays must stop, Satanta's reply chilled the Quaker
agent:

> We have tried the White man's road and found it hard; we find nothing on
> it but a little corn, which hurts our teeth; no sugar, no coffee. But we
> want to walk in the white man's road. We want to have guns, breech-
> loading carbines, ammunition and caps. These are part of the white man's
> road, and yet you want us to go back to making arrowheads, which are
> used only by bad, foolish Indians.

On hearing this, the commissioners recommended reinforcements for Fort Sill
in order to control the tribe.[25]

During Tatum's first winter the Indians came peacefully to the agency
every five days to collect their rations. In February, Tatum thought that
giving each Indian an additional ten pounds of sugar and four pounds of
coffee would keep the Kiowas on the reservation. He remained similarly
convinced in May, believing that reported Indian raids had actually been
committed by white men disguised as Indians. The agent's opinion began
to change when Kiowa braves stole eighty mules from the agency corral.
Then one June evening an army sentry at Fort Sill heard cries for help; the
next morning a civilian herder was found scalped a mile from the agency. A
short time later a teamster was shot in front of Tatum's porch, and soon after
that a report arrived telling of the murder of a white man at Beaver Bridge.
The Indian warriors openly challenged the soldiers at Fort Sill to a fight before
leaving to raid the Texas settlements. On June 18 Tatum warned Fort Richardson in Texas that Kiowa braves planned to attack during the full moon.[26]
By the middle of the summer the War Department was receiving urgent appeals from Texas that someone such as Sheridan replace Grierson:

Wild Indians seames to be running at large with out restriction thay seame to be privladge caractures for the want of compatent officers and it is a true saying if thare was a man of Sound sences in the country to Witness the fact While Country is infested with Small bands of Indians prowling about and way laying every thay may chance to lite on So that it is Impossible for a man woman or child to travel. . . . our Quacker missionary seams to take it very easy he dont truble himself much about the Indians he has turned his attention to farming . . . the very same Indians was so trublesom in 1864 that Col. Shivington whiped them so on Sand Creek that the Government suckers called it a massacree.[27]

Far from taking it easy, Tatum was desperate. Following the agency murders he had called a meeting of employees. All the Friends except a married couple resigned, and a month later the agent's own wife departed for the East. On July 22, Tatum learned that while in Texas the Kiowas and Comanches had burned homes, murdered two farmers, and kidnapped six children. Whereas he previously had believed that these raiders were either whites masquerading as Indians or only a few wild Kiowas, he now learned that both tribes were fully involved. When the Indians returned from the south, they demanded ransoms and rations, attacked a herder, and threatened the agent's life. Tatum began a new approach. He decided that the Kiowas and Comanches were exceptionally savage Indians who mistook Grierson's clemency for cowardice and who, believing that Texas existed as free ground for plunder, actually thought the government paid them to attack Texans (did not rations increase after each raid?). Praying for wisdom and trusting "in the Lord who could restrain the evil intentions and passions of the Indians," Tatum, now protected by troops from Fort Sill, resolved to stop the raids by withholding rations until the Kiowas were disarmed and had promised to stay on their reservation.[28]

On September 1, however, Tatum compromised and gave the tribe half of its sugar and coffee. "They thought it was very hard that I should 'get mad just as they had got entirely over their mad' . . . I did it to punish them & I thought the punishment would be the most effectual."[29] He was wrong. Two weeks later Kiowa warriors again crossed the Red River into Texas, this time killing a man and wounding his wife and children; they also kidnapped a brother and sister, eventually killing the girl. In October Tatum reported to his superior that in the spring the Kiowas and Comanches planned to murder everyone at the agency and would raid Texas indefinitely: "They have Carbines, Spencer Rifles, & Needle Guns, & they wish to show that they are more than sufficient for all the soldiers that the Government can raise." Then, in a sentence that must have shocked Quaker superintendent Hoag, who had disbelieved the agent's earlier reports, Tatum observed that the

Indians simply did not comprehend the white man's might and that to stop the raids, the government had to send enough troops to "whip them."[30]

A tense peace settled over the Comanche reserve in December. In his annual report for 1870 Tatum challenged the humanitarian article of faith that maintained that white men always provoked Indians into violence and that no Indian was actually vicious: "The Indians have undoubtedly commended and carried on their depredations this year without cause; everything reasonable has been done for them by the officers and others in this vicinity that could be done; they have received no injustice, indignities, or insults from citizens or soldiers."[31] For Lawrie Tatum, Quaker pacifism had begun to crumble. During the next year he would be forced to battle on a second front against Enoch Hoag and Friends in the distant East.

Although the Kiowas and Comanches stopped raiding Texas during the winter, they continued to threaten the agent and to attack neighboring tribes. In February, Tatum pleaded with the Kiowas not to return to Texas that spring. When they told him that Texans were "but marks for Indians to shoot at," the agent instructed Grierson to protect the white settlements with troops. In May, Tatum heard rumors that Satanta had once more crossed the Red River.

On May 18 a Kiowa and Comanche band attacked a wagon train crossing Salt Creek Flat between Jacksboro and Fort Griffin. Seven teamsters were killed and the fort's grain shipment burned. The attackers barely missed William Tecumseh Sherman's touring party, which had passed along the same road a few hours earlier. Sherman immediately ordered a detachment to pursue the Indians, but Satanta eluded them, and on May 28 he returned to the reservation, where he informed Tatum of his victory. The agent ordered his arrest, during which an Indian was shot to death. Tatum urged that Satanta and other chiefs be held hostage to prevent further depredations: "That they are guilty of murder in the first degree, I have not the shadow of a doubt and approve sending Zatanat, Zatank, and Big Tree to Texas."[32]

During the summer of 1871, his third at the agency, Tatum encouraged Grierson to march six companies back and forth across the reservation. This maneuver seemed to intimidate the tribe until late September, when the Kiowas scalped and cut the ears off an agency herder. Four days later they killed two other employees and one soldier. Rumors circulated of possible Texas raids and, although the raids did not occur, Tatum judged the Indians so treacherous that military occupation of the reservation seemed to be the only hope of preventing war. At the year's end, the commissioner of Indian affairs reported that Kiowas and Comanches had broken all promises and that "lenient measures and forbearance toward these restless and war-loving spirits appear to have no effect in restraining their passions, plunder and war, and a severe treatment would seem to be the only wise and proper course to pursue."[33]

Tatum's attitude and his role in the arrest of the Kiowa leaders had caused Quaker concern in the East. Friends at the Cheyenne-Arapaho agency had opposed Tatum's reliance on the army in 1870 and had expressed their protest to him in person. Enoch Hoag and Cyrus Beede, administrators of the Central Superintendency, remained unable to understand Tatum's plight despite visits to the frontier. A Quaker official on the East Coast, Edward Earle, described Tatum's actions as regrettable, and the *Friend's Intelligencer* deliberately played down the Texas raids. The newspaper admitted that Satanta was "an old hard-faced Indian, and hard as he looked," but it reminded its readers that the frontier whites had created many false rumors about all Indians. An Iowa Friend wrote to Tatum that using the army to make arrests implied soldiers "armed with deadly weapons, guns, swords, and Bayonets, and if Resistence is offered . . . these weapons [would] be used to the taking of life."[34] The Indian committee of the Orthodox Friends agreed that Tatum had waited until further forbearance was impossible before ordering the arrests; nevertheless the committee found it difficult to evaluate and justify his measures. Staunch pacifists contended that everything concerning the agency should be stricken from the Society's annual report, whereas other members on the committee insisted that the truth be published. They pondered a protest from the Ohio Yearly Meeting that declared Tatum himself responsible for an Indian's death. Furthermore, the memorial warned, "the use of military force is a violation of the principles of peace, that the use thereof in the present instance was an act of war . . . that the argument which would justify taking one, would justify taking ten or one hundred lives and thus excuse a protracted war."[35] William Nicholson, a general agent for the Society, defended Tatum and asked that "Friends & Advocates of Peace not get into any war amongst themselves." Nicholson pointed out that most men living within the realities of the West honestly and justifiably viewed matters differently from easterners. His advice was heeded by the committee, which concluded that had Lawrie Tatum not used force, he and the Society could be "justly charged with upholding acts of murder and rapine, and with protecting those who boasted of their guilt." Although Friends lamented all violence, to act other than Tatum had would destroy the Peace Policy. An agent was a public official charged with enforcing the law and "for this end he must use the civil force provided, and if this force is insufficient, he must use the military."[36]

Tatum's victory over the "strong peace men" of his church was as short-lived as his pacification of Kiowas and Comanches. Between September of 1871 and September of 1872 the tribes killed over twenty more Texans. Tatum's request in the spring of 1872 for troops to capture the Indian raiders was denied by Superintendent Hoag, who said it was impractical to keep the tribe on the reservation by military force. Hoag suggested moving Fort Sill to the Texas border.[37] During the summer there were few raids, but in the autumn, after Quaker leaders pleaded for peace at the Fort Cobb and Okmulgee councils, full-scale attacks began anew.

National attention now turned to Indian Territory. Newspapers favored removing Grierson and allowing the army to pursue the Indians onto their reservation sanctuary. Texas congressman John C. Conner deplored that "this bloody peace drama" had resulted in two hundred murders since 1869 and cost his state millions of dollars because "broad-brimmed Commissioners" forced Texans to repurchase goods that Indians had stolen from them. The *New York Herald* joined Conner's attack on Quaker pacifism and demanded that Grant halt the Peace Policy. The *Herald* warned, "It is nonsense to be sending . . . soft-soaping Quakers to deal with the false and treacherous savages. . . . The people of this country are heartily sick of the canting peace policy with its hectacombs of innocent victims barbarously slain by the cowardly redskins." Later *Herald* editorials told of "Horrible Outrages by Red Devils in Texas" and recommended using "Little Phil's Radical Cure for Bad Injun." In September, while praising Friends in Nebraska and Kansas, the paper declared that "a Kiowa will wear a Quaker hat, but he will never carry a Quaker head. If the military had been left to deal with the refractory Indians even the Kiowas would now be quiet and on the reservation; but the President yielded to the pressure of the churches and we now see the consequences. The pat-em-on-the-back policy has never succeeded with warlike tribes and never will."[38] Lawrie Tatum was ready to agree. His report for 1872 insisted that Indians alone were responsible for bloodshed. Warriors regarded his and Grierson's patience as cowardice or imbecility. Only punishment and military control, Tatum advised, could tame the Kiowas and Comanches.[39]

The agent had been equally frank with the Friends. When he told the Society that in certain circumstances patience and kindness were not virtues but crimes, demands for Tatum's censure arose. The *New York Tribune* reported that Quaker officials had harshly reprimanded Tatum and planned to force his resignation. The climax came in March of 1873. Tatum felt that Satanta's life sentence in a Texas state prison had helped the government subdue the Kiowas and that if the chief were released, as requested by Friends in the East, it would be seen as a sign of weakness. When pressure finally forced Texas governor Davis to commute Satanta's sentence, Tatum feared "a dark and rolling cloud in the Western horizon." Exhausted by direct threats on his life, by processing more than two hundred depredation claims from Texas, by responsibility for the lives of others, and by quarrels over Quaker principles, the agent resigned. He told Friends that if they could find a pacifist able to control Comanche warriors, such a man surely ought to have the opportunity. The Society expressed its disappointment that he had been so harsh with the tribes.[40]

Tatum left Fort Sill convinced of his failure. General W. B. Hazen, however, described Lawrie Tatum as one of the most courageous men he had ever known. Indians, soldiers, Texans, and Quaker missionary Thomas Battey regretted his resignation, and Battey later remembered how the agent had gained the respect of everyone he met.[41]

The Society of Friends sent James H. Haworth to replace Tatum. They believed that Haworth was reliable, a true pacifist, and they gave him special instructions to be lenient. Just as Haworth arrived at Fort Sill, Governor Davis of Texas, in a fit of rage over the Modoc War in California, reversed his decision to free Satanta. The Kiowas responded by kidnapping the Quaker missionary Battey and threatening to do likewise with the new agent. After extracting a promise that all raiding would cease, the governor released one hundred Kiowas but retained the chief. Haworth and the Friends continued to press for Satanta's unconditional pardon. The agent's first report assured Hoag that if they accomplished this he was confident that the Indians would become peaceable. "I presume," he continued, "thee will begin to think I am a little enthusiastic on the Indian subject. I confess my mind has become deeply interested for them and the success of the Peace Policy, believing as I firmly do, that it will work out right and prove a blessing to many, in spite of the opposition of the bad, as well of some of the misinformed good."[42] Haworth worked all summer for the release of the Kiowas, persisting in his belief that they were ready to pound spears into pruning hooks and praising Indian patience with whites. The tribe's sporadic farming encouraged him that Indians would listen to "the sweet name of Jesus spoken [and] learn war no more."

In August a survey crew moved onto the reservation and alarmed the Indians, a reaction exacerbated by low rations at the agency. A month later Haworth admitted that a few Comanches had been raiding again in Texas but he concluded that the tribes generally were "very *friendly* and *peaceable*." When Kiowas admitted stealing Texas livestock, Haworth refused to use coercion or to withhold rations; instead he "simply reminded them of their promises and appealed to their better natures." Indian raiders along the Brazos then murdered a white family, scalping a seven-year-old girl and hanging her in a tree. After a Washington telegram ordered the agent to arrest five Indians, Haworth was visibly shaken. When Comanches attacked the Texas settlements again in November, he declared that they were not from his agency. The reports from Texas, he lamented, came from men "worse and meaner than most Comanches . . . enemies of the Indians [who are]

land-grabbers as well as that worthless class who hover around the frontier. . . .
I hope the Lord will continue to rule in this Territory." Such views pleased
eastern Quakers who had been stung by articles in the *Nation* praising Tatum
and holding the Society responsible for murder. The Orthodox Indian Committee found comfort by now reporting that tales of Indian depredations
were merely unsubstantiated rumors manufactured by border whites and uncritically accepted by the "depraved press." They were confident that Friend
Haworth could preserve the peace.[43]

The eastern Friends had replaced Lawrie Tatum in 1873. They experienced
less success when they tried to force the resignation of their Cheyenne-
Arapahoe agent in 1874. Forty-year-old John Miles had been transferred from
the Kickapoo agency to the Upper Arkansas, or Cheyenne-Arapaho, reservation following the death of agent Brinton Darlington in the spring of 1872.[44]
Like Tatum and Haworth, Miles originally believed that Indians did little
wrong and that the Cheyennes, who traditionally raided settlements to the
north, in southern Kansas, would rapidly accept farming. Conditions at the
agency encouraged Miles as he outlined plans for a large Sunday school
on the reservation. The peace lasted one year.

Early in 1873 Miles had a disagreement with his superintendent, Enoch
Hoag, when the agent reported fifteen hundred drunken, brawling Indians.
Miles, though not certain whether the Cheyennes or the Kansas settlers were
to blame, requested a large police force to halt the liquor traffic. In Lawrence, Hoag somehow translated this message to mean that the army had
attacked innocent Cheyennes who wandered off the reservation. Even after
intoxicated Indians killed four white surveyors, Miles's requests for troops
went unheeded. Then the tension subsided and 1873 passed without further
incident. Miles and Wichita agent Jonathan Richards prayed that "with the
blessing of Divine Providence" their tribes would continue to improve.[45]
Hoag and his assistant Cyrus Beede continued to ignore the violence and to
rationalize tribal raiding as "retaliatory depredations" by the Indians.[46]

The next year brought sudden violence and carnage to all of western Oklahoma. It began with Comanche and Kiowa raids into Texas. Busy with his
spring plowing, agent Haworth reported no danger signals, although he did
admit that the Indians were unhappy with his refusal to supply ammunition.
In May an Indian prophet who led medicine dances and claimed an ability
to produce cartridges from his stomach excited Comanche warriors by promising to make them bullet-proof or, that failing, to raise them from the dead.
As Haworth watched agency rations dwindle, he began to fear a new out-
break. After Indians ransacked the boarding school and stole livestock from
the agency corral, Haworth followed Tatum's example and sent for troops
from Fort Sill. Realizing that war was about to break out once more, the

eastern Friends sent a peace delegation to reason with the Kiowas and Comanches and to persuade them of the folly of their ways. After the eastern peacemakers departed, Haworth reported that many Indians had disappeared from the reservation. He hoped that "this cloud [would] like many others . . . pass away without a storm." Enoch Hoag responded by blaming the tribe's disappearance on Congress's failure to provide rations. At the agency, rumors soon reached Haworth that the Indians were ready to fight, already having killed a woodcutter. The agent confessed that "the sky [looked] considerably hazy."[47]

At the upper Arkansas agency John Miles had no difficulty in perceiving the gathering storm. He reported to Hoag in December of 1873 that the Kiowas had murdered a white man on the Cheyenne reserve. Hoag doubted the report, ordered an independent investigation, and refused to send the agent's report to Washington. Hoag's persistent refusal to honor requests for troops or to report murders forced Miles to bypass the superintendent by writing directly to the Indian Office. Reprimanded by Quakers for insubordination, Miles replied that he could not serve two masters. The Indian Office upheld the agent.[48] At the same time, Miles had to contend with buffalo hunters who were decimating the southern herds. After pursuing white horse thieves and quarreling with drought-stricken Kansas homesteaders searching for food on the reservation, the embattled agent read attacks against him in Kansas press and heard rumors of white gangs that planned to lynch him. The first week in June, Indians killed several buffalo hunters, attacked a survey crew, and the Comanche chief Quanah Parker fought a three-day battle at Adobe Walls in the Texas Panhandle. The Red River War of 1874 had begun in earnest.[49]

Following the Battle of Adobe Walls, Miles received reports that the Cheyennes, Kiowas, and Comanches planned to combine in a general uprising. On June 16 the agent informed Washington that Indians had challenged him to fight. He requested soldiers to protect the agency and whites on the Kansas border. A week later John Holloway, son of the agency physician, slumped over a patient after an Indian fired a pistol through the hospital window, hitting young Holloway in the back. With young Holloway's death and the father's grief, Miles realized how desperate his situation was. All persons at the agency were in danger, he mused bitterly, because no one had punished white men who stole Indian horses. Miles was convinced that the tribes would have remained peaceful had it not been for hide-hunters and horse thieves, "all of which *could* have been done and *would* have been done could [the agency] have had the timely assistance of sufficient *force*." He blamed Hoag for ignoring "the many appeals that have been made from this office for a sufficient *power* to *crush*" the desperados. "We are required," Miles wrote to Commissioner E. P. Smith, "to cry aloud for a *force* and for the strong arm of the Govt."[50]

When the force still did not arrive, John Miles stalled the Indians and prayed for time. On the second evening in July two Cheyennes rode into the agency and displayed the ring of a white man, William Watkins; they informed Miles that war parties were already heading north toward Caldwell, Kansas. The next morning the agency learned that the Indians had killed and scalped Watkins thirty miles to the north. The agent sent a messenger to Fort Sill and, without waiting for troops to arrive, armed the agency employees and set out on the wagon road to Caldwell.

At the Lee and Reynolds's ranch Miles was told that Indians had fired on both houses before riding off to the north. Near Buffalo Springs another ranch had been hastily abandoned. Then, three miles along the road, the agent and his men sighted a black smoking hulk. Miles and his small band anxiously approached:

We found four men Pat Hennessy Geo Fand Thomas Calloway & one more unknown lying in the road murdered their three wagons loaded with sugar & coffee for agent Haworth all of which was destroyed or taken away all the men were scalped Hennessy had been tied to his wagon & burned fire still burning . . . body of Hennessy was still roasting in the fire. Indications were that he had been tied and sacks of oats and corn piled around & on his person while he was yet alive—his feet and ankles were yet out of the fire & indicated a death struggle. . . . We gave them hasty burial & proceeded to next ranch here we found teamsters stages concentrated.

The teamsters reported that they had driven off the warriors. Miles left these men all the ammunition his group could spare and rode all night to warn ranchers, reaching Caldwell the following noon. At 12:30 he telegraphed Smith: "& now I ask & shall expect to receive at once two or three companies of cavalry . . . as quickly as possible . . . no hostile Indians shall be quartered at agency & I must have the troops to back it up let the hostile Element be struck from every point at once & with such power as shall make the work quick & effective."[51] The images of mutilated men haunting him, Miles traveled to Wichita, Kansas, where he found General John Pope prepared to campaign but unable to proceed without permission from the Interior Department and the Central Superintendency of the Indian Office. Meeting with Hoag, Miles found the superintendent "not disposed to assume such responsibility." Finally, on July 10, Hoag reluctantly requested Pope to protect the agencies and to provide military escorts for all wagon trains.[52] Relieved, John Miles now turned to face the attack from his own church.

Enoch Hoag was furious over reports that he had refused to protect Miles and that he had told the agent that if he could not succeed without the army, Hoag would find a man who could. The superintendent maintained that all requests for a "police or Marshall force" had been honored and that blame for the deaths rested on Kansas whites who by breaking the law had forced the Indians to strike back.[53] At the same time, Hoag asked the Friends' Executive Committee to meet in Lawrence on July 17.

The committee met and learned that, except for tribes on the southern plains, all Indians under Quaker care prospered, with schools and farms flourishing everywhere. Then the committee turned to the matter of violence. John Miles accused Hoag of deliberate falsehood and charged that the superintendent had intentionally misled General Pope in order to prevent the deployment of troops to Indian Territory. The agent firmly denied Hoag's and Haworth's claims that the Kiowas and Comanches had not been involved in raiding and that only the Cheyennes were guilty.[54] The committee listened courteously and conceded that it was true that "small war parties [had] attacked one train, a few ranches, and the buffalo hunters in the Pan Handle of Texas" but, they counseled, that problem should not alarm anyone because order and quiet would soon be restored. The executive committee then formally approved its minutes:

> Whilst we recognize the exigencies of the situation in which our agent John D. Miles had been placed . . . and considered that great allowance is due to him under these trying circumstances, yet it is the conclusion of this committee, after having given him a full personal hearing, that some of his actions and the warlike tenor of [his telegram], show that he is not sufficiently in harmony with the principles upon which our work among the Indians is based, and hence we would kindly request his resignation. It is with great regret that the committee have been forced to the above conclusion, and they desire to assure him of their feelings of personal kindness toward him.[55]

Miles listened to the verdict, rose, and left the room. During a sleepless night he thought about the past and the future, about his friends among the Cheyennes, about Orthodox Friends in Philadelphia, about his family, his church, and his personal convictions. Early in the morning he made his decision and wrote to the Indian Office.

> I have endeavored to form my conclusions from a personal knowledge of the whole situation & must say that I deem it the *only* remedy to make use of the military & *force* the Hostile Bands into subjection. This is due to Loyal Indians, loyal settlers, Govt. Employees, Govt. interests, and common humanity. While I sympathize very much with our Friends in the present trying hour when it seems necessary to forsake some of our true honored peace principles, yet it will not do for us to remain *quiet* &

permit the horrid butchering of innocent persons—this would have been criminal negligence. I claim there was a time when all this trouble could have been prevented *but* the remedy was refused by the same authority (including the central superintendency) who now request my resignation for an act forced upon me on account of *their own inaction.* It is utterly impossible for *distant* Friends to realize the situation & to know what remedy to apply. I have therefore much charity for them in their conclusion. I now return to the Agency & for the present shall endeavor to "do justice & love mercy" but cannot tender my resignation at this time for performing an act which I believe to be right.[56]

News of the war and the Quaker rift spread rapidly. It elated the *New York Tribune,* which ran headlines such as "HORRIBLE ATROCITIES COMMITTED BY THE SAVAGES" and, after E. P. Smith endorsed Miles, "THE COMMITTEE OF FRIENDS REBUKED." The *New York Times* reported "FRIEND MILES IN TROUBLE" over the "Gunpowder Flavor of his Actions." *Advance* blamed the entire war on Quaker meddling, and the *Unitarian Review* found itself filled with anxiety and dismay.[57] The new Board of Indian Commissioners joined the chorus against Quaker pacifism. Public humiliation of the Friends was official and complete when Smith published a letter accusing the Quakers of injustice to Miles and of harming the Peace Policy:

> If it comes to be understood that the moment an agent takes a position like that of Agents Miles and Tatum, he is to lose his position in a kind of disgrace with the Society of Friends, it will be impossible to administer affairs through the Society. . . . I regard Agent Miles as the best agent that Friends have . . . and he has done nothing more than ordinary prudence required him to do, and certainly nothing that the Government does not thank him for doing.[58]

With these rebukes in mind, the executive committee of the Orthodox Friends gathered for its annual meeting in Richmond, Indiana. Enoch Hoag voiced his skepticism about the south-central tribes and William Nicholson, the Society's chief lobbyist, reported that the war was caused by whites. Informed that Miles had refused to resign, some delegates recommended that the Society withdraw from the violent agencies, which, they insisted, the Friends had never requested. Nicholson reminded them that Ely Parker had warned the Society in 1869 that Kiowas and Comanches were "totally different from [the Indians] with whom William Penn dealt." Parker had advised not accepting responsibility unless Quaker agents could cooperate with the army. This prospect, Nicholson said, had made the Society reluctant to enter the Peace Policy. In the fall of 1870 Nicholson had finally persuaded the Friends to abandon these agencies, only to have Parker refuse permission to withdraw. Nicholson concluded that the only solution now was destruction of the buffalo and removal of the tribes eastward. If this were not done, the Society of Friends should retire from the Peace Policy to avoid "complications with the military." The Washington subcommittee supported Nicholson, but the executive committee was divided over immediate withdrawal. A large majority finally voted to remain.

No one suggested how to eliminate Miles; instead the committee members praised other agents "who fully represent us" and who had been "preserved faithful at heart to peace principles." After a long debate, the committee drafted a statement on religious duty and the use of force. It sanctioned the vigorous use of government power against lawless whites and Indians, and it allowed Quaker agents to transmit information leading to the arrest of criminals. Sole responsibility for capture and arrest, however, was the federal government's and under no circumstances could a Friend use weapons. The compromise resolution did not satisfy everyone, especially extreme pacifists, who renewed their demand for withdrawal from the Peace Policy. Unsuccessful in this, they argued that the Department of Interior should be petitioned to retract its support of Miles and Smith.[59]

John Miles considered the new policy a step toward what "*good common sense*" demanded, but he observed that the law required an agent to *request* troops, not simply inform the army that problems existed. In other words, Indian agents, being responsible for the use of force, could have "no compunctions of conscience in calling upon the military or any other lawful force to maintain law and order." Also irritated that the Society of Friends would publish its request for his resignation, Miles reiterated his conclusion of a month earlier: it was immoral to disavow military force when doing so meant sacrificing innocent lives; it was immoral to neglect those whom one was pledged to protect, whether Indians, border whites, government employees, or one's own family. "An Indian on the *Warpath* respects neither *friend* nor *foe*," he told E. P. Smith. "I have done nothing more than *peaceable* and *law-abiding* citizen would do in a city were he to witness a *mob* destroying the *lives* and *property* of innocent persons—He would call (loudly too) for the 'Police'—especially if some *loved one* was soon to fall a victim to their savage cruelty."[60]

One can imagine that to Orthodox Friends in Indiana and Ohio, as in Baltimore, Washington, and Philadelphia, Miles's reasoning seemed limited and short-sighted. He apparently needed greater faith and "a spiritual vision cleansed from the mists of self and expanded beyond the atmosphere of Earth."

General Pope's troops did not rapidly quell the violence on the frontier. As Quakers in Indiana debated resolutions about an agent's duties, James

Haworth and Jonathan Richards faced more trouble. Late in July of 1874 a combined Kiowa-Comanche-Cheyenne raiding party rode into southern Colorado, killing more than sixty Americans and Mexicans. Prolonged drought strained the temper of both the Indians and the army during August as creeks ran dry and blast-furnace winds drove temperatures past 112 degrees. Then violence hit Jonathan Richards's Witchita and Caddo agency on Saturday, August 22. Forty-eight hours earlier Indians had killed a teamster, resulting in General J. W. Davidson's departure from Fort Sill with four companies of cavalry on Friday. Davidson had feuded bitterly with James Haworth since January, when the general accused the Quaker agent of breaking annuity laws. Now Davidson discovered that Haworth, with his "preaching and pandering" to the Comanches, had refused to segregate his reservation into hostile and peaceful classes of Indians. On Saturday the sweltering soldiers arrived at Richards's agency on the Washita River. When Davidson demanded that all Kiowa warriors surrender their rifles, an Indian fled and was fired on. Lone Wolf and Satanta fired at Davidson and a gunfight broke out that lasted through Sunday. The cavalry dug in behind a hill and, after repulsing a charge led by Lone Wolf, watched the Indians loot and burn the commissary, school, and farm. On Sunday evening the soldiers recaptured the agency. Agent Richards departed for Lawrence, the army counted ten men lost, and the Indians, Haworth reported to Washington, were "on the warpath in earnest."[61]

By mid-September 190 whites had been killed, fifteen of them at the three agencies. When John Miles found herder Ed O'Leary shot three times in the face, he called for troops, and the war continued amid torrential rainstorms that ended the drought. Nothing dampened the fighting spirit of the Cheyennes, who once more rode toward Caldwell, attacking ranches, burning bridges, and killing railroad crews along the way. "Thou will not wonder at my anxiety," Miles wrote in a plea for more soldiers, "when I say that my wife & three little ones are now between here and Caldwell detained by High waters." Miles worked closely with army officers and, unlike Richards and Haworth, refused to allow Indians to use the agency as a refuge: "My idea is that they should surrender to the *troops in the field after* they have *felt* the *power of the Govt.*" As winter set in, the raiders decided to return, and with permanent troops at the agency by the end of November, and with Satanta returned to prison again, Miles was convinced that the Indian resistance had been broken to the point where the Kiowas and Comanches were ready for permanent reconciliation.[62]

During the winter the army pushed its relentless pursuit until the tribes were disarmed, dismounted, and "completely humiliated." In March 1875, seventy warriors were shipped to the federal prison in St. Augustine, Florida; those remaining faced the complex problem of adopting an alien culture. With the threat of violence decreasing, John Miles and the Society of Friends strove to forget their differences. In 1877 the Friends gave Miles an enthusiastic endorsement for renomination. Agent James Haworth agreed to cooperate with Fort Sill and to initiate an Indian police force.[63]

John Miles, his health nearly broken, did not retreat from his hard-earned belief that physical force, whether exercised by the army or by Indian police, was required on reservations. In 1878 the government deposited 350 Northern Cheyennes at his agency. Led by Dull Knife and Little Wolf, they escaped in September and headed north. Although Miles earlier had disagreed when the government forced the tribe to move south, he now called for the army, which pursued the Northern Cheyennes toward their eventual destruction in the ice and snow of a Nebraska winter.

Men learned different lessons from the Cheyenne and Comanche wars of 1870-74. General Hazen said in the *Nation* that moral persuasion had failed, though he admitted that the raiding had begun long before Quakers arrived. General Davidson felt *"a good thrashing"* would tame the Indians. The Indian Office confessed that it had been overlenient. The Board of Indian Commissioners allowed that kindness and good faith produced positive results with most tribes, but the board confessed that radical errors had been made with the violent groups. Westerners wrote to their congressmen that meekness and turning the other cheek had failed, and the Red River War gave ammunition to those who wanted Indian administration returned to the War Department. During the subsequent House debate over transfer, Texas congressman Roger Quarles Mills read aloud from Thomas Battey's *Adventures of a Quaker* to prove how feeble the Indian Office was. Martin Townsend of New York said that Comanche Indians should not be treated as lambs: "Why, the Society of Friends, the men of peace, they who would resist nothing, have in their plan *'an adequate police force.'* . . . What kind of police would you send there? Would you send to the Indian country a man with a broad-brimmed hat and locust club?" "Police" meant "army" in the Far West, Townsend argued, and without the army, Christian missionaries would be murdered or, at best, hairless.[64]

Indians, too, learned several lessons between 1869 and 1876. If anything paid, violence did. Wichita Indians, who did not resist, saw white men turn their lands over to Kiowa and Comanche warriors. Poncas, who did not resist, watched and starved as boatlands of food passed up the Missouri to pacify angry Sioux. Pawnees who scouted for the army were repaid with expulsion from their Nebraska homeland. The Osages stopped fighting in the early seventies, and their Quaker agent was honest enough to admit that "the highest virtue [nonviolence] . . . placed this people between the upper and lower millstones . . . one great cause of their decline [was] their fidelity to pledges." The Hopis were fondly described as a law-abiding, peace-loving people; in 1877 they were also a vanishing people. As Meacham commented, only the violent aggressive tribes secured anything from the white man; only warlike Indians gained a fraction of justice.[65] Military defeat broke the Navajos, Yakimas, Comanches, Sioux, Kiowas, and Nez Perces, yet because their leaders fought and died, these tribes retained larger reservations than the peaceful Indians, who mainly received the white man's accolades and peace medals.

Friend John Miles learned what he called a "wholesome truth"—teaching respect for law could legitimately require force and coercion. If this wholesome truth was self-evident to Miles, other Friends found it a bitter lesson. Under pressure in 1874, the Orthodox Friends conceded that the army was sometimes necessary. They confessed in 1875 that four years experience had taught them that force must be employed, sometimes. In 1877 they credited the army with helping to open the way to Indian assimilation, and the next year they endorsed the Indian police, providing it did not mean a "parade of deadly weapons." Privately, many Quakers refused to surrender their faith that, as the *Friend's Intelligencer* put it, "true believers" who practiced peace needed no weapons. William Nicholson blamed the Cheyenne-Arapaho War on hide-hunters and liquor, and arch-pacifist Edward Earle refused to admit that civil authorities should ever cooperate with the army in any way. Enoch Hoag argued that the Red River War could have been averted had the Indians been removed from the Kansas border.[66]

To most Quakers, pacifism was an unquestioned truth, a dogma beyond critical examination, and against which evidence to the contrary was inadmissible. "All war is forbidden by the gospel of Christ" ... "a total abnegation of personal carnal protection" . . . "perfectly untinged by the ensanguined hue of war," so they preached and so read the Society's tracts, letters, and reports during the 1870s and after. The most unloving element in this doctrinaire pacifism was not cowardice, servility, or escapism, but an intolerance toward dissent and a meanness of spirit that distorted events and words to accord with absolutes, a rigid and crabbed mind-set that opposed coercion but twisted and coerced facts to prove the dogma of peace. In 1756 the Friends in Pennsylvania had shipped gunpowder and called it grain. In 1872 eastern Friends justified Lawrie Tatum's use of the army by calling it a posse. In 1878 the *Intelligencer* reported that after 1871 no Indian under Quaker control had killed a white man—"They have been murdered, yet they have not murdered." Friend Barclay White boasted that he never carried weapons or used military escorts in the Indian country, except when he requested two armed U.S. marshals to accompany him across the "uncanny country on the frontier of Kansas." Even the sensible John Miles felt better when he designated the military as "our National Police."[67]

In 1882 an article in the *Friend's Intelligencer* lauded the Quaker quest for freedom and justice and told the old story of how William Penn founded the City of Brotherly Love:

> The tomahawk dropped from the red man's hand
> When he saw the Quaker advance and stand
> Presenting his purse but to share the land.

In 1891 a tract entitled *Address on Behalf of the Indians* related the Quaker view that every war since 1870 had been precipitated by white men. The tract spoke of Piegans, Sioux, Bannocks, Nez Perces, Apaches, and Utes, but neglected to mention Cheyennes, Kiowas, or Comanches.

The Friends had made a basic error in their pacifism. They, like other Americans, assumed that all men—Sioux, Kiowas, Pueblos, Salishes, and Orthodox Quakers—were the same. The idea that charity and nonresistance might be taken as weaknesses no more occurred to the Friends than did the idea that farming, private property, and schools could be repugnant to another culture. But, as Ely Parker knew, controlling warriors and raiders meant crushing their culture:

> That you must love your enemies, do good to them that dispitefully use you, that when one smiteth you on the cheek you should turn to him the other, or that when a chief steals your coat you should give him your cloak also, are doctrines so abstruse that the [Indian] mind does not readily comprehend them. The mind must first be educated and refined. . . . and I am not prepared to allow that all who profess this belief are always found to carry their belief into practice. Try any of them upon any one of these points and see what the result will be.[68]

8. Gentle Genocide: The Impact on the Indian

I do not care whether any civilized, semi-civilized, or barbarous Indian tribe does or does not consent. . . . I do not believe it is necessary to consult with savages as to the best mode of civilizing them.

James R. Waddill,
U.S. Congress (1880)

No more Indians *should be raised.*

Missionary Herald
(November 1877)

After the Cheyennes and Comanches were subdued, eastern Friends recommended the removal of these tribes from the West to an eastern location where hunting and wandering would be impossible. When the government decided to keep most of the Indians at western agencies, the Society complained but stayed on to teach the white man's agriculture. For three years the Indians sowed, corn sprouted, and drought destroyed: "Their hopes were blasted, for no more rains fell." The new path meant starvation, and slowly the burned-out land began to affect even the most rational men. John Miles ironically observed that the reservations could never support agriculture: "Except that, as is argued, the breaking up of the soil, the building of railroads, established telegraph lines, and planting forest trees and orchards, have the effect to attract moisture and rains."[1] Indians realized that white culture could accomplish many marvels, but who could believe that it could bring rain to the arid West?

Other tribes found transition to white culture equally difficult. Under the Peace Policy, the Chiricahua Apaches met a tough little agent, John P. Clum, who tried to subdue them, but not until the mid-1880s did they accept domestication.[2] The Sioux futilely resisted the invasion of their Black Hills and were herded onto the barren wastelands of Dakota. Taking the Poncas from their Nebraska home, the government deposited

149

the compliant tribe in Indian Territory. Nez Perces clinging to their old culture were pursued, captured, and sent south to adapt in Oklahoma. When the Colorado Utes revolted against farming in 1879, the government suppressed them and offered a choice: "Work or starve." In 1875 Congress wrote the work ethic into law by requiring that all Indian males between eighteen and forty-five had to labor "at a reasonable rate" in order to pay for their annuities and supplies.[3] Native Americans in the 1870s learned that the alternative to submission was death, and that submission often meant working *and* starving.

Reformers and church leaders of the 1870s brought to the Peace Policy attitudes toward cultures that differed little from those of their predecessors. For a century, the friends of the Indians, whether politician, missionary, philanthropist, or philosopher, had set out to destroy native culture. The reformers' beliefs were abstract theory uninfluenced by realities and therefore simple in their notion of how cultures changed, that is, quickly and easily. Earlier reform hostility to Indian culture was clear in Thomas Jefferson and Thomas McKenney: both men wished to protect Indians, both had little tolerance for native ways of life, and both believed that Indians were children eager for assimilation and adulthood. The native's entire character, McKenney insisted, "inside and out, language and morals, must be changed."[4]

The same attitudes characterized leaders of the Peace Policy. Armed with what Francis Paul Prucha has described as an "ethnocentrism of frightening intensity," the reformers and missionaries strove to completely obliterate all vestiges of native culture—language, dress, food, sex roles, religion, marriage— and to replace it with private property, schools, citizenship, and the work ethic. "The white man's sympathy," Bernard Sheehan has aptly observed, "was more deadly than his animosity."[5] Roy Meyer, in his history of the Santee Sioux at Sisseton, Flandreau, and Devil's Lake, reached the same conclusion:

Not all of the harm done to the Indians was the work of their enemies. So far as the assault on their culture is concerned, perhaps the greatest damage was done by those who regarded themselves as their best friends— the missionaries. Neither the loftiness of their motives nor the selflessness of their devotion to the Indians they sought to convert is questioned here, nor does there seem to be any doubt that many of them knew Indians better than any other white men did. But their single-minded determination to Christianize the Indians, born of their unshakable conviction that Christianity—their own particular brand of Christianity—was the true religion, blinded them to everything good in the Indian character that grew out of or could be identified with the native religions. . . . the greatest crime committed by the white man against the Indian was not in stealing from him a continent, but in denying to him the right to be an Indian—trying to deprive him of his racial and cultural identity.[6]

Felix Brunot, reformer, humanitarian, philanthropist, knew what was required of Indians under the Peace Policy: they must become white men. Brunot told Little Raven, "The white man is like the sun; the Indian is like the camp-fire." And it was obvious how one became "like the sun." Ohio senator George Pendleton preached that for barbarians to develop into civilized men they must accept "the trinity upon which all civilization depends—family, and home, and property." This meant monogamy, stationary life, and private property. Three other necessary cultural values were the work ethic, individualism, and agrarian idealism. Finally, the humanitarians assumed that assisted by proper education and the Christian religion, any society could adopt these values quickly. These assumptions inspired and sustained the Peace Policy.

White men decided, for Indians at least, that "culture" meant agriculture. Churchmen, legislators, and government officials alike believed that if they could inculcate loyalty to a small piece of land, convince the Indians to live and labor there year around, and forgo tribal traditions and nomadism, the old ways would drop away like an ancient skin and from this earthy chrysalis would emerge model Anglo-American homesteaders. This, they were certain, would take only a few years. The trick was to persuade Indians to try it, and the not-so-gentle means of persuasion was severalty, which required dividing reservations into individual land allotments. Episcopalians agreed that private property and plowing one's own farm struck "a death blow to heathenism, barbarism, and idleness . . . a medicine absolutely necessary to restore health." For William Welsh, severalty signaled an Indian's first giant step toward civilization, and Bishop Whipple thought that in surrendering unused land, Chippewas had exchanged useless reservations for a superior way of life. Bishop Hare solicited all possible haste in making tribal land sales and individual allotments; reservations, he declared, were only "great squares of granite" blocking American progress and sustaining Sioux identity, their racial pride, and "manners of their own . . . and hence [were] an obstruction, a gravel-stone in the machinery of our political and social life." Quakers too believed that private farmland, like cleanliness, was essential for human happiness. The Hicksites's goal in the Peace Policy was to transform naked, scrofulous Indians into educated, self-sufficient Christians "living in comfortable houses on land held in fee simple."[7]

Private property, as it turned out, was not the whole solution. Once an agent scattered the Indians onto assigned land, he still had to convince them to work. That entailed combating tradition and village loyalties, seasonal activities, pressures from unconvinced "renegades," and the general unsuitability of alloted lands for intensive cultivation. J. A. Stephan, a Catholic agent at Standing Rock, complained that "sufficient unto the day" was the unfortunate motto of American Indians, and Indian Commissioner E. A. Hayt condemned Indians as lazy, slothful aristocrats who despised toil. Montana agent William Alderson lectured the Flatheads on world history: "The greatest men that ever lived have labored. The first great Father of all people labored and so the first great chief of all the whites was not ashamed to work. . . . And the Great Father that some of you saw in Washington worked real hard when he was a boy. . . . And whenever whites want anything they go to work and raise it out of the ground or make it . . . it makes a man strong to labor and it makes him rich."[8] Most whites employed on reservations knew that Indians were not weak or lazy—the tribes labored hard at hunting, fishing, fighting, and moving. Indians simply did not work as white men wanted them to work, as individuals and as tillers of the soil.

The inculcation of individualism required blinders of another sort because, in many ways, native cultures were highly individualistic. Most chiefs possessed far less authority over their people than the president of the United States, or a territorial governor, had over theirs. In the struggle for the continent, whites won because they cooperated and Indians lost partly because they practiced extreme individualism. Yet a purpose of the Peace Policy was to demolish the Indians' communal life, to wreck tribal identity and values, and to implant a different individualist ideology. Reformers used almost any method to achieve these goals. Quakers tried to depose chiefs and thereby break tribal systems. Episcopalians and Presbyterians encouraged removals, arbitrary division of Indian land, and separation of families; Sioux, Omaha, Ponca, and Makah children were literally kidnapped and placed in reservation or eastern boarding schools. The American Missionary Association deliberately upset kinship systems and created factionalism. Quakers, contrary to their original intentions, justified educational coercion and psychological brutality when they found Indians "slavish to fashion's rule, so tenacious of old-time custom, and sensitive to ridicule." Friends could not understand why converted natives wearing pants and hats writhed under the jeers of "pagan" Indians. John Miles at the Cheyenne-Arapaho agency, though more understanding and flexible than most agents, forced the tribes into a radical rejection of what he considered the superstition, idleness, and vagrancy of camp life. Trying to "kill much of the 'Indian' in the Indians" in his school, the Quaker agent insisted on haircuts; he enforced separation of families, enforced the use of English, and compelled name changes. Miles issued military uniforms, taught discipline through military drills, and advocated destruction of the buffalo. Elsewhere, a Methodist mused that since humans were naturally gregarious and communistic, Christianity had to accept the task of training Indians to accumulate private property and to cultivate *"want . . .* the entire difference between the savage and the civilized man . . . *want* is the great motive power of civilization."[9]

A traditional method of weakening Indian culture and opening land for settlement was removal. The removal of the Poncas (1877) cast an ugly shadow on the Peace Policy when it became a national scandal, but few if any persons protested the removal of the Osages (1870); Kaws, Modocs, and Kickapoos (1873); Pawnees (1875); Nez Perces (1877); Utes and Iowas (1879); or Otoes (1881). Aside from the question of whether to use force, nothing caused the Society of Friends more internal dissension and external conflict than removal policy. Isaac Gibson denounced the Osage removal as a crime, other Quakers said the Indians had the right to decide for themselves, and Samuel Janney thought that Indians possessed far too much land. Janney argued that the Friends should encourage Indians to avoid eventual exploitation by selling quickly under Quaker guidance. Friends antagonized the Pawnees by endorsing their removal in order to secure funds for farm equipment. The Society also believed that reservations allowed Indian children to grow up in barbarism, whereas severalty provided a "kindly and familiar intercourse with civilization."[10]

When severalty, consolidation of reservations, and forced removal proved disastrous for tribes such as the Northern Cheyennes and Nez Perces, the Peace Policy leaders began to have doubts. The Board of Indian Commissioners voiced concern over respecting the Indians' attachment to their homeland, and Hicksites opposed Nebraska removals even when the Indians supposedly favored moving. In 1878 the *Baptist Watchman* denounced termination of tribal ownership as having the ulterior motive of appropriating Indian land. The American Home Missionary Society also objected to the consolidation of Pacific Northwest tribes. Realizing that Indians cared neither for individual property nor for white culture, and questioning whether white Americans had any right to force an agrarian culture on an unwilling people, the *Unitarian Review* opposed both severalty and consolidation. Indian agents increasingly realized that, faced with drought and forced to cultivate poor soil, Indians could never become successful individual farmers. After four years at Cheyenne River, Hiram Bingham decided farming was impossible: "If the same misfortunes year after year were the reward of white men's labor, I venture to say that despair would supplant hope." The agent at Standing Rock recorded the same experience; his Indians "planted and cultivated, but heat, wind, and grasshoppers harvested." At Pine Ridge, agent V. T. McGillycuddy realized that trying to make Indians into self-sufficient farmers was "a waste of time, labor, and money, for the simple reason that this is not an agricultural country."[11]

Another humanitarian oversimplification during the Peace Policy was the practice of taking Indian chiefs on excursions through New York, Boston, and Washington, D.C. Reformers and government officials hoped that these eastern visits would convince Indians to renounce their own culture. The Board of Indian Commissioners frequently advocated this as "one of the most effective peace measures." The carefully manipulated tours avoided slums and skimmed past immigrant districts in an effort to convince the Sioux, Kiowas, Apaches, and Crows to exchange their life on the plains for the white man's "ease, comfort, and luxury." The board fooled itself more than it did the Indians. Navy yards, arsenals, and mansions did not dazzle Chief Red Cloud nearly so much as Grant's lavish feast at the White House, complete with "so much good eat and so much good squaw." The eastern tours grew out of a culture egotism and pride that expected outsiders to gasp in envy. Only a few reformers realized that a thousand years of culture could not be eradicated quickly, not by schools, missions, or by grand tours through the East.[12]

Whether by individual allotments in the West or by trips to the East, never before had the U.S. government so intensively and deliberately set out to dismantle native cultures: cultural destruction was by far the major impact of the Peace Policy on the majority of Indians. Indians were sent to manual labor schools; endlessly told about the virtues of farming, private property, and individualism; torn from their land and families and tribal customs; and confused about the expected relationship between men and women.[13] Indians felt the crush of humanitarian love; it was a love officially expressed in policy and doctrine, but it was not a love for the person as Indian. Felix Brunot warned the Umatillas, "Some of you here are trying to be Indians still. All such will soon be gone like their fathers; but if the Indians listen to the white man's teachings and become like the white man, instead of getting fewer every day they will increase like the white man, and will have become like the white man." And he told the Skokomishes that learning the right way was very simple: "The Bible has the words in it that made the white man what he is and . . . the same words will make the Indians like the good white man." The Society of Friends emphasized thrift, comfort, and cleanliness, rejoicing whenever an Indian ceased sleeping on the ground, built a home, and used bedsheets. Quakers taught the Pawnees how to dig graves, a strange and revolting custom to the tribe.[14]

Yet it is often overlooked that there were other Americans who, though they failed to influence official policy, protested against forced assimilation. They did so for many reasons. Some were racists, whereas others believed in noble savages, in toleration, and in cultural diversity. Still others disliked or rejected their own Anglo-Saxon culture. Among these were a number of frontiersmen, army officers, and western congressmen who, unlike the humanitarians who believed change could be easily accomplished, recognized the barriers to assimilation. The motives of these antiassimilationists could be racial. Preston Plumb, for example, argued that it was impossible to educate any full-blood Indians. Others who thought assimilation was impossible used that belief as a rationale for removal—as a way to protect native culture. Military men and westerners often had directly experienced the complexities of Indian life. Whatever their reasons, these skeptics understood culture change better than eastern humanitarians and government officials who acted as if a plow, wagon, 160-acre tract, and a few years at Carlisle could create white men and women. Schools alone could end the Indian problem in ten years, "perhaps in five," Senator George Hoar of Massachusetts told the Forty-seventh Congress. Henry Teller of Colorado answered that if Hoar or anyone else expected a thousand-year-old culture to vanish overnight, he simply did not know one single thing about Indians: "To take from them their pride, and their prejudice, and their passions, and put them on the plane occupied by intelligent, educated people, in five or ten years . . . is a moral impossibility. It cannot be done."[15]

Awareness of ethnic diversity and the problems of forced change occasionally appeared in the Board of Indian Commissioners and Indian Office proceedings. Francis Walker, perhaps the most sensitive of Peace Policy administrators, appreciated that Indians had their own culture, that change required time, and that white men respected defiant tribes more than submissive ones. Although Walker believed Anglo-Saxon culture to be superior, he could have doubts. In his book, *The Indian Question,* he wrote, "A wall was built across Manhattan Island [in 1653] to keep out the savages [along] the present course of Wall Street; our readers may not fail to wonder whether the savages were not the rather kept in by it." E. P. Smith's successor, J. Q. Smith, likewise could condemn Anglo-Saxons as a greedy race, argue that civilization was relative, and warn that future Americans would view the 1870s as a crude and destructive era.[16]

At times a few others expressed a more tolerant view. Quakers in Kansas might consider Indian clothing the "garb of the uneducated," yet an agent in Arizona defended the Pimas who discarded uncomfortable government pants and coats. A number of army officers came to appreciate Indian life. John Bourke's *On the Border with Crook* and other writings, though filled with prejudice, provided a more objective description of native cultures than most church publications. O. O. Howard's expressions of tolerance for the Nez Perces, Apaches, and Flatheads led some fellow whites to condemn him as an Indian lover. A lieutenant named George Ford scorned the stupidity and vices of Caucasians while praising the intelligence and good government of the

Pueblos: "Here we find a race with dark skins . . . whose lessons of morality, industry and integrity may well be learned and practiced by their so-called Christian neighbors of a superior race." With similar sentiments the House Committee on Indian Affairs condemned the *"greed and avarice of professed Christians."*[17]

Other critics of Anglo-Saxon superiority were even more vehement. Lydia Marie Child urged toleration of polygamy and native languages, denounced white racial pride, and pointed out that her culture exceeded the red man's in violence; Indians professed revenge and practiced it, she said, while Christians professed forgiveness and practiced hate. Richard MacMahon praised noble savages who lived in a primitive paradise until they learned injustice and treachery from white men. Tribes that accepted civilization, MacMahon felt, exchanged their freedom for vices and for the artificial life of Europe's "ten thousand superfluous wants."[18] The same views could be found in the circular *Council Fire*, which was published by the retired minister and social activist, T. A. Bland. Columbus Crocket's broadside told the president,

> It's my opinion, *Gen'l Grant*
> That, take the Indian all in all,
> He's a better sample of our kind
> Than the cut-throat, frontier, human wolves
> That civilization vomits forth —
> The very refuse of our land.

Criticism of American culture, sporadic and ineffective though it was, found a few voices in the Christian churches. Bishops Hare and Whipple, Samuel Janney, and others earnestly tried to understand why Indians required so long to change. Several churchmen and missionaries—Gilfillan at White Earth, Eells at Skokomish, Williamson in Dakota—could see the weaknesses and limitations in white civilization, though few could agree with Episcopal missionary E. A. Goodnough, who after twenty-five years with the Oneidas positively appreciated and defended Indian ways. William Welsh, when he perceived that destroying native religion would demoralize the Poncas and Sioux, advocated modifications in Episcopal ritual in order to appeal to Indians. Welsh also advised the use of "minor civilizing agencies . . . such as Base Ball, Croquet, &c" to wean Indians from sun-dancing and fighting "and also to show that Christianity does not mar the joy of the young." Hare, too, spoke of missionaries needing to understand Indian customs and to modify certain mission methods. With insight that was rare in nineteenth-century Christianity, the *United Presbyterian* could argue that both Indian and white culture derived from nature and not the gospel.[19]

Yet the majority of Christians assumed that Anglo-Saxon culture was inseparable from Christianity and the gospel, an assumption that led to bitter policy debates during the Peace Policy. In 1874 James Wilbur told the Board of Indian Commissioners that Indians needed the Bible and the plow, and clergyman B. Rush Roberts added soap, water, and "proper standards of cleanliness." Dr. John Lowrie, forgetting that a year before he had argued that mission progress in the Southwest was impossible until railroads brought more white settlers to New Mexico, responded that religion alone could change the Indian, "not the plow, not money gifts, not these civilizing processes, but the simple making known of the story of the Cross of Christ."[20] Lowrie's viewpoint found its clearest expression in the policy of the American Board of Commissioners for Foreign Missions.

At the beginning of the Peace Policy, the American Board's Rufus Anderson published a book on mission policy. Anderson argued that Christians had erroneously identified their religion with social mores and thus mistakenly used their own manners, morals, and education to measure the growth of various races in the faith. Citing the American Indians as an example, Anderson said that modern European and American culture had become identified with the Christian faith and thereby had weakened missionary trust in simple gospel methods. If men and women would rely on the Holy Spirit and the gospel alone, many more souls could be saved at less expense. Rufus Anderson believed that culture advanced as a by-product of Christian faith, gradually coming to native peoples through education and their own efforts. In the meantime, Christians had to tolerate differences in custom and morals among new brethren.[21]

However appealing Rufus Anderson's formula appeared on paper, the American Board missionaries found it difficult to apply in Dakota. The Riggs family taught Indian men to labor in potato patches and Indian women to comb their hair, sweep their houses, and wash and iron—"the gospel of cleanliness is emphatically taught." When the Riggs brothers requested one hundred thousand dollars to build a school at Santee the American Board's Prudential Committee answered that the Sioux must build their own schools and reprimanded the missionaries for being embarrassed by Presbyterian and Episcopal affluence. Instead, the Riggses were admonished to adhere to the "pure missionary ideal" of evangelism apart from culture and use apostolic methods. The board recalled that Paul preached without pay; it had no intention of copying the false examples of Hampton or Carlisle, who competed with the government in secular work. The Riggses shot back that Paul enjoyed the luxury of preaching to civilized Greeks and Romans, and that the Prudential Committee in Boston knew nothing about barbarous Indians.[22] This retort did not impress the committee, nor did letters from a Miss Pike, their missionary at Fort Berthold. She told the board that some missionaries, like Indians, were lazy and unclean. She prayed to escape such disgrace:

Here on this unbroken prairie I want to be a truly *refined Christian woman* in everything, in manners, dress & way of living, as I would want to be anywhere. I feel that we are representatives to the heathen, of the best that the Gospel can do for women & . . . if our house is not neatly kept, the children well managed, and all cheerful & happy, these ignorant, filthy, degraded, half-naked heathen will perceive it *quite* rapidly. . . . [I want] bread *always* light and sweet and neither raw nor burned, potatoes mealy, and cooked *just* enough. . . . I have *seen* Mr. Hall *eat* pudding which was partly *raw dough*—not even *warmed through*, with as smiling a grace as though it were a thing fit to put into the stomach of a Christian. . . . [I] hope I may never become so depraved.[23]

The vast majority of nineteenth-century American Christians would have supported the Riggs family and Miss Pike against Rufus Anderson, Charles Lemon Hall, and John Lowrie. Weekly prayer meetings, rote Bible reading, and worship on Sunday were the means to convert Indians into model businessmen, into farmers with clean hands and shirts, short hair, and land in severalty. In 1872 the Board of Indian Commissioners reported that whenever the Indian accepted Christianity, "he abandons all the cherished customs and traditions of his nation, cuts off his scalp-locks, adopts civilized garments, and goes to work for his living."[24]

The government and the churches generally ignored the advice of agents such as J. C. Tiffany at San Carlos and James Wilbur at Yakima, who urged that only by living and working *with* native Americans, only by eating food that one did not care to eat, only by sharing, could an agent or missionary succeed. The official Protestant theory and practice was just the opposite: unless a man were married, well-paid, and comfortable, he would be ineffective. Baptists warned in 1871 that Protestants should not copy Jesuits who compromised the gospel and put on "masks of pagan civilization" by adopting non-Christian customs. The American Missionary Association agreed that one could not lift fallen men by stooping to their level, and E. P. Smith, who observed that "pure heathen" Indians had nothing in common with Christian citizens, rejoiced when Christianity caused Indians to loathe their old way of life. Quaker John Miles felt that Kickapoo children must be forcibly separated from their parents; otherwise school lessons were forgotten "*lounging in the old Wigwam* at night among the dirt, dogs, and tobacco spit." The Missionary Association similarly praised Hampton's Indian students, who no longer smoked or spit or drank, but who prayed, spoke of Jesus, "and [could] be seen digging ditches or picking potatoes with all the energy of an Anglo-Saxon."[25]

Episcopal leaders were probably more sensitive to Indian culture than

other Protestant denominations, yet they too thought that cultural trans-
formation was a natural consequence of conversion.[26] One Episcopalian
wrote that Christian merchants should support African missions because
they created a market for dry goods: "The first step toward civilization is to
introduce garments [and] who does this so effectually as the Missionaries?"
Nude children, he observed, were barred from mission schools and converts
wore clothing "instead of the shameful, yet shameless, state of nudity in
which wild heathen live." Episcopal missionaries to Indians also insisted that
proper clothing was a sign of true conversion. Bishop Henry Whipple preached
at William Hare's ordination that the tipi could never be a Christian home,
that vassals of tribal chiefs could never be free men, and that common property could not be tolerated by Christians. Hare, who caused resentment
among the Sioux by forbidding their Grass Dance, warned the churches that
spiritual salvation by itself would fail. Missionaries, he said, must cooperate
in building houses, towns, and cities, and "in advancing the price of corner
lots."[27]

The theology of American manufacturing and the gospel of plows and shoes,
of knives, forks, and spoons, of balloon-frame houses and rising real estate
values, had a forceful impact on one tribe in Washington Territory, the
Yakimas, and it completely baffled another, the Makahs.

At Fort Simcoe, below the eastern foothills of the Cascade Mountains,
labored the model agent, "Father" James Wilbur. Wilbur, though he worked
closely with the Yakima people, rejected Indian customs and religion. To him
Indians were simply undisciplined children and his duty was to transform
them into Protestant white men and women as rapidly and as efficiently as
possible. In this he was more effective than any other agent in the service.

In 1871 Wilbur reported that the year the agency spent under army control (1869-70) had disrupted reservation farming and made the Yakima Indians paupers while the military agent stole cattle and robbed the agency.
Wilbur set out to help the Yakimas recover their pride by teaching them
about *"industry, God, and heaven."* By 1878 he had done so. Wilbur trained
Indian blacksmiths, harness makers, carpenters, and painters; he built, with
no aid from the government or the Methodist church, a shingle mill and sawmill that cut ten thousand board feet of timber a day; he watched over six
hundred native Methodists who owned sixteen thousand horses in addition
to thirty-five thousand head of cattle and who lived in good houses with
"sewing machines, bedsteads, cook-stoves, mirrors, clocks, watches, crockery,
the newspaper, and the Bible." In accomplishing this, Wilbur, unlike many
other agents, labored hand in hand with the tribe as they cut logs, plowed,
erected homes. A credo inspired his sacrifices, and in 1871 he wrote:

I believe in the manhood of the Indian, and in the possibility of elevating him to a high state of civilization. True, he is ignorant, treacherous, and cruel by nature; he is destitute of moral character; he is poor in every respect . . . his first great want is character. Failing to give him character, all material rights but hasten his degradation and his future destruction. . . . As a Christian teacher, I have believed in the possibility of giving him the first indispensable condition of civilization. I have known I could inspire virtue in the Indian only by the plain, open, unequivocal manifestation of virtue on my own part. . . . I find the result of my labors a perfect justification of my theory.[28]

And seven years later:

Indians must have men of God, full of business enterprise . . . men who are awake to the interests of this and the world to come. . . . With such men upon the reservations, instructing and governing them, there *can be no failure*. . . . They must have *practical business men* who can instruct them how to live by the cultivation of the soil, and the teachings of God's Word; any and everything else connected with the service is a failure.[29]

Wilbur was an egotist, certainly a religious zealot, and a very effective Indian agent. He was hard on Indians, harder on local whites, and, most of all, hardest on himself. Poverty and despair eventually returned to Fort Simcoe after the blizzard of 1880–81, but in terms of his beliefs, beliefs that were also the basic assumptions of the Peace Policy, few agents achieved as much or made as deep an impact on their reservations.[30]

On the far northwestern corner of Washington Territory's Olympic Peninsula no one would dominate Neah Bay as Wilbur domineered Yakima. The six hundred Makah Indians were still a sea-faring people when the Peace Policy began. Trading and fishing increased their tribal wealth to more than one hundred thousand dollars by 1873; a good sealing season could boost the tribal income by almost twenty thousand dollars. From January to May hand-hewn cedar canoes moved from the Strait of Juan de Fuca into the Pacific Ocean searching for whales, often ranging as far as forty miles out.

The Makahs' first Peace Policy agent, Lieutenant J. H. Hays, understood their economy and he recognized that the poor soil at Neah Bay made it foolish to insist on farming. Lieutenant Hays, prudish as any missionary, disliked the Makah manner of attire: "The simplicity of Eden, as respects dress, is one of their peculiarities . . . the men and women are naked, and are not ashamed. One of my first efforts was to make them cover their nakedness. I have succeeded in accustoming a majority of the men to wear trousers

when out of doors. This I regard as one great point gained."[31] Hays also induced the tribe to adopt white burial customs.

In 1870 a Disciples minister, Elkanah Gibson, replaced Hays. Gibson at
first thought there was little need for farming and realized how much the
Makahs disliked tilling the soil. He reported no school on the reserve—Indian
parents seemingly did not want their children to become like white people.
Nature, the agent reported, supplied the tribe with life's every necessity:
"They are the most happy and independent people I have ever seen." Gibson
built a jail and planned to add a hospital and sawmill. Eventually he changed
his mind about farming and cultivated eight acres. The agent reasoned that by
draining and diking a tidal marsh near the ocean, land could be farmed. Once
agriculture was fully pursued, summer sports and fishing festivals no longer
would distract Makah children from the agency school. Washington's Indian
superintendent, Robert Milroy, a Methodist minister, opposed Gibson's plans,
considering it futile to force agriculture on the tribe. Instead, Milroy recommended that the government purchase boats, nets, and weirs, and that the
agent teach the tribe to can and pack salmon rather than farm. In 1873 Milroy ordered a fifty-ton schooner for Neah Bay.[32]

The commercial fishing program encountered problems in 1874, when the
Methodists removed Gibson and appointed a former Congregational minister
named Charles A. Huntington. A close friend of Wilbur, Huntington for five
years had been deeply enmeshed in Indian Office politics. His slander of
Superintendent Samuel Ross in 1869, and his opposition to army control
had split his parish in Olympia and resulted in his dismissal as minister of that
church. After politicians blocked his appointment as Skokomish agent, he
joined the Methodist Church. Two years later Methodist officials assigned him
to Neah Bay.[33]

Huntington arrived on the Olympic Peninsula filled with plans for improvement. The Makahs lacked "pocket-handkerchief, comb, brush, knife and
fork," and their morals filled him with revulsion. Seeing the Makahs with
only "a surfeit of such food as savages desire," he resolved to teach Christian
eating habits and a love of good food, which meant farming. After failing to
reclaim Gibson's tideland, Huntington realized that fertile soil did not exist
at Neah Bay and, acknowledging that "the first disciples of Christianity were
fishermen," he abandoned farming. Despite the concession to Indian ways,
the agent considered the Makahs a depraved, selfish people and sought to save
the children by forcing them into his boarding school. Here young people
would witness Huntington's own exemplary home life, a blessing that would
enable them "to steer clear of all barbarism and insure them the blessings of a
civilized life."[34]

The agent's optimism disappeared in 1877, when he concluded that redemption of the Makahs required at least a generation of Christian labor. The separation of children from parents had been especially trying. After a year of unsuccessfully attempting to persuade parents with kindness, the minister-agent decided "to take high ground with them and carry the point by force":

> The first trial was a severe one and was made a test of the principle of coercion. It resulted in the surrender of the child demanded after [the father] had lain two nights and one day in prison. . . . Seeing that I was in earnest, that withholding their children would only subject them to punishment, they yielded to the requirement with great reluctance. . . . The children finding themselves comfortably situated and kindly treated, soon became content and happy.[35]

Again shifting goals, Huntington was instructing Indian boys in the arts of "gardening, hauling and cutting wood."

Meanwhile the agent had run afoul of investigators from the Board of Indian Commissioners and the Indian Office. The agency carpenter and blacksmith testified to Inspector E. C. Watkins that Huntington illegally sold agency fruit trees and offered to divide profits gained from false vouchers. The Makahs considered Huntington their worst agent yet and accused him of taking their money through fines and of stealing their supplies and cattle. Churches in Portland had sent clothing packets that the agent sold to the tribe, keeping the money for himself. Watkins reacted with alarm as he toured the neglected farm and the filthy agency and school. He also sighted several nude young people bathing in the surf, proof that the tribe lacked chastity and modesty. When Huntington conceded that most of these charges were true, Watkins suspended him as "a disgrace to the public service and a sham to his profession as a minister of the Gospel."[36]

Huntington's Episcopal successor, Charles Willoughby, continued to separate children from their parents and, like Watkins, was horrified by Makah nudity and "pernicious free-love." Yet their industry and bravery at sea impressed him. Willoughby's effort to force agriculture on the tribe failed and he concluded that the reservation possessed great wealth in cod, salmon, and halibut that should be marketed. Despite his advice, the Indian Office persisted in futile efforts to transform the Makahs into farmers.[37]

The Makahs, whom Elkanah Gibson once considered the happiest people he had ever met, never again had an agent like the Reverend Mr. Huntington to implement the "Christian and humane peace policy." According to Willoughby, Huntington's only accomplishment was inspiring Makah elders to detest Christianity.[38]

Indians expressed few opinions, at least to non-Indians, about the Peace Policy—unless we accept the Sioux, Cheyenne, Ute, Apache, and Nez Perce wars as testimony. Years later there were both bitter and positive native recollections of the Peace Policy. The Arapahos cherished their memory of Brinton Darlington, but the Apaches remembered the 1870s at the San Carlos and Mescalero agencies as a time of starvation, violence, and poverty that bred a century-long hatred of whites and the federal government. At the time, many who expressed their views spoke through white men such as William Welsh and usually said exactly what William Welsh expected them to say: they admired Grant (in 1870), were enthusiastic about the new Policy, and requested Christian agents and teachers.[39]

Most Indians who knew of the Peace Policy probably were as misinformed about Grant's reform as frontier white men. Not surprisingly, most tribes identified the Church with the government. One reason for this confusion may have been that local tribal communities could not conceive of a society that compartmentalized public and private life, government and religion. Another reason was that agents and missionaries and peace commissioners repeatedly encouraged the identification of Church and State. Welsh told the Poncas and Sioux that Indian agents were sent by the Church in answer to Christian prayers. When southwestern tribes asked Vincent Colyer if God had sent him he answered, "It was God." Felix Brunot opened his treaty councils by praying for the president, the governor, the agent, and the agency employees.[40] The identification took hold. Informed that they had to leave their land, Hoopa Valley Indians bitterly blamed the agent, deserted his Sunday school, and abandoned Christianity en masse. When the government broke its promises at Round Valley, the agent soon discovered that the tribe's eight hundred Christians deserted the Church. After the end of the Peace Policy, Episcopal missionaries in Dakota complained that anti-Christian Sioux "confounded [the missionaries] with the government."[41]

Missionaries, reformers, and school teachers believed that Indians actually desired what the Quakers called "the sweetness and light of Christian culture," and therefore the humanitarians could not understand the tenacity with which native Americans held to traditional ways or the violence that some Indians directed against others who did adopt white culture.[42] To most Indians, the white man's way, especially schools, farming and religion, made little sense. As a Nevada agent finally realized, not all were "children of the forest or fertile valley, but [some were] of alkali plains, barren mountains, and sage-brush deserts." They proved to be difficult, indifferent, or justifiably hostile pupils. White intolerance and racial prejudice offered them only two choices: assimilation or extermination.[43] The Grant Peace Policy embraced the solution of assimilation, with few of its paternalistic founders having any more sympathy for Indian ways than did the exterminationists. Instead, as the Honorable Isaac Parker of Missouri observed, white men saw Indians only from a white viewpoint, acted only on white assumptions, and solved problems with white solutions. Most reformers assumed that the key to the problem was the Gospel and, as the American Missionary Association said, the Gospel "is very unlikely to abide in a bark house."[44]

White cultural intolerance manifested itself at all levels of the Peace Policy. Even Quakers required that Indians possess more than the inner light. After twenty Wichitas repented and accepted Christ, agent Jonathan Richards faced a difficult problem—what to do with Christian Indians? The agent and his wife, as Lawrie Tatum later recalled, were refined, intelligent Philadelphia Friends and "it would hardly seem consistent to take these Indians . . . into church membership with those living in the City of Brotherly Love."[45] Bishop William Hare, after ten years in Dakota, likewise concluded that the preservation of Indian land and traditional culture would only produce indigestion in American civilization. Felix Brunot bargained hard, seldom listened to Indian opinion, and used small deceptions in negotiation because he knew that the Crows and Utes did not understand their own best interests. Requests by tribal leaders for control over agency employment and for the right to name their own agents were uniformly ignored by the government and by reformers.[46] And according to Secretary of the Interior Carl Schurz, Indian culture, religion, and "old-fogy chiefs" had to succumb to the white man's will: "We must in a great measure do the necessary thinking for them, and then in the most humane way possible induce them to accept our conclusions."[47]

Had Indians been allowed to do the necessary thinking that Carl Schurz denied them, it is not altogether certain they would have chosen the white man's path. An Indian reading *Harper's Weekly* or the *Baptist Watchman* might have wondered about a civilization that needed Ladies Undervests, or Madam Foy's Corset Skirt Supporter, or Allan's Anti-Fat—"the Great Remedy for Corpulence." The Indian could have learned that accepting the superior culture would bring cheap cigarettes and Dr. Jno. V. Burton's TOBACCO ANTIDOTE, or Dr. A. J. Flagg's Medicated Inhaling Balm. Exchanging a longhouse and buffalo robes for Reed and Barton's Silver Plated Table Ware might possibly appeal to native women, but they would puzzle over advertised cures for sour stomachs, ear diseases, pimples, and "Piles—Itching Piles."

The effects of forced cultural assimilation on social behavior and personal health were hardly recognized in the 1870s as rapid change took a huge toll in human misery and suffering among Indian tribes. Despite treaties that provided for medical services, and even though the Bureau of Indian Affairs finally created a division of Indian medicine in 1873, native mortality rates during the Peace Policy are shocking. The government's failure to issue food and clothing after aboriginal supplies had been destroyed resulted in chronic malnutrition and disease. The trauma of military defeat, the emotional dislocation caused by an unfamiliar lifestyle, the abrupt shift from a hunting economy to farming, the contact with diseased whites, and the official suppression of tribal medicine men helped produce ideal conditions for endemic tuberculosis, typhoid, malaria, pleuropneumonia, syphilis, and whooping cough.[48]

Some Indians decided that civilization was worth that price. Others did not. Even the model Episcopal convert, Enmegahbowh, had doubts toward the end. Years of cooperation with whites and the Episcopal church had brought destruction and despair. In 1878 he wrote to Henry Whipple:

> Please let me talk with you again for one minute only as regard the health of my people. . . . all my youngest children have died since I came here. I have in my Register the number of children who have *died with worms*. . . .
>
> The worms that are destroying [our] children caused by using the stagnate water &c &c. . . . Yesterday I have just buried our daughter's oldest boy a boy that you Baptized three years ago & boy was named after you. Before he died I saw 6 regular water Leeches that passed through him.
>
> Dear Bishop, as you well know & saw our old homes & country since the dawn of our earliest days—we have always drank the purest & Running water—that is while living with our innocent lives & before the palefaces brought the devil Spirit . . . which not only destroyed our smaller children but the older persons both body & soul—Bishop we tried to run away from the effect of this bad drink—But this Bad drink Bishop and its effects will thin our Rank and there will only a few to remain to tell the fate of the nation. . . .
>
> In really Bishop my people are groaning with the deep recesses in their hearts. . . . My wife is much effected. She ask me what if we go back to our old country . . . poor woman I feel deeply effected when I think of her. She has entirely quit attending our church.[49]

In 1835 Alexis de Tocqueville wrote that despite shameful atrocities and bloodshed in Latin America, the Spanish had not entirely destroyed the native race. "But," he observed, "the Americans of the United States have accomplished this . . . with singular felicity, tranquility, legally, philanthropically, without shedding blood, and without violating a single great principle of morality in the eyes of the world. It is impossible to destroy men with more respect for the laws of humanity.[50]

Forty years later, at the collapse of the Peace Policy, experienced army officers would agree. The churches, the government, and the Board of Indian Commissioners, they would contend, were mistaken in anticipating that Indians eagerly awaited missions, schools, and civilization. The Christian Church and western civilization had required centuries to evolve their complex social and intellectual systems; to expect that a people could change cultures in four years, as the board predicted in 1869, was foolish. Indian culture, these military men knew, had grown as slowly as Anglo-Saxon culture and was just as complex and deeply ingrained.[51] Only gradually did a few humanitarians realize the truth in these observations, but by then it was too late. At the end of the century James Mooney recorded the same story in "Song of the Ancient People":

> For the fires grow cold and the dances fail
>   And the songs in their echoes die;
> And what have we left but the graves beneath,
>   And, above, the waiting sky?[52]

Benjamin West, *Penn's Treaty with the Indians*, 1771. The myth that Quakers never injured Indians provided a motive for adopting the Peace Policy. Quakers often gave reproductions of this painting to native leaders; a copy of it hung in the office of the Northern Superintendency. Courtesy Pennsylvania Academy of the Fine Arts.

Ulysses S. Grant, c. 1869, at the beginning of the presidency. This was his favorite portrait. Courtesy Chicago Historical Society.

ROBINSON CRUSOE MAKING A MAN OF HIS FRIDAY

INDIAN CHIEF. "Mr. President, we call here to-day to offer our fealty to you as our recognized Guardian and Ward, and to pray you, Sir, to continue our Good Friend and Father."

THE PRESIDENT. "You are welcome; and in reference to continuing your 'Good Father,' as you say, I must answer that I have long thought that the two nations which you represent, and all those civilized nations in the Indian Country, *should be their own Wards and Good Fathers. I am of the opinion that they should become Citizens*, and be entitled to all the rights of Citizens—cease to be Nations and become States."

Grant's policy of assimilation and citizenship for all Indians. Thomas Nast, *Harper's Weekly*, February 12, 1870.

"LET US HAVE PEACE." — [*Drawn by C. S. Reinhart.*]

The Peace Policy was a year old and accepted by the eastern press when *Harper's* reported this reception of a Sioux delegation including Red Cloud, Spotted Tail, and Swift Bear. The man standing behind Grant is unidentified. *Harper's Weekly*, June 18, 1870.

Jacob D. Cox, Grant's first secretary of the interior. Cox resigned after differences with the president over reform measures. Courtesy Library of Congress.

Columbus Delano. Delano replaced Cox as head of the interior and symbolized a return to traditional politics in the Grant administration. Courtesy Library of Congress.

Ely S. Parker, Seneca Indian, commissioner of Indian affairs, 1869–71. Parker was the first Native American to administer the Indian Office. Courtesy National Archives.

Edward P. Smith, commissioner of Indian affairs, 1873–75. Smith, a Congregational minister, earlier served as Chippewa agent at White Earth. Courtesy Edward Parmelee Smith Papers, Amistad Research Center.

NON-RESISTANCE.

Big Red Brother. "Owgh! owgh! owgh! Scalpee—owgh!"
Friend Obed. "Take all thee finds, friend—thee's quite welcome."

This cartoon appeared the month after Quaker agents occupied their new agencies. The artist points to the incongruity between Quakers and Indians, pacifism and frontier violence, east and west. *Harper's Weekly*, August 21, 1869.

Samuel D. Hinman, 1867, Episcopal priest and Dakota missionary. Hinman, a translator, treaty negotiator, and friend of Bishop Whipple, eventually caused scandal and controversy within his church. Courtesy South Dakota State Historical Society.

William Hobart Hare, bishop to the Dakotas. Hare's aggressive leadership in establishing native churches and schools helped to make the Protestant Episcopal church one of the most effective denominations in the Peace Policy. Courtesy South Dakota Historical Society.

William Welsh, Episcopal layman and Philadelphia businessman. Zealous, temperamental, and suspicious, Welsh drove Commissioner of Indian Affairs Ely S. Parker from office and constantly attacked corruption in government and Indian affairs. Courtesy Historical Society of Pennsylvania.

Felix Reville Brunot, Episcopal layman and philanthropist, replaced William Welsh as the chairman of the Board of Indian Commissioners in 1869. Courtesy State Historical Society of Wisconsin.

Henry B. Whipple, 1871, Episcopal bishop and the church's most effective advocate of Indian reform during the 1860s and '70s. Courtesy Minnesota Historical Society.

Vincent Colyer, Episcopal layman and well-known landscape painter. As the first secretary of the Board of Indian Commissioners, he often became the target of abuse on the western frontier. Courtesy National Archives, Record Group 48.

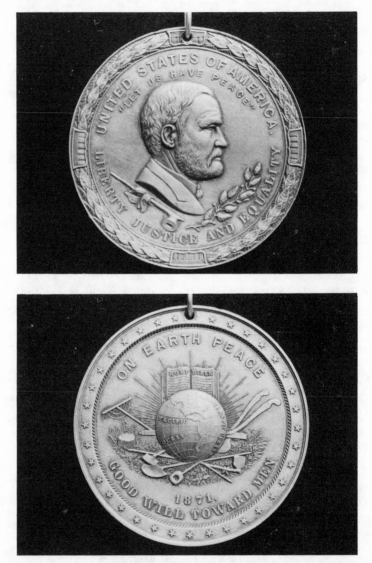

It was customary for government officials to distribute medals with the president's likeness to tribal leaders at treaty negotiations and when delegations visited Washington. All of the so-called peace medals emphasized friendship with the Indians, but Grant's medal (obverse above, reverse below) was particularly elaborate, carrying symbols of his program to civilize the Indians. Courtesy Historical Photography Collection, University of Washington Libraries. Photograph by E. H. Latham.

James H. Wilbur, Methodist minister and Yakima agent, 1870–82. Government officials and reformers often referred to "Father Wilbur" as the Peace Policy's ideal Christian agent.

Wilbur's home at Fort Simcoe was one of the best in the Indian service. Courtesy Oregon Historical Society.

Orthodox Quaker agents photographed in Lawrence, Kansas, 1872. Sitting, left to right: Hiram Jones, John Miles, Brinton Darlington, Mahlon Stubbs, Joel Morris. Standing, left to right: Isaac Gibson, Rueban Roberts, Enoch Hoag, Jonathan Richards, John Hadley, Lawrie Tatum. Courtesy Quaker Collection, Haverford College Library, Haverford, Pennsylvania.

John P. Clum, center, San Carlos Apache agent appointed by the Dutch Reformed Church. As one of the most controversial and tough-minded Peace Policy agents, Clum forced defiant Apache bands onto the reservation, resisted army control, and battled with Arizona politicians. Courtesy Arizona State Museum, University of Arizona.

Issue of rations to three thousand Indians at Camp Supply, Oklahoma, 1870. Sacks of flour and sugar to the right. Courtesy BAE Collection, Smithsonian Institution.

Fort Sill schoolhouse, Kiowa-Comanche reservation, 1872. Courtesy Oklahoma Historical Society.

THE POPE'S BIG TOE: "If we are to have another contest in the near future of our national existence, I predict that the dividing line will not be MASON and DIXON's."
—GRANT's speech on our Public School System.

A typical Thomas Nast cartoon, *Harper's Weekly*, October 30, 1875, entitled "The Pope's Big Toe."

AN EXPERIMENT WORTH TRYING.

A Nast cartoon supporting transfer of the Indian Office to the War Department, *Harper's Weekly*, April 22, 1876, two months before the Little Big Horn.

THE SECRETARY OF THE INTERIOR INVESTIGATING THE INDIAN BUREAU.
GIVE HIM HIS DUE, AND GIVE THEM THEIR DUES.

THE SECRETARY OF THE INTERIOR INVESTIGATING THE INDIAN BUREAU.
GIVE HIM *HIS DUE, AND GIVE THEM THEIR DUES.*

Schurz, a liberal Republican appointed by President Hayes in 1877, disliked
the Peace Policy but could not repeal it, so he began his own reform of alleged
corruption in the Indian "bureau." Thomas Nast, *Harper's Weekly*, January
26, 1878.

9. New Views of Church and State

The United States government in 1875 imprisoned a Cheyenne Indian named Howling Wolf at St. Augustine, Florida. Stifled by confinement and bewildered by the jail, Howling Wolf found comfort in holding a Bible, which he could not read. Slowly, he realized the sinfulness of the Cheyenne way. He would "throw away all of [his] bad deeds" and return to his people: "I asked God to take away my bad heart, and give me a good heart. Then I felt happy. . . . I threw away my old road, and took the road of the Bible. . . . I urge all the Indians, Cheyennes and Arapahoes, to take the Bible road that they also may be happy."[1] This, to men such as Felix Brunot, William Welsh, James Wilbur, and Lawrie Tatum, was the primary goal of Grant's Peace Policy. An illiterate Christianity was preferable to any form of Indian culture or religion, and they felt that the federal government should fully cooperate with the Christian Church to set Americans like Howling Wolf on the right road.

In 1869 only a few persons wondered whether constitutional barriers might block that road. By 1882, there was increasing discussion of walls between Church and State because it had become evident that the road could also lead to Rome. Indian affairs and the Peace Policy must be understood in the context of a Church-State controversy throughout the decade, a constitutional controversy over religion unparalleled in American history to that time and not repeated until nearly a century later.

167

At the end of the Civil War, Protestant Americans had begun to worry about Roman Catholic immigration and the role of religion in public institutions, especially in public schools in Catholic areas. Evangelical Protestants and nativists were convinced that it was necessary to limit or eliminate Catholicism, considered an undemocratic and antirepublican religion, and to enhance the traditional supremacy of Protestantism in society. The latter concern found expression in an effort to amend the U.S. Constitution by stamping explicitly Christian language onto the fundamental law of the land. The new preamble, first proposed in 1864, would have affirmed the existence of God, confessed Christ as savior, and acknowledged true religion as the sole basis for civil government. Led by Felix Brunot, the Christian preamble movement reached a peak in the mid-seventies. Then it was stunned by unexpected opposition from Grant. Speaking in 1875 to the Army of the Tennessee, Grant advocated the complete separation of church and state and the end of all tax exemption for churches. "Encourage free schools," said the founder of the Peace Policy, "and resolve that not one dollar . . . shall be appropriated to the support of any sectarian schools. Resolve that neither the state nor the nation nor both combined, shall support institutions . . . with sectarian, pagan, or atheistical dogmas. Leave the matter of religion to the family altar, the church, and the private school supported entirely by private contributions. Keep the church and the state forever separate."[2] A month later Grant asked Congress to pass what came to be known as "the Blaine Amendment." The amendment would have banned all aid to religion, all religious oaths, and all teaching of religion in public schools. It defined the troublesome word *establishment* and would have guaranteed religious freedom in the states. Congress voted on the controversial matter a dozen times between 1876 and 1888, never passing it.

Amid all of this, the relationship of the federal government to Indian missions and to religious liberty on Indian reservations was largely ignored. Whenever Americans did stop to reflect on that particular problem, they treated it exactly as they did the ethics of property, contract, and conquest—the First Amendment, like the ethics of property rights and contracts, did not apply to Indians.

Under the Peace Policy, churches nominated federal agents, operated Indian schools, and persistently labored for religious conversion. When the churches at first responded slowly to Grant's invitation, the Board of Indian Commissioners called for new "faith in the Gospel, especially when [they had] the Government to protect us." By 1872 the churches effectively controlled some nine hundred government employees. Indian agents reported statistics on missions, church membership, and Sunday school attendance to Washington, D.C. As Thomas Cree remarked, it was "a power which has never been placed in the hands of the church before."[3]

From sermonlike prayers at treaty councils to the singing of Moody and Sankey hymns at Indian boarding schools, Church and State were joined. Beginning in 1869, men such as Felix Brunot of the board, presenting himself as a delegate of the Great Spirit, would officially mix polemic and prayer, piety and government policy, whenever he urged tribes to accept Christ and cede land.[4] Episcopalians held worship services in government buildings, and Bishop William Hare could criticize Catholics for their failure to evangelize in government schools. Congregationalist Myron Eells refused to come to Skokomish until reassured his appointment would not interfere with preaching the gospel. As Skokomish agent, Eells distributed Bibles in the government school and instructed Indian children that it was a sacred book. Government payrolls at Warm Springs, Kamiah, and Lapwai listed ministers and missionaries as teachers. In Idaho, where the federal government built chapels and churches, someone asked General O. O. Howard if Presbyterian missionary Kate McBeth taught theology at the Lapwai school. "Certainly not theology in the way of 'isms' of any kind," he replied. "I told her to call it *theophily*, if a high sounding name was needed for God's love." A Presbyterian missionary in Wisconsin reported that the government day school was "no mere secular affair, but a genuine Evangelizing agency. We are rejoiced that we have access to so many and can have them under Mission influence."[5]

An 1877 Indian Bureau circular asserted that under the Peace Policy the federal government did not promote religion. Yet in 1869 the Quakers had been told that Christianization of Indians would receive the president's support insofar as he could legally give it, an offer that created no conflict in principle for most churchmen. A year later the American Missionary Association assured its members that the Peace Policy was nonsectarian, that it created nothing new, and that it was "free from all legal or constitutional objections." A Unitarian magazine advocated complete separation of Church and State, then blandly described the Peace Policy in the same issue and found no contradiction. The Quakers worried momentarily about Church-State relations when Benjamin Hallowell argued for separation, but no Friend pressed the issue.[6] Only Episcopalians, Presbyterians, Roman Catholics, and the American Board of Commissioners for Foreign Missions had raised serious constitutional questions when the Peace Policy began.

In 1878 an army officer questioned the *Churchman*, an Episcopalian journal, about cooperation between Church and State required under the Peace Policy. Bishop Henry Whipple answered the inquiry by saying that the Episcopal church had never used government funds, that it never would, and that he personally had not accepted a single dollar from the Indian Office. Whipple likewise wrote to President Rutherford B. Hayes to assert that among clergymen responsible for Indian missions, he alone opposed "any & all uses of public money by religious bodies."[7] The Minnesota bishop's 1877 statements accurately reflected the position taken by the Episcopal church eight years earlier, when William Welsh told President Grant in March of 1869 that the government must not give money to the denominations. Welsh promised that salaries of teachers and missionaries as well as expenses of schools and hospitals would be "freely proffered" by the churches. The following year, disheartened by meager Episcopal contributions, he realized that federal money posed a great temptation. Welsh still refused aid and insisted that no Episcopal missionary accept wages from the United States. His reasons were threefold: missions should operate on "pure Gospel principles"; Indians distrusted everyone paid by the government; and larger denominations could outmaneuver Episcopalians in competition for tax money.[8]

Opposition to Welsh's scruples gradually grew in his own and other churches. At an 1870 meeting of the Episcopal Mission Board, Welsh introduced a resolution refusing all government aid. Asked if Episcopalians should decline money from the government's Civilization Fund, which had supported missions since the 1820s, he reiterated that they must accept nothing. A bishop interjected that this was unwise—when the government offered to build hospitals it was "exceedingly expedient" for the church to make them Christian hospitals. Welsh answered that such cooperation led to discrimination and denominational jealousy, limited the Church's mission, and distorted the gospel. Bishop William Whittingham joined Welsh and reminded the mission board that the eternal conflict between the flesh and the spirit, the temporal and the eternal, meant that Church and State must ultimately remain rivals. Before Constantine, Whittingham said, the Christian Church was "entirely separate from the secular Government. . . . How did evils creep into the Church? They came with the 600 purses which Constantine gave. The reasoning then was just as specious as now. The Church was to be the Almoner of the State, and the Church accepted the bribe." Another bishop protested that chaplains set a precedent for cooperation, and a board member said that the Church *must* be the almoner of the State because "we need government money for the Freedmen and for hospitals." Welsh withdrew his resolution.[9]

William Welsh encountered further opposition to his principles at the 1871 church conference with the Board of Indian Commissioners. After voting against him, the majority requested the federal government to provide school buildings at agencies. In 1872 Welsh reluctantly agreed to lobby in Congress for funds to build Episcopal schools and chapels, even though he realized that for the government to pay for missions would antagonize Indians and frontier whites. Privately, he expressed his chagrin over a united Church and State.[10]

The American Board in Boston similarly opposed government aid, though its workers in the field often held a different view. Board secretary Rufus Anderson wrote in 1869 that unlike "Romish missions," Protestants never accepted state aid except for personal protection. The board endorsed strict separation and supported its Dakota missionaries when they denounced what seemed to be Episcopal attempts at establishment.[11] Later in the decade, after Episcopalians signed contracts to operate government schools, the American Board at first was tempted to apply for funds, but then decided to avoid "entangling alliances" and to have "just as little to do with the government as possible in every way." The board considered government schools too secular and it anticipated that some day the public would resent tax money spent on missions. It also realized that competition from Catholics and Episcopalians would be severe.[12]

Dr. John Lowrie of the Presbyterian church shared these concerns of William Welsh and the American Board. Early Presbyterian conflicts with the Quaker agent at Omaha had alerted Lowrie to the dangers inherent in the Peace Policy and he soon developed guidelines to maintain a correct view of government relations. Presbyterians announced that they would request no funds for missionaries and religious instruction, although they did expect to use government school buildings. The Presbyterian concern was not so much a theory of separation as a desire to avoid investing heavily in land and buildings to which the church might eventually lose title.[13] In practice, religious instruction dominated the curriculum of the Presbyterian government schools. Lowrie allowed missionaries Henry Spalding and Henry Cowley to accept federal salaries and he did nothing about the many missionaries hired as agency teachers in the Southwest. Nevertheless, Presbyterians consistently professed an official aversion to any combination of Church and State.[14]

Few other Protestant denominations asked any constitutional questions. The Quakers contented themselves with euphemisms: their cooperation with the government was "not formal, but [was] full, generous, and cordial"; their agents eliminated Indian superstition but did not teach sectarianism. Methodists looked on the Indian Office itself as a missionary enterprise that helped them introduce "at the expense of the Government, all the Gospel Appliances." When Roman Catholics complained that this meant reversion to "the old Colonial *State Church* . . . a feeler and experiment in *State*-Church-ism," Methodists shrugged that such cooperation indeed was hazardous but "justified by the extreme necessities of the case . . . as a lesser evil."[15] E. P. Smith, even after the scandals and wars under the Peace Policy, still believed that the government needed religious help. Secularism alone, the Indian commissioner declared, would fail: "When I look over the field, I believe it to be simply impossible, morally impossible, for this Government, unaided, to furnish that kind of an agent which is required. This cannot be done without some such cooperation from . . . the Christian bodies of this country."[16] Smith paid no heed to warnings from the *Independent*, which thought that having the churches collaborating with government in the Peace Policy created unnecessary evils and violated cherished principles of American freedom.[17]

Such criticism as the *Independent*'s was infrequent until after 1876. In that year, during a long debate in Congress over whether to transfer the Indian Office to the War Department, Representative Martin Townsend of New York demanded an end to "clerical control of the government." Townsend warned of men like Hildebrand, Wolsey, and Richelieu rising to power in the United States. Two years later the Hayes administration informed the churches that the Indian Office could no longer support missions.[18] After 1878 legal attacks on the Peace Policy grew sharper as both the House and Senate committees on Indian affairs viewed the Policy as a clear violation of the Constitution and complained of religion becoming entangled in the "meshes of state policy." On the floor of Congress, Representative Alfred Scales of North Carolina described the Peace Policy as a malignant growth that violated religious liberty and rendered the federal government a paymaster of churches. Citing the Constitution, Texas Senator Sam Maxey proclaimed that church domination of the Indian Bureau made men hypocrites and produced weak agents. Henry Teller, a senator from Colorado who would soon become secretary of the interior, nodded in agreement.[19]

Outside of Congress tension also mounted. Richard Dodge assailed the religious selection of agents as unconstitutional, discriminatory, ridiculous, and absurd. When William Tecumseh Sherman in 1876 argued for an end to religious monopolies, the editor of the *New York Tribune* supported the general with a sarcastic column about the return of Official Religion.[20] In an especially emotional onslaught, former agent John Ayers complained in a pamphlet that he had been pressured to join the Presbyterian church in New Mexico. The Peace Policy, Ayers wrote, made dogma a test for public office and allowed "fanatics . . . designing men . . . and unscrupulous votaries" such as John Lowrie to worm into government. The Indian Office, Ayers exclaimed, told whites, Indians, and Mexicans that the United States would totally ignore them unless they renounced their faith, accepted predestination, "and in short, became a Presbyterian. Good God!"

> The Presbyterian body [is] simply fattening on Government pap, and enjoying a monopoly of its patronage, while scarcely a murmur is uttered in any quarter, unless, mayhap, by some ill-advised Catholic, who is at once utterly overwhelmed and snuffed out of existence by the righteous indignation of sleek, pampered Presbyterians and their loud-mouthed organs. Friends and fellow citizens . . . give the Presbyterian no more show than the Jesuit, but give each what he is fairly entitled to *under the Constitution,* and no more.[21]

As criticism increased in the press and in Congress, and as Catholics became more aggressive, a number of Protestants began to endorse Ayers's sentiments. At the 1881 Board of Indian Commissioners conference, American Board representative John Means pushed for radical separation. When he asked "Father" Wilbur to distinguish between his civil and clerical roles at Yakima, Wilbur spoke of a "double position" but saw no conflict in serving as a missionary and as an Indian agent at the same time.

DR. MEANS: Suppose your principal responsibility centered beyond the seas, and you wrote "S.J." after your name, and you were a government agent, and that all the agents were in such a position, do you think there would be any risk to the government or the Indian?

AGENT WILBUR: I do not know.

John Means then forced Wilbur to admit that the dual role provided much more power than any agent or a missionary alone possessed.[22]

In July of 1882, after Dr. John Reid had written his letter requesting Methodist appointments in Oregon and Michigan, Secretary of the Interior Henry Teller officially halted the Peace Policy. Allowing any additional religious appointments, Teller concluded, would be an abdication of responsibility and would create a system in which federal employees owed allegiance to churches and church policy instead of to the federal government. In so reasoning, Teller assumed that the government should be autonomous in employment and spending, that religious institutions ultimately act in their own best interests, and that the interests of the United States and the Christian churches were not necessarily identical. After receiving Teller's reply, Reid explained the new government policy to Oregon Methodists and then uttered one of the most remarkable statements of the entire period: loss of the agencies would not harm missions, he said, "[for] upon a moment's reflection, you will perceive that the peace policy has no relation at all to the spiritual and religious interests of the Indians. The Government could not, in any way, be cognizant of religious matters."[23]

Many Protestants would have added to Reid's comments that the Church likewise should not be cognizant of politics. Although some religious periodicals gave considerable space to political scandal and reform in the 1870s, religious quietism and a belief that words constituted action constantly overshadowed Protestant concerns for society. The First Amendment provided a simple rationalization for those who thought religious liberty meant that the Church should not speak out on civic affairs. *Harper's Weekly* accused clergymen of violating separation of Church and State when a group of New York ministers petitioned Grant to reform the Customs House. After Baptists and Methodists supported a political candidate in Massachusetts, the same magazine warned that the Christian ministry must be entirely divorced from politics. In 1876, when Bishop Gilbert Haven asked fellow Methodists to support Grant for a third term, the *Independent* feigned shock and *Harper's* attacked Haven for acting like a pope. The First Amendment, one Unitarian said, made it un-American to mix religion and politics except in one's private meditations. Enhancing this moral quietism was a desire for personal purity and a distrust of power, attitudes that partially explain why, to cite a notable example, Felix Brunot refused the responsibility of being commissioner of Indian affairs despite pleas from Jacob Cox, Bishop Whipple, William Welsh, and Grant.[24]

The Peace Policy forced Protestants to confront political problems in a religious context and thus made many persons uneasy. "A Quaker is very much out of place in Washington," wrote one correspondent; "their smooth, clean, pure faces, look strange upon our dirty streets." Many Friends thought so too. Benjamin Hallowell considered politics alien to the piety and practice of religion, and the Society itself traditionally discouraged acceptance of public office.[25] Other organizations such as the American Missionary Association entered the Peace Policy with high hopes, then veered away from political demands and gradually withdrew from responsibility. In 1881 the Association sullenly reflected on the "infelicities" of government business: "We have no wish to discuss the subject, nor to press upon the Administration . . . the continuance of the Peace Policy."[26]

A man who did advocate church involvement in politics was William Welsh. Welsh knew that Protestants had to overcome contractors, railroads, spoilsmen, rings, and corruption in and out of Congress if the Peace Policy were to succeed. He and Henry Whipple cautioned the Friends not to trust anyone in Washington and both men understood political infighting. Other Episcopalians were less comfortable. After Welsh's attacks on Ely Parker and E. P. Smith, the *Churchman* warned that worldly affairs, "caucuses, wire-pulling and political trickery" defiled the church.[27]

Episcopal disagreement over political action reached its climax two years after Welsh's death. At Henry Whipple's suggestion, the House of Bishops asked for a special committee to lobby for Indian civil rights. At the church's 1880 General Convention, U.S. Senator Robert Withers of Virginia objected to activism in Indian affairs. Episcopal interference with Congress, he argued, had violated separation of Church and State and had involved the clergy in temporal affairs beyond their competence. Felix Brunot's pastor answered Withers by saying that the Church must respond to society and that unless

Christians acted on their ideals, Christianity would remain ineffectual. Another clergyman supported Whipple's plan by labeling as absurd any equation of lobbying with a state church. He declared that Withers did not want separation, but a mindless, silent estrangement from the state, in which false purity and asceticism required the Christian Church to "kneel in her high places and offer up her prayers for Congress without descending, for fear of defilement, into the valley of Sodom." Withers, undismayed by this opposition, contended that lobbying was not the same as moral preaching, that the Episcopal church had always avoided "allusions to politics," and that Bishop Whipple's lobbying proposal was a radical departure from tradition. After a luncheon recess, Withers returned with support from a Kentucky priest, who said that Christians as individuals might be politicians, but the Church itself had no right to meddle directly or indirectly in government: legislators must legislate and the Church must preach the gospel. A layman declared that only the cure of souls concerned the Christian faith and anything else violated the U.S. Constitution. At this point Columbus Delano rose to inform the convention that Episcopalians had not only influenced but controlled the Indian Service, and if that violated the Constitution, then they had steadily violated it for an entire decade. Kentucky senator John Stevenson agreed that the Peace Policy's "glorious fruits" proved Withers's fears groundless. The General Convention passed Whipple's resolution seventy-one to thirteen.[28]

Other churches at times struggled to move beyond quietism. The Malheur Indian agent told Disciples that missions and Sunday donations were worthless as long as politicians despoiled the Indians. A Dutch Reformed spokesman, boasting that his church could remove any New York congressman at will, urged other denominations to apply similar pressure. E. P. Smith informed his American Missionary Association that lobbying was essential, and even some Quakers came to acknowledge that political activism must undergird moral reform.[29] Stephen Riggs tried to convince the American Board that Episcopal success had resulted from effective political pressure which gained contracts, appointments, and preference. The Dakota missionaries of the American Board suggested copying the Episcopalian example by placing a permanent secretary in Washington, D.C. "Nothing," Riggs complained, "comes in Washington without *personal persistence* in applying, reiterating, pressing and in fact worrying through. . . . Everything has weight in Washington according to its *political importance*." Riggs's ideas met a cool reception in the Boston offices; the board's official unconcern for politics was best expressed in the title of an 1877 *Missionary Herald* article on the Sioux: "The Indian Problem Solving Itself."[30]

At the annual Board of Indian Commissioners conferences with the churches, only John Lowrie seemed to grasp political realities. He told the

1879 meeting that merely to denounce politicians gained nothing, and that to fling moral platitudes at men in public office, men required to weigh conflicts and make complex decisions, was unfair. Lowrie reminded his colleagues of their Christian duty to understand politicians as well as Indians. Faced at this point with discontinuing the Peace Policy or making political concessions, the majority rejected Lowrie's advice and joined with the American Missionary Association's M. E. Strieby, who contended that a "mixed affair" was morally impossible: "It must be either one thing or the other—either . . . take it out of the hands of the politicians . . . or the nominating boards will as a body retire. . . . Either the country does want this Indian policy to be carried on . . . or it does not. Our religious societies do not want to be mixed up with a thing that is partly clay and partly iron."[31]

Human affairs, unfortunately, are usually mixed with clay and iron, plus many other impurities. Effective reform required working with all elements. It also required organization and persistence. Failing to realize this, Protestants increasingly remained silent or substituted proclamations and conferences for action. Joseph of the Nez Perces knew what that meant:

> I have heard talk and talk, but nothing is done. Good words do not last long unless they amount to something. Words do not pay for my dead people. They do not pay for my country. . . . Good words will not give me back my children. Good words will not make good the promise of your War Chief General Miles. Good words will not give my people good health and stop them from dying. Good words will not get my people a home. . . . I am tired of talk that comes to nothing.[32]

The Grant Peace Policy replaced the spoils system with church patronage, provided federal support for sectarian missions and worship, violated the constitutional ban against religious tests for public office and, perhaps most serious of its legal transgressions, denied religious liberty as guaranteed by the First Amendment.

Religious tests for federal office holding were an obvious part of the Peace Policy. Hicksite Friends quarreled over whether they should hire competent persons regardless of religion, or whether they ought to restrict all positions to Quakers. Osage agent Isaac Gibson fired any employee who drank, swore, fought, played poker, or did not attend Sunday school. In Oregon and Montana, the Methodists insisted that all agency employees must be professing Christians.[33] Despite a few isolated complaints, these requirements caused little controversy during the 1870s. What did bring turmoil was the assumption that the federal government guaranteed to each denomination a restrictive and exclusive right to control access to Indian reservations—the right to deny religious liberty. This problem first arose when Protestants excluded

Roman Catholics; it was not resolved until Roman Catholics began to exclude Protestants.

Prior to the Peace Policy the government had at times allowed a single church's missionaries to occupy a reservation to the exclusion of other denominations. In 1866, for example, the Indian Office refused to permit Lake Superior Chippewas to build a Catholic chapel because they were already served by a Methodist mission. In 1869, at the beginning of the Peace Policy, Commissioner Ely Parker firmly established the occupancy rights of earlier missionaries and did not mention the status of new missions. Nevertheless, Hicksite Friends warned their first agents to avoid conflict at all costs, never to criticize other denominations on a reservation, and to *"let them entirely alone."*[34]

What little trouble arose during these first years was easily contained. Unitarian Jebez Neversink Trask argued that Indians should be afforded a wide choice of denominations. Episcopalians clashed briefly with the American Board, and Quakers with Presbyterians. Otherwise conflict among Protestants was negligible. Jonathan Richards and Lawrie Tatum informed all missionaries on their reservations that the Friends had no desire to monopolize the Wichita and Cheyenne tribes. Samuel Janney invited anyone to bring Christianity to Hicksite reservations, and Enoch Hoag praised Catholic missions in Kansas. Methodists, Baptists, Mennonites, Episcopalians, and Presbyterians labored on Quaker reservations, and the Friends happily reported that love for "wretched and afflicted" Indians seemed to reunite Christian hearts. The American Board, Episcopalians, Methodists, and Presbyterians cooperated with the American Missionary Association in Wisconsin. Baptist agents in Indian Territory aided Episcopalians, Methodists, northern Presbyterians, and Moravians. Presbyterians and Congregationalists pursued their missions at Episcopal agencies, and at the Catholic Colville agency, Henry Harmon Spalding in 1874 claimed 253 Protestant converts.[35]

The spirit of toleration often became more strained whenever Protestants and Catholics had to work together. The Friends reprimanded their agent Isaac Gibson for anti-Catholic sectarianism; Gibson responded by advising the Osage to send their children to Catholic schools and by allowing priests to use the agency chapel. Sisseton and Wahpeton Sioux in Minnesota complained that Jared Daniels discriminated against Catholics. The newly organized Catholic Bureau of Indian Missions filed similar complaints and besieged the government with accounts of abuse in Washington, Oregon, Idaho, Montana, California, and the Southwest.[36] By 1872 Father Pierre DeSmet and the Catholic Bureau had begun to openly protest their expulsion from Protestant reservations. Both the words and deeds of various Protestants gave substance to their accusations. Several Congregational Indian agents deliberately ignored Indian requests for priests, and a Presbyterian in

Wisconsin, after successfully proselytizing five Catholics, spoke of priests as an evil and a cause of factionalism on his reservation. Inspectors from the Board of Indian Commissioners and the Bureau of Indian Affairs would recommend protection for Indians from Catholic intrusions onto the assigned reservations. After further conflict at the Yakima, White Earth, Lapwai agencies, and among the Pueblos, exclusion of competing denominations became official government policy in 1874.[37]

No church more strongly believed in such exclusion than the Methodists. At Fort Peck they did nothing to promote Indian education for ten years, yet the threat of a Roman Catholic school in 1880 prompted immediate action. In Oregon, the Methodist conference stated that since agencies actually were missions, all whites on Methodist reservations had to be Methodist. A bitter conflict occurred at Round Valley, California, where a Methodist agent was accused of arresting and flogging a priest named Father Osuna. After inspector William Vandever condemned Osuna as an "enthusiast or lunatic" who annoyed the agent, the Indian Office prohibited further Catholic services at Round Valley. Vandever also reported, "The patent fact [is] that there can be no coalescence of Catholics and protestants on the same reservation."[38]

Yakima's James Wilbur firmly endorsed and implemented anti-Catholic plans. Wilbur blamed the Catholics for Marcus Whitman's massacre in 1847 and he had tried to ban priests from the Yakima reservation before the Peace Policy began. Wilbur's army replacement in 1869 reported that three of every four Yakimas were Catholic and that Wilbur as agent had grossly discriminated against them in distributing food and supplies.[39] After he regained control, Wilbur again excluded priests from Yakima because they made the tribe "feverish and dissatisfied." The minister-agent also tried to prevent Indians from worshipping at the St. Joseph mission, a Roman Catholic chapel off the reservation. When the Catholic bishop of Nisqually secured government permission to build a new chapel on the Yakima reserve, Wilbur and Washington superintendent Robert Milroy protested to the Indian Office that the ruling violated a Peace Policy agreement that gave each church complete jurisdiction over agencies assigned to it. Wilbur said that this included the right to shut out other churches, "most of all" Roman Catholics. Milroy cited the 1855 Yakima treaty, which required the agent's permission before any white man could enter the reservation. These arguments convinced Secretary Delano, who then rescinded permission for the chapel. Repeated Catholic demands were rejected because, the federal government maintained, Yakima was a Methodist agency.[40]

Protestant-Catholic relations at the White Earth and Pueblo agencies involved similar sectarianism and became even more complicated. No one questioned the effective Catholic presence on the White Earth reservation. Indeed, the Board of Indian Commissioners in this instance contradicted the

Indian Office by ruling that agency assignments did not imply a religious monopoly and that Indians could receive any mission group they desired. Problems arose when the White Earth agent and Bishop Whipple charged that a Catholic priest named Tomazine was attempting to disrupt the agency school and incite rebellion. The ensuing struggle, which included Tomazine's military arrest in a church, nearly drove Whipple to despair.[41]

In the Southwest, Protestant agents to the Pueblos had to contend with a long, complex Catholic tradition. Presbyterian agents and teachers were accused by the Roman church of insulting the Catholic faith and of forcing Protestant creeds on helpless Indians. The Presbyterians declared that two hundred years of Catholic influence had left Pueblo heathenism untouched, and Protestants branded Catholic priests as malicious, cunning liars. The "Romanish Church . . . breathing out annihilation" wanted the Indians suppressed as deluded and superstitious slaves under a "brainless, cringing Mexican agent." At Laguna Pueblo in New Mexico the struggle for power between Catholic bishop Jean Lamy and Presbyterian missionaries eventually resulted in violence.[42] Compounding these difficulties were language barriers, conflicts between Mexicans, Indians, and whites, conflicts between American and Mexican priests, and conflicts between the U.S. army and civilians. In the Southwest, no one admired the Indian Office, and there was a perennial Protestant-Catholic-secular battle over all public schools in Arizona and New Mexico.[43]

Presbyterian agents in the Pacific Northwest also stumbled against the Catholic problem. Smarting over the Lapwai agency's unfair transfer in 1870, Roman Catholics were determined to establish schools and missions on the Nez Perce reservation. In 1873 agent John Monteith denied the Catholics permission to use the agency school or to build a chapel. Missionary Joseph Cataldo then conducted open-air services. Under pressure from Henry Spalding and the Reverend A. L. Lindsley of the Portland Presbytery, Monteith requested permission to expel Cataldo in order to protect Nez Perce "morals." E. P. Smith replied that this would be an abuse of government power. If Indians wanted Catholic priests, the commissioner warned Monteith, "it is not in accordance with *public policy* or the spirit of religious toleration to forbid or hinder such services in any way."[44] Smith's reply, together with attacks against him in the local press, angered Monteith, who insisted that he opposed equally the Jesuits and the Methodist revivalists who disrupted Indian farming. In Portland, Lindsley and Wilbur vehemently denounced both Monteith and the Indian Office. If an agent allowed "popish priests" on the Nez Perce reserve, Lindsley fumed, it would mean that any missionary could enter any reservation. E. P. Smith's betrayal was "manifest political bidding for cheap popularity with the press and papists" that would embolden Catholics to build even more churches—a fatal stab at the Peace Policy. "Rome," said Lindsley, "is utterly & intolerably unscrupulous."[45]

Monteith eventually came to agree that a Catholic threat made religious monopoly necessary, and he was supported by an 1874 Interior Department ruling that granted exclusionary rights to the denomination in charge of each reservation. In November of 1875 Monteith halted construction of a Jesuit school near the agency. Two years later he reported that Catholics were still "straining every nerve and exerting themselves to break into our ranks." The priests, he told Lowrie, taught Indians to lie: "I would rather see an Indian remain in his native religion than join the Catholics."[46]

Even though the Indian Office did allow Roman Catholics to maintain a church and rectory on the Nez Perce reservation, it never clearly defined the limits of religious liberty. Columbus Delano wrote an ambiguous statement about the Round Valley controversy in which he asserted that Indians enjoyed complete freedom to attend any church they wished, but agents had the duty to expel sects that caused discord. The same confused thinking was apparent when the Red Cloud Commission asked E. P. Smith if the Peace Policy guaranteed exclusive control. Smith answered that it did not, though the assigned churches did have "possession" of their reservations.[47]

Dissatisfaction with such evasive answers increased after 1875. Violation of religious liberty, for instance, provided an excellent target for congressmen seeking to transfer Indians to army control. The transfer bills usually required religious freedom for all denominations on Indian land. Congressional supporters of army control quoted E. P. Smith to prove that the churches had religious monopolies and that this interfered with a missionary's divine duty to go wherever the Gospel called. A representative from Oregon asserted that even Indians must be allowed freedom of conscience.[48] Failure of the army transfer bills did not end the debate. The *Catholic World* continued to protest that the Peace Policy's "sectarian fanaticism, Protestant bigotry, and anti-Christian hatred" violated America's principles of "absolute freedom." In 1878 Representative Alfred Scales introduced a bill providing complete freedom of religion on Indian reservations. Opposed by Protestants, Scales's bill died in a House committee but was reintroduced before each Congress until the end of the Peace Policy.[49]

Conflicts on the reservations continued as the decade of the seventies drew to a close. Orthodox Friends evicted a Baptist missionary from the Wichita agency and opposed a Mormon mission at the Kiowa-Comanche agency. In northern Montana, Methodist opposition to Catholic missions and the banishment of priests from the Blackfeet reserve began during the Peace Policy and continued into the 1880s.[50] The Green Bay agent rebuked and threatened a Catholic mission, while Episcopalians sought some means to stop Catholic "interloping" at the Sioux agencies.[51] Bishop William Hare learned that Chief

Spotted Tail, having "gotten a R.C. maggot in, or on, the brain," wanted Black Robes. When Father Meinrad McCarthy was expelled from Pine Ridge by Episcopal agent V. T. McGillycuddy, the Indian Office once again backed the agent. William Welsh considered such practices unwise, but other Episcopalians argued against open reservations and "the baneful picture of contending Christians . . . the warfare of jarring creeds . . . shattering and scattering Christianity." According to Nebraska's Bishop Robert Harper Clarkson, "one minister of God saying 'Lo, Christ is here' and another saying to the very same Indians, 'No, Christ is there,'" would bewilder the Sioux and produce the impression that Christians were not united. Asked if the church could avoid this liability in a free land, Clarkson scoffed that silly talk about Church and State need not scare or repel anyone: "Now I do not think it would be an infringement on the rights of a free Church in a free State, for the Government to say to these same religious bodies: 'Keep away from all other Indian tribes.' [Applause] I hold that the Government has precisely the same right in the premises as the policeman against the peace-breaker."[52]

The problem of religious liberty came before the public in March of 1879, when the *New York Tribune* printed a letter from William Tecumseh Sherman. Only the rivalry and diversity of different faiths, Sherman said, could stimulate genuine religious activity, and this could only happen on Indian reservations under army control. The *Independent* responded that Sherman failed to realize that Indians were "infants in law" and needed protection from religious controversy. While admitting that protection meant government control of religion, the *Independent*'s editor felt it was unavoidable, a necessary condition of wardship—"they are taken care of as children." The *Baptist Watchman* warned Sherman that priests at Yakima "tend to insurrection and bloodshed," and that Catholics opposing exclusion did so because "the Protestant drives out the Romish priests, and uses the civil power to compel his silence. Is this wrong? At first glance it seems to be an outrage. But a little thought will suggest that it may be an actual necessity."[53] At the same time, and unknown to the *Watchman* and the *Independent*, the American Board of Commissioners for Foreign Missions was preparing a missionary invasion of the Catholic agency at Devil's Lake. The encounter there would give Protestants another opportunity to decide whether government restrictions on religious liberty were an outrage or an actual necessity.

Early in the Peace Policy the Riggs family urged the American Board to use its influence in Congress to secure appointments at the Devil's Lake agency. When this appeal failed, the missionaries continued to ask the board to support expansion of the Dakota mission. In 1874 the board's office in Boston denied the missionaries' request to enter the Standing Rock Reservation, but when the Catholic agent reported that the Sioux could never become

Christians, the Riggs group sent native convert David Greycloud to Standing Rock. At first he was welcomed. Then a new agent arrived who said that Greycloud must obtain permission from the resident Catholic priest if he were to remain. The priest refused and Greycloud returned to Cheyenne River. During the next winter the Standing Rock agent ordered all Protestant missionaries to leave. This disturbed the board in Boston, yet it did nothing and let the matter drop. Four years later the board's missionaries in Dakota again appealed for help in breaking down reservation barriers. Although the board itself still did not act, its Indian committee responded that any denial of complete religious freedom was regrettable.[54] With this encouragement, the Riggs family decided to expand its work to Fort Peck, Rosebud, Pine Ridge, Standing Rock, and Devil's Lake.[55]

At Devil's Lake, five nuns staffed an Indian hospital and two Benedictine fathers preached daily in the vernacular, taught confirmation classes, and conducted three Sabbath services. Catholic agent James McLaughlin felt that the religious life of his agency was in good hands; even so he had welcomed Protestant Daniel Renville in 1878, and in 1879 he asked the Indian Office if he could issue government rations to Protestant missionaries. Commissioner of Indian Affairs Ezra Hayt informed McLaughlin and the Riggses that mixing denominations was against federal regulations and that the Protestants must leave.[56]

In an abrupt letter that served only to irritate Secretary of the Interior Carl Schurz, the Riggs family demanded that Hayt's ruling be voided as unconstitutional. Their Presbyterian friend, John Williamson, asked John Lowrie to support the protest and to defend the First Amendment. Lowrie seemed to agree, and this time the American Board also decided to aid its Indian missionaries. In May of 1880 the Indian Office, now administered by R. E. Trowbridge after Hayt had departed in a flurry of scandal, polled the mission boards regarding exclusionary rights to reservations. Two (including Lowrie) declined to commit themselves, one opposed all restrictions, and six gave their "unqualified approval" to Hayt's restrictive ruling. Trowbridge and Schurz, considering this a confirmation of government policy, reiterated that Protestants must leave Devil's Lake.[57]

It dumbfounded the Riggses to learn that other Protestants, especially Presbyterians and the American Missionary Association, had not supported them against the "missionary monopoly rule [which] crept in like Satan into Eden." Determined to take their cause before the nation, the Riggses professed even greater shock when they learned of opposition within the American Board itself and the Congregational church. The *Missionary Herald*'s editor said that in attacking the government the Dakota missionaries cast blame in the wrong direction—the truly guilty parties were the Riggses themselves, the American Board, and any Protestant who had agreed to the Peace

Policy in the first place. American Board secretary N. G. Clark, aware that the board desired Indian school contracts, cautioned the Riggs family and deplored any public turmoil that might embarrass the Hayes administration. A final jolt came from a national committee of the Congregational church. Originally appointed to support the Riggses, it arrived at the opposite conclusion and supported closed reservations. In a memorial to Congress the Congregational church declared that since Indians were not citizens and could not own individual property, the tribes were unprepared for religious freedom.[58]

It would require more than committees and memorials, however, to deflect Alfred, Stephen, and Thomas Riggs. The Dakota missionaries had no intention of being cautious and were hardly concerned about embarrassing the national government, their own board, or the Congregational church. In an act of civil and ecclesiastical disobedience, they ordered Daniel Renville and Charles Lemon Hall back to Devil's Lake. Venerable Stephen Riggs published an article in the *Missionary Herald* assaulting the Peace Policy for its failure to produce agents and for building *"a wall of exclusion"* that allowed some churches to "stand as the dog-in-the-manger, to keep everybody else out of their *patch*." Such a policy, he said, must end.[59] His arrow hit the target.

At the Board of Indian Commissioners conference in January of 1881 the American Board's J. O. Means submitted a formal protest against all restrictions. This time the Presbyterians stood firm and presented a General Assembly memorial demanding religious liberty for Indians. In the debate that followed, Quakers, Methodists, and the American Missionary Association fought to retain closed reservations. The Friends observed that a tolerance policy in Indian Territory had produced denominational conflict and backbiting. Means answered that although the American Board disliked Roman Catholic missions, the Catholics had equal rights with other churches. Methodist John Reid disagreed, vowing that as soon as Catholics officially entered Yakima, the Methodist church would leave. Reid observed that Indians cleverly played competing churches against each other, and he pointed out that there were enough Indian reservations for everyone. Christians practiced comity abroad, Reid argued, and with American Indians "in a state of pupilage [they] have not the same rights as us." The Methodist secretary also reminded the board that exclusion always had been the Methodist position because, under the Peace Policy, an agency was assigned to a church "with a view to its working there and covering it with education and religious influence." M. E. Strieby of the American Missionary Association said that Indians were wards of the government needing special protection. One member of the Board of Indian Commissioners announced that the first church to reach a reservation had "squatter rights." Means answered that the American Board really preferred voluntary comity agreements and only opposed control by the government. Supported by Board of Indian Commissioners chairman Clinton Fisk, who was a Methodist, and by John Lowrie, Means won the debate and the conference passed a resolution favoring open reservations.[60]

A week later the Board of Indian Commissioners informed the American Board in Boston that Secretary Schurz would remove all restrictions if the churches agreed. Means quickly composed a letter endorsing religious freedom for missionaries and circulated it to thirteen mission boards. The Presbyterians, Baptists, American Missionary Association, Episcopalians, Unitarians, Lutherans, and Orthodox and Hicksite Friends signed within two weeks. The Catholics, United Presbyterians, Methodists, and Disciples did not reply.[61] On February 15, 1881, Means wrote to Alfred Riggs that Schurz had revoked the "obnoxious ruling of Com. Hayt." In March the Indian Office issued a formal confirmation: "In the future, in all cases except where the presence of rival religious organizations would manifestly be perilous to peace and good order, Indian reservations shall be open to all religious denominations providing that no existing treaty stipulations would be violated thereby."[62] Presbyterians immediately made plans to enter Standing Rock. Their Sioux missionaries rejoiced: "Religious liberty is now the law for Indian reservations as well as the rest of the country."[63]

Ideals, theories, and principles conflicted with practical needs in the contest over religious liberty. Opponents of open reservations correctly pointed out that many Indians had no missions at all, and they knew from experience that Christian competition could cause more religious harm than the violation of abstract doctrines of liberty. Insofar as constitutional principles of disestablishment were concerned, even the American Board was competing for federal funds to operate its Dakota schools.[64]

As the Methodists predicted, the new ruling brought religious diversity to the Indians. The results were varied. At the Cheyenne-Arapaho agency, Friends, Mennonites, and Episcopalians considered one another brothers in Christ and reported themselves to be "so full of cheery Christian feeling." But while eighteen reservations enjoyed two or more denominations, thirty-five still had no missions by 1886. True to their word, Methodists dropped virtually all Indian work; nine of their agencies were without a missionary within five years.[65]

The wrongs that people fail to protest are often more significant than those that they do protest. Throughout the debate on open reservations, no one mentioned the exclusion of Jews and Mormons from the Peace Policy. Jewish leaders did secure one appointment in 1870. The Mormons were never considered. A Mormon attempt to reach the Navajos had been opposed by the Presbyterians, and in 1877 a Mormon request to establish a Kiowa mission was rejected by the Quakers and the Bureau of Indian Affairs.[66] Likewise, the noisy battle for religious liberty was a battle for the white man's rights, not the Indian's. Few Americans of the period believed that the First Amendment protected non-Christian "heathen" ideas and practices. Humanitarian reformers differed little from the most orthodox clergy in their lack of comprehension of and tolerance for native religions.[67] When the Society of Friends spoke of religious freedom, it was freedom "to reclaim [Indians] from a debasing paganism," not freedom and tolerance for that so-called paganism. The *Catholic World* could attack Protestant bigotry and call for absolute freedom of conscience, yet it too neglected to extend this liberty to potlatches, kiva ceremonies, sun dances, grass dances, or Smohalla's dreamers.

Instances of a relentless Anglo-Saxon prejudice against native American religion are legion throughout the Peace Policy. William Welsh said that Indian customs must be destroyed "by those whom the Indians [would] recognize as their true friends." When a peace delegation to the Nez Perces learned that Indian unrest in the Pacific Northwest was caused by a "new fangled religious delusion," the commissioners recommended repression of all native beliefs. In Washington Territory the superintendent of Indian affairs set the destruction of native customs as his first goal. Aiding him was the Reverend Elkanah Gibson, who labored to "obliterate . . . vague ideas of morality and religion" by forcing the Makahs to plow their salt marshes. Baptist Calvin Bateman at Utah's Pyramid Lake ridiculed Shoshone beliefs as a farce and their religious dances as a "great fandango." Few Quakers expressed any tolerance for Indian faith; instead most agreed with Santee agent Joseph Walker, who opposed use of the vernacular because it preserved Indian customs and so-called superstitions.[68] The religious agents and the missionaries were not alone in such sentiments. When Lieutenant J. H. Hays attempted to suppress Indian religion at Neah Bay he considered it impossible to reason with the Indians: "I have found that ridicule, to which they are exceedingly sensitive . . . was much more efficacious." Several exponents of army control described Indian religion as a vulgar polytheism and they recommended that medicine men be ruthlessly crushed. Roman Catholic agents reported banning "orgies [which] call up memories of past prowess."[69]

The identification of contemporary culture—the gilded age—with the Christian religion accounted for a portion of the intolerance. It was not an ascetic era that looked to St. Francis as a patron saint. For many Protestants wealth, comfort, health, neatness, and personal hygiene seemed essential to the gospel. Calvin Bateman happily reported that a "marked desire to be clad" demonstrated Shoshone progress in the true faith. A teacher in Oklahoma who denounced Indian dancing and sorcery as completely incompatible with Jesus Christ also complained that native Creek preachers taught the people two heresies: that private property was evil, and "that the kingdom of heaven is for the poor." Myron Eells wanted to eradicate Indian religion at Skokomish, especially the potlatch ceremony, in which wealthy chiefs gained social status by giving away their possessions. Potlatching, Eells observed, required Indians to "deny themselves so much for years, to live in old houses and in so poor a way, that the self-denial becomes an enemy to health, comfort, civilization, and Christianity."[70]

Yet the gilded age had its cultural heretics, and during the 1870s several men did consider unassimilated Indians as equal human beings. Methodist agent H. J. Armstrong, born and raised among the Crows, argued that Indians had a God-given and constitutional right to worship as they pleased. J. O. Means advised the Board of Indian Commissioners conference of 1880 that Christians had no business forcing their doctrine on others. Bishop William Hare appreciated several aspects of Sioux religion, and Jared Daniels pursued a lifelong interest in native worship and ritual.[71] A few Christians realized that the destruction of native ways not only broke men and women's spirits but could also weaken missions. In 1881 John Williamson noticed that as native ceremonies declined on the Yankton reserve, so did his own accomplishments, for without competition "the devil lulls the Christian to carelessness."

In 1669 John Locke drafted a constitution for the colony of Carolina. In it he guaranteed religious freedom for "the natives of that place . . . utterly strangers to Christianity, whose idolatry, ignorance, or mistake gives us no right to expel or use them ill." Almost three hundred years later an order from the United States Government, Bureau of Indian Affairs, read: "No interference with Indian religious life or ceremonial expression will hereafter be tolerated. . . . The fullest constitutional liberty, in all matters affecting religion, conscience, and culture, is insisted on for all Indians."

Between 1669 and 1934 white Americans practiced an almost unrelieved history of repression and intolerance toward American Indian religions. Bigotry and intolerance breed the same, and no one should have been surprised when Ely Parker wrote that the misery of his people resulted not from their tribal customs, their religion, or their race,

> but solely, wholly and absolutely from the unchristian treatment they have always received from Christian white people who speak the English language, who read the English Bible, and who are pharisaically divested of all the elements of vice and barbarism. The tenacity with which the remnants of this people have adhered to their tribal organizations and religious traditions is all that has saved them thus far from inevitable extinguishment; when they abandon their birthright for a mess of Christian pottage they will then cease to be a distinctive people.[72]

Chief Joseph demanded the same thing: "Let me be a free man—free to travel, free to stop, free to work, free to trade where I choose, free to choose my own teachers, free to follow the religion of my fathers."

10. Termination of the Peace Policy

On March 4, 1873, a late winter storm blew into the nation's capital from the northwest. Thermometers touched four degrees at sunrise, barely creeping up to twenty degrees by the time Ulysses S. Grant took his oath of office shortly after noon. Raw freezing winds from the west obliterated the president's voice as he delivered his second inaugural address. In it Grant denounced wars of Indian extermination and insisted that the United States must provide its native people with education and fair treatment if the nation were to stand before the world with a clear conscience. Grant, in 1873, promised that the Peace Policy would continue.

The Peace Policy labored on for nine more years after 1873, including the five years following Grant's retirement from office. They were years of decline and faltering reform as Grant's second term in office degenerated into a national scandal and as pressures against Indian reform grew in magnitude and intensity. The later years of the Policy witnessed the gold rush into the Black Hills and Custer's disaster on the Little Big Horn; they saw national embarrassments over the forced removal of the Poncas, a shameful war against a long-time United States ally, the Nez Perces, and an uprising in which the Colorado Utes killed their agent, the nominal Unitarian appointee Nathan Meeker. Half a dozen other major Indian wars marred the last half of the Peace Policy as well. Working against the idealism of 1869 were military pressure for control of the Office of Indian Affairs, frontier desire for cattle ranges, and petty bickering among the churches. The election of 1876 brought in a poorly informed president, an antagonistic secretary of the interior, and an arrogant commissioner of Indian affairs recruited from the former ranks of the Board of Indian Commissioners. As patronage pressures increased under the Hayes and Arthur administrations, exhausted and jealous mission boards withdrew one by one from the remarkable policy that Grant had started. The Peace Policy, the *Independent* had predicted in 1875, would eventually cause "sectarian jealousy [and] those who believe with us in the utter separation of church and state do not feel . . . that it will be long-continued."[1] Yet when the Policy did end in 1882, the reason was not because it harmed the Republic by undercutting the principle of Church-State separation. The Peace Policy died because it had become a political liability and had not accomplished the impossible reform goal established for it: a swift and painless conversion of North American natives into United States citizens.

Between 1876 and 1882 the series of Indian wars and tribal removals in the West made Grant's policy seem ineffective and, to some, nonexistent. Reformers such as Helen Hunt Jackson deplored white plunder and Indian suffering as if there were no Peace Policy. Most distressing was the forced removal of the peaceful Ponca Indians from Nebraska, a national scandal that embarrassed the leaders of the Episcopal church as well as the new secretary of the interior, Carl Schurz. When Jackson wrote her *Century of Dishonor*, it would include the seventies.

Widespread opposition to the Peace Policy had grown steadily since Grant's reelection in 1872. The 1874 mass resignation of the original Board of Indian Commissioners coupled with pervasive scandals in other departments during Grant's second term had alarmed reformers such as Bishop Whipple. Yet when attacks on the president increased, most Indian reformers rallied firmly behind him. After Custer's defeat in 1876, public criticism became intense. The *Nation*, whose opinions on Indian affairs habitually shifted to harmonize with its other political goals, became anti-Grant and the magazine began to attack the Peace Policy as an absurd failure. Editor E. L. Godkin asked why Grant had not surrendered the Treasury Department to the Bible Society and the Post Office to the American Board.[2] Advocates of transferring the Bureau of Indian Affairs to the army fired nearly as many salvos at the Peace Policy as soldiers fired bullets at Indians. General John Pope said that while the morale of Indian agents had improved, otherworldly, naïve, and impractical Christians had caused the tribes to suffer more than ever. A starving Indian, he argued, was unimpressed by theory and Bible lessons from the Church's "well-fed apostles." Other officers attacked the

Policy as "shuffling and perfidious to the last degree" and they ridiculed corrupt agents who "dressed in purple and fine linen and sat high up in the temple of the Lord."[3] Well-informed civilians such as George Manypenny, Lewis H. Morgan, and Francis Parkman began to disparage the Peace Policy, whereas congressmen declared that there never had been so much violence or fraud in Indian affairs as there was under church control. Senator George Vest had only contempt for "cheap philanthropy" and "the northern press and pulpit filled with lecture-room gush and namby-pamby sentiment." Western congressmen defined the Policy as an eastern plot against the development of the frontier.[4] Democrats feared that Grant would seek a third term in 1880 and accused him of being a Napoleon, "a reptile of the most poisonous character . . . a monster more venomous than the tarantula."[5] One tract described Grant as a despot who had murdered the innocent Custer to protect

> Rings of schemers, rouges, and defrauders,
> And many rings for robbing the farmers . . .
> And rings for stealing in the swamp lands,
> And Rings for stealing in school fund bonds,
> Rings for stealing from the poor Indians . . .
> There were rings of trappers and Indian traders,
> And rings to buy up Territorial Legislatures.[6]

Frontier skeptics complained that the president had given patronage to the churches in order to train theological students. To some critics, the Peace Policy, a "very God Moloch," proved the fallacy in the Golden Rule, and in Wyoming and Montana, cattle-owner associations cursed eastern bureaucrats for knowing nothing about conditions in the Far West. Richard Dodge found Christians as greedy as other men, and Richard MacMahon pronounced the Peace Policy a disgrace to the nation.[7]

Churchmen, too, grew dissatisfied with the Policy. John Lowrie experienced no joy in this perplexing work, and Bishop Henry Whipple listened to his friend H. H. Sibley describe how since 1869 Indians had come inexorably closer to extermination. Myron Eells concluded that Christians generally had not responded well. Montana's "Brother Van," the Reverend William Wesley Van Orsdel, told the General Conference of the Methodist church (1880) that the Peace Policy was an evil that obstructed his own work with whites; Van Orsdel made a motion calling for complete withdrawal from the program. Roman Catholics unsparingly attacked the government for its "idiotic policy . . . imbecility and blunders." They castigated the Peace Policy as "a monstrous piece of folly, conceived in the strange brain of President Grant," whom they considered a pawn of the Methodist church.[8]

The more positive opinions seemed faint against the outpouring of church criticism. Since 1870, reformers and government officials alike had resented the hostility and silence in much of the religious press. Church periodicals, E. P. Smith remarked, discredited the government and indulged in "careless sneers" about the Peace Policy. E. E. Whittlesey, a Congregational leader, could think of few denominational publications that supported the reform. One religious paper that did strongly support the Peace Policy was the *Friend's Intelligencer* and in 1876 its writers recommended Grant for a third term. Quaker Gideon Frost said that Grant was the first president to protect Indians, with the result that "almost immediately upon his accession, Indian wars and massacres ceased, or nearly so." A Methodist publication also commended Grant for solving the Indian problem, and in Congress, Representative James Burnie Beck said that no one had helped Indians so much since the Pilgrims, "nay, since Columbus!"[9] After 1875 these voices became weaker and less frequent amid the wars with Sioux, Bannocks, Nez Perces, and Utes.

To survive, the Peace Policy needed dedicated, influential friends to overcome two persistent challenges. The first challenge was a movement for military control of Indian affairs, and the second a political struggle to regain patronage. The Policy survived the first threat; it succumbed to the second.

In February 1876, *Harper's Weekly* reassured its readers that the one trustworthy branch of the United States government was the army, a "proverb of honesty." One month later a scandal involving Secretary of War William W. Belknap excited Washington gossip. *Harper's* threw its hands up in dismay and proclaimed "a national calamity . . . a national shame." The Belknap scandal broke at an unfortunate time for the army generals and their supporters, who were finally approaching success at the end of a twenty-year battle to regain control of the Indian Office.[10] The pro-army or "transfer" movement, stymied when Congress canceled Grant's military assignments in 1870, gained momentum with every agency scandal and every Indian war during the Peace Policy. To its supporters, army control meant that firm, honest military supervision could discipline Indians into citizenship. To many humanitarians, transfer meant surrendering tribes to the mercy of men like Chivington, Sheridan, Baker, and Custer. To the Department of the Interior, it meant losing control of large appropriations. To Congress it meant loss of patronage.[11]

The struggle over military control was nowhere more vicious than on the reservations of the Southwest. It simmered beneath the surface during Vincent Colyer's tour in 1871, became intense with the appointment of the tough and independent Apache agent John P. Clum, and culminated when General George Crook obtained special permission to enter Apache lands without the consent of the Indian Office. Idealism and hatred, bravery and corruption, economics and politics, all combined to create a situation so confusing and unstable as to make humane federal management of the Apaches impossible. Nowhere was the influence of the church so remote, and no church was more bitter toward the army than the Dutch Reformed responsible for Apache agencies.[12] Similar, if less violent, civilian-military struggles occurred elsewhere. At Cheyenne-Arapaho the army unsuccessfully tried for years to discredit John Miles following the Red River War.[13] On the northern plains various Peace Policy agents were incessantly embroiled with military politics, backstabbing, defamation, threats, charges, and counter-charges as the army sought control of the Sioux agencies.[14]

Committee hearings had already convinced some congressmen that Christianity had failed and that religious agents had fallen into all the system's vices. The House Committee on Indian Affairs declared that military control was needed to replace an ailing Peace Policy and to rid the Indian service of "those heartless scoundrels who infest it."[15] A Democratic landslide in 1874 encouraged army hopes for passage of a transfer bill. Felix Brunot and Bishop Whipple were tempted to advocate the change after civilian catastrophes at Red Cloud and White Earth, and in 1876 William Welsh was courted by generals William T. Sherman and John Sanborn. Following a three-day weekend with the new secretary of war, Alphonso Taft, Welsh abruptly turned against the Peace Policy, urged his church to support transfer, and added that he could guarantee the appointment of Episcopal army officers as Indian agents. Despite the growing pressures, Brunot, Whipple, and the president defended civilian control.[16]

Further committee hearings revealed that those who favored army control could be just as vague, idealistic, irrational, evasive, and narrow as proponents of church control. Their arguments were that the army understood Indians; army officers were religious and honorable men; a Methodist agent was an adulterer; the army was frugal; Indians respected soldiers; and civilians were helpless. By a six to five vote the Indian Affairs Committee recommended passage of the transfer bill. Debate in the House began on April 5, 1876, and at issue was the success or failure of Grant's Peace Policy. William Sparks of Illinois referred to agent J. J. Saville as a typical example of how Christians had failed. New York's Samuel Cox responded by citing the Belknap scandal, by playing on fears of militarism, and by blaming every Indian war on the army. Proponents of transfer told of civil bungling, referred to the plight of Lawrie Tatum, condemned corruption at White Earth, and denounced forced removals. Their opponents countered with references to the Sand Creek and Piegan massacres and praised Wilbur's progress at Yakima and the Quakers' progress at Santee. When territorial delegate Orange Jacobs from Seattle said that religious agents in his territory had not stolen a dollar from the government, he was answered with attacks on "disgusting . . . pretended Christian gentlemen . . . high priests of the moral-suasion school" who carried Bibles with the Eighth Commandment stricken. LaFayette Lane of Oregon resented church criticism of the Indian Office, declaring that the Peace Policy humiliated the government and at the same time turned Indians against the Christian faith. So-called Christian agents, Lane charged, canted creeds to obtain agencies in "this humbug management by the church." Omar Conger of Michigan replied that to vote for transfer would be to sneer at Christianity. On April 25 the House voted for transfer, 130–94.[17]

With the transfer bill passed in the House, Episcopal leaders thought the Peace Policy was doomed. Yet the Board of Indian Commissioners, the churches, and pacifist groups rallied to bury the bill in a Senate committee for four years. In 1876 the only floor debate occurred when one senator attached a transfer rider to the Indian appropriations bill. Defeating this amendment, proponents of the Peace Policy argued that Grant's reform had produced the best Indian agents in American history. Other senators said that to vote for an army "crimson with blood" was to vote against the New Testament. Illinois senator John Logan accused army officers of merely seeking personal glory. Such, he said five days before the Seventh Cavalry charged across the Little Big Horn, was their motive in the Black Hills: "Doubtless ere long we shall receive more news perhaps of some brilliant campaign and a splendid victory."[18]

Custer's defeat, the Belknap scandal, and the valiant flight of the Nez Perces added powerful arguments to the antitransfer arsenal and dimmed the army's luster, even though the transfer debate continued until any hope was finally killed by Congress in 1879.[19] The center of congressional debate shifted to Indian Territory and severalty, not transfer. The churches, aided by the pen of Helen Hunt Jackson, sustained a determined campaign against military control while the army tarnished rather than improved its image. An officer at Fort Robinson announced that the only way to discipline the Northern Cheyennes was to starve and freeze them, which he did. In 1882 an essay by a Captain Butler won an award from the Military Service Institution. Butler described Indians as a dying people much like wild animals. After reading the book, humanitarian Edward E. Ayer penned inside the front cover of his personal copy: "Diabolical . . . by all odds the coldest blooded book I have ever read. . . . that anyone with the shape of a man should hold these views is beyond my comprehension." In the 1870s and '80s the American military knew less than the churches about public relations.

Baptists had been reluctant to join the expanded Peace Policy in 1870. Nathan Bishop told Vincent Colyer that if Grant could remain in office for twenty years, the Baptist church would gladly cooperate, but it feared that after Grant's retirement the spoilsmen and political sharks would regain control of the Indian Bureau. Others shared their concern. Although few reformers liked Grant's appointment of Zachariah Chandler as secretary of the interior in 1875, Chandler did honor most church nominations. Grant remained faithful to his policy even though vilified from all directions at the end of his second term. In 1876 no one knew what to expect from his successor.

After seven ballots, the Republican convention nominated Rutherford B. Hayes for president. The party then adopted a platform that did not mention the Peace Policy.[20] Hayes, though aware of Indians when he wrote a history of his native Ohio, knew very little about the Peace Policy. He believed in the Penn Myth, confessed that white men often had wronged Indians, and realized that justice and good faith were needed. His first message to Congress deplored Indian wars and stressed that more money should be appropriated by Congress.[21] After Hayes's inauguration, Hicksite Friends visited the White House to protest interference by Nebraska politicians. They were pleased to learn that the new president intended to firmly enforce the Peace Policy. When representatives of the Board of Indian Commissioners and mission boards called on Hayes in January of 1878, he repeated his concern, assuring them that he planned no changes. This, coupled with Hayes's private pledge to Bishop Whipple, led the churches to believe that Grant's policy was secure.[22]

Rutherford B. Hayes selected Carl Schurz as secretary of the interior. An advocate of civil service reform and a liberal Republican, the German-born Schurz knew almost nothing about Indians when the Senate confirmed him in 1877. Despite detractors who considered him a freethinker and "dreamer among the stars," Schurz by 1880 had become one of the most informed and articulate defenders of American Indian rights, at least as he understood them. He planned to slowly eliminate Indian culture, consolidate the reservations, and replace whites in the Indian service with natives. Schurz seldom mentioned the Peace Policy, which, he felt, tended to install "broken-down ministers" as Indian agents. His administrative reforms resulted in tight centralized control over employees, contracts, and annuity funds. Schurz, ignoring the Board of Indian Commissioners' role under Grant, appointed a three-man commission in 1877 to investigate the Office of Indian Affairs. This body returned with charges against agents in the West and the central administration in Washington, D.C.[23] One result, and a very unpopular measure with the churches, was Schurz's creation of a secret Interior detective bureau to observe agents and trap them in any malfeasance. But the decision that the churches most disliked was Schurz's replacement of Grant's last commissioner of Indian affairs, John Q. Smith, with Ezra Ayers Hayt.[24]

The Dutch Reformed mission office had appointed Ezra Hayt to the Board of Indian Commissioners in 1874. They recommended him as the wealthy treasurer and chairman of their Board of Foreign Missions, "a first rate businessman . . . firm, courageous, clear-headed, and a hearty Republican."[25] But Hayt clashed with Zachariah Chandler, then secretary of the interior, and resigned from the board one month before Grant left office. Hayt claimed that J. Q. Smith had insulted him and, after Hayes's inauguration, Hayt quietly worked for Smith's removal. By August not only had he succeeded, but he had also obtained the commissioner's position for himself. Certain board members applauded his appointment; others considered Hayt self-seeking and unfair.[26]

Once in office, Hayt rapidly became unpopular with all the churches. During his first year he "purified" the Indian service by removing thirty-five agents. He attacked nepotism, especially at the Quaker agencies, and he assumed a tough, anti-Indian attitude, maintaining, for example, in the case of the Ute tribe that all of Colorado's arable land was needed by white men. The commissioner pushed the removal of Poncas, Northern Cheyennes, and Southern Apaches, and he terminated the Wichita and Omaha reservations. Hayt refused to appoint ministers as agents, advising them to stay in their pulpits, and he further irritated the churches by dismissing a number of reliable agents for probable cause. When an inspector wanted to suspend an honest agent who was the subject of vague local rumors at Green Bay, Hayt consented. It was unjust, he admitted, but such a policy was "absolutely necessary to put the service on such a basis as . . . will remove every suspicion of weakness."[27]

Ezra Hayt earned the enmity of most persons who knew him. The Presbyterian missionary at Green Bay said that the commissioner's "highhanded, worse than despotic tyranny" was supported by the Wisconsin timber barons: "Alas for fair play, justice and righteousness. Call in the Coffin maker, and engage the grave digger. . . . the Indian is doomed."[28] When the Indian Office refused to reappoint John Monteith in 1879, the long-time Nez Perce agent filed accusations of fraud against the commissioner, whom he found "better qualified to manufacture butter from dirty grease than manage Indians." Representative John Luttrell of California matched Monteith's rhetoric when he told Congress that Hayt knew no more about Indians "than a hog does about a holiday." Hayt angered Episcopalians by attacking their agents and with sarcastic letters to Bishop Henry Whipple. The Episcopal Indian Commission expressed disappointment over the commissioner's dishonesty, ignorance, and egotism.[29]

Despite frequent attempts to limit church control during the Grant administration, the mission boards had retained varying degrees of influence. Under Hayes, Schurz, and Hayt, they swiftly lost all control. As Hayt purged another set of agents in 1878, the churches gradually perceived an overall strategy by someone to dismantle the Peace Policy. Presbyterians were requested to dismiss two experienced agents at Lapwai and Uintah Valley. Nathan Meeker, a friend of Carl Schurz, was appointed at White River without the knowledge of Unitarians. A man unknown to the Baptists, J. Q. Tufts, took charge of the Union agency after the church consented to his appointment at Hayt's insistence. Church agents found themselves harassed and spied on by the Indian Office inspectors and by their own agency employees. When Benjamin Thomas suspended a clerk whom he believed in league with fraudulent contractors, Hayt ordered the clerk rehired. By the end of 1878 many churchmen agreed that the Peace Policy was in abeyance.[30]

The government reports of 1880 contained snide, anti-Christian comments about missionaries. One agent attacked the Quakers, and another suggested that Indians could do without religious confusion.[31] Troubles between and within the denominations, declining mission support, the temporary retirement of William Hare, and minuscule attendance at the annual board conferences, attested to American Protestantism's exhaustion with Indian reform. This withdrawal was most apparent in the two denominations that had spearheaded the Peace Policy in 1869, the Friends and the Episcopalians.

Since the beginning of the Peace Policy, the Society of Friends had been uneasy over its relationship with the government. Numerous times they considered withdrawal. Trouble over Osage lands, political attempts to abolish the Northern and Central superintendencies, establishment of the inspection system, Senate rejection of Quaker nominations, and the Red River War frequently tempted the Quakers to retire from the Policy during Grant's administration.[32]

Under Hayes, the Orthodox Quakers encountered difficulty in June of 1877, when James Haworth resigned from the Kiowa-Comanche agency and Friend William Mitchell was nominated to replace him. J. Q. Smith, still serving as commissioner of Indian affairs, approved Mitchell's nomination and forwarded it to Schurz. Hayt in the interim replaced Smith in the Indian Office, Mitchell's nomination was misplaced, and a person unknown to the Friends was appointed. During this same period Hayt suspended or fired three Quaker agents with whom he differed over hiring policies.[33] Hurt and ready to withdraw from the Peace Policy, the Orthodox Friends requested an interview with Schurz and Hayes in the spring of 1878. On April 18 Hayt wired Schurz from New York that Quakers would arrive that morning "to talk about withdrawing which is not desirable at this juncture. I think you will have no difficulty in retaining them."[34] Two long sessions with Schurz and the president convinced the Friends that both men opposed Hayt's policies. "We feel that the blessing of the Lord was with us in these interviews," one Friend related to Henry Whipple; "may he continue to give us all wisdom & guidance in our efforts to help the poor Indian to a Christian life."[35]

When the Orthodox Friends met with other mission representatives, they were surprised to discover that each mission board had similar complaints against Hayt. "Other toes besides our own have been trodden on," noted the Episcopal secretary; "the Friends feel deeply aggrieved by the treatment they have received. The Methodists have gone so far as to present a square issue to the Dept. in the form of an *ultimatum* . . . the next instance of deviation on the part of the Govt. from the origional status will cause a break."[36] Having no intention of allowing Quakers, Episcopalians, or Methodists to manage his department, Hayt ignored the pledges of Schurz and Hayes. After another tense year, the Orthodox Friends officially withdrew from the government service on May 20, 1879.[37]

Hicksite experience was much the same. Liberal Friends found unrelenting political pressure against their agents and were irritated by an 1873 attempt to abolish the Northern Superintendency.[38] Congress reduced appropriations for the Nebraska agencies in 1875. When the government eventually did eliminate the superintendency a year later, the Friends paid the superintendent's salary in order to keep a man in the position. During 1877 and 1878 politicians blocked every agency nomination that the Society made. As Schurz's "system of secret service spies"—agency clerks and physicians—filed charges against Hicksite agents, alarm and distrust spread throughout the bureau. Near the breaking point, the Baltimore Yearly Meeting concluded that under Hayes they had "met a lion in [their] path." They contended that Ezra Hayt ignored or subverted the church, made false accusations against their agents and deliberately discredited Quakers with the Indians.[39]

The Hicksite Friends debated whether they should follow the example of their Orthodox brethren or persist until forced out. They decided to remain. After another confrontation with Hayt in 1880, they refused to nominate anyone for the Winnebago agency but tenaciously clung to other assignments. Garfield's election offered new hope and, until his assassination, liberal Friends planned to begin the Peace Policy anew. With Chester Arthur in the White House a few Hicksite and Orthodox Friends lingered, retaining agency positions until 1884 and 1885, but the Society discouraged its members from becoming Indian agents.[40]

Although the reforms of Carl Schurz and the administration of Ezra Hayt overtly forced the Orthodox Quakers to withdraw from the Peace Policy and the Hicksite Friends to retreat, a vague weariness, apathy, and growing unconcern for Indians preceded the departure of the Society. Toward the end of the seventies the annual reports of Quaker committees became terse, mechanical, tired, and melancholy. After 1874 the Friends remained dutiful but no longer seemed to envision the grand calling of 1869: the Peace Policy had become an obligation more than a blessing. Accusations, lack of money, and the ordeals of warfare had made the Society at least unconsciously aware of its limitations and weaknesses. The early leaders had died by the end of the decade, and once vigorous executive committees, now "sadly broken up," no longer met or recruited new members. In 1880 only four editorials in the weekly *Friend's Intelligencer* discussed Indian problems; in 1881 there were none. Friends read about good manners, women's rights, immigrants, slums, fairs, Jews, opium, fish, and drought. Having finally and officially retired from Grant's Peace Policy, the Orthodox Friends rejoiced greatly over "having been providentially relieved from responsibility to the Government, and thus withdrawn from the complications involved."[41]

The Episcopal church's struggle against political patronage began during Grant's final year in office. After the battle on the Little Big Horn, Zachariah Chandler yielded to William Tecumseh Sherman and used the Sioux war as an excuse to replace civilian agents with army officers at the Cheyenne River, Red Cloud, and Spotted Tail agencies. When the church protested and refused to endorse the officers, both Chandler and John Smith pleaded ignorance of the Peace Policy. Although William Welsh and other Episcopalians were relieved because the replacements excused the church from aiding the army in the Sioux war, they disagreed over how to regain control of the Upper Missouri agencies once armed conflict ended. An emergency meeting of the Episcopal Indian Commission was delayed until Hare returned from Europe and until Welsh finished serving on a Sioux commission. When the church leaders finally did meet, some were reluctant to criticize the government for fear of jeopardizing Indian school contracts. The Episcopal Indian Commission voted to defer action on the Sioux problem.[42]

For the next six months the church unsuccessfully tried to reinstate its own men at the Red Cloud and Spotted Tail agencies. Hare and Welsh called on Hayes and Schurz as soon as the new president took office. The meeting was cordial enough, yet a week later the administration created a new superintendency in Dakota and appointed a non-Episcopalian to the post. In addition, the government sent a special inspector to investigate Episcopal Yankton agent Henry F. Livingston. After Livingston was indicted, frontier merchants strongly backed the agent and the Peace Policy against the Schurz reform efforts. The Indian Bureau's actions and new appointments, the church protested, negated the role of Bishop Hare in Dakota and were a "serious breach of the compact." Privately, Episcopalians believed that Hayt's Dakota reorganization was a plot by the Indian Ring, but they decided not to resist if the Indian Office would accept church nomination of agents.[43]

Early in 1878 church nominations were threatened at other agencies. Welsh then asked the Interior Department if it planned to revoke the Peace

Policy, and the Episcopal Indian Commission delegated Bishop Hare to confer with Schurz. The Indian Office promised Hare that it would not remove any agents without Episcopal consent, a promise quickly broken "in one fell swoop" as the church lost control of three more Dakota agencies. In addition, inspector Edward Kemble, an Episcopalian, was fired. Since 1876 Hare had cautioned his church against any open confrontation with the government, but now the Episcopal Indian Commission, suspecting "*at the bottom* not merely the Army but Rome!" and seeing its bishop maligned on the frontier, decided to act. It sent a sharp letter to Schurz and to its relief received a request to nominate agents. When their new nominations were ignored, the Episcopal officials voted to settle the issue in one way or another.[44]

Meanwhile, Congregationalists were having similar problems at Fort Berthold, where American Board missionary Charles Lemon Hall protested that the licentious men who controlled the agency had threatened to kill him. Later Hall complained that infidels and the adulterous relatives of Ezra Hayt had evicted him from the agency school. The Riggs family asked their board to terminate "the farcical partnership [with the government] which brings . . . nothing but insults and ill savor." The American Missionary Assocation told the American Board that it no longer had control over Fort Berthold. The American Board then reprimanded Hall for criticizing Hayt.[45]

On November 6, 1878, a meeting was held in John Lowrie's office to discuss such problems. Episcopalians, Friends, Baptists, Methodists, Congregationalists, and Presbyterians discovered that they shared grievances in common and unanimously concluded that "endurance had ceased to be a duty." At this meeting the Friends announced their immediate withdrawal from the Peace Policy. Other denominations rejected this drastic action, deciding to try one last time to force Hayes and Schurz to acknowledge the conditions established by Grant. Robert Rogers, M. E. Strieby, and Lowrie were selected to draft a memo that would be "virtually an *ultimatum*. If the Govt. is willing to go back to *first principles*, well & good. If not, then the Missionary Societies retire."[46]

The churches did not retire, nor was the Peace Policy reinstated. Hayt forced out the Wind River Shoshone agent in January and continued to harass Episcopalians.[47] The church patiently sent more names to the Indian Office for endorsement until May of 1882, but by 1879 its leaders had realized that their recommendations carried no force in Washington.

The Episcopal experience clearly illustrated important changes in the role and responsibility of the churches under the Peace Policy. In the beginning, Jacob Cox had told Bishop Whipple that any man named by the churches would be appointed. Columbus Delano altered this to mean that mission boards had a right to nominate agents, but the government would control appointments. Under Carl Schurz, the right to nominate was reduced to an endorsement of men already selected by the department.

Many examples confirm what had happened. Charles Medary, son of a former governor of Ohio, informed the Episcopal Indian Commission that Hayt had promised him an agency as soon as he could obtain a church recommendation. When Episcopalians approved Cicero Newell as Rosebud agent ("under the circumstances, the most available man") they approved a man whose appointment had been urged on Chandler, Hayes, Schurz, and Hayt by Episcopal, Baptist, and Reformed clergy, by a mayor, a former mayor, the Saginaw postmaster, the editor of the *Saginaw Morning Herald*, the Ypsilanti postmaster, an official in Washington, D.C., two Michigan tax collectors, and the pastor of the New Jerusalem Church. In 1880 the Episcopalians were pressured into appointing another Rosebud agent, this candidate backed by Detroit banker and Senator Henry Baldwin.[48]

One of Commissioner Hayt's tactics in undermining the churches was to make extremely urgent requests for nominees; another impediment was to require all church candidates to come to Washington at their own expense for interviews and rigorous examinations, tests that usually resulted in their rejection. Churchmen soon realized that whenever Hayt sent a mission board a request for endorsement, certain names could not be rejected. Bishop Whipple encountered the new practices as early as 1877, when former senator Henry Rice of Minnesota forced the removal of agent Lewis Stowe from White Earth and replaced him with Charles Ruffee. Whipple had blocked Ruffee's appointment earlier and he suspected that Rice and Ruffee had been behind William Welsh's attack on E. P. Smith. After Stowe's removal, Whipple refused to participate in the Peace Policy.[49]

Episcopalians, like the Quakers, had grown disillusioned with Indian reform. In 1877 Jared Daniels refused to be nominated for White Earth because he felt that an Indian agent's job was a "humiliating farce."[50] One month after the 1878 meeting in Lowrie's office, the Episcopal church abolished its Indian commission. Episcopal interest in the Peace Policy had reached a peak in 1873. Then a scarcity of missionaries, the impact of the 1873 Panic, the Welsh-Smith feud, embarrassment at the Red Cloud agency, Indian factionalism, Hare's illness and long-festering quarrel with Samuel Hinman, and the death of William Welsh dispirited the Episcopal church, the church of Whipple and Colyer and Brunot and Welsh, which had so strongly supported Ulysses S. Grant in 1869.

By 1879 the Peace Policy was in ruins and nothing demonstrated that more compellingly than the ridicule heaped on the Board of Indian Commissioners by Congress. Legislators called the board a well-meaning but useless "convocation of barnacles." Alfred Scales of North Carolina said that because Carl

Schurz had reformed the Indian service and because Indian inspectors since 1874 had duplicated board duties, the board had no work to do except "charter a palace car and make an excursion over the Indian country . . . their expenses all paid, they have a good time, and they return in good humor." The House prevented the board's abolition by a vote of ninety to thirty-three in 1879, but a year later the House and Senate renewed the fight against the board. Senators Teller and Ingalls insisted that the board was fraudulent and destructive of good government. Others said the Peace Policy had ended and thus the board served no practical purpose. In April the House voted to discontinue board funding. The Senate compromised by cutting the appropriation by a third.[51]

The board, like the churches, had lost its strongest leaders. Awed by Schurz and divided within itself, the commissioners at best made only a fumbling defense of the Peace Policy. Their confusion and lack of leadership became evident at the joint conference with the mission boards in 1880. Here, as the churches for once openly admitted their problems, the last great debate over Grant's Indian policy occurred.

On January 8, 1880, the Board of Indian Commissioners, Commissioner Hayt, and the mission officials met. The Ute war was first on the agenda. Unitarian Rush Shippen explained that his denomination had wanted to send devoted, religious men to Colorado, yet their nominations had been uniformly ignored. Shippen accused Hayt of dishonesty in his comments about White River agent Nathan Meeker. Hayt retorted that when he had opposed Meeker's appointment he was overruled by Schurz. When Shippen persisted that Hayt had been unfair in public statements about the Unitarians, the commissioner challenged him to name someone who could fill the Colorado vacancies. Shippen named a minister and Hayt sneered that clergy were not acceptable. The commissioner's reply jolted the mission representatives and they began to discuss whether or not to continue cooperating with the Peace Policy. The Dutch Reformed admitted that for several years they had been unable to place any of their own members at agencies, and that their nominations had been "exclusively political recommendations." Baptists confessed that Hayt had seduced them in appointing "an imbecile, a man utterly incompetent," and the board blamed Zachariah Chandler as the person most guilty in undercutting Grant's original plan. It gradually became apparent that each denomination felt that it alone had been bullied by Hayt. They discovered, as Shippen exclaimed, "We are all in the same balloon and are kept dangling in the wind together." Shippen, shocked and dismayed by these revelations, told the churches to resolve the issue by either demanding complete control or pulling out in favor of the spoilsmen.[52]

It proved easier to dangle than to puncture the balloon, especially a Christian balloon floating over a Christian Nation. The next day the Board of

Indian Commissioners and the mission boards met at the White House. They requested Hayes to continue the Peace Policy and to enforce "strict compliance" with church nominations. Board chairman Clinton Fisk, commending Carl Schurz for his investigations, admitted that the churches had been lax. Schurz answered that certain "perplexities and embarrassments" hindered his relationship with the churches, but he now felt a strong obligation to cooperate and in the future would heed church advice "except in such exigencies as demand a different course."[53]

Chairman Fisk had another concern, one that gave considerable satisfaction to mission officials and that caused Carl Schurz further perplexity and embarrassment. In some ways it represented a brief revival of the reform spirit that had animated the Peace Policy during its initial years.

In 1875 Clinton Fisk and E. P. Smith had regarded Ezra Hayt as perhaps the most capable member of the reconstituted board. Fisk told one disappointed contractor that Hayt, as chairman of the board purchasing committee, was one of the most honest and untiring workers he had ever known. But when Hayt forced the highly respected J. Q. Smith out of office and then hired detectives to duplicate board work, Fisk grew disillusioned.[54] After conflicts in the Southwest led to the resignation of San Carlos agent John Clum, Hayt had blocked every nomination from the Reformed church and insisted on placing his own men at the agency. By the autumn of 1879 Fisk alerted the board that something was awry—the Indian Office seemed more devoted to southwestern mining ventures than to protecting Apaches. After Fisk's suspicions reached the *New York Tribune*, Hayt accused the board chairman of slander and challenged him to produce evidence and facts. Fortunately Fisk had followed a hunch and struck silver. He learned from San Carlos agent H. L. Hart that in May of 1879 an Indian inspector named General J. H. Hammond had knowingly devaluated a mine on the reservation from forty thousand dollars to ten thousand dollars and had afterward bribed the agent to remain silent. Fisk in November of 1879 concluded that Hayt indeed was corrupt and had made the Bureau of Indian Affairs "a stench in the nostrils of honest men."[55]

Hayt denied Fisk's allegations at the tumultuous board meeting on January 8, 1880. When the board hesitated to pursue the matter, Fisk went to the *New York Tribune*, which immediately published the charges and denounced the board. In addition to saying that Hayt conspired with his son to purchase the Apache mine under an assumed name, Fisk accused the commissioner of neglecting his duties, destroying official documents, and casting contempt on the churches. He added that Hayt had insulted government creditors, caused the Ute war, and allowed the seduction of Indian girls. Hayt demanded a fair investigation—until Inspector J. H. Hammond confessed. Carl Schurz refused Hayt's resignation and fired him.[56]

In January of 1881 Secretary Schurz warned president-elect James Garfield that one of the most difficult and critical tasks facing him would be the selection of an honest, capable commissioner of Indian affairs. Garfield replied that he hoped to persuade former commissioner Francis Walker to accept the post. He also made a promise to the mission boards that Grant's Peace Policy would continue and that the agencies would be reapportioned, with southern Protestant churches being brought into the program. The board endorsed the new president's plans.[57] In the meantime, however, many denominations had withdrawn. Following departure of the Dutch Reformed (1878), Orthodox Friends (1879), and Episcopalians (1879), the American Missionary Association also retired. The association in 1879 decided that the Peace Policy actually harmed Indians by impeding Christians from preaching the Gospel; therefore it returned the privilege of nominating agents to the government. Baptists too talked about the "so-called peace policy" and Presbyterians pronounced the Policy dead, its demise releasing them from a "difficult and delicate duty." Only the Methodists expressed any interest in retaining agencies.[58]

Charles Giteau shot James Garfield on July 2, 1881. Two months later any hope for a new or revitalized Peace Policy died with the president. His successor, Chester Arthur, pledged to cooperate with the board, but demands from office seekers drove his secretary of the interior, Samuel Kirkwood, to distraction. Then Arthur appointed Henry Teller to replace Kirkwood. As a senator, Teller had supported army control, opposed severalty, and defended his Colorado friend, fellow Methodist, and Indian-hater, Colonel John Chivington. Teller knew all about the Peace Policy and was determined to sweep "incompetent sectarians" out of the service.[59]

By April of 1882, one month before Congress finally relieved the board of every official duty and power,[60] all denominations except Teller's own, the Methodist, had abandoned the Peace Policy. When Dr. John Reid inquired why Teller did not honor the Mission Board's nominations for Michigan and Yakima, Teller answered that church selection of agents not only had failed to improve the Indian Office, but it had resulted in some of the greatest frauds in American history. As for a "peace policy," he knew nothing about it. This, as Clinton Fisk observed, clearly meant that Methodists like everyone else were "mustered out of service."[61]

In 1882 only a few slight barriers to white settlement on the once awesome Indian frontier remained. Gone were the buffalo, the wide sweep of open plains, the tribes free on native land—all had fallen before railroads, barbed wire, cattlemen, repeating rifles, and farmers. Gone too were the idealistic reformers of the 1860s. Lydia M. Child, William L. Garrison, Samuel Janney, Lucretia Mott, and William Welsh were dead. Peter Cooper was ninety. Bishop Henry Whipple by the 1880s had become a symbol more than a participant, and his pronouncements on Indians indicated a man out of touch with actual conditions. In 1882, after a twelve-year struggle, Grant's Peace Policy expired.

11. Aftermath and Appraisal

Ulysses S. Grant's Indian Peace Policy began in 1869 with the appointment of Quaker agents and the creation of the Board of Indian Commissioners. In 1870 it expanded to include nine other denominations; it nearly collapsed the same year when Secretary of the Interior Jacob D. Cox resigned. For many of its founders, the true Peace Policy did collapse in 1874 with the resignation of the original board. It staggered on weakly under Zachariah Chandler, Rutherford B. Hayes, Carl Schurz, and Ezra Hayt. In 1882, with President Chester Arthur reminding Americans that all previous Indian policies had failed, and with Congress more interested in excluding Chinese than in saving Indians, Henry Teller buried the Peace Policy. By the end of that year, two and one half centuries of frontier bloodshed had all but ceased, "Father" Wilbur was gone from Yakima, and the Presbyterians reported that a man of low character had replaced John Critchlow, an outstanding agent at Uintah Valley for well over a decade.

The legacy of the Peace Policy was considerable. Just as Grant's experiment was rooted in previous American history, so Indian affairs for the next seventy years reflected what happened between 1869 and 1882. The creation of a division of education and medicine in 1873 within the Bureau of Indian Affairs reflected the humanitarian concerns of the era and signaled an expanded concept of government responsibility

205

for native Americans. An essential ingredient in Grant's thinking was Indian education, and by the time the churches withdrew in the late seventies, educational programs had become institutionalized within the Indian Bureau. Also as a result of the Peace Policy, American Indians gained and retained powerful allies within white society. By 1882 Helen Hunt Jackson was belaboring the nation about its century of dishonor, and from Pike's Peak in Colorado to Lake Mohonk in New York a score of philanthropic organizations stood ready to fight for the Indians' cause. Moral-religious idealism had shifted outside the Church: the Indian Humanitarian Association; Indian Hope Association; Ladies National Indian League; Indian Treaty Keeping and Protective Association; Boston Indian Citizenship Association; New York Indian Peace Commission; Women's National Indian Association, with its eighty-three branches by 1886; and Indian Rights Association. Almost all of these groups were motivated by Protestant evangelical Christianity, they included many clergy, and they were in agreement on the destiny of American Indians.[1]

There was still much to do. Under Presidents Chester A. Arthur and Grover Cleveland the patronage system returned full-sized. Henry Pancoast of the Indian Rights Association complained in 1883 about Indian agents who were "ignorant, conceited, and narrow-minded in their office, and openly irreligious and immoral in their private lives."[2] In *The Murrain of Spoils in the Indian Service* (1898), Herbert Welsh, a nephew of William Welsh, would accuse Cleveland of removing all but two agents in 1885. Presidents Arthur and Cleveland also continued the policy of opening tribal lands. The sanctity of Indian Territory had begun to crumble under Grant and Hayes; by 1890 the land promised to the Cherokee, Choctaw, Pawnee, Ponca, and many other tribes was open for white settlement.

Indian education, promoted by the board and receiving its first significant government aid under the Peace Policy, expanded rapidly after 1876. Schools on reservations and at Hampton, Carlisle, Haskell, and Forest Grove were guided by the same principles and ideals that directed the Peace Policy. The complete eradication of Indian culture remained the goal of the United States long after 1882. If officials now emphasized the Christian gospel less than they had in the seventies, a cult of nationalism took its place. Thomas Jefferson Morgan, Baptist scholar and the commissioner of Indian affairs under Benjamin Harrison (1889-93), ordered Indians to accept white national purity and superiority: "A fervent patriotism should be awakened in their minds. The stars and stripes should be a familiar object in every Indian school, national hymns should be sung, and patriotic selections read and recited. They should be taught to look upon America as their home ... they should hear little or nothing of the 'wrongs of the Indians' and of the injustices of the white race."[3] The American Missionary Association celebrated the same spirit when it exulted over the fatal shooting of Sitting Bull. The great Sioux warrior made his last stand "against a band of Christian Indians, and not against white soldiers . . . it was the supreme effort of paganism arrayed against Christianity, and paganism went down."[4] With Indians killing their brothers in the name of Christ, the triumph of a Christian Nation appeared complete.

Another way to make an Indian "look upon America as his home" was to assign deeds for land in fee simple. When the Dawes Act of 1887 allowed Indians to own individual farms, it accomplished a long-standing goal of Indian reformers, one for which the churches, Grant, and the board had constantly striven during the 1870s. The American Missionary Association applauded the General Allotment Act, saying that as soon as red men accepted God they would "be ready to go to work . . . the taking up of the hoe and the spade is [the] first confession of faith."[5]

Throughout the Peace Policy the denominations had worried about title to the land on which they built chapels and missions. Although the Peace Policy encouraged churches to settle on Indian reserves, no one answered the question of who owned the land or the buildings. Despite Episcopal and Presbyterian concern, early legislation securing Church title failed to pass. The Dawes Act and later legislation provided the secretary of the interior with authority to confirm mission title to Indian land, thereby making legal the gains of the 1870s.

Intimate relations between Church and State continued in many other ways. Denial of Indian religious liberty led to the Ghost Dance controversy of 1890. One government report described the Sioux killed at Wounded Knee as "notoriously the very ones who have been least affected by the missionaries and teachers."[6] Nor did the Peace Policy's failure induce either Church or State to abandon cooperation with each other, for in 1882 the Indian Office promised that the federal government would continue to support missions.[7] A Quaker wrote in 1887 that government schools must be church-controlled in order to enlist the "most potent force in civilization," Christianity. The superintendent of Indian schools said in the same year that education "cuts the cord that binds [Indians] to a Pagan life, places the Bible in their hands, substitutes the true God for the false one, Christianity in place of idolatry . . . cleanliness in place of filth, industry in place of idleness."[8] At Haskell Institute the curriculum included communion, Sunday school, and prayer meetings. Government teachers constantly reminded Crow children that Jesus Christ lived and died for them, and the principal at the Chilocco school reported that the Saviour found his way into young Indian hearts. The same educator rejoiced when a dying Pawnee girl told him, "I think of Jesus. 'I love to think of Jesus, His name is so sweet.' With this simple trusting faith . . . she ascended to her home beyond the stars, to be with God forever."[9] Religion permeated government schools and the federal government aided church schools. Of all Grant's policies, none brought so much continuing conflict as this legacy that came to be called the contract school system.

During the 1860s Methodists and Quakers had been awarded government contracts that provided funds to educate Shawnee and Chippewa children; in 1869 Father Eugene Chirouse at Tulalip signed a similar agreement to support a Catholic school near Seattle. Government funding of denominational schools rapidly increased under the Peace Policy. In 1871 the Presbyterians received funds for their Odanah school in Wisconsin, and on Christmas Day, 1874, Bishop Hare signed contracts providing up to one thousand dollars for eight Episcopal schools at Yankton, Ponca, and Crow Creek. By March of 1875, Hare had accepted additional contracts for schools at Red Cloud, Spotted Tail, and Lower Brule. Soon the program spread to Catholic and Presbyterian programs in the Southwest, to the Presbyterians' Omaha school, and to the American Missionary Association's Hampton Institute. The American Board of Commissioners for Foreign Missions debated the issue before deciding to seek funds whenever possible.[10] Even the Baptists, who protested in 1892 that they had *"never drawn any of this money,"* in 1881 were operating schools in Indian Territory under contract and had rejoiced that the government would give churches substantial aid for Indian education.[11] At the end of the Peace Policy, every major denomination except the Dutch Reformed and the Unitarians had signed federal contracts. Twenty-nine of the 139 government schools were operated by denominations in 1883; by 1886 this figure had doubled.

Toward the end of the 1880s, with Roman Catholics obtaining almost two-thirds of all contract funds, it became apparent that Protestants had to rethink their constitutional principles. Baptists and other denominations suddenly became purist in reading the First Amendment. Nativists, frightened by an increase in Catholic parochial schools throughout the Northeast, formed organizations such as the National League for Protection of American Institutions, the Sons of the American Revolution, the Immigration Restriction League, and the American Protective Association. These groups, which included men such as John D. Rockefeller, Rutherford Hayes, Francis Walker, Charles Adams, and Henry Whipple, lashed out at Catholicism and renewed their efforts to pass the Blaine Amendment to ensure strict separation of church and state.

The battle over Indian schools began in earnest with Thomas J. Morgan's appointment as commissioner of Indian affairs in 1889. Aroused by Morgan's anti-Catholic warnings, the Methodists, Congregationalists, Presbyterians, and Episcopalians withdrew from Indian school contracts in 1892. The attack on the Roman Catholic church reached its peak in Morgan's speech in the Boston Music Hall, April 16, 1893. After protesting that he was no bigot or demagogue, Morgan began by accusing Catholics of violating the Constitution. He contrasted their "audacity and wickedness . . . their elaborate efforts, their adroit scheming, their secret plotting, their infamous lying," with Protestant loyalty to American principles, and he called for resistance against "a priesthood plunging into politics for public plunder. . . . an insatiable greed of power . . . an alien transplant from the Tiber . . . recruiting her ranks by myriads from the slums of Europe. . . . Jesuitical cunning . . . un-American, unpatriotic, and a menace to our liberties . . . a corrupt ecclesiastico-political machine masquerading as a church. . . . Its spirit that of the Inquisition."[12] Wildly cheered, Morgan's Boston address resembled in tone and emotion the 1874 *Catholic Address on President Grant's Indian Policy in its Bearing upon Catholic Interests at Large.* Only the names were changed. The Peace Policy had faded into the dim and distant past by 1893. Thomas J. Morgan ended his polemic with a plea for patriots to rise again and defend the Republic: "I long to hear the voice of a James Otis, a Samuel Adams, a Patrick Henry . . . I remember Concord and Bunker Hill, Washington and Jefferson, Gettysburg and Appomattox, Sumner, and Lincoln, and Grant."[13]

Many factors complicate an evaluation of the Peace Policy. Its history includes seventy different reservations spread across twenty states and territories in settings as diverse as Arizona deserts and Puget Sound forests. It encountered Indian cultures as different as the Hopi and Lummi. Three hundred Indian agents were assigned by thirteen different mission boards. The Peace Policy involved the Congress, the Department of the Interior, the White House, many ministers, philanthropists, bishops, reformers, and various scoundrels.

Furthermore, Grant's Peace Policy was only part of a larger national debate over Indian affairs, a single program among many undertaken by the government. Government goals in the 1870s were to protect tribal lands, destroy Indian culture, promote white settlement, build railroads, stop treaty making, consolidate reservations, provide good agents, exterminate buffalo, and pacify resisting tribes by feeding or defeating them. Such complexity convinced many critics of Grant's hypocrisy. General H. H. Sibley complained that the government pursued a "shifting, uncertain, miserable policy," and Chief Joseph of the Nez Perce observed, "Such a Government has something wrong about it . . . the white people have too many chiefs. They do not understand each other . . . I cannot understand why so many chiefs are allowed to talk so many different ways and promise so many different things."[14]

A confusing muddle of idealism and destruction, of altruism and greed, limits any historical judgment which one can make about the Peace Policy's success or failure. Measured by certain standards of the period, it was a success. According to the Board of Indian Commissioners, almost one-half of all Indian men and women wore European-style clothing in 1876; between 1868 and 1876, the number of houses on reservations increased from seventy-five hundred to fifty-six thousand; schools and teachers tripled; acres under cultivation increased sixfold; and Indians owned fifteen times more livestock in 1876 than they had in 1869. Churches and Indian aid associations had donated tons of food, clothing, and books to tribes.[15]

Yet by 1876, or even 1882, other goals had not been attained. Liquor dealers, speculators, traders, and squatters still made Indian reservations "Beelzebub's domain," many congressmen and humanitarians believed the Indian race was doomed, and Christian ministers preached about red men caught between the upper and nether millstones. Senator George Pendleton of Ohio predicted in 1881 that the Anglo-Saxon "car of civilization" would roll over all reservations "even though the wheels are axle deep in individual suffering and ruin." The Indian problem persisted. In some crucial ways it was quite different from the problem of 1869, and in other important ways it remained exactly the same. In 1882, for example, the commissioner of Indian affairs still searched for "*honest, industrious,* and *intelligent Christian* men," and the Indian Rights Association pleaded for federal agents of superior character.[16]

Even good men can be destroyed by an unfair or incompetent system and by the forces of history. Even excellent agents, which the Peace Policy supplied in surprising number, could not save Indian tribes or make Grant's policy the instant success that reformers planned. One limit was that the Policy inherited past problems. By 1869 the institutions and habits of Indian-white relations were so deeply ingrained in American practice that it would require decades, if not a century, of genuine reform to dislodge and change them.[17] No reform policy, for example, could have reversed the years of disaster experienced by the Kaws. The Kansas tribe's unhappy forced migration to Indian Territory under Quaker Myron Stubbs in 1873 can by no means be considered a failing of the Peace Policy; it was the end result of disastrous decisions and actions of previous decades.[18] In another instance, the Flandreau Colony of Santee Sioux under missionary Thomas Williamson possessed all the ingredients for success on the eve of the Peace Policy: the agent was religious, honest, and efficient; the Indians were Christian and self-sufficient in agriculture; the tribe had rejected its original culture. Yet Flandreau suffered from starvation, alcoholism, grasshoppers, and the loss of land to lawless whites.[19]

Few men could withstand the demands placed on an Indian agent in the nineteenth century. Between 1869 and 1900 complaints about the agents' living conditions on Indian reservations were commonplace. An especially desperate tale came from Charles Willoughby, stationed at the Quinault agency, where the rainfall was 136 inches in 1887. "Our buildings are rotten from the ground up; every storm gust threatens to topple them; the rain drips in upon us from the roofs, and the wind cuts keenly through the chinks in the walls; in some of them the beds have to be covered with our waterproof clothing, and buckets placed to catch the water . . . it becomes necessary to mop the floors or place old sacking to soak up the rain falling upon everything, and being driven through the side walls at every gust."[20] Most Indian agents were, as one historian has concluded, simply "ordinary people up against an extraordinary task and hampered in its execution by extraordinary difficulties." In the 1870s both the temptations and the tasks were perhaps more extraordinary and overpowering than at any other time.

Failure to correct defects in Indian administration also contributed to the demise of the Peace Policy. Advocates of reform naïvely believed that good faith toward Indians and nonpolitical, honest, religious appointees could transform the system. A related error occurred early in the Peace Policy: Grant's arbitrary and indiscriminate removal of men who, like the agent at Umatilla, had a decade of successful experience and who wished to remain at their posts. The sweeping removal of all experienced agents in 1869 and their replacement with army officers and Quakers, revealed a cold, unimaginative, and insensitive side to the new reform. Nor did the government improve living conditions or reform its administrative procedures. Leaders in Indian reform in the seventies spoke mainly about justice, honor, and trust; the Peace Policy was based too largely on vague principles, and too little on proper bookkeeping, accounting, inspection, and equity in salaries.

The Black Hills provided another symbol of failure. Grant, caught in a contradiction of policy, was cold and rude to Sioux chiefs who came to Washington to save their land, and even Episcopal bishops Hare and Whipple would buckle under the pressure of gold in the Hills. Angry Sioux, five times removed from lands five times promised forever, asked that their people be placed on wheels so the white man could push them around more easily. The disheartened peace commissioners and religious leaders listened, blushed, and averted their eyes: "Admiration would have kept us silent had not shame and humiliation done so."[21]

A brighter side to the Peace Policy was the time, money, and effort volunteered by the Board of Indian Commissioners and the missionary societies. These men, repeatedly distressed and discouraged by their impossible task, gained an appreciation for the problems of secular government. They also learned new lessons in church apathy. In failing to accomplish what was devoutly expected, the Christian Church again proved itself a human institution, subject to human limits and imperfections. With agents and missionaries beguiled by temptation, with internal conflicts arising in every major denomination, the Peace Policy tested the limits of the Church and of a Christian nation.

Protestant opposition to Catholics, Mormons, Biblical criticism, and infidels obscured efforts to help the Indian. The churches were more intent on revivalism than on Indian missions, more concerned about a shortage of ministers than about the quality of Indian agents, and more worried about Chinese immigration, divorce, liquor, Darwinism, Henry Ward Beecher's adultery, Bible wars, and slums than about the Poncas, Crows, and Chippewas. An 1858 treaty had opened China to Protestant missions for the first time, and throughout the 1870s Asia was the most urgent field for many foreign mission boards. The Peace Policy thus never became a Protestant crusade, or even a major concern. Men such as Whipple, Welsh, and Hare were exceptions, not the rule. For the *Baptist Watchman* temperance was "The Great Question" of the age, and admonitions against the sin of listening to an opera, "An Awful Way to Spend the Sabbath," filled as much space in church journals as reports about Sioux raids or the Modoc War. Limited in devotion, time, and money, the Christian Church performed no minor miracles to redeem a conquered people; it accomplished no mass conversion of its own members to an unpopular cause.

The evangelical Christian reformer had ways to explain the mixed results of the Peace Policy. Success was due to the gospel and failure to bad men and liquor. Thus Senator Oliver Morton of Indiana accounted for the failure of the Peace Policy as simply the "failure of ourselves," thereby reducing social reform to individual decision and effort. Few churchmen comprehended the powerful and complicated forces against which they struggled, and most humanitarians overlooked what William Tecumseh Sherman recognized: that the onrush of railroads, industry, and settlement rendered Indians, agents, and peace policies irrelevant.[22] "Time is rapidly solving the problem," one supporter of the Peace Policy said in 1872. The solution did not favor Indian tribes.

Although the Board of Indian Commissioners and Grant had warned from the start that success would require years of patient, long-suffering effort, even they had no accurate idea of how many years were required or how rapidly time was running out for the tribes. When the board reluctantly approved the Ute treaty of 1873, it did so because the treaty provided land "for many years" of white expansion in Colorado. The "many years" numbered six.

Besides a lack of time, there were Protestant misconceptions of society and politics. Grant, the reformers, and the Protestant leaders naïvely if typically believed that piety produced secular competence and that professions of individual morality were substitutes for force and political power.[23] The

Peace Policy, an attack on corrupt politics in the name of religious idealism, labored under the mistaken notions that believers can remain pure, that compromise is unnecessary, and that presidents need not exercise power. This idealism, a desire for moral purity, was apparent in the Friends' attack on John Miles and in their repeated threats to withdraw from participation. It was apparent in the 1880 board conference, when mission secretaries rejected any "mixed affair" of clay and iron. Skill, technology, and strength determined the course of Indian-white relations, not ethical purity. Construction of railroads, sod houses, repeating rifles, and windmills were instruments and actions more powerful than Quaker morals and petitions. As Emmet John Hughes has commented, "The deed—however simple—counts in politics for more than the word—however eloquent. To rely on a speech for some kind of triumphant substance is, of course, nonsense."[24]

The most powerful deeds and driving forces in America in the 1870s concerned the massive accumulation of land and wealth, forces that the government, the Board of Indian Commissioners, and the churches seldom had a desire to oppose or even question. There was much talk of Indian depredations, of squatters, whiskey sellers, and corrupt men. There was little effective discussion, in the last third of the nineteenth century, of corporate depredations involving railroad and telegraph right-of-ways, timber, grazing permits, illegal surveys, and fraudulent land grants. For its part, the Grant administration had the ultimate goal of eliminating Indian reservations and vastly reducing native land holdings, including Indian Territory. The goal was firmly supported by most reformers, who seldom protested when several dozen tribes made huge land cessions to "restore" their land to the public domain.[25]

The protection of Indians required the organization and application of power equal or superior to that of white settlers and the powerful financial institutions promoting migration. This the churches were unable and unwilling to do. Protestants failed to establish any effective organization to apply pressure through lobbyists and lawyers. One irony of the Peace Policy was that the Roman Catholic church, incorrectly believing that Protestants were highly organized, built an Indian Mission Bureau far more effective than anything that their rivals developed. Beginning with the advantage of the government-sponsored Board of Indian Commissioners, Protestants, with the exception of William Welsh, failed to maintain effective pressure for reform.

As for the relationship between Church and State, the Peace Policy can be viewed equally as the culmination of the idea of a Christian Commonwealth and as a flagrant violation of the First Amendment, but the second possibility simply did not occur to many people in the 1870s. Nineteenth-century Protestants assumed that government would reflect spiritual values and that it could cooperate with religion in achieving them. It was understood, of course, that the United States must never have a federal church and that established churches in the states were gone forever, but times of national crisis could link evangelical religion with patriotism and government. Formal and enduring ties, or direct government aid to a specific church, might cause misgivings, yet not until American Catholicism began to grow in size did "strict separation" become a Protestant constitutional doctrine. Certain traditional patterns describe Grant's Indian policy: cooperation was assumed, officials and reformers agreed on Christian goals, and only a Catholic threat disturbed the peace. Finally, it must be acknowledged that Indian affairs always seemed minor and remote in the scope of national concerns and therefore little indignation was expressed when Indians' rights were violated. The Peace Policy, in theory, was a staggering exception to the First Amendment, but Indians did not count.

That Grant should at once create the Peace Policy and then more than any other president insist on absolute separation of Church and State may seem bewildering. Grant saw no contradiction and thereby revealed one of his intellectual weaknesses as president. No one is ever well prepared to assume leadership of the United States, but few presidents have come so ill-prepared to the White House as he did. In 1869 it was easy for the public to admire Grant, a solid man of courage and good will, and it was comfortable to believe in his sincerity. But, lacking political experience outside the military and, like a later general who became president, distrustful of "all struttings of power, all histrionics of politics . . . so odd a mixture of force and weakness," Grant was reluctant to act when necessary and hesitant to use his office when events demanded it. When the economic pressures became great he would retreat from principles of fairness toward Indians, as in the case of the surrender of the Sioux's Black Hills and the Nez Perce homeland in the Wallowas. For victorious commanding generals, the American presidency can be an emotional disappointment, an anticlimactic office of less intensity that therefore requires less close attention than the ordering of troops in combat. Somehow fortitude and resolution seeped from the president during the mid-seventies as not only his Indian policy but his entire administration slid into chaos.[26] One could fairly say of Ulysses S. Grant what has been written of a later president:

> Certain qualities of the man, even virtues in themselves, could be wrenched in the play of politics and made to seem misshapen. Clearly, there was in him a profound humility—a refusal to *use* the full force of his personal authority or political position against a critical consensus. He saw himself realistically as a man of military affairs, a stranger to political affairs, surrounded by Republican leaders who—by their own testimony, at least— were political "experts." He would have abhorred any image of himself

as the man-on-horseback, crudely importing military discipline into a civil arena.[27]

Grant was too cautious, too uncertain, too awed by businessmen, too willing to let the dust settle before acting decisively. This philosophy of government has been consciously and deliberately held by certain presidents. Grant barely sensed it.

Neither Grant, his cabinet, the Indian Office, nor the reformers could break away from the presuppositions of their age. David Halberstam, writing about American involvement in Vietnam in the early 1960s, said that officials in Washington, D.C., "responded with clichés to desperately complicated and serious challenges" and that Americans, both in Washington and in Southeast Asia, experienced the frustration of trying to promote American interests "in a complex world where the best intentioned and most enlightened of policies often carried out by the ablest of public servants do not necessarily work."[28] Grant, however enlightened his Indian policy, did not enjoy the most able public servants, and ruinous clichés in his time were ample.

So the Peace Policy failed. It was an honest attempt by a concerned president, by Christians and men of good will to solve a national problem. It failed because even hard-working, sincere, devout Christian Americans do not necessarily succeed. It failed because Christian nations cannot always be moral. The failure was not entirely caused by malicious politicians or by public indifference, although both played a large part. Participants in the Peace Policy were not all sinners or saints; they certainly were not members in a grand conspiracy to establish a state church. As Protestants, they did believe that religious reform would yield moral conclusions and that peace and love of justice could counterbalance force and injustice. They ignored the fact, or did not realize, that religion is only one element in history. Moral dilemmas, chance, honest error, misunderstanding, lack of time, and alien Indian cultures defeated the Peace Policy. Christians, J. B. Harrison said in 1887, do not "adequately understand or value the other great world forces besides religion."[29] A booming population, greed for gold, human ignorance, fear, disease, deception, suspicion, human resistance to conquest, the human desire to own fertile land, and an endless list of unforeseen difficulties overpowered the good intentions of the Wilburs, Brunots, and Tatums. The reluctance of the churches and the federal government to acknowledge these forces explains many defects and failings in the conception and practice of the Peace Policy. Historian Robert Athearn has written of the American settler's desire for more land, for freedom, for the good life:

As . . . hundreds filtered silently westward, unknown and undistinguished, they were gradually weighting the scales against the natives. . . . In that . . .

lay the answer to the Indian problem. It was not found in the noisier events of cavalry charges, the brassy cry of bugles, or the now romanticized notes of "Garry Owen." Such sounds were heard only by a public whose ear could not pick up the crump of Nebraska sod as it was ripped out and turned grass-side down.[30]

Both Church and government officials had forgotten Sir Edmund Burke's advice to the British government a century earlier: "We must govern America . . . not according to our own imaginations, nor according to abstract ideas of right—by no means according to mere general theories of government, the resort to which appears to me . . . no better than arrant trifling."[31]

Appendix 1: Denominational Apportionment

Denominational Apportionment

Denomination	1870[1]	1872[2]	1875[3]	Previous Work[4]
Friends, Hicksite (Nebr.)	Great Nemaha	Great Nemaha	Great Nemaha	
	Omaha	Omaha	Omaha	Presby.
	Winnebago	Winnebago	Winnebago	Presby.
	Pawnee	Pawnee	Pawnee	Presby.
	Otoe	Otoe	Otoe	
	Santee	Santee	Santee	ABCFM, Episc.
Friends, Orthodox (Kans., Ind. Terr.)	Kaw	Kaw		
	Shawnee	Shawnee		
	Pottawatomie	Pottawatomie	Pottawatomie	R.C., Meth.
	Kickapoo	Kickapoo	Kickapoo	Meth.
	Quapaw	Quapaw	Quapaw	R.C.
	Osage	Osage	Osage	R.C., Prot.
	Sac and Fox	Sac and Fox	Sac and Fox	
	Wichita	Wichita	Wichita	
	Kiowa	Kiowa	Kiowa and Comanche	
	Upper Arkansas	Cheyenne and Arapahoe	Cheyenne and Arapahoe	
Roman Catholic (Wash., Oreg., Mont., Dakota, Ariz.)		Flathead	Flathead	R.C.
		Tulalip	Tulalip	R.C.
		Colville	Colville	R.C., ABCFM
		Grand Ronde	Grand Ronde	R.C.
		Umatilla	Umatilla	R.C.
		Grand River	Standing Rock	R.C.
		Devil's Lake	Devil's Lake	
			Papago	R.C.

Denomination	1870[1]	1872[2]	1875[3]	Previous Work[4]
Baptist (Utah, Idaho, Nev., Ind. Terr.)	Pyramid Lake	Walker River	Pyramid Lake	
	Walker Lake	PiUte	PiUte	
	PiUte			
	Fort Hall			
	Cherokee and Creek	Cherokee and Creek	Union	Bapt., Meth., ABCFM, Presby.
Methodist (Wash., Oreg., Mont., Idaho, Cal., Mich.)	Puyallup			
	Quinault	Quinault	Quinault	Meth., R.C.
	Yakima	Yakima	Yakima	R.C.
	Umatilla			R.C.
	Grand Ronde			R.C.
	Blackfeet	Blackfeet	Blackfeet	R.C.
		Hoopa Valley	Hoopa Valley	R.C.
		Round Valley	Round Valley	R.C.
		Tule River	Tule River	R.C.
		Skokomish		Presby., R.C.
		Warm Springs	Alsea	R.C.
		Siletz	Siletz	R.C.
		Klamath	Klamath	R.C.
		Crow	Crow	R.C.
		Fort Hall	Fort Hall	R.C.
		Milk River	Fort Peck	ABCFM, R.C.
			Lemhi	R.C.
			Neah Bay	AMA, Meth., Presby., R.C.
		Michigan	Michigan	

American Missionary Association (Minn., Wis., Mich.)	Chippewa, Minn.	White Earth	LaPointe	Episc., Meth., R.C.
	Lake Superior	Lake Superior	Green Bay	R.C.
	Green Bay	Green Bay		R.C., Episc.
	Michigan			AMA, Meth., Presby., R.C.
			Red Lake	AMA
			Sisseton	ABCFM, Episc.
			Fort Berthold	
			Skokomish	R.C.
Dutch Reformed (Ariz.)	Colorado River	Colorado River	Colorado River	
	Pima	Pima	Pima	Meth., Presby., R.C.
		Camp Grant	Maricopa	
		Camp Verde	San Carlos	
		White Mountain		
Presbyterian (N.Mex., Idaho, Colo., Ariz.)	Navajo	Navajo	Navajo	Presby., R.C.
	Mescalero	Mescalero	Mescalero	R.C.
	Southern Apache	Southern Apache	Southern Apache	
	Cimarron		Cimarron	
	Hopi	Hopi	Hopi	R.C.
	Uintah Valley	Uintah Valley	Uintah Valley	Mormon
		Choctaw and Seminole		Meth., Bapt.
		Abiquiu	Abiquiu	
			Apache	R.C.
			Pueblo	ABCFM, R.C.
		Nez Perce	Nez Perce	
Episcopal (Nebr., Dakota, Minn.)	Ponca	Ponca	Ponca	
	Crow Creek		Crow Creek	ABCFM
	Whetstone	Whetstone	White River (Dakota)	
	Cheyenne River	Cheyenne River	Cheyenne River	ABCFM
	Spotted Tail	Upper Missouri	Spotted Tail	

221

Denomination	1870[1]	1872[2]	1875[3]	Previous Work[4]
Episcopal	Red Cloud	Red Cloud	Red Cloud	Episc., R.C.,
		Shoshone	Shoshone	ABCFM, Presby.
		Yankton	Yankton	
			White Earth	Episc., Meth., R.C.
Unitarian (Colo.)	White River	White River	White River	
		Los Pinos	Los Pinos	
United Presbyterian			Warm Springs	R.C., Presby.
Free Will Baptist			Leech Lake	Episc.
American Board (Ind. Terr., Dakota)	Seminole			Bapt.
	Chickasaw	Sisseton		Meth., Bapt.
	Choctaw			ABCFM, Meth., Bapt.
				ABCFM, Episc.
Evangelical Lutheran (Iowa, Nev.)		Sac and Fox	S. E. Utes (1877)	
Christian Union (Wash., Oreg.)		Neah Bay	Malheur (1876)	

1. BIC: LR, J. Cox to F. Brunot, August 20, 1870.

2. CIA, *Annual Report*, 1872, pp. 73-74.

3. Ibid., 1875, p. 172.

4. This column is based on two criteria: incidence of Indians belonging to a church and recorded claims of different denominations.

Appendix 2: Church Performance

Evaluation of the Peace Policy presents difficult methodological problems. Except for Whitner's detailed study of the Methodists and Milner's work on the Hicksites, most studies repeat generalizations from official reports, the press, and other writers. The major hindrances are (a) the difficulty in determining which agents and teachers actually were church-appointed; (b) the lack of criteria to define "religious progress"; (c) the incompleteness and inaccuracy of much official data; and (d) the error of comparing data (e.g., church membership, conversion, mission) based on different definitions.

The following summary rests on official reports. In general, I found that these reports provide a brighter picture than warranted by the facts. Schools that may appear strong in the official reports of the Indian Office, BIC, and churches often were weak and inadequate, according to private correspondence and inspection reports.

Missions and Schools

Denomination	Total Indian Missionaries		Missionaries at Assigned Agencies		Total Indian Schools		Schools at Assigned Agencies	
	1873	1882	1873	1882	1873	1882	1873	1882
Friends (Hicksite, Orth.)	0	10(?)	0	10(?)	21	6	21	0
Episcopal	15	28	7	18	11	14	4	6
Methodist	6	1	3	1	18	1	15	1
Presbyterian	10	26	7	7	10	15	5	7
Dutch Reformed	0	*	0	*	2	*	2	*
Baptist	0	1	0	1	0	0	0	0
Unitarian	0	*	0	*	1	*	1	0
American Missionary Association	10	12	3	4	4	11	2	3
Roman Catholic	18	34	16	18	11	23	6	10

Source: From the Commissioner of Indian Affairs, *Annual Reports*, 1873, 1882; excluding Indian Territory. Schools are those in operation; missionaries are those not supported by government.

* = No report for the year.

Denominational Expenditures[†]

Denomination	1873	1874	1876	1877	1878	1879	1881	1882
Friends (Hicksite, Orth.)[**]					5,000	11,500	8,000	
Hicksite Friends	7,500	6,000	3,400	2,000				*
Orthodox Friends	10,000	11,000	7,500	*				8,000
Roman Catholic	*	*	*	*	*	*	*	*
Baptist	5,000	*	4,900	8,000	4,400	8,000	3,000	2,500
Methodist	5,000	*	3,500	*	*	3,500	3,600	*
Dutch Reformed	*	800	*	*	*	*	*	*
Presbyterian	22,500	17,000	11,000	10,700	11,500	28,300	64,000	75,300
Unitarian	*	*	*	*	*	*	*	*
Episcopal	68,000	48,000	46,300	48,200	39,300	48,700	38,500	41,700
ABCFM	*	16,000	14,900	17,100	12,100	12,600	20,000	20,600

Source: From the BIC, *Annual Reports*, 1873-82 (1875 and 1880 not reported).

† = In dollars.

* = No report for the year.

** = From 1878 to 1881, the government made no distinction between Hicksite and Orthodox Friends.

Missionaries and Schools by Agency

		1873		1877	
Denomination	Agency	S	M	S	M
Hicksite Friends	Great Nemaha	2	0	2	0
	Sac and Fox	0	0	**	**
	Omaha	3	0	1	1
	Winnebago	4	0	3	0
	Pawnee	0	0	2	0
	Santee	1	0	8[a]	4[a]
	Otoe	1	0	1	0
Orthodox Friends	Kaw	0	0	**	**
	Kickapoo	1	0	**	**
	Pottawatomie	1	0	*	*
	Wichita	2	0	1	0
	Osage	0	0	2	2

Denomination	Agency	1873		1877	
		S	M	S	M
	Cheyenne and Arapaho	1	0	1	0
	Kiowa-Comanche	**	**	1	0
	Quapaw	4	0	5	0
Roman Catholic	Tulalip	1	3	2	2
	Umatilla	1	1	1	0
	Papago	1	1	**	**
	Flathead	2	2	2	7
	Grand River	0	0	2	4
	Devil's Lake	0	1	1	1
	Grand Ronde	2	1	2	3
	Colville	2	3	1	5
Methodist	Hoopa Valley	1	0	0	0
	Round Valley	1	0	2	1
	Tule River	1	0	2	1
	Yakima	1	3	2	1
	Quinault	1	0	1	0
	Alsea	0	0	**	**
	Siletz	2	1	1	0
	Klamath	1	0	1	0
	Warm Springs	1	0	**	**
	Michigan	7	4	6	6
	Crow	1	0	1	0
	Fort Peck	0	0	0	0
	Fort Hall	0	0	0	0
	Blackfeet	1	0	1	0
Baptist	Cherokee-Creek	(191)[b]	*	*	*
	Walker River	0	0	0	0
	PiUte	1	0	0	0
American Missionary Association	Green Bay	5	0	3	2
	LaPointe	2	0	3	1
	Sisseton	4	0	3	2
	Fort Berthold	0	0	1	2
	Skokomish	1	1	1	2
	White Earth	5	0	**	**
Unitarian	Los Pinos	0	0	0	0
	White River	0	0	1	0
Dutch Reformed	Colorado River	0	0	0	0
	Pima	2	0	1	1
	Maricopa	0	0	0	0
	San Carlos	0	0	0	0

Denomination	Agency	1873		1877	
		S	M	S	M
Presbyterian	Abiquiu	0	*	0	0
	Navajo	0	1	1	0
	Mescalero	0	0	0	0
	Apache	*	*	*	*
	Southern Apache	*	*	*	*
	Cimarron	*	*	*	*
	Pueblo	*	*	6	0
	Nez Perce	2	2	4	0
	Uintah Valley	0	0	0	0
	Hopi	1	0	1	0
Episcopal	White Earth	**	**	1	5
	Ponca	0	1	0	0
	Yankton	7	1	11	2
	Whetstone	0	0	**	**
	Upper Missouri	2	2	**	**
	Crow Creek	*	*	3	4
	Cheyenne River	3	1	3	0
	Spotted Tail	**	**	1	1
	Red Cloud	0	0	0	0
	Shoshone	1	0	0	0
Evangelical Lutheran	Sac and Fox	1	1	**	**
Christian Union	Neah Bay	2	1	**	**

Source: U.S. Department of the Interior, *What the Government and the Churches Are Doing for the Indians* (Washington: Government Printing Office, 1874); CIA, *Annual Report*, 1877, pp. 288–305.

a = + Episcopal and ABCFM   * = No report for the year.

b = + Annuity schools   ** = Agency did not exist or was consolidated.

S = Schools

M = Missionaries

Evaluation: 1880

The following attempt to evaluate performance after ten years is based on agent reports (CIA, *Annual Report*, 1880), which often are biased for or against the state of the agency depending on the agent's prior relation to the reservation (long-term agents are too positive; first-year agents are usually very critical). The rating assumes Yakima was a model agency. The ratings do not necessarily measure the success or failure of the Peace Policy, for the system does not take into account removals, military control, condition of the agency in 1870, or the different attitudes, location, and strength of the tribes. For a much more sophisticated statistical analysis of the Peace Policy's success, see Milner, "With Good Intentions," chapter 10. My evaluation is based on: (a) civilization (cleanliness of Indians, Indians in houses, white dress, peaceful conditions, white morals, etc.); (b) farming activity; (c) schools; and (d) religious and missionary activity.

Excellent

Devil's Lake	Kansas	Cheyenne-Arapaho	LaPointe
Standing Rock	Michigan	Umatilla	Colville
Yankton	Flathead	Warm Springs	Green Bay
Nez Perce	Santee	Skokomish	Grand Ronde
Omaha	Tulalip	Yakima	

Good

Cheyenne River	Pawnee	Great Nemaha	Klamath
Crow Creek	Ponca	Winnebago	Siletz
Sisseton	White Earth		

Fair

Tule River	Shoshone	Pueblo	Kiowa-Comanche
Fort Berthold	Quapaw	Uintah Valley	Blackfeet
Rosebud	Sac and Fox	Neah Bay	Osage-Kaw
Fort Hall			

Poor

San Carlos	Lower Brule	Fort Peck	Navajo
Hoopa Valley	Pine Ridge	Otoe	Quinault
Round Valley	Crow	Abiquiu	

Very Poor

Colorado River	Los Pinos	Walker–Pyramid	Mescalero
Pima	White River	Lake	Shoshone

Evaluation of Agencies by Denomination

Denomination	Excellent	Good	Fair	Poor	Very Poor
Friends	4	3	4	1	0
Roman Catholic	7	0	0	0	0
Baptist	0	0	0	0	2
Methodist	2	2	4	5	0
American Missionary Association	3	2	1	0	0
Dutch Reformed	0	0	0	1	2
Unitarian	0	0	0	0	2
Presbyterian	2	0	2	2	1
Episcopal	1	3	2	2	0
Total	19	10	13	11	7

Appendix 3: Peace Policy Agents

Robert Whitner, in his study of the Methodist reservations, assumed that long tenure signified a "good" agent. George Betts's five years at Michigan leads one to question that assumption, since Betts proved to be a corrupt agent. It is also clear that honest agents often faced immediate defamation and what V. T. McGillycuddy called the "star-chamber treatment" from dishonest contractors. Keeping these limits in mind, turnover rates at different reservations indicate how unstable the Indian service was under the Peace Policy.

Tenure of Agents

Denomination	Agency	Years	No. of Agents
Hicksite Friends	Great Nemaha	1869–82	4
	Omaha	1869–78	3
	Winnebago	1869–82	5
	Pawnee	1869–82	7
	Otoe	1869–82	7
	Santee	1869–82	4
Orthodox Friends	Pottawatomie	1870–79	2
	Shawnee	1869–72	1
	Kickapoo	1869–74	2
	Quapaw	1871–79	1
	Osage	1870–77	3
	Sac and Fox	1870–82	7
	Wichita	1871–77	2
	Kiowa-Comanche	1869–82	3
	Cheyenne and Arapaho	1869–82	2
Roman Catholic	Tulalip	1871–82	4
	Colville	1873–82	1
	Grand Ronde	1872–82	1
	Umatilla	1871–82	3
	Flathead	1871–82	5
	Grand River	1871–82	7
	Devil's Lake	1871–82	4
	Papago	1871–76	2
	Fort Hall	1871	1
Methodist	Hoopa Valley	1871–78	5
	Round Valley	1871–82	3
	Tule River	1871–82	3
	Yakima	1871–82	1
	Quinault	1871–82	2

233

Denomination	Agency	Years	No. of Agents
	Alsea	1871–75	1
	Siletz	1871–82	4
	Klamath	1871–82	4
	Blackfoot	1871–82	6
	Crow	1871–82	7
	Fort Peck	1871–82	6
	Fort Hall	1872–82	5
	Michigan	1871–82	2
	Neah Bay	1873–78	2
	Lemhi	1878–80	2
	Warm Springs	1871–73	1
Baptist	Cherokee	1871–75	1
	Creek	1871–73	2
	Union	1875–81	3
	Walker River	1871–82	5
	S.E. Pi-Ute	1871–74	2
	N.W. Shoshone	1871–79	3
ABCFM	Sisseton	1871–73	1
	Fort Berthold	1871–73	1
American Missionary Association	Green Bay	1871–82	5
	LaPointe	1871–82	5
	Red Lake	1873–78	2
	Sisseton	1873–82	4
	Fort Berthold	1873–82	7
	Skokomish	1871–82	1
	White Earth	1871–73	1
Dutch Reformed	Colorado River	1873–77	3
	Pima-Maricopa	1871–78	2
	Camp Grant	1872–75	3
	Camp Verde	1873–74	2
	San Carlos	1874–78	2
Presbyterian	Choctaw	1871–73	2
	Seminole	1871–73	1
	Abiquiu	1871–80	6
	Navajo	1871–82	6
	Mescalero	1871–82	7
	Southern Apache	1871–77	4
	Cimarron	1871–78	5
	Pueblo	1875–78	1
	Moquis Pueblo	1871–80	12
	Nez Perce	1871–82	3
	Uintah Valley	1871–82	1

Denomination	Agency	Years	No. of Agents
Unitarian	Los Pinos	1871–78	6
	White River	1871–79	3
United Presbyterian	Warm Springs	1874–82	1
Episcopal	White Earth	1874–82	5
	Ponca	1871–77	6
	Crow Creek	1871–77	1
	Cheyenne River	1871–77	3
	Yankton	1871–82	6
	Spotted Tail	1871–77	5
	Red Cloud	1871–82	5
	Shoshone	1871–82	4
Evangelical Lutheran	Sac and Fox (Iowa)	1873–75	2
	S.E. Ute	1877–82	4
Christian	Pueblo	1871–73	3
	Neah Bay	1871–72	1
	Malheur	1876–81	1
Free Will Baptist	Leech Lake	1875–78	2

The average Peace Policy agent remained at his post for 2.3 years. Among the major denominations, Orthodox Friends (3.3) and Roman Catholics (3.1) had the longest tenure, and Presbyterians (1.9) and Episcopalians (1.9) the shortest. Agents who served for most of the Peace Policy years were: Hiram Jones (Quapaw, 1871–79); J. Miles (Kickapoo, Cheyenne-Arapaho, 1869–82); J. Simms (Colville, 1873–82); Patrick Sinnot (Grand Ronde, 1872–82); N. Cornoyer (Umatilla, 1871–74 and 1876–80); J. Wilbur (Yakima, 1871–82); E. Eells (Skokomish, 1871–82); J. Monteith (Nez Perce, 1871–78); J. Critchlow (Uintah, 1871–82); J. Smith (Warm Springs, 1866–82); H. Livingston (Crow Creek, 1871–77). The possible importance of climate is indicated by seven of the eleven long-term agents being in the Pacific Northwest.

Agent Salary

It is difficult to make valid comparisons of prices and real wages for the period 1869–82, but a few statistics indicate how well or poorly Indian agents were paid. Between 1860 and 1890 the real daily wage of factory workers increased 50 percent despite the exceptionally hard depression of 1873; more important, the cost of living decreased in the same period. In 1870 foundry workers earned $690 a year ($2.30 a day) and clothing workers $420. In 1875 blacksmiths earned $2.50 a day or about $750 a year; a machinist would be paid $810 and a carpenter $1,050 (Clarence D. Long, *Wages and Earnings in the United States, 1860–1890*, pp. 3, 13, 27–28, 37, 59, 62, 69, 79).

If it is correct that western wages were at least 30 percent higher than those in the East, then fifteen hundred dollars in the West would equal one thousand dollars in the East. An Indian agent who made fifteen hundred dollars was assured of an annual income; he also worked twenty-four hours per day, seven days per week, every week of the year.

If food consumed 50 percent of one's income and shelter 20 percent (1883), then an agent for whom the government provided these items actually received twenty-six hundred dollars. If he employed a wife or child as clerk or teacher, his income could reach four thousand dollars. Allowing a 33 percent reduction for western inflation, this leaves a real income of about twenty-two hundred to twenty-seven hundred dollars.

In 1879 there was the following salary schedule for the Indian service (from *House Exec. Doc.* no. 5, 45th Cong., 3d sess.):

$1,000   Warm Springs, Grand Ronde, Malheur, Quinault, Hoopa Valley, Tule River, Flandreau, Uintah, Great Nemaha, Otoe, Santee, Pottawatomie

$1,100   Klamath, Neah Bay, Skokomish, Lemhi

$1,200   Siletz, Umatilla, Devil's Lake, Lower Brule, Abiquiu, Sac-Fox, Quapaw, Macinac, White River, Ponca, Pawnee

$1,300   Crow Creek, Moquis

$1,400   Fort Berthold

$1,500   Sisseton, Shoshone, Pueblo, Mescalero, Green Bay, Colville, Tulalip, Round Valley, Fort Hall, Flathead, Cheyenne River, Colorado River, Red Lake, Leech Lake

$1,600   Nez Perce, Yankton, Los Pinos, Omaha-Winnebago, White Earth

$1,700   Standing Rock

$1,800   Nevada, Blackfoot, Papago, Pima

$2,000   Yakima, Crow, Fort Peck, Navajo, Kiowa-Comanche, LaPointe, San Carlos

$2,200   Red Cloud, Spotted Tail, Cheyenne-Arapaho

Indian agents were underpaid when compared with the military or with the director of the New York Customs House—the latter made forty thousand dollars per year based on moieties of fines collected (after the Phelps-Dodge scandal, the position paid an annual wage of twelve thousand dollars). Compared with ministers and missionaries, the agent did well. Episcopal bishops were paid three thousand dollars per year; Samuel Hinman's salary was fifteen hundred dollars and native preacher Enmegabowh received twelve hundred dollars; most Episcopal missionaries were paid seven hundred to one thousand dollars (1875). Salaries of ABCFM officials averaged about two thousand dollars in 1870 and dropped to sixteen hundred by 1878. The ABCFM paid promotional ministers three thousand dollars. Other government salaries during the Peace Policy years include:

Supreme Court Justice	$8,000
U.S. Senator	5,000
Territorial Governor	2,600
Clerk of the House	4,500
Sergeant at Arms, House	4,000
Clerks, House	1,800–2,500
Janitor, House	1,200
Secretary, BIC	3,000
Clerk, Board of Indian Commissioners	2,400
Commissioner of Indian Affairs	3,000
Indian Inspectors	3,000
Lieutenant General, U.S. Army	13,600
Brigadier General	7,500
Colonel	3,500
Major	2,500
2d Lieutenant	1,500
Chaplain	1,500

Appendix 4: Federal Officials, 1869–85

Federal Officials, 1869-85

President	*Secretary of the Interior*	*Commissioner of Indian Affairs*	*Secretary of War*
Ulysses S. Grant 1869-77	Jacob D. Cox 1869-70	Ely S. Parker 1869-71	John A. Rawlins 1869
	Columbus Delano 1870-75	Francis Walker 1872	William T. Sherman 1869
		Edward P. Smith 1873-75	William Belknap 1869-76
	Zachariah Chandler 1875-77	John Q. Smith 1875-77	Alphonso Taft 1876
			James Cameron 1876-77
Rutherford B. Hayes 1877-81	Carl Schurz 1877-81	Ezra D. Hayt 1877-80	George W. McCrary 1877-79
		R. E. Trowbridge 1880	Alexander Ramsey 1879-81
James Garfield 1881	Samuel J. Kirkwood 1881-82	Hiram Price 1881-85	Robert Todd Lincoln 1881-85
Chester A. Arthur 1881-85	Henry M. Teller 1882-85		

Notes

Abbreviations Used in the Notes

ABCFM	American Board of Commissioners for Foreign Missions
AHMS	American Home Missionary Society
AMA	American Missionary Association
BIC	Board of Indian Commissioners
CIA	Commissioner of Indian Affairs
EIC	Episcopal Indian Commission
FHL	Friends Historical Library
LR	Letters Received
LS	Letters Sent
NA	National Archives
OIA	Office of Indian Affairs (Bureau of Indian Affairs)
PHS	Presbyterian Historical Society
RCA	Reformed Church Archives
RG	Record Group
SI	Secretary of the Interior
WP	Whipple Papers

Introduction

1. A good introduction to Indian mission history is James R. Ronda and James Axtell, *Indian Missions: A Critical Bibliography* (Bloomington: University of Indiana Press, 1978). Henry Warner Bowden's *American Indians and Christian Missions: Studies in Cultural Conflict* (Chicago: University of Chicago Press, 1981) provides an excellent overview and interpretation of five centuries; Bowden is one of the few historians who has successfully placed Christian missions in the context of Native American religion. The leading historian of Protestant missions is R. Pierce Beaver; see the first chapter in his *Church, State and the American Indians* (St. Louis: Concordia Publishing House, 1966). Valuable sources are Wade C. Barclay, *History of*

Methodist Missions, 3 vols. (New York: Board of Missions of the Methodist Church, 1949-57); Isaac McCoy, *History of Baptist Indian Missions* (Washington: William M. Morrison, 1840); Myron Eells, *History of Indian Missions on the Pacific Coast* (Philadelphia: American Sunday School Union, 1882); and Clifford Drury's published documents and many writings on Presbyterian missions, including *Marcus and Narcissa Whitman, and the Opening of Old Oregon*, 2 vols. (Glendale, Calif.: Arthur H. Clark, 1973). In few missions did the reality contrast as starkly with the ideal as in the American Board's Oregon mission; see the account in Alvin M. Josephy, Jr., *The Nez Perce Indians and the Opening of the Northwest* (New Haven: Yale University Press, 1965). A behavioral analysis of missions and culture is found in Robert F. Berkhofer's *Salvation and the Savage* (Louisville: University of Kentucky Press, 1965). For a summary and analysis of Indian mission failure, see R. Keller, "Christian Indian Missions and the American Frontier," *American Indian Journal* 5 (April 1979): 19-29.

Protestant denominations such as the Lutherans and Disciples had virtually no Indian program prior to 1870. For example, see David E. Harrell, Jr., *Quest for a Christian America: The Disciples of Christ and American Society to 1866* (Nashville: Disciples of Christ Historical Society, 1966), pp. 207-10. Both Ronald N. Satz, *American Indian Policy in the Jacksonian Era* (Lincoln: University of Nebraska Press, 1975), p. 275, and Herman J. Viola, *Thomas L. McKenney: Architect of America's Early Indian Policy, 1816-1830* (Chicago: Swallow Press, 1974), pp. 193ff., describe Indian resistance to missions and distrust of missionaries. Baptist opposition to Indian mission programs is discussed by George A. Schultz, *An Indian Canaan* (Norman: University of Oklahoma Press, 1972), pp. 42-43. For the failure of Presbyterian missions with the prairie tribes in the 1830s and 1840s, see Robert A. Trennert, Jr., *Alternative to Extinction: Federal Indian Policy and the Beginnings of the Reservation System, 1846-1851* (Philadelphia: Temple University Press, 1975), pp. 134ff. Roy W. Meyers's *History of the Santee Sioux: United States Indian Policy on Trial* (Lincoln: University of Nebraska Press, 1967), pp. 53, 66-67, tells of the lack of success in Protestant Minnesota missions before 1862. For one of the most dismal stories of missionary incompetence, frustration, despair, and exploitation of Indians, see William E. Unrau, *The Kansa Indians: A History of the Wind People, 1673-1873* (Norman: University of Oklahoma Press, 1971), pp. 168-70, 179-82, and chap. 5. The collapse of the American Board mission to the Five Civilized Tribes is described in Robert T. Lewitt, "Indian Missions and Anti-Slavery Sentiment: A Conflict of Evangelical and Humanitarian Ideals," *Mississippi Valley Historical Review* 50 (June 1963): 39-55.

2. Sidney E. Mead, "Church and State in the United States," *Religion in Life* 20 (Winter 1950): 37.

3. Mark Dewolfe Howe, *The Garden and the Wilderness: Religion and Government in American Constitutional History* (Chicago: University of Chicago Press, 1965), and Sidney E. Mead, "Neither Church Nor State: Reflections on James Madison's 'Line of Separation,'" *Journal of Church and State* 10 (Autumn 1968): 349-63, convincingly argue that Thomas Jefferson's "wall" metaphor has become an inaccurate and unfortunate legal fiction with which to describe Church-State separation in America. The social reality has been a religious establishment, or what Robert Bellah and others call civil religion. Howe contends that the First Amendment actually served to advance *de facto* establishment of evangelical Protestant Christianity in the nineteenth century. His book is a sound historical analysis; had Howe included Indian affairs in it, he would have found in American Indian history ample confirmation of his thesis. See R. Keller, "Church Joins State to Civilize Indians, 1776-1869," *American Indian Journal* 5 (July 1979): 7-16, and Beaver, *Church, State and the American Indian.*

4. *Missionary Herald* 17 (December 1822): 377.

5. John C. Fitzpatrick, ed., *The Writings of George Washington,* 39 vols. (Washington, D.C.: U.S. Government Printing Office, 1931-44), 30:355; Robert Walker, *Torchlight to the Cherokees* (New York: Macmillan, 1931), pp. 16-18, 98-99; James D. Richardson, ed., *A Compilation of the Messages and Papers of the Presidents,* 10 vols. (Bureau of National Literature and Art, 1904), 11:415-516.

6. McCoy, *History,* p. 575 (italics in text); statistics indicating church dependence on federal aid are in Francis Paul Prucha, *American Indian Policy in the Formative Years* (Cambridge: Harvard University Press, 1962), p. 220. Virtually every denomination sought this aid between 1790 and 1860.

7. *Annual Report,* Massachusetts Missionary Society, 1802, p. 55. For Red Jacket's famous rejection of Christian missions, see "Red Jacket and the Missionary" in Wilcomb Washburn, ed., *The Indian and the White Man* (Garden City: Doubleday, 1964), pp. 209-14.

8. *Panoplist and Missionary Herald* 14 (January 1818): 46.

9. ABCFM, transcripts of correspondence, 1827-78, in the Newberry Library, Chicago, F. Ayer to D. Greene, October 31, 1838, MS 141. Ayer also complained, "The affairs of Govt with Southern Tribes has reached their ears and excited new jealousies."

10. Andrew J. Blackbird, a hereditary Ottawa chief, declared that he opposed assigning government funds to missions at the Treaty of Detroit in 1855 because such money never reached the Indians. Blackbird protested that the missionaries lied in their reports to the government and were guilty of fraud in their use of treaty money for Indian education. Andrew J. Blackbird (Mac-ke-te-pe-nas-sy), *The Indian Problem from the Indian's Standpoint* (n.p., 1900). For Sioux resentment of treaty funds being given to mission-

aries, see Meyer, *History of the Santee Sioux,* pp. 65-66. Schultz in *Indian Canaan* describes Christian efforts to secure treaty annuities, pp. 54-56.

11. *American State Papers* 2:150-51, 274-75, 446-48; William T. Hagan, *American Indians* (Chicago: University of Chicago Press, 1961), pp. 87ff.; Prucha, *American Indian Policy in the Formative Years,* p. 220ff.; Thomas L. McKenney, *Memoirs* (New York: Paine and Burgess, 1846), pp. 32-35; and Anson Phelps Stokes, *Church and State in the United States,* 3 vols. (New York: Harper and Bros., 1950), 1:704-5.

12. L. Schmeckebier in *The Office of Indian Affairs* (Baltimore: Johns Hopkins Press, 1927) asserts that between 1818 and 1845 the federal government provided more than half the money required by Indian missions (p. 40); also see Berkhofer's *Salvation and the Savage,* chap. 3; George Harmon, *Sixty Years of Indian Affairs* (Chapel Hill: University of North Carolina Press, 1941), pp. 165ff.; R. Pierce Beaver, "Church, State, and the Indians: Indian Missions in the New Nation," *Journal of Church and State* 4 (May 1962): 23-29, and *Church, State, and the American Indians,* p. 79; Schultz, *Indian Canaan,* pp. 33-35, 73, 134; Satz, *American Indian Policy,* pp. 247ff.; Viola, *Thomas L. McKenney,* chaps. 3, 10. Civilization Fund disbursements for 1824 were as follows:

United Brethren	$ 300
ABCFM	4,450
Baptist General Convention	1,950
United Foreign Mission Society	1,400
Ohio Conference, Methodist Church	500
Synod So. Carolina and Georgia	800
Cumberland Missionary Society	400
Catholic Bishop of New Orleans	300
Hamilton Baptist Mission Society	800

The ABCFM operated thirteen schools; the Baptist General Convention and the United Foreign Mission Society had four each. All other organizations had one. Four new applications were received in 1824. National Archives, RG 75, Data Book for the Civilization Fund, 1824-32.

13. ABCFM, MS 245, Newberry Transcripts, Commissioner of Indian Affairs to Governor Ramsey (Minnesota), c. 1850.

14. ABCFM:LS, Houghton Library, Harvard University. ABC 1.3.2., vol. 20, S. B. Treat to the Commissioner of Indian Affairs, July 30, 1857.

15. In 1875 Justice David Davis noted that proceeds from Osage land sales had been placed by the government into the Civilization Fund, but he offered no opinion on the matter. *Leavenworth, Lawrence and Galveston R.R. Co.* v. *United States,* 92 U.S. 733, at 750 (1875).

16. *American State Papers*, 2:273.

17. ABCFM, MS 244, Newberry Transcripts, Adams to Treat, November 1851.

18. Government recognition of the central role of the churches is frankly stated by Commissioner of Indian Affairs William Medill in his *Annual Report* of 1847, p. 749. See Francis Paul Prucha, *American Indian Policy in Crisis: Christian Reformers and the Indian* (Norman: University of Oklahoma Press, 1976), p. 32; and Prucha, "American Indian Policy in the 1840s: Visions of Reform," in John G. Clark, ed., *The Frontier Challenge: Responses to the Trans-Mississippi West* (Lawrence: University Press of Kansas, 1971), pp. 81-110.

19. Albert D. Richardson, *Beyond the Mississippi* (Hartford: American Publishing Co., 1869) gives the flavor of the times. For secondary sources, see Allan Nevins, *The Emergence of Modern America: 1865-1878* (New York: Macmillan, 1939); Arthur M. Schlesinger, Sr., *The Rise of the City: 1878-1898* (New York: Macmillan, 1933); Everett Dick, *The Sod-House Frontier: 1854-1890* (Lincoln: Johnsen Publishing, 1954); Henry May, *Protestant Churches and Industrial America* (New York: Harper and Bros., 1949); Aaron Abell, *The Urban Impact on American Protestantism, 1865-1900* (Cambridge: Harvard University Press, 1943); and Richard Hofstadter, *Social Darwinism in American Thought* (Boston: Beacon Press, 1955).

20. B. J. Lossing, "Our Barbarian Brethren," *Harper's Monthly* 40 (May 1870): 810. The Joint Special Committee of Congress, or the Doolittle Committee, named after its chairman, James R. Doolittle (Wisconsin), was formed in March of 1865; its membership consisted of two other senators and four representatives and its findings are in *Senate Report* no. 156, 39th Cong., 2d sess., *Condition of the Indian Tribes.* Members of the Peace Commission were more prestigious: N. G. Taylor, Commissioner of Indian Affairs; Senator John Henderson of Missouri; Samuel F. Tappan, a Boston philanthropist; John B. Sanborn, a wealthy Minnesota lawyer; Gen. Alfred Terry; Gen. W. S. Harney (ret.); Gen. William T. Sherman. The *Report of the Indian Peace Commissioners* is in *House Executive Document* no. 97, 40th Cong., 2d sess. Sherman's cynical attitude toward the commission is described in Robert Athearn, *William Tecumseh Sherman and the Settlement of the West* (Norman: University of Oklahoma Press, 1956). Athearn's book remains one of the best presentations of the western and military viewpoint, 1865-80.

21. *Condition of the Indian Tribes*, pp. 10, 21, 405-10, 478, 481; Whipple, "Our Indian System," *North American Review*, 1864, pp. 452-53; William Welsh, *Sioux and Ponca Indians* (Philadelphia: McCalla and Stavely, 1870), p. 24.

22. Grant's Peace Policy can be seen as a reform of the patronage system. The *Nation* (December 31, 1868, p. 544) had argued that only civil service

reform and the removal of "rag-tag-and-bobtail" agents would solve the Indian problem, but the attitude of the United States, especially the western states, was that spoils were essential for grass-roots politics. Also see Leonard D. White, *The Republican Era, 1869–1901: A Study in Administrative History* (New York: Macmillan, 1958), pp. 1, 5–8, 26, 291, 318.

23. R. Satz, *American Indian Policy in the Jacksonian Era*, chaps. 6–7; Viola, *Thomas L. McKenney*, pp. 104, 223; Meyer, *History of the Santee Sioux*, chap. 3.

24. John C. Paige, "Wichita Indian Agents, 1857–1869," *Journal of the West* 12 (July 1973): 403–13.

25. Gerald Thompson, *The Army and the Navajo* (Tucson: University of Arizona Press, 1976).

26. Whipple, *Lights and Shadows of a Long Episcopate* (New York: Macmillan, 1900), pp. 510–14.

27. Modern historians frequently accept the corrupt agent mythology. See, for example, Edmund J. Danziger, Jr., *Indians and Bureaucrats: Administering the Reservation Policy During the Civil War* (Urbana: University of Illinois Press, 1974). What is needed, as William Unrau has argued, are specific agency studies that carefully examine what actually happened on a reservation apart from the constant accusations and claims of fraud that beset almost every agency. Gerald Thompson's work on Bosque Redondo is a good example of such research, as are John Bret Harte's publications and doctoral dissertation on San Carlos. Unrau has sought to do this using southern plains agent Jesse Leavenworth as an example of an intelligent, sensitive man caught up in the complex dilemmas of Indian administration on the frontier. See his "Indian Agent vs. the Army," *Kansas Historical Quarterly* 30 (Summer 1964): 129–52, and "The Civilian as Indian Agent: Villain or Victim?" *Western Historical Quarterly* 3 (October 1972): 405–20. Thompson in *The Navajo and the Army* (Tucson: University of Arizona Press, 1976), however, reaches very different conclusions about Leavenworth, and Unrau's sympathy for agents is somewhat compromised by the evidence in his history of the Kansas Indians, who, for example, suffered under nine terrible agents between 1848 and 1855. Also see *Condition of the Indian Tribes*, p. 460; U.S. Commissioner of Indian Affairs, *Annual Report*, 1869, p. 305. Job hunters and new agents often discredited the work of their predecessors in order to exalt themselves, character assassination being a common way to gain control of an agency. In 1887 J. B. Harrison reported that "one hears in the Indian country all kinds of vague, incoherent and absurd rumors about everybody," *The Latest Studies on Indian Reservations* (Philadelphia: Indian Rights Assoc., 1887), pp. 20, 199.

28. For a careful defense of early government policy and administration, see Prucha, *American Indian Policy in the Formative Years*. Official corruption

and duplicity is revealed in Paul Gates's *Fifty Million Acres* (Ithaca, N.Y.: Cornell University Press, 1954), an account of graft, betrayal, lying, and outright theft during the occupation of Kansas. Gates shows how white settlers lost their lands, too, as corporations, speculators, and even missionaries cheated Indians and white men in land schemes. The impact on Indians is made specific in Unrau's *Kansa Indians*. Howard Lamar's *Dakota Territory, 1861-1889* (New Haven: Yale University Press, 1956), and *The Far Southwest, 1846-1912* (New Haven: Yale University Press, 1966), demonstrate the dependence of the federal government on frontier cooperation.

29. See Sandra Sizer, *Gospel Hymns and Social Religion* (Philadelphia: Temple University Press, 1978), and "Politics and Apolitical Religion: The Great Urban Revivals of the Late Nineteenth Century," *Church History* 48 (March 1979): 81-98. William G. McLoughlin's *American Evangelicals* (New York: Harper and Row, 1968) is a helpful anthology and his *Revivals, Awakening and Reform* (Chicago: University of Chicago Press, 1980) integrates religion and social change. A recent analysis of the churches in the 1860s is James H. Moorhead, *American Apocalypse: Yankee Protestants and the Civil War, 1860-1869* (New Haven: Yale University Press, 1978).

30. John F. Finerty, *War-Path and Bivouac* (Chicago: Donohue and Henneberry, 1890), p. 145.

31. Niebuhr's critique of moral pride and idealism is best stated in *The Irony of American History* (New York: Charles Scribner's Sons, 1952), where he argues that Americans fail to recognize the fortuitous elements in their national prosperity and therefore mistakenly congratulate themselves on controlling history. Two essays by Woodward on the same subject are in his *Burden of Southern History* (New York: Vintage Books, 1961). Also see Martin E. Marty, *Righteous Empire* (New York: Dial Press, 1970).

32. Robert Patterson, "Our Indian Policy," *Overland Monthly* 11 (September 1873): 201.

33. *The Holyoke Transcript* (1873), quoted in Thomas Cochran and William Miller, *The Age of Enterprise* (New York: Harper Torchbooks, 1961), p. 231. Confessions of moral failure in Indian affairs and a determination to achieve justice appear frequently in official government statements. See Francis Paul Prucha, ed., *Documents of United States Indian Policy* (Lincoln: University of Nebraska Press, 1975), documents 9-11, 14-15, 28, 35, 38, 41, 44-45, 62-64, 67-69, 74-75.

34. Francis Parkman, *The Oregon Trail* (New York: Modern Library, 1949), pp. 51-52.

35. Franklin Littell, *From State Church to Pluralism: A Protestant Interpretation of Religion in American History* (Garden City, N.Y.: Doubleday Anchor Books, 1962), pp. 92-95. Robert Bellah makes similar comments in *The Broken Covenant* (New York: Seabury Press, 1975): Indian dispossession is

"the primal crime on which American society is based" and the plight of Indians is "the most damning testimony against the course of American history" (pp. 36–37, 146). Littell and Bellah's observations are typical of a long-standing approach to Indian history that began with Helen Hunt Jackson's *Century of Dishonor* (1881; reprint ed., New York: Little, Brown and Co., 1903) and which continued with Dee Brown's *Bury My Heart at Wounded Knee: An Indian History of the American West* (New York: Holt, Rinehart and Winston, 1970).

36. F. D. Huntington, *Two Ways of Treating the Indian Problem* (Indian Commission of the Protestant Episcopal Church, 1875), pp. 2–4.

Chapter 1

1. At times historians have made too sharp a distinction between Grant's Peace Policy and his Quaker Policy, the former being defined as his entire Indian administration, including the use of force to suppress tribes, and the latter being the appointment of Quakers and adherence to pacifistic principles in the Northern and Southern superintendencies. Such a distinction obscures more than it reveals and imposes a more careful definition of terms than was used in the 1870s. Robert Winston Mardock in *The Reformers and the American Indian* (Columbia: University of Missouri Press, 1971) employs the term *Peace Policy* to refer to goals of the entire Indian reform movement, and Prucha, in *American Indian Policy in Crisis*, says the expression refers to "a state of mind." My definition emphasizes that the Grant Peace Policy was first of all a Church-related reform program.

2. Not included in my definition are two other important goals for the Grant administration and Indian reformers: the abolition of the treaty system, which was achieved by 1871, and the termination and consolidation of reservations in favor of individual allotment. See Prucha, *American Indian Policy in Crisis*, chaps. 4, 13, and pp. 63–71, 110, 231–34.

3. *House Misc. Doc.* no. 37, 39th Cong., 2d sess., E. S. Parker to General U. S. Grant, January, 1867. Also see A. C. Parker, *The Life of General Ely S. Parker: Last Great Sachem of the Iroquois and General Grant's Military Secretary* (Buffalo: Buffalo Historical Society, 1919); and William H. Armstrong, *Warrior in Two Camps: Ely S. Parker, Union General and Seneca Chief* (Syracuse: Syracuse University Press, 1978). Parker, the grandson of Red Jacket, had worked with Lewis H. Morgan on *The League of the Ho-de-no-sau-nee, or Iroquois*; in 1867 Parker had also advocated Indian territorial government and the need for closer inspection of agencies. See Armstrong, pp. 119–21, for a description of Parker's plan for reform of the Indian Office.

4. See Prucha, *American Indian Policy in Crisis*, chap. 9, for a description of the reformers' uncritical faith in education.

5. FHL:RG 2, William Macy to B. Hallowell, October 27, 1868; WP, O. H. Browning to Whipple, December 26, 1868; E. A. Washburn to Whipple, December 28, 1868; A. Badeau to Whipple, February 13, 1869; B. Hallowell to Whipple, January 7, 1869.

Henry Benjamin Whipple was born in Adams, New York, where he grew up as a Presbyterian before joining the Episcopal Church at the age of twenty in 1842. Before his ordination in 1849, Whipple had worked in his father's business and had been active in the Democratic party; between 1849 and 1859, when he was appointed as Minnesota's first bishop, he served parishes in New York and Chicago. After coming to Minnesota, he learned to respect the Indians and their way of life, at the same time recognizing that their culture was doomed. As a reformer, Whipple combined zeal and devotion with a Calvinist intuition for human limits. Always a tough, eloquent fighter, he had the personal political connections, and direct influence in official government circles and in the business world, that most reformers and missionaries lacked. Among his friends he could count John J. Astor, J. P. Morgan, Arthur Peabody, William Vanderbilt, and William Tecumseh Sherman. Whipple corresponded regularly with cabinet members and knew all the American presidents since Jackson, being especially close to Lincoln, Grant, Hayes, and Cleveland. Appointed by the federal government as Minnesota's acting superintendent of Indian affairs in 1868 and 1869, Whipple accepted this and other Indian Office assignments as a trust from God. He respected Indians as men and women, and they in turn called him "Straight Tongue." He understood the injustices that they suffered, and in a frontier parish he defended them against racist whites, developing a rapport with tribes that frequently inspired the government to appoint him as a treaty commissioner and to seek his advice, as Browning did here. Two years before his death in 1901, Whipple remarked, "I seem to have been a man of war from the beginning. Circumstances forced me to be so." The papers and correspondence of this remarkable reformer, held by the Minnesota Historical Society, constitute a crucial source for study of the Peace Policy.

6. Thomas Battey in the introduction to Lawrie Tatum, *Our Red Brothers and the Peace Policy of President Ulysses S. Grant* (Philadelphia: John C. Winston, 1899), p. xvii; written thirty years later, this stylized account of the meeting is obviously influenced by Battey's imagination.

7. The letter was published in an 1879 reprint of the *Brief Sketch of the Efforts of the Philadelphia Yearly Meeting* (emphasis in text).

8. National Archives, SI:LR, Appointments Division, Baltimore Convention of Hicksite Friends to President Grant, April 19, 1869; FHL:RG 2, F. W. Cook to B. Hallowell, March 29, 1869. For a critical survey of Quaker history and the Society's relations with Indian tribes, see Clyde A. Milner II, *With Good Intentions: Quaker Work among the Pawnees, Otos, and Omahas in the 1870s* (Lincoln: University of Nebraska Press, 1982).

9. For the issues dividing the Friends, see Samuel Janney, *The Separation of the Religious Society of Friends in America in 1827-28* (Philadelphia: T. Ellwood Zell, 1868 [?]), and Robert W. Doherty, *The Hicksite Separation: A Sociological Analysis of Religious Schism in Early Nineteenth Century America* (New Brunswick: Rutgers University Press, 1967).

10. Whipple, *Lights and Shadows,* pp. 516-18; Henry Fritz, *The Movement for Indian Assimilation, 1860-1890* (Philadelphia: University of Pennsylvania Press, 1963), pp. 34-55; Society of Friends (Orthodox), Western Yearly Meeting, *Minutes,* 1861, pp. 31-32; Edward D. Neill, *Efforts and Failure to Civilize the Aborigines* (Washington: Government Printing Office, 1868); Martha L. Edwards, "A Problem of Church and State in the 1870's," *Mississippi Valley Historical Review* 11 (June 1924): 45.

11. Charles J. Kappler, *Indian Affairs: Laws and Treaties,* 2 vols. (Washington: Government Printing Office, 1904). Provisions for boards of visitors were made in the following treaties: Treaty with the Chippewas of the Mississippi and Pillager and Lake Winnibigoshish bands (1863), art. 7; ibid., (1864), art. 7; treaty with the Red Lake and Pembina Chippewas (1863), art. 6; treaty with the Chippewas of Saginaw, Swan Creek, and Black River (1864), art. 4. The Pillager and Red Lake treaties provided for a board of three members "selected from . . . Christian denominations" and empowered to inspect agencies, attend annuity payments, oversee the morality of the reservations, and report annually to the government. The Saginaw treaty required the Michigan superintendent of education, the lieutenant governor, and a representative of the Methodist Missionary Society to inspect agency schools and report on the qualifications of teachers.

12. National Archives, SI:LS: Cox to William Welsh, April 15, 1869; on the U.S. Christian Commission, see Stokes, *Church and State,* 2:230-33. Leaders in the Peace Policy who served on the Commission were Felix Brunot, E. P. Smith, George Stuart, James V. Farwell, William Dodge, Clinton Fisk, Nathan Bishop, and E. S. Tobey.

13. *Condition of the Indian Tribes,* pp. 8-10.

14. The six influential citizens were George Stuart, Eli K. Price, S. R. Shipley, J. S. Hilles, Thomas Wister, and Judge Strong.

15. WP, Welsh to Whipple, March 26, 1869; George H. Stuart, *The Life of George H. Stuart* (Philadelphia: J. M. Stoddart, 1890); the report of Welsh's committee is in Welsh, *Journal of S. D. Hinman* (Philadelphia: McCalla and Stavely, 1869), pp. 73-78.

16. *Churchman,* March 30, 1878, p. 342, and George Hinman, *American Indians and Christian Missions* (New York: Fleming H. Revell, 1933), p. 97, gave the credit to Whipple and Welsh; others later claimed that they had originated the Policy. Superintendent T. J. McKenney said he had advocated the Peace Policy as early as 1867 (CIA, *Annual Report,* 1872, p. 346); A. C.

Parker hinted that Ely S. Parker submitted the ideas to Grant (*Parker*, p. 147) and A. B. Meacham, Oregon Superintendent, is cited in Keith Murray, *The Modocs and Their War* (Norman: University of Oklahoma Press, 1959), p. 44, as having "presented" the Policy to Grant. The best life of Grant is William S. McFeely, *Grant: A Biography* (New York: W. W. Norton, 1981). Chap. 19 on Grant's Peace Policy is based almost entirely on secondary sources. McFeely suggests that John Rawlins may have had a humane influence on Grant in regard to Indian tribes, p. 299.

17. Henry G. Waltmann, "Circumstantial Reformer: President Grant and the Indian Problem," *Arizona and the West* 13 (Winter 1971): 323-42, is the best study of Grant's motives and attitudes in Indian affairs. Waltmann argues that Grant has been greatly overrated as an Indian reformer. Robert Mardock in *Reformers and the American Indian* fails to explain Grant's actions and Mardock's evidence that the president had "thought a great deal about the Indian question" (p. 49) is weak. Mardock's generalizations about "most reformers" do not fit Grant. The argument for a de facto transfer to the army is made by Milner, "With Good Intentions: Quaker Work and Indian Survival, the Nebraska Case, 1869-1882" (Ph.D. diss., Yale University, 1979), pp. 33-40.

18. Ulysses S. Grant, *Personal Memoirs* (New York: Grosset and Dunlap, 1962), pp. 20-29, 88.

19. *Harper's Weekly*, March 13, 20, 1869; also see the *Congregationalist*, March 4, 11, 1869.

20. M. M. Cramer, *Ulysses S. Grant: Conversations and Unpublished Letters* (New York: Eaton and Mains, 1897), pp. 74-75, 108; Adam Badeau, *Grant in Peace from Appomattox to Mount McGregor: A Personal Memoir* (S. S. Scranton, 1887), chap. 17.

21. John Y. Simon, ed., *The Papers of Ulysses S. Grant, 1837-1861*, 5 vols. (Carbondale: Southern Illinois University Press, 1967-), 1:14; Lawrence A. Frost, *U. S. Grant Album: A Pictorial Biography of Ulysses S. Grant* (Seattle: Superior Publishing, 1966), p. 22. The painting was probably copied from the work of another artist as part of a class exercise; Grant's piece is in the West Point Museum.

22. Grant, *Memoirs*, pp. 15, 102-4. Some of his contemporaries believed that Grant's experience in the Northwest inspired the Peace Policy; see the *Congressional Globe*, 42d Cong., 3d sess., January 10, 1873, and *Harper's* editorial on August 5, 1876. George Childs, a close friend, said in 1890 that at Fort Vancouver Grant had resolved to help the Indians; according to Childs, Grant was a talented artist and had painted a portrait of a "noble" chief on the Columbia (George W. Childs, *Recollections* [Philadelphia: J. B. Lippincott, 1890], pp. 71-72, 100-101). Felix Brunot reported to Whipple in 1870 that Grant's experience in Oregon made him knowledgeable about

Indians (WP, Brunot to Whipple, February 11, 1870) and Brunot's biographer, Charles Slattery, wrote in 1901 that a "shocked" Grant vowed at Fort Vancouver to attack the corruption of the Indian system (*Felix Reville Brunot* [New York: Longmans, Green, and Co., 1901], p. 142). Childs and Slattery are undocumented.

There were also rumors that Grant had an Indian mistress while stationed on the Columbia. Click Relander, in a history of the Yakima nation, *Strangers on the Land* (Yakima, Wash.: Franklin Press, 1962), asserts that Grant lived with an Indian woman at Fort Vancouver, that she once saved his life, and that he then deserted her (p. 78). Relander provides no documentation for his assertions, but the story is very similar to the one recorded in Lucullus V. McWhorter's research notes, which reads: "Grant had an Indian 'wife' at Vancouver, who in all probability saved the young Lieut. to the Presidency of the U.S. He and some of the officers, or privates, were worsted in a saloon broil, and Grant going to his quarters, procured his pistol and was returning to the fray, when he was seized by his 'wife,' who dragged him down on her lap on the ground and was holding him thus when found by some of his companions and returned to his quarters. He was too drunk to overcome the opposition of the Indian woman. Grant left two half-blood children at Vancouver, issue from this 'marriage'; a boy and a girl" (Lucullus V. McWhorter, "'Lieutenants' Grant and Sheridan's Indian wifes," typescript, file 1544, L. V. McWhorter Papers, Washington State University Library, Pullman, Washington). McWhorter's annotation gives David Longmire, an early Washington Territory pioneer, as his source. McFeely, in *Grant,* discounts the story of an Indian daughter, p. 282, but he did not evaluate the stories by Relander and McWhorter.

23. Simon, *Papers,* Grant to Julia Dent Grant, March 19, 1853, 1:296.

24. Ibid., Grant to Cross, July 25, 1853, p. 310. The Yakima Indian War of 1855-58 would prove Grant wrong.

25. Richardson, *Messages,* 7:38.

26. Fritz, *Movement for Indian Assimilation,* pp. 69ff.; Athearn, *Sherman,* p. 228; Donald J. Berthrong, *The Southern Cheyennes* (Norman: University of Oklahoma Press, 1963), pp. 284, 388; Richard N. Ellis, *General Pope and U.S. Indian Policy* (Albuquerque: University of New Mexico Press, 1970), pp. 118-21, 235; Ralph H. Ogle, *Federal Control of the Western Apaches, 1848-1886* (Albuquerque: University of New Mexico Press, 1940), p. 69.

27. Meyer, *History of the Santee Sioux,* p. 263.

28. Robert M. Utley, *Frontier Regulars: The United States Army and the Indian, 1866-1891* (New York: Macmillan, 1973), p. 198.

29. Gerald Thompson, *The Army and the Navajo,* pp. 107, 121, 148.

30. Ibid., p. 129; James C. Olson, *Red Cloud and the Sioux Problem* (Lincoln: University of Nebraska Press, 1965), p. 72.

31. Gertrude Stein, *Four in America* (New Haven: Yale University Press, 1947); Edmund Wilson, *Patriotic Gore: Studies in the Literature of the American Civil War* (New York: Oxford University Press, 1962), pp. 140-41.

32. Simon, *Papers*, 1:7.

33. Grant, *Memoirs*, pp. 107-10; Richardson, *Messages*, 7:151. Know-Nothing secrecy and opposition to freedom repelled Grant and he never returned after his first meeting.

34. Francis Paul Prucha, *Indian Peace Medals in American History* (Madison: State Historical Society of Wisconsin, 1971), pp. 125-29. The Arizona Historical Society in Tucson holds a silver 1871 Grant peace medal that was taken from the body of Noch-aye-det-Klin-ne, a White Mountain medicine man killed in 1881 at the Battle of Cibicu Creek.

35. Richardson, *Messages*, pp. 221-22. Grant sincerely hoped this was God's will, but knew better. "To maintain peace in the future it is necessary to be prepared for war" (Grant, *Memoirs*, p. 587).

36. Mark Twain, *Autobiography*, 2 vols. (P. F. Collier and Son, 1925), 1:69.

37. BIC Journal (NA:RG 75), 1873, p. 64; Library of Congress, Grant Papers, Grant to George Stuart, October 26, 1872, October 9, 1873; also see Stuart, *Life of George H. Stuart* (Philadelphia: J. M. Stoddart, 1890), p. 279. McFeely, in *Grant*, makes it convincingly clear that Grant was not a racist, even though he and his wife had once owned slaves, and though his administration of Reconstruction policy in the 1870s would have negative effects on blacks for a century to come.

38. Cramer, *Conversations*, pp. 7-8, 28-29, 41-43, 55, 106-7, 129, 166.

39. Library of Congress, John P. Newman Papers, Mrs. C. B. Strong to Newman, April 6, 1885; also see Richard Goldhurst, *Many Are the Hearts: The Agony and the Triumph of Ulysses S. Grant* (New York: Reader's Digest Press, 1975), p. 190; Twain, *Autobiography*, 1:68-70; Thomas M. Pitkin, *The Captain Departs: Ulysses S. Grant's Last Campaign* (Carbondale: Southern Illinois University Press, 1973), pp. 34, 72.

40. Grant Papers, Library of Congress, Grant to Stuart, October 26, 1872.

41. Richardson, *Messages*, 7:38-39, 200, 222.

42. J. F. C. Fuller, *Grant and Lee: A Study in Personality and Generalship* (Bloomington: University of Indiana Press, 1957), p. 58; Pitkin, *The Captain Departs*, from the foreword by John Simon, p. xiii.

43. Goldhurst, *Many Are the Hearts*, p. xxi.

44. Quoted in Pitkin, *The Captain Departs*, p. 93. Grant has an unusual following of literary admirers: Twain, Gertrude Stain, Hamlin Garland, Owen Wister, Matthew Arnold, Edmund Wilson.

45. Wilson, *Patriotic Gore*, pp. 164-67.

46. CIA, *Annual Report,* 1872, p. 10; this report, also published as part of a book, *The Indian Question* (Boston: James R. Osgood, 1874), is the most balanced and perceptive contemporary analysis of Grant's policy.

47. Richardson, *Messages,* 7:109.

48. PHS, American Indian Correspondence, J. D. Cox to J. Lowrie, August 19, 1870; B. Cowen to Lowrie, May 18, 1872; SI, *Annual Report,* 1872, p. 9; ibid., 1873, p. iii; CIA, *Annual Report,* 1872, p. 7.

49. Orthodox Friends, Associated Executive Committee, *Annual Report,* 1870, p. 2; Friends, *Joint Delegation;* Barclay White, *Friends and the Indians* (Oxford, Pa.: published for the convention, 1886), pp. 6-9.

50. BIC:LR, Questionnaire of the Presbyterian Foreign Mission Society, 1871; *Spirit of Missions* 37, 1872, "What is the New Peace Policy?" p. 279; WP, Letterbooks, Whipple to H. H. Sibley, November 25, 1870.

51. Methodists later said they had joined the program only after being assured that they did not have to provide missionaries; the American Missionary Association also supplied few missionaries. As the Peace Policy gradually expired under the Hayes administration, the churches complained that their obligations were ambiguous, "a little like the British constitution—unwritten." This was true at the end, not at the beginning.

52. CIA, *Annual Report,* 1871, p. 266. Also see BIC, *Annual Report,* 1869, p. 10; 1872, p. 168; 1874, p. 10.

53. FHL:RG 2, S. Janney to Hallowell, April 2, 1869; W. Dorsey to Hallowell, April 3, 1869; WP, H. B. Denman to Whipple, April 6, 1869.

54. FHL:RG 2, Wharton to A. G. Cattell, March 30, 1869; Wharton to Hallowell, March 30, 1869; the FHL also has Hallowell's rough draft of his speech to Grant on April 8.

55. April 10, 1869, 16 Stat. 40, sec. 4.

Chapter 2

1. *Senate Document* no. 49, 41st Cong., 3d sess., 1870; *Executive Document* no. 269, 41st Cong., 2d sess., 1870; BIC:LR, F. Brunot to Colyer, April 13, 1870; Colyer to Brunot, July 16, 1870; Newberry Library, Grierson Papers, F. Brunot to Grierson, May 12, 1870. Also see Athearn, *Sherman,* pp. 277-82. Robert Utley states that the Peace Policy at first had army approval and that Grant had accomplished a rare harmony between the BIA and the army, but the Piegan Massacre, according to Utley, eliminated the military from any further constructive role with the Bureau. *Frontier Regulars:* pp. 190-91. Robert Mardock in *Reformers and the American Indian,* pp. 67-74, concurs, also pointing out that the Piegan affair eliminated any possibility of transfer in the early 1870s and increased public support for the Peace

Policy. Another interpretation of the affair is Robert J. Ege's *Strike Them Hard* (Bellevue, Nebr.: Old Army Press, 1970).

2. *Harper's Weekly*, March 19, 1870; Newberry Library, Ayer Collection, MS no. 149, George Catlin to Professor Harper, 1870; *Independent*, March 17, 1870; *Baptist Watchman*, March 3, 1870.

3. *Congressional Globe*, 41st Cong., 2d sess., p. 1581.

4. I am indebted to Mr. Gerald D. McDonald of the New York Public Library, American History Division, for information on Colyer. Also see the New York Historical Society's *Dictionary of Artists in America*, and Appleton's *Cyclopedia of American Biography* (1887); Colyer's controversial trip is described in the BIC, *Annual Report*, 1869, pp. 30-55.

5. BIC:LS, Colyer to Rev. Mr. Anthony, June 20, 1870; Colyer to F. Brunot, July 12, 1870; WP, W. Welsh to Whipple, June 24, 1870; BIC, *Annual Report*, 1870, pp. 4, 93-96. Felix Brunot and Thomas Cree later claimed that Grant had intended from the beginning to use other churches and that army agents had simply been an "opening wedge." There is no other evidence for this. When William T. Sherman testified to a Senate hearing in 1878 he recalled Grant's displeasure over the 1870 law and said that the president then turned to the churches to outflank the politicians. *Senate Misc. Doc.* no. 53, 45th Cong., 3d sess., p. 227. Henry G. Waltmann concluded that expansion of the Peace Policy to other churches was Grant's slap at Congress for removing the army; Waltmann interprets Grant as being stubborn and spiteful, acting out of frustration. Waltmann's evidence is a quotation attributed to Grant in Sherman's *Memoirs*. H. G. Waltmann, "Circumstantial Reformer: President Grant and the Indian Problem," *Arizona and the West* 13 (Winter 1971): 323-42. Ralph Ogle in *Federal Control of the Western Apaches* had a different theory, holding that the 1869 mining boom in Arizona caused eastern capitalists to support the Peace Policy, p. 88. Also see Richardson, *Messages* 7:38.

6. *Congressional Globe*, 41st Cong., 2d sess., p. 4083.

7. Richardson, *Messages* 7:109.

8. BIC:LR, J. Cox to F. Brunot, August 20, 1870.

9. There was no correlation between church membership distribution by state and agency allocations. See Edwin Scott Gaustad, *Historical Atlas of Religion in America*, rev. ed. (New York: Harper and Row, 1976), pp. 46-51.

10. BIC:LS, V. Colyer to J. Cox, August 11, 1870 (emphasis in text).

11. Charles Ewing, *Petition of the Catholic Church for the Agency of the Chippewas* (Washington: Polkinhorn and Co., 1873), pp. 6, 16-17; Ewing, *Circular of the Catholic Commissioner for Indian Missions* (Baltimore: John Murphy and Co., 1874), pp. 10-12. Also see Peter J. Rahill, *Catholic Indian Missions and Grant's Peace Policy* (Washington: Catholic University Press,

1953), pp. 53, 89. For Presbyterian use of this argument, see CIA, *Annual Report*, 1871, p. 171; 1874, p. 193. Secretary of the Interior Delano verified the principle in a letter to the Dutch Reformed, February 25, 1871.

12. SI:LR, N. Bishop to Ely S. Parker, December 2, 1870. Although this is the only criterion that made sense of Methodist assignments, there is no evidence that the government or BIC ever used it.

13. BIC:LR, an undated, unaddressed, and unsigned statement with Felix Brunot's handwriting in the July 1871 to January 1872 folder makes this argument. Also see F. Brunot to T. Cree, February 12, 1873.

14. See R. Pierce Beaver, *Ecumenical Beginnings in Protestant World Missions: A History of Comity* (New York: Thomas Nelson and Sons, 1962), chaps. 1, 2. Denominational competition on the frontier and attempts to limit it through comity agreements are traced in Colin B. Goodykoontz, *Home Missions on the American Frontier* (Caldwell, Idaho: Caxton Printers, 1939), pp. 351–54. Comity agreements sought to avoid the situation that came to exist on the Navajo reservation, where not only Mormons, Episcopalians, Baptists, Presbyterians, and Methodists now compete for the Indians' attention, but also Seventh Day Adventists, Nazarenes, Plymouth Brethren, the Good News missionaries, Gospel Missions, Free Methodists, and the Wycliffe School of Bible Translators.

15. RCA, R. C. McCormick to E. S. Parker, February 16, 1871; C. Delano to J. M. Ferris, February 25, 1871; E. Palmer to Ferris, March 1, 1871; Delano to Ferris, March 3, 1871.

16. According to the CIA, *Annual Report*, 1869, there were active missions only at the Flathead, Umatilla, Tulalip, Yakima, Lake Traverse, Seminole, and Creek reservations. There was little information in Catholic publications. Henry Fritz defended the apportionment system by showing that of seventy-five missionaries mentioned in the 1861 CIA *Annual Report*, only nineteen were Catholic, whereas twenty-five were Methodist and many others probably Presbyterian; *Movement for Indian Assimilation*, p. 91. The error in this analysis is neglecting to define *missionary*.

17. See Appendix 1 for a list of agency assignments and subsequent changes.

18. F. Blanchet to T. Mesplie, September 21, 1871, quoted in Rahill, *Catholic Indian Missions*, p. 54; John G. Shea, "What Right Has the Federal Government to Mismanage the Indians?" *American Catholic Quarterly Review* 6 (1881): 530; A. C. Barstow to H. Dawes, February 13, 1881, quoted in Loring B. Priest, *Uncle Sam's Stepchildren: the Reformation of United States Indian Policy, 1865–1887* (New Brunswick: Rutgers University Press, 1942), p. 52. Whitner's dissertation on the Methodists and the Peace Policy does not discuss this question except to indicate that Methodists expressed dissatisfaction over receiving too few agencies (pp. 81–82).

19. *Independent,* December 16, 1875, p. 14.

20. Twain, who felt that Newman exaggerated and then exploited Grant's supposed piety, intensely disliked the minister. Newman also preached an hour and a half sermon at Grant's funeral. Richard Goldhurst, *Many are the Hearts: The Agony and the Triumph of Ulysses S. Grant,* p. 190; Thomas M. Pitkin, *The Captain Departs: Ulysses S. Grant's Last Campaign,* pp. 72, 109-10.

21. U.S. Library of Congress, Simpson Papers, B. F. Rawlins to Simpson, June 21, 1872; J. E. Parker to Simpson, November 6, 1872; W. Little to Simpson, December 4, 1872; James Wright to Simpson, December 9, 1872; W. Thomas to Simpson, February 15, 1873, and others. For Simpson's career, see James E. Kirby, "Matthew Simpson and the Mission of America," *Church History* 36 (September 1967): 299-307.

22. *Condition of the Indian Tribes,* pp. 392-93, 434, 469, 477, 480.

23. Anti-Catholicism was prevalent not only in the religious press, but also in much of the secular press. See almost any issue of *Harper's Weekly,* 1870-80, especially Thomas Nast's cartoons. For historical background, see R. A. Billington's *Protestant Crusade* and John Higham's *Strangers in the Land.*

24. PHS, Monteith to Lowrie, December 20, 1877; John Reid, *Missions and Missionary Society of the Methodist Episcopal Church,* 2 vols. (New York: Phillips and Hunt, 1879), 1:94-95.

Protestant and government prejudice against Catholics has been sufficiently documented in Rahill's *Catholic Indian Missions and Grant's Peace Policy.* Henry Fritz (*Movement for Indian Assimilation,* chap. 4) sought to refute some of Rahill's contention, but there is no doubt that the Indian Office secretly discriminated against Catholics during the Peace Policy (e.g., see RCA, Cree to Ferris, February 28, 1872; B. R. Cowen to Ferris, February 7, 1874). On the other hand, Catholic historians John G. Shea, John Tracy Ellis, and Rahill tend to overlook Catholic prejudice against and misconception of Protestantism ("the devil's church"), and they praise Catholic Indian missions too highly, forgetting that Catholics suffered the same difficulties and conflicts as Protestants both before and after 1869. See John Fahey, *The Flathead Indians* (Norman: University of Oklahoma Press, 1974), pp. 157, 178-86; Louis Pfaller, "The Forging of An Indian Agent," *North Dakota History* 34 (Winter 1967): 62-76. Cooperation between the two bodies too often has been overlooked; for further discussion, see Chapter 3.

25. BIC:LS, T. Cree to W. L. Harris, February 23, 1872; SI:LR, S. G. Irvine and G. W. Gray to W. Corbett, May 27, 1871; PHS, Executive Committee of the Oregon Presbytery to C. Delano, June 10, 1874. Methodists unofficially controlled the Puget Sound agencies (Puyallup, Nisqually, Chehalis, etc.) through Robert Milroy, a Methodist minister and Washington's

superintendent of Indian affairs. For the shifting of agencies between churches and prior claims, see Appendix 1.

26. The Methodists did not establish a permanent Blackfeet mission until 1893; Harrod, *Mission Among the Blackfeet* (Norman: University of Oklahoma Press, 1971), pp. 25–29. Also see Francis J. Weber, "Grant's Peace Policy: A Catholic Dissenter," *Montana the Magazine of Western History* (Winter 1969), pp. 56–63. Weber asserts that John P. Newman manipulated the appointment of Methodist agents prejudiced against Catholics.

27. BIC:LR, C. H. Hall to Brunot, January 20, 1872; W. C. McKay to Cree, January 20, 1872; Brunot to Rev. S. Parrish, February 22, 1872; Brunot to Cree, February 12, 1872.

28. Spalding Papers, Washington State University Library, Spalding to O. Marshall, May 2, 1870.

29. Spalding Papers, Spalding to Marshall, December 30, 1870, January 24, 1871; BIC:LR, Spalding to Colyer, May 31, June 3, 1871; PHS, Spalding to Colyer, November 30, 1871.

30. BIC, *Annual Report*, 1870, pp. 93–95, 106; PHS, J. Cox to Lowrie, August 19, September 8, 1870.

31. The *Report on the Condition of the Indian Tribes* frequently referred to Catholicism as the "religion of the country" and the only one able to influence Indians in the Southwest (pp. 106, 108, 112, 148, 187, 224, 323, 356–57, 307–11).

32. SI:LR, Lowrie to C. Delano, April 22, 1873; BIC, *Journal*, 1873, p. 15; BIC, *Annual Report*, 1875, p. 154; Presbyterian Board of Foreign Missions, *Annual Report*, 1873, pp. 15–17. Colyer's deliberate efforts against the Catholic church are most evident in his correspondence with the Dutch Reformed. He said that Catholics were "scheming" for agencies and used this threat to push Reformed nominations. He received a blunt reply from Dutch Reformed officials: *"We will not be hurried one day by Roman Catholics."* BIC:LS, Colyer to Stout, January 24, 1872; BIC:LR, J. Ferris to Colyer, February 27, 1872 (emphasis in MS).

33. FHL, Janney Papers, S. Janney to Elizabeth Janney, June 27, 1869; Wm. Dorsey to S. Janney, December 17, 1870; OIA:LR, Welsh to C. Delano, December 15, 1870; PHS, S. B. Treat to Lowrie, December 24, 1870; WP, J. Cox to Whipple, September 3, 14, 1870; *House Report* no. 39, 41st Cong., 3d sess., p. 121.

34. Jared W. Daniels (1827–1903) was employed as a government physician at the Upper Sioux agency in 1855; in 1862 he became a surgeon in the 5th Minnesota Infantry. He fought in the Sioux uprising and was cited for bravery at Birch Coolie; afterwards Daniels joined campaigns to the Bad Lands and the Yellowstone before returning to private practice in Faribault

in 1865. Under the Peace Policy he became Red Cloud agent in 1872 and an inspector in 1873. He also served on the Black Hills Commissions of 1875 and 1876. I am indebted to Mrs. Karen Daniels Petersen of St. Paul for the use of family papers.

35. SI:LR, H. Dyer to Delano, March 29, 1870; H. B. Whipple to Delano, April 21, 1871; H. H. Sibley to Delano, May 3, 1871; PHS, Treat to Lowrie, May 10, 1871; ABCFM:LR, S. Riggs to Treat, October 19, 1871, January 16, March 26, 1872.

36. WP, Daniels to Whipple, May 22, 1871.

37. Meyer, *History of the Santee Sioux*, pp. 204-7, describes Adams's harsh bigotry, use of physical violence, and destructive division of Sisseton into a church faction and a "scout party." Adams helped to sell valuable reservation lands for ten cents per acre. Also see Everett W. Sterling, "Moses Adams: A Missionary as Indian Agent," *Minnesota History* 35 (December 1956): 167-77.

38. ABCFM:LR, T. Riggs to Treat, June 6, September 11, 1872; S. Riggs to Treat, August 10, 1872; A. Riggs to Treat, September 12, 1874; SI:LR, Treat to Delano, May 13, 1872.

39. SI:LR, Welsh to Delano, July 15, 1872; ABCFM:LR, T. Riggs to Treat, July 8, 1872.

40. "High Church Episcopal Non-Cooperation," *Missionary Herald* 47 (June 1872): 193, and "Intrusion at Ahmednuggur—a Protest" (June 1873), pp. 180-81.

41. *Missionary Herald*, November 1872, "Annual Report of the Indian Committee," pp. 335-36; ABCFM:LR, A. Riggs to Treat, March 20, July 6, 1872; Dakota Mission memorial to the Prudential Committee, May 1, 1875.

42. Episcopal Board of Missions, *Proceedings*, 1874, pp. 2-4; C. L. Hall, Journals and Scrapbook. Riggs and Welsh debated in the *Congregationalist*, September 7, 21, 1871.

43. Daniels Papers, Reminiscences, Sisseton Agency.

44. ABCFM:LR, A. L. Riggs to Treat, February 2, May 15, 1872.

45. WP, Welsh to Whipple, November 23, 1871; SI:LR, Welsh to Delano, July 15, 1872.

46. There was at least one Jewish appointment. In November 1870, a Jewish delegation called on the president to protest their exclusion from the Peace Policy, and Grant responded by promising a superintendency, a promise that he fulfilled the next month by appointing Dr. Herman Bendall of Albany, N.Y., as superintendent of Indian affairs in Arizona. *New York Herald*, November 1, December 9, 1870; cited in personal correspondence from William H. Armstrong, March 3, 1981.

Chapter 3

1. Rufus M. Jones, *A Boy's Religion* (Philadelphia: Ferris and Leach, 1902).

2. For Quaker goals and organization, see: Rayner W. Kelsey, *Friends and the Indians* (Philadelphia: Executive Committee of Friends, 1917), pp. 171-98; Philip S. Benjamin, *The Philadelphia Quakers in the Industrial Age: 1865-1920* (Philadelphia: Temple University Press, 1976); Barclay White's Journal in the FHL; Orthodox Friends Assoc. Exec. Comm., *Annual Report*, 1870; U.S. Office of Indian Affairs, *Report upon the Orthodox Friends* (Washington: Government Printing Office, 1877), pp. 36ff.; and Milner, "With Good Intentions."

3. Friends Assoc. Exec. Comm., *Annual Reports*, 1872, 1873; the first full-time Orthodox missionary appeared in 1878, when Elkanah Beard went to the Pottawatomies (Tatum, *Red Brothers*, p. 297); also see Jeremiah Hubbard, *Forty Years Among the Indians* (Miami, Okla.: Phelps Printers, 1913).

4. Meyers, *Santee Sioux*, pp. 163-74; Webster S. Robbins, "The Administrative and Educational Policies of the United States Federal Government with Regard to the North American Indian Tribes of Nebraska from 1870-1970" (Ed.D. diss., University of Nebraska-Lincoln, 1976). Milner's dissertation (later published in revised form) is a detailed ethnohistorical study of Quaker relations with Indians, local whites, and each other in the Northern Superintendency. By carefully reconstructing everyday life at three agencies, Milner reveals the tension between eastern Quaker idealism and frontier reality in the 1870s.

5. Accounts of daily life at the agencies may be found in the published diaries of two Quaker physicians, William Nicholson in the Central Superintendency, "A Tour of Indian Agencies in Kansas and the Indian Territory in 1870," *Kansas Historical Quarterly* 3 (August, November 1934): 289-326, 343-84, and Joseph Paxson in the Northern Superintendency, James L. Sellers, ed., "Diary of Joseph A. Paxson, Physician to the Winnebago Indians, 1869-1870," *Nebraska History* 27 (July, October 1946): 143-204, 244-75. For the ill-feelings in Nebraska, see Paxson, pp. 169-83, 195, 204, 268, 273, and Milner, "With Good Intentions," pp. 154-71.

6. PHS, Hamilton to Lowrie, July 26, November 1, 1872; Hoag Papers, Haverford College, Adair to Hoag, May 28, June 1, 1875. Another Quaker/Presbyterian conflict festered for years at the Pawnee agency. See Milner, "With Good Intentions," chaps. 4, 5.

7. FHL:RG 2, Painter to Hallowell, February 4, 7, 1870.

8. Tatum, *Red Brothers*, p. 304. For a careful assessment of charges of fraud and misconduct by Quaker agents in Nebraska, see Milner, "With Good Intentions," pp. 154-71, 199-202, 236-66.

9. U.S. Office of Indian Affairs, *Report upon . . . Agencies now under the Supervision of the Orthodox Friends,* p. 36ff. BIC, *Annual Report,* 1877. Stanley Pumphrey, *Missionary Work in Connection with the Society of Friends* (Philadelphia, 1880), pp. 29-30.

10. FHL:RG 2, S. Averill to B. Hallowell, February 26, 1869.

11. WP, E. A. Washburn to Whipple, November 20, 1868.

12. WP, Brunot to Whipple, August 31, 1870; Welsh to Whipple, June 24, October 4, 1870; BIC:LR, Brunot to Colyer, June 28, 1870; *Spirit of Missions* 35 (1870): 26-28.

13. Protestant Episcopal Church, Board of Missions, *Proceedings,* 1870, pp. vi, x.

14. BIC, *Annual Report,* 1871, p. 176.

15. *Spirit of Missions* 36 (1871): 547.

16. BIC:LR, Welsh to Cree, April 8, 1872; *Spirit of Missions* 37 (1872): 220, 269; BIC, *Annual Report,* 1871, pp. 171-76.

17. The American Church Missionary Society was an independent group of evangelical Episcopal laymen and priests; competition between it and the Domestic and Foreign Board of Missions lasted until the Society was formally recognized by the board in 1877. Examples of women's societies were the Dakota League of Boston, the Niobrara League of New York, the Providence Indian Aid Society.

18. Kenny A. Franks, "Missionaries in the West: An Expedition of the Protestant Episcopal Church in 1844," *Historical Magazine of the Protestant Episcopal Church* 44 (September 1975): 318-33.

19. Lamar, *Dakota Territory,* p. 180.

20. After Hare's thirty-year career, almost half of South Dakota's Indians were Episcopalian. See Hare, *Reminiscences* (Philadelphia: Wm. Fell and Co., 1888); "Christian Schools Among the Indians," and "Further Enlargements of the Work" in *The Church and the Indians* (New York: Episcopal Indian Commission, 1874); M. A. DeWolfe Howe, *The Life and Labors of Bishop Hare* (New York: Sturgis and Walton, 1913).

21. *Spirit of Missions* 45 (1880): 121.

22. BIC, *Annual Report,* 1875, pp. 44-63; the investigation revealed that only 380 of 1,500 Indians at White Earth were Episcopalian.

23. WP, J. A. Gilfillan to Whipple, February 22, 1875.

24. WP, Gilfillan to Whipple, October 1, 1877; Church Historical Society Archives, Austin, Texas, Episcopal Indian Commission Letterbooks (EIC:LS), R. Rogers to Gilfillan, November 7, 1876.

25. WP, Gilfillan to Whipple, October 10, 1877; L. Stowe to Whipple, October 12, 1877; Enmegahbowh to Whipple, September 23, 1878. Also see Joseph A. Gilfillan, "Fruits of Christian Work Among the Chippewas," *The Church and the Indians,* 1873.

26. WP, B. Morris to Whipple, August 14, 1879.

27. "A Communication from Bishop Bedell," *Spirit of Missions* 42 (1877): 457–59.

28. EIC:LS, R. Rogers to Coolidge, January 22, 1877.

29. EIC:LS, Rogers to Welsh, September 5, 1877; Rogers to Hare, August 30, November 13, 1877, March 29, May 17, June 24, 1878; Board of Missions, *Proceedings*, 1877, p. xxvi.

30. Domestic Committee Letterbook, A. G. Twing to R. C. Rogers, January 15, 1879; *Churchman*, January 25, 1879, p. 86.

31. BIC, *Annual Report*, 1879, p. 96; 1882, p. 52; Oregon Conference, Methodist Episcopal Church, *Minutes*, 1882, letter of J. M. Reid, December 9, 1881.

32. Robert Whitner ("Methodist Episcopal Church and Grant's Peace Policy," pp. 77–78) claims that the Methodists, in spite of initial reluctance, entered the Peace Policy with enthusiasm and renewed interest in Indians. Although the Oregon Conference did endorse the "wise policy," which aimed to make the federal Indian service "missionary and religious in its character" (*Minutes*, 1872), most evidence indicates that the church hesitated from the beginning; see BIC, *Annual Report*, 1871, pp. 168, 176; 1873, pp. 15, 183–84, 235.

33. Whitner concluded that the Methodist church shirked its educational work, was chaotically organized, and had little interest in American Indians. "Methodist Episcopal Church," pp. 15–16, 40, 58, 70, 90, 95–96.

34. CIA:LS, [E. P. Smith] to the Secretary of the Interior, January 8, 1875.

35. SI:LR, E. Kemble to H. Dyer, December 5, 1873.

36. Wilbur to McKenney, January 26, 1871, Washington Territory, Superintendent of Indian Affairs, Washington State Library, Olympia.

37. Robert Whitner, "Grant's Indian Peace Policy on the Yakima Reservation, 1870–1882," *Pacific Northwest Quarterly* (October 1959), pp. 135–42; Flora Seymour, *Indian Agents of the Old Frontier* (New York: Appleton-Century, 1941), chap. 7; Andrew J. Splawn, *Ka-mi-akin: Last Hero of the Yakimas* (Portland: Binfords and Mort, 1944), chap. 42; BIC, *Annual Report*, 1880, pp. 102ff.; CIA, *Annual Report*, 1881, p. 173. For sympathetic accounts, see Erle Howell, *Methodism in the Northwest* (Nashville: Parthenon Press, 1966), pp. 120–26, and Maurice Helland, *There Were Giants: The Life of James H. Wilbur* (Yakima: Shields Bag and Printing, 1980).

38. Harrod, *Mission to the Blackfeet*, pp. 42–46, chap. 5.

39. BIC, *Annual Report*, 1875, pp. 152–53; 1880, p. 67; CIA, *Annual Report*, 1875, p. 310; 1876, p. 44.

40. In 1870 the Methodists had three home missionaries, three local preachers, and fifty members in Montana (*Annual Report*, Missionary Society

of the Methodist Church, 1870, p. 131). Significantly, one of the few men coming to Montana to save Indians, William Wesley Van Orsdel ("Brother Van"), immediately concluded that he had to save the white population before he could do anything for native Americans. During Montana's first fifty years there was little evidence of Methodist Indian missions.

41. Methodist Episcopal Church, Journal of the Rocky Mountain Annual Conference (MS in the Rocky Mountain College Library, Billings, Mont.), 1876, pp. 151-52.

42. Ibid., 1874, pp. 58, 64, 84-85; 1875, pp. 96, 105; Journal of the Montana Conference (MS, Rocky Mountain College Library), 1877, pp. 114, 119.

43. Churchman, December 13, 1879; July 31, 1880.

44. CIA, Annual Report, 1878, p. 136.

45. PHS, MacElroy to Rev. Dr. Ellinwood, May 18, 1872.

46. PHS, MacElroy to Lowrie [partial letter, date missing, c. May 1872]; W. D. Crothers to Lowrie, February 23, June 9, 1872; MacElroy to Lowrie, March 19, 1872; A. Irvine to Lowrie, November 15, 1875. This painful struggle continued throughout the seventies. MacElroy eventually turned against Lowrie, declaring that all Presbyterian agents were murderers, that missionary Roberts was immoral, and that Presbyterian ministers ("political scamps") in New Mexico had been bribed by Benjamin Thomas (the Southern Apache agent), who controlled the church "by his hypocrisy and tact." MacElroy to Lowrie, January 18, 1879.

47. Charles Ewing, Petition of the Catholic Church in Behalf of the Pueblos and other Indians of New Mexico (Washington: S. and R. Polkinhorn, 1874), pp. 10-11. The Navajo mission was the main reason for Presbyterian cooperation with the government in 1870; with the mission crumbling, Lowrie had reported to his board that the Navajo future depended on federal support, although there were also "such contingencies and matters beyond the control of the Board, some of them not now to be stated for reasons of prudence" (Board of Foreign Missions, Annual Report, 1870, p. 12). It became Presbyterian policy that the government had to first provide school and mission buildings before the church would assign a missionary. For this reason the Presbyterians ignored the Uintah agency, where James Critchlow, the only Presbyterian to retain his agency for the duration of the Peace Policy, constantly pleaded for a school and missionary.

48. BIC:LR, Spalding to Colyer, November 30, 1871; Lowrie to Cree, June 4, 1872; BIC:LS, Cree to Brunot, May 2, 1872; PHS, Colyer to Lowrie, May 22, 1871; Spalding to Lowrie, May 21, 1872; Monteith to Lowrie, November 19, 1872; also see Drury, Henry Harmon Spalding (Caldwell, Idaho: Caxton Printers, 1936), pp. 362ff., and Francis Haines, The Nez Perces (Norman: University of Oklahoma Press, 1955), pp. 163-64.

49. See Henry G. Waltmann, "John C. Lowrie and Presbyterian Indian Administration, 1870-1882," *Journal of Presbyterian History* 54 (Summer 1976): 259-76, for a fair and judicious assessment of Lowrie's role in the Peace Policy. The Presbyterian secretary became one of the leading church spokesmen on Indian affairs by the end of the 1870s. Clearly an Indian reformer, Lowrie stands as an exception to Robert Mardock's stereotype of the typical eastern humanitarian. Lowrie's problems with the Peace Policy were due in part, as Waltmann correctly observes, to his lack of direct experience with American Indian missions and to his tendency to rely heavily on his own experience in India. Like most assimilationist churchmen and reformers, Lowrie's blind spot was native culture and its crucial importance for tribal well-being.

50. Waltmann, "Lowrie," pp. 261, 266, 275. The budget figure dropped to 2.3 percent in 1876.

51. Waltmann's "Presbyterian and Reformed Participation in the Indian 'Peace Policy' of the 1870s," Conference Group for Social and Administrative History, *Transactions* 5 (1974): 8-25, is a sound though limited overview of the two denominations. His general assessment is fair and accurate: both denominations were far from vigorous in meeting their Peace Policy obligations and opportunities—to both the Presbyterians and Reformed, the program was more of a burden than an opportunity. Waltmann limited his study to eastern church headquarters and official reports and did not investigate the actual performance and controversies in the field.

52. PHS, Sheldon Jackson Papers, H. Kendall to Jackson, April 10, 20, May 7, 1878; circular from Frank F. Ellinwood to the Women's Foreign Mission Society, January 1878.

53. PHS, Jackson Papers, H. Kendall to Jackson, August 12, 1878, September 18, 1880, March 28, 1881; Critchlow to Jackson, September 22, 1880; PHS, Indian Correspondence, W. S. Robertson to Lowrie, February 17, 1881.

54. Roman Catholic reaction to the Peace Policy is beyond the limits of this book and has been told in detail by Peter Rahill, *Catholic Indian Missions and Grant's Peace Policy* (1953). Rahill tends to ignore internal Catholic difficulties and leaves the impression that Roman Catholics were more successful than Protestants. He does not probe deeply into scandals at Catholic agencies (agents Hughes at Standing Rock, Jones and Shanahan at Flathead) or into conflicts between missionaries and agents. Roman Catholics, in point of fact, were subject to many of the same pressures as Protestants and experienced similar failures; see Fahey, *The Flathead Indians*, pp. 157, 178-86. The worst to be said about Roman Catholics is that they performed no better than most Protestants. If they were belligerent and bellicose, they had reason; if they did not cooperate, one can argue that the ABCFM also sabotaged the

Peace Policy. And when one compares Catholics with Methodists, the latter clearly harmed Grant's reform the most.

55. BIC, *Annual Report*, 1871, pp. 166–67; 1873, pp. 179–80; 1875, p. 160; 1879, pp. 106–7; BIC, *Journal*, 1873, pp. 27, 29; O. O. Howard, *My Life and Experiences Among Our Hostile Indians* (Hartford, Conn.: Worthington and Co., 1907), pp. 137ff.

56. BIC:LR, Cornelius Martin to Colyer, May 6, 1871.

57. ABCFM:LS, Treat to S. Riggs, December 11, 1875; N. G. Clark to T. Riggs, May 11, 1877; *Missionary Herald*, 1870–76.

58. C. L. Hall, Journal, May 9, 1881.

59. ABCFM:LR, Miss S. B. Pike to J. O. Means, October 19, 1881.

60. *Missionary Herald*, November 1878, p. 382. By comparing Indian expenses with per capita foreign expenditures, the ABCFM could claim that it spent ten times as much on Indians as on overseas missions.

61. ABCFM:LR, S. R. Riggs to Treat, February 24, 1873; A. L. Riggs to Clark, October 23, November 19, 1877; ABCFM, MSS, vol. 5, "Memorial of the Dakota Mission," May 1, 1875; "The Opportunity of the American Board," *Advance*, September 16, 1875, p. 926; BIC, *Annual Report*, 1877, p. 65.

62. BIC:LR, N. Bishop to Colyer, June 2, 1870. Northern Baptists had no claim to these agencies; Southern Baptists complained that the government ignored their willingness to cooperate with the Peace Policy.

63. CIA, *Annual Report*, 1880, p. 126.

64. Baptist Home Missionary Society, *Annual Report*, 1877, pp. 11, 19, 38; 1878, pp. 39–40; 1879, p. 18; 1880, pp. 19, 36; BIC, *Annual Report*, 1872, pp. 194–95; 1875, pp. 153–54; 1878, pp. 91–93.

65. *Baptist Weekly*, October 2, 1873.

66. CIA, *Annual Report*, 1871, pp. 261–62; Marshall Sprague, *Massacre: The Tragedy at White River* (Boston: Little, Brown and Co., 1957), p. 106. Sprague is mistaken in believing that Charles Adams was removed because Unitarians protested; the church was as puzzled as the Utes over his dismissal (SI:LR, R. R. Shippen to Delano, March 11, 1874).

67. *Unitarian Review*, September 1874, p. 1974; American Unitarian Association, *Annual Report*, 1876, p. 10.

68. BIC, *Annual Report*, 1879, p. 98. This was the wrong excuse. At the time of the Ute War, Unitarians were ignored by the federal government. Nathan Meeker, the murdered agent, had been selected by Secretary of the Interior Carl Schurz. See Sprague, *Massacre*, and Robert Emmitt, *The Last War Trail: The Utes and the Settlement of Colorado* (Norman: University of Oklahoma Press, 1954).

69. *Unitarian Review*, April 1882, pp. 353–56.

70. Whitner, "Methodist Episcopal Church," pp. 75, 123–27, 135, 151.

Methodists A. B. Meacham and James Wilbur battled constantly (Meacham, *Wigwam and Warpath* [Boston: John P. Dale and Co., 1875], pp. 91-94).
F. B. Pease, a former agent and Montana cattle rancher who appropriated much Indian land, told a House committee in 1876 that Methodist churches in Montana quarreled frequently over the Peace Policy, with the result that it was "very injurious to the Indians, injurious to the country, and injurious to the churches." *House Misc. Doc.* no. 167, 44th Cong., 1st sess., p. 202.

71. Eells, *History*, pp. 54-56, 80-81, 93; W. H. Gray, *The Moral and Religious Aspect of the Indian Question* (Astoria: Astorian Book Printers, 1879), pp. 3, 11-12; *Unitarian Review*, June 1875, pp. 571-75; Rahill, *Catholic Indian Missions*, pp. 98-99, 119, chap. 5.

72. *Independent*, September 9, 1875; *Advance*, August 24, 1873.

73. BIC, *Annual Report*, 1871, pp. 108, 112, 127-28. One may wonder what Father Chirouse thought of this Christian universalism, but it reveals a different side to Brunot and Protestantism than that given by Peter Rahill and Loring Priest.

74. CIA, *Annual Report*, 1874, p. 190; BIC, *Journal*, 1873, p. 29; CIA, Inspectors' Reports, J. Daniels to CIA, November 13, 1873; EIC, Minutes, December 19, 1871, January 18, 1872, February 11, 1873.

75. *Spirit of Missions*, October 1869, p. 645; Welsh, *Ponca and Sioux*, p. 13; *Baptist Home Mission Monthly*, 1878, pp. 92-94; C. L. Hall, Journals; Oregon Conference of the Methodist Episcopal Church, *Minutes*; CIA, *Annual Report*, 1872; PHS, W. Arny to Lowrie, March 8, 1875; American Missionary Association, *Annual Report*, 1874, p. 60; Kenneth Holmes, "Bishop Daniel Sylvester Tuttle in the West," *Historical Magazine of the Protestant Episcopal Church* 23 (1954): 54-64.

76. WP, Letterbooks, Whipple to "Dear Brother," November 25, 1870; Whipple to J. Cox, September 8, 1870; Whipple, *Lights and Shadows*, pp. 148-49, 204-5, 353ff.

77. WP, A. W. Williamson to Whipple, July 22, 1877. The Riggs family, however, never reconciled itself to Episcopal missions in Dakota. After the ABCFM's *Missionary Herald* published a tribute to Episcopal work in 1879, Alfred Riggs mailed a protest to the journal, condemning all Episcopalians. The *Herald* responded by printing a discourse on missions by F. D. Huntington, Episcopal bishop of New York.

78. Ayer Collection, Newberry Library, MS no. 676, E. S. Parker, c. 1882; Charles Lowe, "The President's New Indian Policy," *The Old and the New*, April 1871, p. 503.

79. FHL:RG 2, Lightner to Cyrus Blackburn, November 14, 1881.

80. CIA, *Annual Report*, 1875, p. 356.

81. See Appendix 2 for statistics.

82. See Appendix 2.

83. *Independent,* July 1, 1880, p. 15.

84. Ibid., July 15, August 5, 12, November 11, December 9, 1880.

85. Ibid., May 19, 1881.

Chapter 4

1. U.S. Board of Indian Commissioners, *Acts of Congress Relating to the Board of Indian Commissioners and Bylaws of the Board* (Washington: Government Printing Office, 1875), p. 5; 16 Stat. 40 (April 10, 1869); 16 Stat. 360 (July 15, 1870).

2. There is no record in the Missouri Historical Society of Campbell's church membership; two Presbyterian ministers officiated at his funeral in 1874.

3. As the board's bookkeeper and accountant, Stuart would spend long hours in detailed examination of vouchers. He was a close friend of Dwight L. Moody, Matthew Simpson, Brunot, and Grant; he had declined treasury and navy posts in the cabinet. Stuart vigorously supported the Evangelical Alliance and in 1868 was suspended from a lay office in the Presbyterian church for communing outside his denomination.

4. Farwell became a Presbyterian in 1873.

5. Lang was named to the board in June to fill the vacancy created by William Welsh's resignation.

6. Stuart, *Life,* p. 240. Also see Mardock, *Reformers,* p. 58.

7. RCA, B. H. Cowen to Ferris, December 24, 1874; *Independent,* January 7, 1875, pp. 17-18. The new BIC members of 1874 included a Methodist, a Friend, a Dutch Reformed, a Baptist, and four Congregationalists.

8. In 1875 E. P. Smith, commissioner of Indian affairs, testified that the churches never had had any voice in naming members, but that selection was done entirely by the administration. Later it was asserted that each denomination sent a member at the president's request. Henry Fritz's conclusion that all board members were nominated by the churches until 1880 conflicts with Smith's testimony and with that of C. Delano and A. C. Barstow. BIC:LS, Cree to Brunot, February 12, 1873; Red Cloud Commission, *Report of the Special Commissioner Appointed to Investigate the Red Cloud Agency* (Washington: Government Printing Office, 1875), p. 51; *Senate Misc. Doc.* no. 53, 45th Cong., 3d sess., pp. 236, 247, 351; Fritz, "Humanitarian Background," p. 130, and *Movement for Indian Assimilation,* pp. 75-84.

9. Richardson, *Messages* 7:23-24. Grant in effect made the BIC the overseer of the Indian Office in Washington as well as in the West. His orders went well beyond those listed by E. S. Parker on May 26, 1869: agency inspection, evaluation of the annuity system, and relations with the army.

10. *Lay Cooperation in St. Mark's Church* (1861); *Letters on the Home Missionary Work of the Protestant Episcopal Church* (1863); *Women Helpers in the Church* (1872).

11. Welsh's theology of lay activism is clearly stated in *Women Helpers in the Church* (Philadelphia: J. B. Lippincott and Co., 1872), p. 11. A sketch of Welsh is in *Appleton's Cyclopedia of American Biography* (1887). Obituary clippings are in the Pennsylvania Historical Society; also see M. A. DeWolfe Howe, *Memorial of William Welsh* (Reading, Pa., 1878). FHL, MS, Journal of Barclay White, 1:322. The minutes of the Episcopal Indian Commission give a more favorable impression of Welsh's attitude toward other churches than is found in Fritz's *Movement for Indian Assimilation*, pp. 152-54, which sees Welsh as compulsive and sectarian.

12. WP, H. Dyer to Whipple, October 29, 1870.

13. *Nation*, August 19, 1875, p. 109.

14. Fahey, *Flathead Indians*, p. 165. Writing as the chairman of the BIC, Welsh had advised a spokesman for the Flatheads: "If the Indians cannot get their rights any other way, they are justified in combining for defense against coercion."

15. Olson, *Red Cloud and the Sioux Problem*, p. 248.

16. "William Welsh and Indian Missions," *Churchman*, April 6, 1878.

17. WP, Hinman to Whipple, April 29, 1869; *Congressional Record*, 42nd Cong., 3d sess., p. 912; 43rd Cong., 2d sess., pp. 441, 443; Hare, *Reminiscences*, p. 14; *Churchman*, February 23, 1878, p. 197; *Spirit of Missions* 43 (1878): 148, 155-56, 121-22, 127. Carl Schurz, *Speeches, Correspondence and Political Papers*, F. Bancroft, ed., 6 vols. (New York: G. P. Putnam's Sons, 1913), 4:57.

18. Welsh, *Journal of Samuel Hinman*, pp. xii-xiii; *Spirit of Missions* 36 (1871): 404, 474; *House Report* no. 39, 41st Cong., 3d sess., p. 120; Herbert Welsh, *The Indian Problem* (Philadelphia: H. F. McCann, 1881), p. 6.

19. WP, Welsh to Whipple, March 26, 1869.

20. WP, Welsh to Whipple, March 26, May 14, 1869; W. Welsh, *Summing Up of Evidence Before a Committee of the House* (Washington: H. Polkinhorn and Co., 1871), pp. 60-67; Welsh, *Indian Office: Wrongs Doing and Reforms Needed* (open letter to Grant, January 8, 1874).

21. FHL:RG 2, Welsh to B. Hallowell, September 16, 1869; FHL, Forbush Papers, Welsh to Hallowell, December 14, 1869; WP, Welsh to Whipple, June 24, 1870.

22. WP, Brunot to Whipple, July 3, 1869; SI:LR, N. Bishop to Cox, July 2, 1869; BIC:LR, Cox to Brunot, July 5, 1869; BIC, *Annual Report*, 1869, pp. 4-5; *House Report* no. 39, 41st Cong., 3d sess., pp. 13, 160.

23. See Slattery, *Felix Reville Brunot*. The Pittsburgh firm was Singer, Hartman and Company; in 1852 Brunot also became a director of the Allegheny Valley Railroad.

24. See Sprague, *Massacre*, p. 95, for a typically mistaken description of Brunot as naïve.

25. Grierson Papers, Newberry Library, Brunot to Grierson, February 15, 1870; WP, Brunot to Whipple, February 11, 1870.

26. BIC:LR, Brunot to Cree, May 4, 1872. For the Sioux council, see Olson, *Red Cloud*, chap. 8.

27. Potts to Brunot, quoted in Slattery, *Felix Reville Brunot*, pp. 212-13; similar praise came from the *Denver Daily News* after the Ute Treaty of 1873. Slattery gives little indication of Brunot's doubts and inner turmoil.

28. BIC:LR, Brunot to Cree, April 11, 1872.

29. See Olson, chap. 8, for the conflicts between the BIC and BIA over administrative decisions such as agency location.

30. BIC, *Acts*, pp. 5-8.

31. On the last point there was disagreement within the BIC. Vincent Colyer claimed that Indian lands should be kept intact, and he lobbied for this goal in Congress (BIC:LS, Colyer to Bishop Armitage, March 7, 1871). Officially the board endorsed the administration's consolidation policy.

32. Welsh, *Summing Up*, p. 26; Stuart, *Life*, pp. 242-43.

33. BIC:LR, Farwell to T. Cree, June 20, 1872.

34. BIC, *Annual Report*, 1871, p. 11; 1872, pp. 6, 141-42; 1873, p. 5.

35. BIC:LR, Brunot to [Colyer?], February 26, July 11, 1870; January [?], April 1, 1871; Lang to Colyer, April 14, 1870; Farwell to Colyer, March 12, 1870.

36. BIC:LR, Bishop to Colyer, January 2, 1871.

37. BIC:LS, T. Cree to the Second Auditor of the Treasury, February 11, March 7, 1874. Correspondence between Colyer and John Stout (BIC records, 1871) indicates a surprising amount of petty maneuvering between the board, the Indian Office, and the Interior. Loring Priest interpreted these differences as an attempt by the board to eliminate the Indian Office (*Uncle Sam's Stepchildren*, chap. 4) but, except for Welsh, there is little evidence of any such board ambition.

38. WP, Welsh to Whipple, January 28, February 17, April 15, 1870; SI:LR, Welsh to Delano, October 21, 1871; U.S. Dept. of the Interior, *Report of the Commission . . . to Investigate Certain Charges Against Hon. E. P. Smith* (Washington: Government Printing Office, 1874), p. 93.

39. WP, Welsh to Whipple, April 22, 1871; BIC:LR, Brunot to Colyer, April 1, 1871; Welsh to Colyer, April 29, 1871; *Union Dakotian*, March 2, 1871.

40. SI:LR, A. Wright to S. B. Treat, April 9, 1869; Treat to Cox, April 10, 1869.

41. CIA, *Annual Report*, 1869, p. 6. Ely Parker considered his own successful career a model for all Indians. See Armstrong, *Warrior in Two Camps*, for a full analysis of how Parker viewed his Seneca heritage.

42. *Congressional Globe*, 41st Cong., 2d sess., June 4, 1870, p. 4083.

43. Newberry MSS 676, 677, Ayer Collection, Parker to Mrs. Converse, n.d.

44. *House Report* no. 39, 41st Cong., 3d sess., p. 62.

45. In 1875 W. J. Kountz of the Kountz Line Steamers of Allegheny City, Pa., declared that he was responsible for the removal of Parker. Under investigation as a shipper to the Santee, Ponca, Yankton, and Upper Missouri agencies, Kountz asked that Brunot and Campbell be called to testify on his behalf (*House Misc. Doc.* no. 167, 44th Cong., 1st sess., pp. 23-24). Kountz may have been Welsh's main source of information, though rumors were rife in all quarters. Jay Cooke allowed Welsh to examine Parker's personal bank account.

46. BIC:LR, Welsh to Colyer, January 2, 1871.

47. WP, Welsh to Whipple, January 28, December 10, 1870; BIC:LS, Colyer to Brunot, July 7, 16, 1870; BIC:LR, Brunot to Colyer, April 13, 1870.

48. *House Report* no. 39, 41st Cong., 3d sess., "Affairs in the Indian Department"; N. P. Chipman, *Argument of N. P. Chipman on Behalf of Hon. E. S. Parker* (Washington: Powell, Ginck and Co., 1871); Welsh, *Summing Up of Evidence Before a Committee of the House of Representatives Charged with the Investigation of Misconduct in the Indian Office* (Washington: Polkinhorn and Co., 1871). Other actions of E. S. Parker that may have alienated reformers were Parker's reversal of agent Lawrie Tatum's decision to bar trader E. H. Durfee from the Kiowa-Comanche reservation and the commissioner's support of railroad development through treaty lands in Indian Territory. Lee Cutler, "Lawrie Tatum and the Kiowa Agency, 1869-1873," *Arizona and the West* 13 (Autumn 1871): pp. 221-44; Miner, H. Craig, *The Corporation and the Indian: Tribal Sovereignty and Industrial Civilization in Indian Territory, 1865-1907* (Columbia: University of Missouri Press, 1976), pp. 32-33. Jacob Cox reversed Parker's railroad decision, for which Miner praises Cox as a rare model of a government official willing to protect tribal resources.

49. BIC:LR, Brunot to Colyer, February 1, 1871; BIC:LS, Colyer to Brunot, February 11, 25, 1871.

50. BIC:LR, Welsh to Colyer, April 29, 1871; Campbell to Brunot, May 26, 1871; Brunot to Colyer, June 7, 1871; Lang to Colyer, June 29, 1871; BIC:LS, Colyer to Brunot, June 13, 1871; Stuart to Parker, May 26, 1871; WP, Welsh to Whipple, July 8, 1871.

51. WP, Welsh to Whipple, July 29, September 8, 1871.

52. *Nation*, August 17, 1871, pp. 100-101, reprinted in the AMA's *American Missionary*, October 1871. The undocumented A. C. Parker biography of E. S. Parker blamed his removal on the Indian Ring and the "venom" of

misguided zealots. According to this account, Parker quit because "his heart was broken." Parker himself wrote to Harriet Converse (Gayaneshagh) that, although he had been vindicated, he resigned because the constant attacks made the position a thankless burden: "I put an end to all wars . . . and I sent [out] professed Christian whites who waxed rich and fat from the plundering of the poor Indians, nor were there teacherships enough to give places to all the hungry and impecunious Christians . . . [and for this reason] they made their onslaught on my poor innocent head and made the air foul with their malicious and poisonous accusations." A. C. Parker, *Ely S. Parker*, pp. 154–59, 166–67. Grant apparently accepted at least some of the charges against Parker, for he wrote to George Stuart, "I will be careful that no one is appointed who is not fully in sympathy with a humane policy towards the Indians. I will see too that he has the full confidence of the Peace Commissioners." Quoted from a letter of July 22, 1871, in the George H. Stuart papers, Library of Congress, cited in Mardock, *Reformers and the American Indian*, p. 106. See also Armstrong, *Warrior in Two Camps*, chaps. 12–13. Armstrong concludes that Welsh was well intentioned but overzealous and unjust to Parker. Cox had known of Parker's purchases without bids and had raised no objection; the law also provided for such procedures in emergencies. Armstrong argues that Parker's demise resulted from his inexperience and from his refusal to bow to the BIC.

53. BIC Scrapbook, random clippings; BIC:LS, Colyer to Brunot, July 20, 1871; C. L. Sonnichsen, *The Mescalero Apaches* (Norman: University of Oklahoma Press, 1958), pp. 136–39.

54. Quoted in the BIC, *Annual Report*, 1871, pp. 57–58.

55. *Tri-Weekly Ely Record*, August 4, 1872. Dan L. Thrapp, *The Conquest of Apacheria* (Norman: University of Oklahoma Press, 1967), has a full description of Colyer's tour and the frontier reaction, but the most detailed account is in John Bret Harte's doctoral dissertation, "The San Carlos Indian Reservation, 1872–1886: An Administrative History" (University of Arizona, 1972), pp. 44–79. Harte describes Colyer as impetuous, short-sighted, over-confident, ill-informed, defensive, and contemptuous of Tucson citizens. The net result of his trip was to enhance General George Crook's hard-line policy in Arizona Territory. For other accounts, see Ralph Ogle, *Federal Control of the Western Apache*, chap. 4, and John U. Terrell, *Apache Chronicle* (New York: World Publishing, 1972), pp. 271–91.

56. BIC:LR, Brunot to Colyer, January 19, 1872; Delano to Brunot, January 12, 1872; BIC:LS, Colyer to Brunot, January 22, February 18, 1872; Colyer to Stout, January 24, 1872; SI:LR, Colyer to Delano, February 19, 1872; Colyer's report on New Mexico is in the BIC *Annual Report*, 1871. Also see CIA, *Annual Report*, 1872, pp. 157–59, 174–75. O. O. Howard asserted that he was sent to the Southwest at the suggestion of John Lang and

that the duty there in 1872 was his most difficult experience on the frontier. Howard, *My Life and Experiences Among Our Hostile Indians*, pp. 11, 23. For an account of Colyer's failure and Howard's success in Arizona, see John A. Carpenter, *Sword and Olive Branch: Oliver Otis Howard* (Pittsburgh: Pittsburgh University Press, 1964), pp. 209-19. Bret Harte concluded in his dissertation on San Carlos, pp. 81-113, that despite their errors, despite opposition from local whites, and despite interference from the army and Department of the Interior, both Colyer and Howard contributed positively to peace in Arizona.

57. WP, Welsh to Whipple, December 22, 1873; *House Report* no. 778, 43rd Cong., 1st sess., pp. 82-83, 227, 232; *Congressional Record*, 43rd Cong., 1st sess., May 9, 1874, pp. 3740-45.

58. Library of Congress, Grant Papers, Grant to Brunot, May 18, 1874. Grand disagreed with Brunot's proposal for changing the tenure and manner of appointment of the commissioner of Indian affairs, correctly pointing out that the Constitution gave this power to the president.

59. BIC:LS, BIC to Grant, May 27, 1874.

60. Thomas Cree later told Carl Schurz that fraud and lack of power were the main reasons for the mass resignation (Library of Congress, Schurz Papers, Cree to Schurz, December 17, 1879). The Red Cloud Commission of 1875 agreed that autonomy was the real reason; they failed to find any firm evidence and Delano denied all conflict with the BIC, though he confessed to reprimanding Brunot for secretly investigating the Red Cloud agency and then refusing to share the information with the government (Red Cloud Commission, *Report*, pp. 745-46, 753-57). After his resignation, William Dodge told the *New York Tribune* that the board quit because Delano consistently awarded contracts rejected by the BIC (*Nation*, June 11, 1874, p. 372). A year later the same newspaper said the reason was the Indian Ring's control of the Interior (*New York Tribune*, April 29, 1875).

61. For the subsequent history of the BIC, see Henry Fritz, "The Board of Indian Commissioners and Ethnocentric Reform, 1878-1893," in *Indian-White Relations: A Persistent Paradox*, Jane F. Smith and Robert M. Kvasnicka, eds. (Washington: Howard University Press, 1976), pp. 57-78, and Prucha's excellent account in *American Indian Policy in Crisis*.

62. BIC, *Annual Report*, 1877, pp. 13, 16-17.

63. Ibid., 1879, pp. 12-13.

64. *Congressional Record*, 43rd Cong., 2d sess., January 14, 1875, p. 470; 46th Cong., 3d sess., January 11, 1881, pp. 528ff.; 44th Cong., 2d sess., January 27, 1877, p. 1062; BIC, *Annual Report*, 1879, p. 119; 1880, p. 95. My conclusions here, made in view of the original role of the BIC, may be excessively harsh. For a more sympathetic view of the BIC after 1880, see Prucha, *American Indian Policy in Crisis*.

65. BIC:LS, BIC to Grant, May 27, 1874.

Chapter 5

1. Mardock's *Reformers and the American Indian,* pp. 110-15, provides a full summary of the role of the Peace Policy in the 1872 campaign. Grant's promise of support was given to George Stuart in a letter of October 26, 1872.

2. BIC, Minutes, August 8, 1885.

3. The *Frontier Index* was quoted in the *Union Dakotian,* December 5, 1868; Pierre DeSmet, *Life, Letters and Travels* (New York: Francis P. Harper, 1905), pp. 1544-45; Richard MacMahon, *Anglo-Saxon and the North American Indian* (Baltimore: Kelly, Piet and Co., 1876), p. 46.

4. See Spencer L. Leitman, "The Revival of an Image: Grant and the 1880 Republican Nominating Campaign," *Bulletin: Missouri Historical Society* 30 (April 1974): 196-204.

5. The best assessments of the Grant administration are in Leonard White's *Republican Era,* Allan Nevin's *Hamilton Fish,* William B. Hesseltine's *Ulysses S. Grant: Politician,* and William McFeeley's *Grant.*

6. W. Welsh, *Sales of Indian Pine Timber* (Philadelphia, March 13, 1874), p. 14.

7. M. A. DeWolfe Howe (ed.), *Home Letters of General Sherman* (New York: Charles Scribner's Sons, 1909), p. 381, Sherman to his wife, from Vienna, June 13, 1872.

8. WP, O. H. Browning to Whipple, February 8, 1869.

9. *Boston Commonwealth,* August 16, 1869.

10. *Nation,* October 6, 20, 1870.

11. See White, *Republican Era,* chap. 9. In 1881 Hayes's secretary of the interior, Carl Schurz, concluded that the department was "the most dangerous branch of the public service . . . more exposed to corrupt influences and more subject to untoward accidents than any other. . . . It is a constant fight with the sharks . . . and a ceaseless struggle with perplexing questions" (quoted by White, p. 180).

12. In 1868 Republicans outnumbered Democrats 61-11 in the Senate; in the House the Republican majority was 170-75. By 1876 Democrats had reversed the count in the House and by 1878 the Senate was evenly divided.

13. BIC:LS, Colyer to Brunot, February 1, 11, 1871; Colyer to H. Dyer, February 21, 1871.

14. BIC, *Annual Report,* 1879, pp. 108-12.

15. Ibid., 1870, p. 112.

16. Waltmann, "Circumstantial Reformer," p. 340; Lamar, *Far Southwest,* pp. 286-87. The Denver agency is discussed in Sprague, *Massacre,* pp. 121-24, and in S. Walker to Cree, July 5, 1873 (BIC:LS).

17. *House Misc. Doc.* no. 167, 44th Cong., 1st sess., pp. 329-30; *Congressional Record,* 43rd Cong., 2d sess., January 14, 1875, pp. 441-42; B. H.

Grierson Papers, Ayer Collection, Newberry Library, Grierson to Brunot, November 1, December 17, 1869; February 15, 1870; November 22, 1872; BIC, *Annual Report,* 1879, p. 112.

18. *Congressional Record,* 44th Cong., 1st sess., June 21, 1876, p. 3947.

19. See Angie Debo's *A History of the Indians of the United States* (Norman: University of Oklahoma Press, 1970), in which she claims that after Senator Samuel Pomeroy of Kansas forced the dismissal of Franklin F. Lyon, the first Baptist appointment in the Indian Territory, all subsequent agents were "strictly political," pp. 172-73. Lawrence R. Murphy's biography of Navajo agent W. F. M. Arny demonstrates how successfully the old patronage system adapted itself to the requirements of the Peace Policy.

20. Haverford College, Garrett Collection, Edward Earle to Garrett, May 19, 22, June 21, 1871; Friends Exec. Comm., Minutes, 1874, report of the general agent; FHL:RG 2, J. Saunders to White, May 26, 1873; BIC, *Annual Report,* 1876, p. 76.

21. WP, Welsh to Whipple, October 12, 1870.

22. Welsh to J. D. Cox, October 18, 1870, quoted in Welsh, *Supplementary Report of a Visit to Spotted Tail's Tribe* (Philadelphia: McCalla and Stavely, 1870).

23. WP, J. D. Cox to Whipple, October 3, 1870. It is not consistently clear why Cox resigned. According to Allan Nivens, Cox was ridden out of office by Zachariah Chandler and "the pack" because of the secretary's effective reforms not only in the Indian Office, but in the Census Bureau, Land Office, and Patent Office (Nevins, *Hamilton Fish: An Inner History of the Grant Administration,* pp. 465ff.). William Hesseltine ascribes less lofty motives to the secretary. Hesseltine questions Cox's claim that he was testing Grant and shows discrepancies in the secretary's account of his action, concluding that Cox tried to embarrass a surprised Grant (Hesseltine, *Ulysses S. Grant: Politician* [New York: Ungar Publishing, 1957], pp. 217ff.). Cox's letter to Grant did mention the Peace Policy as one reason for his resignation: "The removal of the Indian Service from the sphere of ordinary political patronage has been peculiarly distasteful to many influential gentlemen in both houses; and in order to enable you to carry out your purposes successfully, I am satisfied that you ought not to be embarrassed" (Nevins, *Fish,* p. 467). Waltmann in "Circumstantial Reformer" traces Cox's disagreements with Grant from 1870, pp. 339-40, and largely blames the president. Also see Carpenter, *Grant,* p. 115, and McFeely, *Grant,* pp. 300-301.

24. SI:LR, Senator Howe to Cox, September 1870; Senator A. S. McDill to Delano, August 2, 1871; C. H. Sight to Delano, August 8, 1872; A. H. Emanuel to Delano, August 6, 1872; A. S. McDill to Delano, August 12, 1874; Backus to Delano, June 21, 1872, August 2, 1871; BIC:LS, Colyer to Brunot, February 11, 1871; Colyer to Farwell, June 30, 1871.

25. Washington Territorial Papers, H. D. Gibson to Hon. J. M. Edmunds, July 14, 1875; BIC:LR, A. A. Sargent to Brunot, February 28, 1871; J. High to Cree, November 26, 1872; A. B. Meacham to Cree, January 19, 1872; BIC, Minutes, January 13, 1871, and March 30, 1876; BIC, *Annual Report*, 1875, p. 160; 1879, pp. 99-101, 109; SI:LR, Ferris to Delano, January 17, 1871; RCA, E. S. Parker to Ferris, November 8, 1870; Delano to Ferris, January 19, 1871.

26. BIC:LR, Wilbur to Brunot, November 17, 1870; March 18, 1872; Simpson Papers, S. T. Wilson to Simpson, February 13, 1873; C. Clippinger to Simpson, April 12, 1873; W. S. Thomas to Simpson, February 15, 1873. One can almost make a case for a Methodist ring; Methodist preachers sought postal positions, judgeships, Indian agencies, and foreign consulates by urging Simpson to use his influence with Grant, Delano, Cowen, Newman, Senator Harlan, and Postmaster General Creswell.

27. BIC, *Journal*, 1873, p. 14; BIC, *Annual Report*, 1873, p. 185.

28. Rahill, *Catholic Indian Missions*, pp. 63, 67-68, 72, 92. WP: Sibley to Whipple, March 8, 1876. For an account of political patronage in Montana, see Fahey, *Flathead Indians*, pp. 156, 160, 175.

29. PHS, McFarland to Lowrie, March 13, 1873; Arny to Lowrie, November 30, 1873; MacElroy to Lowrie, May 18, 1877.

30. E. Pluribus Unum, *A Democrat's Reasons* (New York: Golden Age Office, 1872); Theodore Tilton, *Self-Condemned: Or, Grant's Platform* (New York: Golden Age Office, 1872); Nelson Cross, *The Modern Ulysses* (J. S. Redfield, 1872); Charles Sumner, *Republicanism vs. Grantism: the Presidency a Trust, not a Plaything and Perquisite* (Washington: Rives and Bailey, 1872); *Cleveland Herald*, November 12, 1872.

31. *New York Herald*, July 23, 1872.

32. B. J. Lossing, "Our Barbarian Brethren," *Harper's Monthly*, May 1870, pp. 810-11; BIC, *Annual Report*, 1870, pp. 2, 11, 26; 1871, pp. 11-12, 23ff.; 1872, pp. 5-6, 24-25, 28-29, 144-46.

33. OIA:LR, Charles Sanard to Grant, July 15, 1872; *Junction City Union*, June 12, 1869, quoted in Athearn, *Sherman*, p. 249; Howard, *Life*, pp. 143ff.

34. "Fenimore Cooper had a wrong idea of the Indian, our eastern Puritan croakers have formed their opinions of them from his works." *Montanian*, August 3, 1871.

35. Ibid.

36. Ibid., August 24, 1871.

37. *Bismarck Tribune*, August 27, 1873.

38. Henry Fritz, for example, asserts that the frontier opposed the Peace Policy: "The Peace Policy had little support west of the Mississippi River and there is much doubt that it was ever understood." "Humanitarian

Background," p. 192, and *Movement for Indian Assimilation,* chap. 5. Fritz neglected to mention the divergent opinions of congressmen from Iowa, Minnesota, California, Oregon, New Mexico, and Missouri. Robert Mardock offers a much better survey of public opinion in *Reformers and the American Indian,* chap. 6. His analysis of the East-West split, however, neglects to consider the South as a distinct region in attitudes toward Indian policy. Further complicating any analysis of public opinion in the West were the mixed and usually unstated motives of many frontier leaders. Westerners often disliked the army because the military was less susceptible to patronage and corruption than the BIA, and for this reason western politicians and speculators could join forces with eastern humanitarians in supporting the Peace Policy. Howard Lamar in *Dakota Territory* and *The Far Southwest* shows the frequent use of humanitarian language in the service of economic goals.

39. SI:LR, J. A. Lyman to Ferris, November 9, 1872.

40. [H. Clay Preuss], *Columbus Crocket to General Grant on the Indian Policy* (Washington: J. Bradley Adams, 1873).

41. *Montanian,* October 12, 1871; BIC, *Annual Report,* 1872, pp. 145-46; Potts to Brunot, quoted in Slattery, *Brunot,* p. 213; *Omaha Daily Herald,* August 29, 1869; *Denver Daily News,* February 6, 1873; *Grand Rapids Eagle,* February 11, 1873; *Sacramento Union,* February 11, 1873; Welsh, *Sioux and Ponca,* p. 23; CIA, *Annual Report,* 1872, p. 346; Presbyterian Board of Foreign Missions, *Annual Report,* 1870.

42. *Independent,* March 18, April 22, May 13, 1869; November 7, 1872.

43. *Watchman,* March 18, 1869; June 16, 1870; November 30, 1871; *Old and New,* April 1871; November 1872; *Congregationalist,* November 3, 10, 1870. The vast majority of the religious press gave the Peace Policy little space but officially supported it, e.g., *Advance; Churchman; American Missionary; Missionary Herald; Christian Mirror; Christian Secretary; Atlanta Methodist Advocate;* the [Methodist] *Christian Advocate* of New York, Buffalo, Pittsburgh, and Portland, Oreg.; *Sunday School Times; United Presbyterian; Friend's Intelligencer; Friends Review.*

44. J. N. Trask, "Indian Affairs," *Old and New,* August 1873, pp. 232-39; Catholic Clergy, *Address,* pp. 7, 14; ABCFM:LR, A. Riggs. to Treat, July 26, 1872; *Missionary Herald,* November 1872, p. 357; T. Williamson in the *North American Review* (1873), reprinted in the *Princeton Review* 5 (1876): 612-13.

45. BIC:LR, John D. Lang to Brunot, April 21, 1873.

46. Welsh, *Sioux and Ponca,* pp. ii, 5; BIC:LR, Welsh to Cree, April 8, 1872.

47. WP, Letterbooks, Whipple to Cox, October 14, 1869; *Spirit of Missions* 35 (1870): 657; BIC, *Journal,* 1873, pp. 19-20, 27, 34; AMA, *Annual Report,* 1871, pp. 20, 22, 64-68; 1872, pp. 9, 21; *American Missionary* 14

(October 1870): 227-28; (December 1870): 272-74; (January 1873): 9; Board of Foreign Missions, Presbyterian Church, *Annual Report,* 1873, p. 17.

48. FHL:RG 2, Hallowell to agents and Northern Superintendent, June 12, 1869; FHL, Green MSS, Hallowell to Green, April 20, 1871.

49. *Congressional Globe,* 41st Cong., 1st sess., p. 167; 41st Cong., 2d sess., pp. 738, 1578-79, 1642, 4006.

50. Ibid., 41st Cong., 2d sess., pp. 479-87. The June 4 debate indicates considerable support for the Peace Policy after its first year. Twenty-seven eastern senators voted for it, eight against; six westerners favored the special appropriation and four opposed it, with West defined as states beyond the Mississippi. No clear East-West cleavage appears because some western congressmen wanted federal income for their states, while some easterners opposed Indian appropriations on fiscal grounds.

51. Ibid., 42d Cong., 3d sess., p. 655.

52. Ibid., p. 731.

53. Ibid., 41st Cong., 2d sess., p. 5010; 41st Cong., 3d sess., pp. 731-35, 1812, 1492-94; 42d Cong., 2d sess., pp. 2195-96; 42d Cong., 3d sess., p. 433.

Chapter 6

1. *Independent,* January 7, 1875, pp. 17-18; *Senate Misc. Doc.* no. 53, 45th Cong., 3d sess., p. 249.

2. Speech of Wabonoquet (White Cloud), quoted in C. A. Ruffee, *Report of the Condition of the Chippewas of Minnesota* (St. Paul: Pioneer, 1875), pp. 28-29.

3. See Appendix 3.

4. CIA, *Annual Report,* 1874, p. 190; 1875, pp. 298, 351, 355, 363; 1877, p. 181; 1880, pp. 70-72; 1881, p. 155.

5. Agents often employed a dozen whites and as many Indians as clerks, doctors, teachers, blacksmiths, plow and wagon makers, gunsmiths, millers, carpenters, cooks, and farm hands.

6. William Unrau has argued that historians attempting to account for Indian problems are often guilty of bias and prejudice against the BIA and have especially maligned its agents. He contends that scholars uncritically accept the contemporary scapegoating and the "devil theory" of Indian agents, neglecting to carefully investigate charges and objectively analyze the actual life and conditions at the agencies in relation to the entire system. Unrau would assign greater responsibility to the army for Indian troubles, particularly the difficulties that enlisted men caused from day to day on reservations. William E. Unrau, "The Civilian As Indian Agent: Villain or Victim?" *Western Historical Quarterly* 3, no. 4 (October 1972): 405-20. For

the evils of the depredation claims system, see ibid., pp. 416-17, and Nicholson, "Tour," p. 302. William T. Hagan, in *Indian Police and Judges* (New Haven: Yale University Press, 1966), describes many of the impossible administrative pressures under which Indian agents lived in the 1870s, among which was the need for legal reform and personal protection. This was true even on the more quiet reservations in Nebraska, Kansas, Minnesota, and Wisconsin. Agents were required to protect neighboring whites from Indians, Indians from whites, and Indians from other Indians. The most frequent crimes were murder, theft, liquor sales, trespassing, and prostitution. Few whites were arrested or punished for crimes against Indians because the Trade and Intercourse Act of 1834 accorded agents little legal authority and less power, leaving them dependent on the army to control violent Indians and whites. Expulsion was the usual punishment for marauding whites. As tribal culture disintegrated, lawlessness increased among the tribes; to end this legal and judicial chaos, the Indian police system evolved slowly during the seventies and was followed by the Indian court system in the eighties. SI, *Annual Report*, 1874, p. viii; Friends Assoc. Exec. Comm., *Need of Law on the Indian Reservations* (Philadelphia: Sherman and Co., 1878).

7. *Spirit of Missions* 38 (1873): 628; Howe, *Hare*, pp. 140ff.; CIA, *Annual Report*, 1881, pp. 39-40, 127.

8. OIA:LR, E. Walsh to E. P. Smith, June 15, 1875; *Senate Misc. Doc.* no. 53, 45th Cong., 3d sess., passim; BIC:LR, H. Breiner to Colyer, April 13, 1871; Daniels Papers, Malicious Statement. Lawrence R. Murphy, *Frontier Crusader: W. F. M. Arny* (Tucson: University of Arizona Press, 1972), pp. 208-9.

9. PHS, Chas. Roedel to Lowrie, February 15, 1872.

10. SI:LR, W. Defrees to E. P. Smith, February 25, 1875; Geo. Balcom to E. S. Parker, July 26, 1871.

11. CIA, *Annual Report*, 1871, pp. 545-46; 1874, p. 245.

12. Ibid., 1871, p. 528. Not all agencies were so miserable; those in Nebraska and Kansas possessed superior facilities.

13. OIA:LR, 2d Comptroller's Office of the Treasury Dept. to I. A. Galpin, May 23, 1876; C. Hudson to J. Q. Smith, May 3, 1876.

14. PHS, Critchlow to Lowrie, September 23, 1876; B. M. Thomas to Lowrie, October 4, 1876; A. Irvine to Lowrie, October 14, 1876; BIC, *Annual Report*, 1873, p. 30; CIA, *Annual Report*, 1872, p. 158. Nonreimbursible moving costs to remote southwestern agencies could run as high as five hundred dollars; see Waltmann, "Presbyterian and Reformed Participation in the Indian 'Peace Policy' of the 1870s," p. 22.

15. PHS, Baird to Lowrie, February 26, 1880 [emphasis in text].

16. PHS, G. Smith to Lowrie, June 17, 1878.

17. Welsh, *Wrongs Doing*, p. 10; Welsh, *Summing Up*; BIC, *Journal*, 1873,

pp. 21–22, 28, 30; BIC, *Annual Report*, 1871, pp. 167–68; 1873, pp. 186, 198–200; BIC:LR, J. Ferris to Colyer, February 27, 1872; AMA, *Annual Report*, 1871, p. 13; FHL:RG 2, J. Wharton to Hon. A. G. Cattell, March 30, 1869; American Unitarian Association, *Annual Report*, 1874, p. 11; OIA, *Report on Friends*, pp. 39–41.

18. *Congressional Globe*, 41st Cong., 3d sess., pp. 1491, 1495.

19. See Appendix 3. Comparative living costs at different agencies can be measured, for instance, by the price of salt and flour. Salt cost one-half cent per pound in Duluth and one cent per pound delivered to the Rosebud landing in Montana; it cost eight cents per pound at Abiquiu and more than nine cents at the Navajo agency. Flour delivered to Yankton cost two cents a pound; at the Mexcalero Apache agency it was more than seven cents, and at Los Pinos, nearly nine cents. Other prices indicate the general cost of living in the Southwest: beans sold for a nickel a pound, sugar ten cents, and bacon eight cents; a desk cost fifteen dollars, chocolate thirty-five cents a pound, and whiskey sixty cents a quart.

20. CIA, *Annual Report*, 1877, p. 7; OIA, *Report on Friends*, p. 30; BIC, *Annual Report*, 1870, p. 11; BIC, *Journal*, 1873, pp. 4, 8; SI:LR, E. S. Parker to Delano, February 18, 1871; H. R. Clum to Delano, April 22, 1874.

21. Elwell Otis, *The Indian Question* (New York: Sheldon and Co., 1878), p. 219.

22. PHS, A. S. Curtis to Lowrie, March 19, 1872; G. Ainslie to Lowrie, September 6, 1870; Lowrie to Delano, March 11, 1875. Ainslie eventually was sent to the Nez Perce as a government teacher. Exceptionally low wages in the ministry probably explains why many clergymen applied for agencies. Critics of the Peace Policy frequently said that it provided a haven for bronchial preachers, but it should be noted that one person who made this claim, Philip Sheridan, also urged the appointment of retired army officers for reasons of health. SI:LR, Sheridan to Z. Chandler, February 3, 1877.

23. PHS, Baird to Lowrie, February 26, 1880; BIC, *Annual Report*, 1874, pp. 147–48; 1875, p. 158, BIC, *Journal*, 1873, p. 30; *Senate Misc. Doc.* no. 53, 45th Cong., 3d sess., p. 32.

24. BIC, *Annual Report*, 1870, pp. 97, 11; BIC, Minutes, 1871, p. 42; SI:LR, Lowrie to Delano, December 19, 1873; J. P. Durbin to Colyer, June 25, 1870; RCA, Delano to Ferris, February 17, 1872.

25. BIC, *Journal*, 1873, p. 14; Whitner, "Methodist Episcopal Church," pp. 164ff., 178; *Senate Report* no. 693, 45th Cong., 3d sess., p. 8; *Senate Misc. Doc.* no. 53, 45th Cong., 3d sess., p. 33; *House Report* no. 167, 45th Cong., 3d sess.

26. *Congressional Globe*, 42d Cong., 3d sess., pp. 437, 440, 470, 1079–80, 1098.

27. FHL:RG 2, Welsh to Hallowell, April 1, 1870; PHS, Breiner to Lowrie,

March 1, 1873; EIC, Minutes, June 17, 1873; EIC:LS, Rogers to Dart, August 20, 1877.

28. Red Cloud Commission, *Report*, p. 429.

29. SI:LR, P. Sawyer to G. Farnsworth, December 11, 1872; Sawyer to Delano, February 13, 1873; G. Whipple to Delano, December 10, 1872; January 27, February 15, 1873 [George Whipple was the AMA secretary and the uncle of Bishop Henry Whipple] ; G. Whipple to Z. Chandler, May 22, 1876; BIC:LS, Cree to Brunot, February 5, 1873; OIA, Inspector Reports, J. O'Conner to E. P. Smith, September 15, 26, 1873; E. Kemble to Smith, August 28, September 7, 1874; E. Watkins to J. Q. Smith, March 20, 1876; W. Pollock to E. A. Hayt, September 22, 1879; CIA, *Annual Report*, 1872, pp. 23, 204; 1873, pp. 177-78, 180; 1874, pp. 186-89; 1878, p. vi; AMA, *Annual Report*, 1871, p. 13; 1872, p. 82; BIC, Journal, 1873, pp. 6-7. For the role of Sawyer and Howe as timber speculators, see Richard N. Current, *Pine Logs and Politics: A Life of Philetus Sawyer, 1816-1900* (Madison: State Historical Society of Wisconsin, 1950), pp. 72-74, 115, 122-23, 211-13, 217-18. The situation in Wisconsin and Minnesota was typical. Several tribes left Nebraska because the Quaker agents could not protect their timber. The Cherokees during the same period received little help or support from the government in protecting tribal timber. After losing millions of board feet of prime walnut, they eventually legislated control over their timber and enforced some regulation, thereby faring better than the Chippewas in the north. See D. F. Littlefield, Jr., and L. E. Underhill, "Timber Depredations and Cherokee Legislation, 1869-1881," *Journal of Forest History* 18 (April 1974): 4-13. In 1873 the U.S. Supreme Court in *U.S.* v. *Cook* (19 Wallace 591) decided that Oneidas could not cut and sell timber on their land because Indians had only the right of occupancy, whereas the fee title belonged to the government. All standing pine was real estate and since the land could not be sold (*Worcester* v. *Georgia, Cherokee Nation* v. *Georgia*) neither could the timber. An 1876 act of Congress authorized Indian timber sales when approved by the agent, but the income went into a government trust. An act in 1882 allowed Green Bay tribes to sell windfall. This paternalism ended in 1938 when the Supreme Court in *U.S.* v. *Shoshone Tribe* (340 U.S. 111) ruled that Indians had a right to all resources on their land.

30. CIA, *Annual Report*, 1871, pp. 588-94, 686-88. The AMA asserted that Smith saved the Indians more than five hundred thousand dollars from fraudulent "half-breed script" (land allotment certificates issued to mixed bloods in 1856, which speculators duplicated to illegally obtain tribal lands). Smith felt this reform precipitated the "malice and fury" of the pine men against him (AMA Archives, Fisk University, E. P. Smith Papers, Smith to Cravath, August 15, 1872). He also had been critical of E. S. Parker and urged a survey of Red Lake lands to prevent white depredations (BIC:LR, Smith to

H. M. Rice, July 10, 1871; BIC:LS, Cree to Welsh, March 22, 1872). Also see
C. A. Ruffee, *Report of the Condition of the Chippewas of Minnesota.*

31. OIA:LR, E. P. Smith to F. Walker, February 5, 16, August 15, September 18, November 9, 1872; Smith to Hon. H. S. Neal, August 16, 1872; Houlton and Nickerson Lumber Co. to Delano, August 28, 1872; E. M. Wilson to Delano, July 20, 1872; H. B. Whipple to F. Walker, August 25, 1872; C. M. Loring to Whipple, August 17, 1872; *St. Paul Pioneer*, August 23, 1872; Whipple, *Lights and Shadows*, pp. 45–49.

32. BIC:LS, Cree to Brunot, March 12, 1873. Columbus Delano testified in 1875 that Felix Brunot asked him to appoint Welsh after Parker resigned in 1871. Delano declined because he felt that Welsh did not possess "judgment, wisdom, and discretion." Welsh's dislike for Smith, so Delano said, stemmed from this rejection. Red Cloud Commission, *Report*, pp. 757–59.

33. AMA Archives, Smith Papers, Smith to G. Whipple, December 15, 1870; Smith to G. D. Pike, June 9, 1871; BIC:LR, Smith to W. Welsh, August 28, 1871; Welsh to Colyer, September 2, 1871; Welsh to Cree, April 8, 1872; WP, Welsh to Whipple, June 5, September 11, 1873; 3; "Indians Robbed by the Wholesale and Left Starving," *St. Paul Dispatch*, September 18, 1873, and "Smith as a Shah," *Minneapolis Tribune*, October 1, 1873, cited by Rahill, *Catholic Indian Missions*, p. 86. Rahill does not question the veracity of these doubtful accounts.

34. WP, Welsh to Whipple, October 5, 1873.

35. Welsh, *Indian Office: Wrongs Doing and Reforms Needed* (January 2, 1874, a tract published in Philadelphia); Welsh, *Sales of Indian Pine Timber* (March 13, 1874).

36. WP, Welsh to Delano, November 8, 1873; Welsh to Whipple, November 7, 12, 17, December 22, 1873; Delano to Welsh, official and personal letters of November 17, 1873; Welsh to Turney, December 1, 1873; BIC:LS, Cree to Brunot, October 27, November 5, 1873; Cree to Stuart, November 8, 15, 1873; OIA:LR, E. P. Smith to H. R. Clum, December 17, 1873.

37. WP, G. Beaulieu to Whipple, August 21, 1873; Beaulieu to Welsh, September 4, 1873; Whipple to the BIC, December 27, 1873, January 6, 1874; Delano to Whipple, January 13, March 20, 1874; Whipple to Welsh, August 19, 1874; E. P. Smith to Whipple, February 25, 1875; OIA:LS, E. P. Smith to Delano, September 13, 1873. Whipple did suspect Smith's successor and on learning that white loggers had cut seven million feet of Leech Lake pine in 1874, he requested an investigation of the agency. OIA:LR, Whipple to Delano, April 14, 18, 1874; *Lights and Shadows*, p. 49.

38. Ruffee, *Report of the Condition of the Chippewas*, pp. 23–29.

39. Smith testified that lumbermen had been introduced to him by Charles Howard (editor of *Advance*) and Congregational minister Edward Williams, both of Chicago. When asked if the AMA controlled pine sales, Smith answered

that since the association controlled its agents, it "more or less" did. Williams, whose brother-in-law purchased Wisconsin timber, refused to testify. There was no evidence of fraud or of direct benefits to the AMA. U.S. Department of the Interior, *Report of the Commission Appointed by the Secretary of the Interior to Investigate Certain Charges against Hon. E. P. Smith* (Washington: Government Printing Office, 1875), pp. 18, 82, 87, 92, 94, 98, 100-119, 134-35.

40. *House Report* no. 778, 43d Cong., 1st sess., pp. 27, 59, 277, 283; *House Misc. Doc.* no. 167, 44th Cong., 1st sess., pp. 305-6, 355ff.

41. Red Cloud Commission, *Report*, pp. lv-lvi, lxix.

42. *Nation*, November 26, 1874, p. 341; *New York Tribune*, January 26, 1874, May 6, 1875; *Washington Chronicle*, February 14, 17, 1874; *Advance*, December 2, 1875; *American Missionary* 18 (June 1874): 134; 19 (September 1875): 198-99.

43. Grant Papers, Grant to Oliver Hoyt, November 14, 1875.

44. In 1871 Smith promised G. D. Pike and E. M. Cravath that if they visited White Earth he would pay their expenses by listing them as teamsters or cooks. AMA, Smith Papers, Smith to Pike, August 5, 1871; Smith to Cravath, September 2, 1872. To determine Smith's innocence or guilt in the pine sales requires a detailed study of his affairs, of the northern timber frauds, and of the practices of the Land Office. On the Land Office, see L. White, *The Republican Era*, pp. 196-208; for the timber industry, see Robert Fries, *Empire in Pine* (Madison: State Historical Society of Wisconsin, 1951).

45. *House Report* no. 778, 43d Cong., 1st sess., pp. 217-18; *House Misc. Doc.* no. 167, 44th Cong., 1st sess., pp. 107ff., 116ff., 141, 198-99, 351, 398ff. Anson Dart was a druggist and former superintendent of Indian affairs in Oregon. He said that F. A. Walker and Columbus Delano refused to buy the medicine but that Smith gave in after a "good deal of urging." Endorsements of the Specific read: "Can any philanthropist look with indifference upon this discovery . . . as sure a protection as that water will quench fire." Lust, Dart said, could not be curbed by moral preaching and therefore only "Sanitary Specific" could drive venereal disease out of the United States. It acted "mechanically and chemically" by closing the "pores of the cuticle" and neutralizing the virus. An OIA physician and the surgeon general denounced the fraudulent preparation as "repulsive, degrading and filthy."

46. WP, Hare to Whipple, May 3, 1874.

47. WP, Welsh to Whipple, c. July 1874; Whipple to Welsh, August 19, 1874.

48. Whipple, *Lights and Shadows*, p. 49.

49. Richard I. Dodge, *Our Wild Indians* (New York: Archer House, 1959), p. 93; originally published in 1882 as *A Living Issue*.

50. Although the 1860s are considered an especially corrupt period at the

agencies, attacks against agents in that period were filled with false accusations. William Unrau's dissertation, "The Role of the Indian Agent in the South-Central Plains, 1861-1868" (University of Colorado, 1963), indicates that conditions that make evaluation difficult were present before 1869. For the same problems in an earlier period, see Satz, *American Indian Policy in the Jacksonian Era.*

51. The editor of the *American Missionary* questioned whether the Christian Church could do so. In 1871 he predicted that the Peace Policy must expect trouble because it was perilous to regard any devout churchman "as necessarily a good man in business, or even an upright man . . . one of the old Indian manipulators knows more in an hour than some good men can find out in a month" (*American Missionary* 15 [February 1871]: 33). Ben Simpson, agent at Siletz for eight years before the Peace Policy removed him, also complained that bringing religion into Indian affairs created a danger that piety might replace "certain other very respectable and necessary qualities. . . . Many very good and pious men are but children in the business of the world" (CIA, *Annual Report,* 1871, p. 318).

52. See Appendix 3.

53. Red Cloud Commission, *Report*, p. 609.

54. David Halberstam's *The Making of a Quagmire* (New York: Random House, 1965), demonstrates the consequences of information lag between a Washington desk and a battlefield, even in the age of instant communication. When there is no desire to deceive, there remains the willingness to be deceived—the human temptation to adjust reality to fit theory, myth, and policy. Halberstam argued that this created the American fiasco in Southeast Asia in the 1960s. Or, as one general reportedly said of U.S. army operations in the Pacific during World War II, "When you got out into the field, you learned quickly that although these people had the same problems you had always known about, there was a critical difference to be considered. A problem read in a report is entirely different when the problem is one demanding personal attention and solution. . . . Reading about a shortage of shoes when you're in Washington, and walking barefoot on a hot desert, may be the same problem, but it's a long way different in individual meaning." Quoted in M. Caidin, *The Mission* (Philadelphia: Lippincott, 1964), p. 34.

55. Before Hare arrived at Yankton in 1873, Hinman had been the Episcopal church's model Indian missionary, even though the Riggs family constantly anathematized him as a lewd and licentious man, a seducer and debaucher of Indian girls. After Hare's arrival, Hinman grew jealous of the younger bishop, who criticized his squandering of mission funds. The two men also battled over title to Santee mission land. The death of Hinman's wife led to new problems that culminated in the late 1870s, when Hare dismissed the missionary and requested that the Indian Office banish him from the reservation.

When Himan fought back, Hare published rumors of theft, drunkenness, fornication, and stolen mission funds; he revealed allegations that Hinman had killed his wife by infecting her with venereal disease. Eastern Episcopalians tried to hush everything, but Hinman filed a libel suit against Hare, and a jury awarded the missionary $10,000. The verdict was upheld in the New York Supreme Court (1884) and then reversed in the New York Court of Appeals (1887). Apart from its sensational aspects, the Hinman-Hare dispute deserves further study because it involved legal questions regarding church property, rules of evidence, privileged information, libel law, the relationship between ecclesiastical authority and American civil law, the doctrine of the Church, and the nature of missions. The major sources are the Whipple Papers, records of the Episcopal Indian Commission and the American Board, and Special File 269, Record Group 75, National Archives. The legal citations are *Hinman* v. *Hare*, New York Supreme Court, CCCLVI, 680-88, and ibid. in the Court of Appeals of New York, *Northeastern Reporter*, January 1887, pp. 41-58. Even after the scandal became public, Hinman continued to work for the government in securing Sioux land cessions. See Olson, *Red Cloud*, chap. 15, Prucha, *Crisis*, p. 173, and Grant K. Anderson, "Samuel D. Hinman and the Opening of the Black Hills," *Nebraska History* 60 (Winter 1979): 520-42.

Chapter 7

1. "A Universal Verdict," *Omaha Daily Herald*, August 29, 1869.

2. *New York Weekly Tribune*, September 29, 1869; R. B. Marcy to the BIC, June 1869, quoted in BIC, *Annual Report*, 1869, pp. 70-79; Richardson, *Messages* 7:38-39; Friends Assoc. Exec. Comm., *Annual Report*, 1870, p. 12. Opponents of the Peace Policy also called on the Quakers to test their principles in practice: "Now that the prominent Indian superintendencies and agencies have been assigned to the broad-brims and shad-bellies, we hope that a fair trial will be given to the 'brotherly love' system. That the practice of these benignant gentlemen may comport with their precepts, it is to be hoped that they will forego the protection of military escorts, and trust entirely to the humanizing and Christianizing influences of greenbacks, brown sugar, burnt coffee, wooden beads, striped calico and blue blankets," *Kansas Daily Commonwealth*, May 6, 1869, quoted in Lonnie J. White, "Indian Raids on the Kansas Frontier, 1869," *Kansas Historical Quarterly* 38 (Winter 1972): 372.

3. Grant commuted the death sentences of two Modocs, an act that did not increase his popularity in the West or with the army, and he allowed four to hang, which did not enhance his standing with the radical reformers and pacifists. The BIC felt privately that the war would turn public opinion

against the army. Although the board denied responsibility for the Modocs, they had urged the peace talks and if Canby had succeeded, one suspects that the BIC would have claimed credit. BIC:LS, Cree to Brunot, March 10, 24, April 18, 1873; BIC, *Annual Report*, 1873, pp. 3-4, 197, 204, 217-20; Hare, *Reminiscences*, p. 12; *Spirit of Missions*, 1873, p. 370. The fullest account of the war is Keith Murray, *The Modocs and Their War*; also see Athearn, *Sherman*, chap. 15.

4. *New York Herald*, April 14, 1873; *Watchman*, January 30, April 24, May 8, 1873; *Philadelphia Inquirer*, April 15, 1873; *Friend's Intelligencer*, May 10, 1873.

5. *New York Times*, April 20, 1873; *Harper's Weekly*, May 3, 1873, pp. 364-65; *Nation*, April 17, 1873, p. 259; *Cheyenne Daily Leader*, June 25, 1873; *Congregationalist*, April 17, 1873. Mardock's *Reformers* contains the best account of public reaction to the Modoc War. He concludes that it significantly undercut public support for the Peace Policy and that only A. B. Meacham's altruism, self-sacrifice, and devotion to the Policy after the war sustained the program's credibility (pp. 115-28, 134-37). Also see Prucha, *Crisis*, pp. 88-90. The Battle of Remolino did not attract public attention to the extent that Sand Creek, the Piegan Massacre, and the Modoc War did, yet Remolino, according to Robert Utley, was "one of the rare instances in which the Regular Army stands convicted of warring purposely, rather than incidentally or accidentally, on women and children" (Utley, *Frontier Regulars*, pp. 347-49).

6. Mardock, *Reformers*, pp. 39-42, describes the role of Love and his union in the Peace Policy. Love supported Grant, but believed that any use of the army in the West signified a failure to pursue a true peace policy. Also see Mardock, "Alfred H. Love," *Kansas Quarterly* 3 (Fall 1971): 64-71.

7. *Spirit of Missions* 40 (November 1875): 696-99; also see Episcopal Board of Missions, *Proceedings*, 1874, pp. 163-71; Hare, "Further Enlargements"; Howe, *Hare*, pp. 110ff., 120, 128; BIC, *Annual Report*, 1874, p. 62.

8. Whipple, *Lights and Shadows*, pp. 166, 195, 386; OIA, Inspector Reports, Kemble to E. P. Smith, January 30, 1875; CIA, *Annual Report*, 1872, pp. 268-69; 1873, p. 244; 1878, p. 24; BIC, *Annual Report*, 1874, p. 62. Despite such abundant evidence, George Hyde in *Spotted Tail's Folk* (Norman: University of Oklahoma Press, 1937), pp. 194-95, wrote that the Peace Policy was a pacifist program, that Episcopal agents were "pilloried by the church people" for using force, and that agents feared losing their jobs if they called on the army.

9. Library of Congress, Grant Papers, Grant to General J. M. Schofield, March 6, 1872. Also see CIA, *Annual Report*, 1871, p. 374; BIC, *Annual Report*, 1869, p. 25; 1871, pp. 5-6; 1877, p. 89. There were more than two hundred military operations against Indians during the Grant administration.

10. *Congressional Globe*, 41st Cong., 2d sess., p. 4087.

11. B. White, *Friends and the Indians*; Janney, *Memoirs*, p. 251; BIC, *Annual Report*, 1873, p. 45; FHL:RG 2, S. Averill to Hallowell, February 26, 1869; FHL, Green Papers, J. Powell to Green, September 25, 1869.

12. FHL, Green Papers, W. Dorsey to Albert Green, July 5, 1869.

13. FHL:RG 2, S. Averill to Hallowell, August 29, 1869; CIA, *Annual Report*, 1873, pp. 196-97; BIC, *Annual Report*, 1874, p. 31; T. Battey, *The Life and Adventures of a Quaker Among the Indians* (Boston: Lee and Shepard, 1875), pp. 61-62. For early Quaker use of Indian police, see James L. Sellers, ed., "Diary of Dr. Joseph A. Paxson, Physician to the Winnebago Indians, 1869-1870," *Nebraska History* 27 (October 1946): 255, 273, and Meyer, *Santee Sioux*, pp. 164-65. For Hicksite compromises of absolute pacificism, see Milner, "With Good Intentions," pp. 129-37, 172-82, 190-94, 314. The issues in Nebraska were the same as in the Central Superintendency, only on a smaller scale.

14. FHL:RG 2, Averill to Hallowell, February 26, 1869; CIA, *Annual Report*, 1872, pp. 233-34.

15. BIC:LR, Lang to Colyer, January 28, 1871; BIC, *Annual Report*, 1870, pp. 83-84.

16. The army could not legally enter an Indian reservation until requested by the Department of the Interior.

17. Friends Assoc. Exec. Comm., *Annual Report*, 1872, p. 5; BIC:LS, Cree to Brunot, April 10, 1872; Cree to Hoag, April 13, 1872; BIC, *Annual Report*, 1872, p. 151; 1872, p. 93; CIA, *Annual Report*, 1874, pp. 226-27.

18. CIA, *Annual Report*, 1869, p. 350; 1870, p. 243; 1872, pp. 213-14; 1873, pp. 40-41; BIC, *Annual Report*, 1875, pp. 40, 64. George Hyde is very critical of Quaker pacifism in *Pawnee Indians* (Denver: University of Denver Press, 1951), pp. 227ff. Another problem for the Friends in Nebraska was the murder of Edward McMurtry by four Pawnees on an island in the North Platte River; the Indians also decapitated Oscar Munson, a Polk County resident. The tribe surrendered the nine murderers after a plea by the agent, but the two incidents belie later Hicksite claims that Indians under their control never killed a white person. CIA, *Annual Report*, 1869, pp. 336-37; S. Janney, *Memoirs*, pp. 266-71, 277-78.

19. *Congressional Globe*, 41st Cong., 2d sess., p. 4079.

20. See Trennert, *Alternative to Extinction*.

21. One of the spectacular scandals of the Grant administration involved the trading post at Fort Sill. In 1876 it was revealed that Secretary of War William Belknap's wife received six thousand dollars in annual kickbacks from the post trader (see McFeely, *Grant*, chap. 25). One fact not brought out at Belknap's trial was that a secret investigation in 1871 revealed how an agency

clerk, George Smith, made more than sixteen thousand dollars in eighteen months. Though a close friend of Quaker agent Tatum, Smith himself was not a Quaker and Tatum apparently had no knowledge of the affair. OIA:LR, Walter Burr to H. R. Clum, September 25, 1871.

22. By far the best history of the agency is William Hagan's *United States-Comanche Relations: The Reservation Years* (New Haven: Yale University Press, 1976). Especially see chap. 4, "The Education of a Quaker." Other accounts of the agency during the Peace Policy include Debo's *History*, chap. 12; Lee Cutler, "Lawrie Tatum and the Kiowa Agency, 1869-1873," *Arizona and the West* 8 (Autumn 1971): 221-24; Aubrey L. Steele, "The Beginning of Quaker Administration of Indian Affairs in Oklahoma," *Chronicles of Oklahoma* 17 (December 1939): 364-92; Martha Buntin, "The Quaker Indian Agents of the Kiowa, Comanche and Wichita Indian Reservation," *Chronicles of Oklahoma* 10 (June 1932): 204-18. Wilbur S. Nye's *Carbine and Lance: The Story of Old Fort Sill* (Norman: University of Oklahoma Press, 1969), chap. 6, a battle history filled with details of bloodshed and murder, is generally fair to Tatum and somewhat prejudiced against the "benevolent pollyannas in the East."

23. Newberry Library, Ayer Collection, Grierson MSS, Grierson to Tatum, September 30, 1869.

24. OIA:LR, Tatum to Friend E. S. Parker, July 24, 1869; Tatum to Hoag, October 16, 1869.

25. BIC, *Annual Report*, 1869, pp. 20-25; Haverford College, Garrett Collection, Tatum to Garrett, January 25, 1870; Tatum, *Red Brothers*, pp. 25, 30.

26. OIA:LR, Tatum to Hoag, February 11, May 14, June 12, 22, July 1, 10, 1870.

27. OIA:LR, Hugh Quipley to Belknap, July 7, 1870.

28. OIA:LR, Tatum to Hoag, July 22, August 6, 1870; Tatum to Parker, August 12, 1870; Tatum, *Red Brothers*, p. 35.

29. OIA:LR, Tatum to Hoag, September 6, 1870.

30. Ibid., October 26, 1870.

31. CIA, *Annual Report*, 1870, p. 264.

32. OIA:LR, Tatum to Hoag, February 10, March 18, May 20, 25, 28, 1871; W. T. Sherman to W. Wood, May 19, 1871; Sherman to E. D. Townsend, May 28, 1871; Tatum to Sherman, May 29, 1871; R. C. Crane, "Damage Claims for Attacks on Warren's Wagon Trains," *West Texas Historical Association Yearbook* 21 (October 1945): 72-76.

33. Grierson MSS, Grierson to S. L. Woodward, September 4, 1871; OIA:LR, Tatum to Hoag, September 23, 26, 30, October 14, 1871; CIA, *Annual Report*, 1871, pp. 3, 502.

34. Quoted in Hagan, *United States-Comanche Relations,* p. 78.

35. Haverford College, Garrett MSS, Ohio Yearly Meeting to the Associated Executive Committee, November 1871.

36. Friends Exec. Comm., *Annual Report,* 1871, pp. 10-16; *Friend's Intelligencer,* September 9, 1871; Garrett MSS, E. Earle to Garrett, June 21, 1871; W. Nicholson to Garrett, September 14, 1871.

37. OIA:LR, Hoag to F. A. Walker, March 6, 1872.

38. *Congressional Globe,* 41st Cong., 3d sess., pp. 715, 735; *New York Herald,* July 18, 23, September 23, 24, 1872.

39. CIA, *Annual Report,* 1872, pp. 136, 248, 251.

40. Friends Assoc. Exec. Comm., *Minutes,* 1872, p. 19; *New York Tribune,* August 17, 1872; OIA:LR, Tatum to Hoag, March 3, 1871; Tatum, *Red Brothers,* pp. 132, 160-66.

41. Battey, *Life and Adventures,* pp. 136-37. Lawrie Tatum returned to Iowa where he became the legal guardian of Herbert Hoover.

42. OIA:LR, Haworth to Hoag, April 7, 1873; Hoag to Smith, April 11, 1873; Battey, *Life and Adventures,* pp. 196, 251ff.

43. OIA:LR, Haworth to Hoag, April 7, 1873; C. Beede to E. P. Smith, July 31, 1873; Haworth to Smith, November 14, 24, 1873; CIA, *Annual Report,* 1873, pp. 200, 219; *Nation,* October 30, 1873, p. 287; November 13, 1873, p. 320; January 1, 1874, pp. 7-8; Friends Assoc. Exec. Comm., *Annual Report,* 1873, p. 13. Haworth's tenure at the Kiowa-Comanche agency is told in Hagan, *U.S.-Comanche Relations,* chap. 5.

44. A twentieth-century Arapaho account, filtered through seventy years of tribal memory, describes Darlington as the ideal Peace Policy and Quaker agent:

President Grant was the Great White Father in Washington when he came to the reservation. Before that time he had been a great warrior. . . . he saw to it that good men were sent to take charge of our agency. There was more than one white man's road . . . and President Grant wanted us to take the right one. He sent Brinton Darlington to be our first Agent. Mr. Darlington belonged to the Society of Friends, the Quakers, and we could tell that he believed many of the things that we believed. . . . He had not been trained in our religious societies and did not know our ceremonies. But he did not try to wipe them all out, as some white people believed in doing. Brinton Darlington came to the Agency as our friend and helper, and we liked him. . . . He brought assistants there, many of them Quakers like himself, who built good buildings and started schools and opened trading posts and laid out farms. . . . He was patient and kind; he managed like a chief; he prayed to the Man-Above when he was thankful and when he needed power. So although he was a white man and did not speak our

language, we could understand him. He died in 1872 . . . and when he was
buried in the cemetery on the hill . . . there were Cheyenne and Arapaho
chiefs, as well as white men, who wept over his grave. Even today when
the Arapaho think of Darlington we think of a place where life was once
happy and good.

From the memoirs of Carl Sweezy, an Arapaho born in 1881, in Althea
Bass, *The Arapaho Way: A Memoir of an Indian Boyhood* (New York: Clarkson N. Potter, 1966), pp. 4, 58. Another positive evaluation of Darlington's
service is in Berthrong, *Southern Cheyenne*, chap. 15. Sandra LeVan's "The
Quaker Agents at Darlington," *Chronicles of Oklahoma* 51 (Spring 1973):
92-99, is an uncritical account of Quakers on the southern plains in which
there is no hint of conflict; for LeVan, the "wild and warlike chiefs yielded
to [the agent's] gentle sway" and she neglects to explain what happened
after 1873.

45. OIA:LR, Miles to Hoag, April 11, May 7, 1873; Hoag to E. P. Smith,
April 15, 1873; CIA, *Annual Report,* 1873, pp. 221, 225.

46. Hagan, *U.S.-Comanche Relations,* p. 113. Quaker gullibility and
naïveté is clear in William Nicholson's "Tour of Indian Agencies" (1870).
Hoag and Nicholson visited the southern agencies, learned directly of the
tense and explosive situations, and glossed over the problems.

47. OIA:LR, Haworth to Hoag, February 9, April 20, May 6, 26, June 3,
July 14, 1874; Haworth to E. P. Smith, April 8, 1874.

48. OIA:LR, Hoag to Smith, February 1874; Miles to Smith, August 8,
1874; Haverford College, Hoag Letterbooks, Hoag to Nicholson, April 27,
May 19, 1874.

49. Donald Berthrong's *Southern Cheyenne*, chap. 16, is the best account
of the Red River War. Berthrong includes as causes of the war: Miles's
coercive use of annuities; the slaughter of the buffalo by white hunters;
trespass on the reservation by surveyors, horse thieves, settlers, and whiskey
traders; and the influence of older Kiowas on the younger warriors. A firsthand account that placed all the blame directly on the "idiotic twaddle" of
the Quakers and peace commissioners is J. T. Marshall's *The Miles Expedition
of 1874-1875: An Eyewitness Account of the Red River War*, ed. Lonnie J.
White (Austin: Encino Press, 1971). Following the rescue of two white girls
on the Staked Plain, Marshall, an army scout, warned: "Here is another theme
for Quaker homilies on the dove-like innocence and tender compassion of the
noble red man of the forest, whose bloody deeds shock the sensibilities. . . .
Is it not time these atrocities were stopped and their merciless perpetrators
brought to certain punishment? Let Quakerism and its abettors answer"
(p. 39).

50. OIA:LR, Miles to Smith, June 13, 16, 23, 30, 1874.

51. Ibid., July 7, 1874, six-page telegram.

52. Ibid., July 10, 1874; Hoag Letterbooks, Hoag to General John Pope, July 10, 1874.

53. Hoag Letterbooks, Hoag to D. R. Anthony, July 14, 1874.

54. OIA:LR, Miles to Smith, August 29, 1874. Miles later told E. P. Smith that he had to speak "a word for truth's sake" by telling General Pope to ignore any artificial line drawn between what Hoag called "the progressive and loyal Kiowas & Comanches" and Miles's unruly Cheyennes and Arapahos.

55. OIA:LR, newspaper clipping with a Lawrence dateline, July 17, 1874.

56. OIA:LR, Miles to Smith, July 18, 1874.

57. *New York Tribune,* July 20, 1874; *New York Times,* July 21, 1874; *Advance,* July 23, 1874; *Unitarian Review* 2 (September 1874): 197.

58. OIA:LR, E. P. Smith to Zadok Street, July 20, 1874 (published in the *New York Tribune,* July 27, 1874).

59. Assoc. Exec. Comm. on Indian Affairs, *Minutes,* August 17, 1874, pp. 3-11, 13, 20; *Annual Report,* pp. 10-12; Hoag Letterbooks, Hoag to Nicholson, August 10, 1874; Hoag Papers, T. Wister to Hoag, August 21, 1874; SI:LR, B. Tatham to Delano, September 1874; SI:LS, Delano to Tatham, September 17, 1874.

60. OIA:LR, Miles to Nicholson, August 15, 1874; Miles to E. P. Smith, August 15, 18, 1874.

61. OIA:LR, Haworth to Smith, August 24, 1874; Connell to Miles, August 25, 1874; General J. W. Davidson to Assistant Adjutant General, Department of Texas, August 10, 1874.

62. OIA:LR, Miles to Smith, September 26, October 12, 1874; BIC, *Annual Report,* 1874, pp. 79ff. On Miles's cordial relations with the army during the war, see Marshall, *The Miles Expedition,* pp. 56-57.

63. Assoc. Exec. Comm., *Annual Report,* 1875, pp. 13, 18-19; SI:LR, J. Rhoads to Z. Chandler, January 4, 1877. Miles remained as Cheyenne-Arapaho agent until he resigned in 1885. For the story of his later conflicts with the BIA and his reliance on the army to control white trespass on the reservation, see Donald J. Berthrong, "Cattlemen on the Cheyenne-Arapahoe Reservation, 1883-1885," *Arizona and the West* 13 (Spring 1971): 5-32, and Berthrong's excellent book, *The Cheyenne and Arapaho Ordeal: Reservation and Agency Life in the Indian Territory, 1875-1907* (Norman: University of Oklahoma Press, 1976). James Haworth also remained with the BIA after the Peace Policy, becoming the first superintendent of Indian schools in 1882.

64. *Nation,* January 15, 1874, p. 40; OIA:LR, Gen. J. W. Davidson to Adj. Gen., U.S. Army, January 10, 1874; CIA, *Annual Report,* 1874, p. 10; BIC, *Annual Report,* 1874, p. 83; Sturgis, *Common Sense View,* pp. 6, 36, 50; *Congressional Record,* 44th Cong., 1st sess., pp. 2567, 2661, 2670, 2682.

65. Meacham, *Wigwam and Warpath*; CIA, *Annual Report*, 1871, pp. 485ff.; 1877, p. 161; Welsh, *Sioux and Ponca*, p. 19.

66. OIA, *Report on Friends*, pp. 36ff.; Friends Assoc. Exec. Comm., *Need of Law*, p. 32, and *Annual Report*, 1875, p. 10; BIC, *Annual Report*, 1874, pp. 126-27; CIA, *Annual Report*, 1874, pp. 236, 215; Hoag Papers, J. Miles to Hoag, May 28, 1875.

67. *Friend's Intelligencer*, November 30, 1878; CIA, *Annual Report*, 1872, p. 143; SI:LR, Miles to E. P. Smith, August 15, 1875; FHL, Barclay White Journal, 2:400.

68. Newberry Library, Ayer Collection, MS no. 676, E. S. Parker, c. 1882.

Chapter 8

1. BIC, *Annual Report*, 1875, p. 149; CIA, *Annual Report*, 1879, pp. 42, 46; 1881, pp. lviii, 68, 79.

2. Woodworth Clum, *Apache Agent: the Story of John P. Clum* (Boston: Houghton Mifflin, 1936); also see John Bourke, *On the Border with Crook*, and *An Apache Campaign in the Sierra Madre*.

3. Kappler, *Indian Affairs, Laws and Treaties* 1:23-24, 18 Stat. 420, March 3, 1875.

4. Sheehan, *Seeds of Extinction*, chaps. 5-6; Viola, *McKenney*, chap. 10, quoted from p. 187.

5. Sheehan, *Seeds of Extinction*, p. 278. Also see Prucha, *Americanizing the American Indian: Writings by the "Friends of the Indians"* (Cambridge: Harvard University Press, 1973), and *American Indian Policy in Crisis*; Waltmann, "John C. Lowrie"; Michael Coleman, "Christianizing and Americanizing the Nez Perce," *Journal of Presbyterian History* 53 (Winter 1975): 339-61. The philanthropic and even the scientific-anthropological inability to overcome cultural stereotypes can be seen in the attitude toward native American displays at the 1876 Centennial Exposition in Philadelphia, where Indian cultures were exhibited as curious relics of the past. See Robert A. Trennert, Jr., "A Grand Failure: The Centennial Indian Exhibition of 1876," *Prologue* 6, no. 2 (Summer 1974): 118-29.

My conclusions about the impact of Protestant missions on native culture differ considerably from recent and more positive interpretations of native reactions to Christianity. See Margaret Whitehead, "Christianity, A Matter of Choice," *Pacific Northwest Quarterly* 72 (July 1981): 98-106. For interpretations similar to mine, see Bowden, *American Indians and Christian Missions*, and Milner, *With Good Intentions*.

6. Meyer, *History of the Santee Sioux*, pp. 362-63.

7. *Spirit of Missions*, 1870, pp. 26, 39, 343; 1880, pp. 416-17; Whipple, *Lights and Shadows*, p. 143; Hicksite Friends, *Joint Delegation*, pp. 35ff.;

White, *Friends and the Indians,* p. 10. Almost alone in his church, Episcopal missionary Goodnough at Green Bay opposed severalty (*Spirit of Missions,* 1872, p. 158). The legal basis for severalty was the Act of March 3, 1871 (U.S. Stat. 18:420) which abolished the treaty system and extended the Homestead Act to Indians who would forsake all tribal relations. Severalty debates in Congress during the next decade provide a rich source for white attitudes toward native cultures. See Prucha, *American Indian Policy in Crisis* and D. S. Otis, *The Dawes Act and the Allotment of Indian Land,* F. P. Prucha, ed. (Norman: University of Oklahoma Press, 1973).

8. W. W. Alderson, "A Talk to the Indians in Council at Fort Peck," January 24, 1874 (transcript in the Montana Hist. Soc., Helena); H. Ludlow and E. Goodale, *Captain Pratt and His Work for Indian Education* (Philadelphia: Indian Rights Association, 1886), p. 6; Whipple, *Lights and Shadows,* pp. 286-88, 517; Hicksite Friends, *Annual Report,* 1871, pp. 4, 8; CIA, *Annual Report,* 1876, p. 77; 1877, p. 4; 1878, p. 141; 1880, p. 57; Wash. Terr. MSS, R. H. Milroy to J. Smith, February 19, 1876; Milroy to Hayt, February 7, 1879. The work ethic is evident throughout the documents collected by Prucha in *Americanizing the American Indian.*

9. R. H. Milroy, "Our Indian Policy Further Considered," *Princeton Review* (October 1876): 624-28; BIC, Minutes, April 23, 1879; Hicksite Friends, *Annual Report,* 1871, pp. 1-4; 1877, p. 13; Washington Terr. MSS, R. H. Milroy to E. C. Axtell, November 16, 1875, letter containing instructions to break up Indian families on the Puyallup reservation. Protestant attitudes toward native culture are also described in Berthrong, *Cheyenne and Arapaho Ordeal,* pp. 78-90; Hagan, *U.S.-Comanche Relations,* chap. 6; Ramon Powers, "Why the Northern Cheyenne Left Indian Territory in 1878: A Cultural Analysis," *Kansas Quarterly* 3 (Fall 1971): 72-81; Joseph E. Illick, "'Some of Our Best Indians Are Friends . . .': Quaker Attitudes and Actions Toward Western Indians During the Grant Administration," *Western Historical Quarterly* 2 (July 1971): 283-94. Roy Meyer in his *History of the Santee Sioux* portrays the Friends as much more extreme assimilationists than either the American Board or the Episcopalians. There is little evidence of any Quaker appreciation of native culture in contemporary documents, e.g., Sellers's "Diary," Nicholson's "Tour," and Thomas Battey's *Life and Adventures.* For an evaluation of Quaker intolerance toward native cultures, see Milner, "With Good Intentions," pp. 277-81, 388, 416-20. Milner's study excels in assessing the impact of the Peace Policy on Indian people.

10. FHL:RG 2, Janney to Hallowell, December 16, 1869; Saunders to B. White, January 20, 1873; BIC:LR, Gibson to Colyer, January 24, 1872; Janney to Cree, December 19, 1872; Garrett to Colyer, February 8, 1870; CIA, *Annual Report,* 1869, pp. 338-40; 1874, p. 201; Hyde, *Pawnees,* pp. 237, 243-44, 252-56.

11. BIC, *Annual Report,* 1878, pp. 9, 60–68; CIA, *Annual Report,* 1876, p. 23; 1881, pp. 46–47, 59; *Unitarian Review* 7 (June 1877): 639–55; *Watchman,* January 24, 1878. An effective attack on contemporary agrarian idealism was General John Pope's *Indian Question* ([Cincinnati], 1878). Pope based his argument on the premise that Indians were as diverse in abilities and interests as whites and that any policy that tried to force an entire race into a single vocation was "absurd, impracticable, and injurious." Even excellent Quaker agents such as John Miles profoundly misunderstood the large acreage required for dry farming and for agricultural survival on the southern plains. After a decade of trying to force farming on the Cheyennes and Arapahos, ten years that included annual crop failures and constant struggles to ease rigid BIA policy, Miles finally recognized the futility of conventional farming. He resigned in 1884 after a dispute over grazing permits. See Berthrong's detailed account, *The Cheyenne and Arapaho Ordeal.*

12. BIC, *Annual Report,* 1872, pp. 5, 123–313; Quakers, who knew Indians were at times escorted to red-light districts at government expense, questioned whether any good resulted from exposing "the children of the forest" to "the glare and turmoil of our boasted 'civilization,'" *Friend's Intelligencer,* March 29, 1873, p. 73. For Red Cloud's bizarre trips to the East, see Olson, *Red Cloud,* chaps. 7, 9, 10. The practice did not begin with the Peace Policy; a description of early Indian tours to Washington, D.C., may be found in Viola, *McKenney,* chap. 7, and Katherine Turner's *Red Men Calling on the Great White Father* (Norman: University of Oklahoma Press, 1951) is a complete history of pacification tours.

13. Agent William Alderson told the Blackfeet that their attitude toward women was "not good. It is all wrong. And the Great Spirit will not give you riches & peace and happiness as long as you do these things . . . the great God made women to be your equal" ("A Talk," 1874).

14. BIC, *Annual Report,* 1871, pp. 92, 110, 137, 162; 1872, p. 192; CIA, *Annual Report,* 1870, pp. 241, 254; 1881, p. 88. Whipple, *Lights and Shadows,* p. 560. Extreme acculturation occurred in the eastern boarding schools, Hampton and Carlisle. See Armstrong, *The Indian Question* (Hampton: Normal School Press, 1883), and Ludlow, *Pratt,* for a critique of Christian missions as being too soft on Indian culture.

15. *Congressional Globe,* 41st Cong., 2d sess., pp. 4015–16; 42d Cong., 3d sess., pp. 139–41; *Congressional Record,* 46th Cong., 2d sess., pp. 4253–62; 47th Cong., 1st sess., pp. 2418–56.

16. See Walker's book, pp. 6, 14, 138–40, and his 1872 *Annual Report*; CIA, *Annual Report,* 1876, pp. vi–vii; BIC, *Annual Report,* 1872, p. 19.

17. Howard, *Life,* p. 454; CIA, *Annual Report,* 1869, p. 252; *House Report* no. 98, 42d Cong., 3d sess., pp. 218–19 (emphasis in text). Also see Thomas C. Leonard, "Red, White and the Army Blue: Empathy and Anger in the American West," *American Quarterly* 26 (May 1974): 176–90.

18. L. M. Child, *Appeal*; MacMahon, *Anglo-Saxon and the . . . Indian*, pp. 7, 19-20, 29; also see Lossing, "Our Barbarian Brethren."

19. Eells, *Ten Years*; Gilfillan, "Fruits"; Whipple, *Lights and Shadows*; Bloomfield, *Oneidas*; Episcopal Board of Missions, *Proceedings*, 1874, p. 168; Welsh, *Journal*, p. xvi; Welsh, *Ponca and Sioux*, pp. 16, 19; Howe, *Hare*, pp. 232, 337; *United Presbyterian*, May 2, 1872. See Everett W. Sterling, "Moses Adams: A Missionary as Indian Agent," *Minnesota History* 35 (December 1956): 176-77, regarding Episcopalian E. C. Kemble's toleration of native culture.

20. BIC, *Annual Report*, 1871, p. 171; 1873, pp. 175-76; 1874, pp. 130, 140-42.

21. Rufus Anderson, *Foreign Missions, Their Relations and Claims* (New York: Charles Scribner's and Co.,1869), pp. 94-98, 109-18. Although he cautioned that acculturation required time and took different forms, Anderson did not doubt that Protestant conversion would help "heathens" grow into Christian civilization. He complained that conversion to Roman Catholicism made little difference in the daily lives of a people: "How small the change required of a Buddhist to be accepted as a true son of the Romish Church . . . how small in the wild African, and in the American Indians," pp. 294, 298. For a full statement of Anderson's thought, see R. Pierce Beaver, *To Advance the Gospel: Selections from the Writings of Rufus Anderson* (Grand Rapids: Wm. Eerdmans Publishing, 1967).

22. ABCFM:LR, A. Riggs to N. G. Clark, November 22, 1877; S. Riggs to Clark, November 26, 1877; ABCFM:LS, Clark to T. Riggs, November 10, 1877; October 24, 1880; May 19, 1881.

23. ABCFM:LR, S. B. Pike to J. O. Means, May 21, October 19, 1881.

24. BIC, *Annual Report*, 1872, p. 5.

25. *Baptist Quarterly* 9 (1871): 257-75, "Romish and Protestant Theories of Missions," by A. J. Gordon; *American Missionary* 15 (March 1871): 58-59; 15 (November 1871): 248-49; 16 (March 1872): 62-63; CIA, *Annual Report*, 1877, p. 177; BIC, *Annual Report*, 1878, p. 78; 1881, p. 83; Haverford College, Garrett Papers, Miles to Garrett, February 21, 1871.

26. Until the mid-eighteenth century the Anglican church had not insisted on cultural conformity as a requirement for membership, but this policy abruptly changed in the 1760s. For a discussion of the shift, see Gerald J. Goodwin, "Christianity, Civilization, and the Savage: The Anglican Mission to the American Indian," *Historical Magazine of the Protestant Episcopal Church* 42 (June 1973): 93-110.

27. *Spirit of Missions*, 1871, pp. 281-84; 1873, pp. 169-77; p. 490; CIA, *Annual Report*, 1880, p. 26.

28. CIA, *Annual Report*, 1871, p. 283.

29. Ibid., 1878, p. 140.

30. Washington Supt. Records, Yakima Agency, Wilbur to T. J. McKenney, January 19, June 26, 1871; CIA, *Annual Report*, 1881, p. 173; Seymour, *Indian Agents*, chap. 7. Homer G. Barnett's unpublished paper, "The Yakima Indians in 1942," describes the long-term failure of Wilbur's plans. Also see Margaret Ann Garretson, "The Yakima Indians: 1855-1935. Background and Analysis of the Rejection of the Indian Reorganization Act," M.A. thesis, University of Washington, 1968.

31. CIA, *Annual Report*, 1870, pp. 36-37.

32. SI, *Annual Report*, 1871, pp. 694-97; CIA, *Annual Report*, 1872, pp. 340, 345, 350-52; 1873, pp. 301-8.

33. BIC:LR, Huntington to Colyer, April 15, 1871; Wash. Supt. Records, Huntington to Hon. James Harlan, November 22, 1869; February 28, 1870; Ross to Huntington, February 22, 1870; Huntington to Ross, February 23, 1870; Huntington to Wilbur, June 4, 6, 9, 1870; Oregon Conf., Methodist Church, *Minutes*, 1874, p. 19. Whitner's dissertation, pp. 120-21, cites evidence to indicate that Gibson's removal was due to his denomination's unorthodox theology and that the agent had been framed by the Methodists and Episcopal inspector Edward Kemble. It is very doubtful that Kemble and the Methodists cooperated; Whitner assumes that the charges by the Disciples were correct and he does not try to adjudicate the issue.

34. CIA, *Annual Report*, 1874, p. 333; 1875, p. 364; 1876, pp. 133-34; BIC, *Annual Report*, 1875, pp. 139-40; 1876, pp. 42-43.

35. CIA, *Annual Report*, 1877, pp. 187-88.

36. OIA, Inspector Reports, file no 1871, Watkins to J. Q. Smith, September 22, 1877; affidavits in file no. 1885. A case similar to Huntington's involved former minister William Arny at the Navajo reservation, where agency employees, post traders, and Indians accused the agent of appropriating flour, beef, and church-donated dry goods for his own use or to sell to the tribe. See Murphy, *Frontier Crusader*, pp. 238-39.

37. CIA, *Annual Report*, 1878, pp. 130-31; 1879, pp. 145-46; 1881, pp. 161-63.

38. Ibid., 1879, p. 146.

39. Welsh, *Sioux and Ponca*, pp. 1, 4, 12; B. F. Overton, *Indians Opposed to the Transfer Bill* (Washington: Gibson Bros., 1878); Bass, *The Arapaho Way*; Eve Ball, *In the Days of Victorio: Recollections of a Warm Springs Apache* (Tucson: University of Arizona Press, 1970), pp. 4-5, 19-30, 43-52; Grenville Goodwin, *Western Apache Raiding and Warfare*, Keith H. Basso, ed. (Tucson: University of Arizona Press, 1971)). One of the most precise Indian definitions and evaluations of the Peace Policy is in a critical letter from Henry Fontenelle (Omaha) to the commissioner of Indian affairs, January 16, 1879, quoted by Milner, "With Good Intentions," p. 382.

40. Welsh, *Sioux and Ponca*, p. 8; BIC, *Annual Report*, 1871, pp. 45, 87,

118-23; 1872, p. 77. Almost any modern anthropological study would support the assertion that native Americans did not distinguish between or separate religion and politics, church and state; e.g., A. Irving Hallowell, *Culture and Experience* (Philadelphia: University of Pennsylvania Press, 1955): Calvin Martin, *Keepers of the Game* (Berkeley: University of California Press, 1978); Bowden, *American Indians and Christian Missions.*

41. CIA, *Annual Report,* 1876, p. 13; 1877, p. 41; 1878, p. 12; BIC, *Annual Report,* 1883, p. 48.

42. See William Nicholson's "Tour"; Berthrong, *Cheyenne and Arapaho Ordeal,* pp. 44-48, 99-106.

43. Senator George Pendleton of Ohio: "The Indians cannot fish or hunt. They must either change their mode of life or they must die. That is the alternative presented. There is none other. These Indians must either change . . . or they will be exterminated," *Congressional Record,* 46th Cong., 3d sess., p. 905.

44. Ibid., 43d Cong., 1st sess., p. 3471; AMA, *Annual Report,* 1871, pp. 66-67.

45. Tatum, *Red Brothers,* pp. 209-10.

46. Olson, *Red Cloud,* pp. 108-9.

47. Episcopal Board of Domestic Missions, *Annual Report,* 1883, p. 133; BIC, *Annual Report,* 1873, pp. 103-24; Carl Schurz's "Present Aspects of the Indian Problem," *North American Review,* July 1881, pp. 1-24, is a closely reasoned argument for paternalism.

48. Virginia Allen, "Agency Physicians to the Southern Plains Indians, 1868-1900," *Bulletin of the History of Medicine* 49 (Fall 1975): 318-30, and "The White Man's Road: The Physical and Psychological Impact of Relocation on the Southern Plains Indians," *Journal of the History of Medicine* 30 (April 1975): 148-63. Allen contends that emotional stress and physical ill-health can account for much of the southern plains violence in the 1870s. Conditions facing agency physicians were as impossible as those facing agents and, at times, doctors became the special object of native hatred. Allen also describes the effective medical work of the volunteer Quaker physician Fordyce Grinnell at Kiowa-Comanche and Pine Ridge, "Agency Physicians," pp. 324ff. For firsthand accounts of suffering in the daily lives of Indians, see Nicholson's "Tour" and Paxon's "Diary."

49. WP, J. J. Enmegahbowh to Whipple, September 23, 1878.

50. Alexis de Tocqueville, *Democracy in America* (New York: Alfred A. Knopf, 1953), p. 354.

51. E. Butler, *An Essay on "Our Indian Question"* (New York: Sherwood and Co., 1882), pp. 221-40; Pope, *Indian Question,* pp. 15-16; Miles, *Recollections,* p. 345.

52. James Mooney, *The Ghost Dance Religion*, American Bureau of Ethnology Reports 14, no. 2 (1896): 643.

Chapter 9

1. L. Tatum, *Red Brothers*, p. 196.

2. Quoted in *Harper's Weekly*, October 23, 1875, p. 860. For the political motivation behind the speech, see Hesseltine, *Grant*, pp. 390-91.

3. BIC, *Annual Report*, 1872, pp. 28, 44-50; 1873, p. 192.

4. Olson, *Red Cloud*, p. 123.

5. PHS, Baird to Lowrie, November 21, 1878; Whipple, *Lights and Shadows*, p. 299; CIA, *Annual Report*, 1882, p. 61; EIC, Minutes, January 13, 1874; Howe, *Hare*, pp. 202-4; AMA Papers, M. Eells to E. P. Smith, February 3, 1871. For further evidence of the government's support of missions, see Williamson's essay in the *Princeton Review*, pp. 612-13; Eells, *History*, pp. 69, 71-74, 105; M. Eells, *Ten Years of Missionary Work* (Boston: Congregational Publishing Soc., 1886), p. 223; Drury, *Spalding*, p. 407; Janney, *Memoirs*, pp. 258-63; C. L. Hall correspondence in the ABCFM archives.

6. WP, Hallowell to Whipple, May 10, 1869; *American Missionary* 15 (March 1871): 57; (April 1871) "Church and State in America," and "The President's New Indian Policy."

7. *Churchman*, February 16, 1878, p. 180; WP, Whipple to W. K. Rogers, August 6, 1877.

8. Welsh, *Sioux and Ponca*, pp. iv, 27; Welsh, *Summing Up*, p. 62; *Spirit of Missions*, 1871, p. 51.

9. *Spirit of Missions*, 1870, "Proceedings of the Board of Missions," pp. 651-53.

10. BIC, *Annual Report*, 1870, p. 111; EIC, Minutes, December 19, 1871; July 18, October 17, 1872.

11. R. Anderson, *Foreign Missions*, p. 283; BIC:LR, Treat to Colyer, January 8, 1872; *Congregationalist*, September 7, 21, 1871.

12. ABCFM:LS, N. G. Clark to A. Riggs, December 28, 1878; Clark to C. L. Hall, November 15, 1879; ABCFM:LR, Hall to Clark, October 20, 1879; January 22, 1880.

13. Title to mission land was not established during the Peace Policy and the issue remained unsettled until much later. *Langford* v. *Monteith*, 102 U.S. 145 (1880), involved mission land at Lapwai, but the Supreme Court only ruled on a narrow jurisdictional question.

14. Presbyterian Board of Foreign Missions, *Annual Report*, 1870, pp. 65-66; 1871, p. 22; 1872, p. 19; 1876, p. 9; 1877, p. 7; BIC, Journal, 1873, p. 16; BIC, *Annual Report*, 1871, pp. 171, 176; 1879, p. 94; PHS,

J. Williamson to Lowrie, January 22, 1879; Baird to Lowrie, January 14, 1881; *Senate Misc. Doc.* no. 53, 45th Cong., 3d sess., p. 28.

15. *Friend's Intelligencer*, August 14, 1875, pp. 387-88; CIA, *Annual Report*, 1876, p. 74; Methodist Church, Oregon Conf., *Minutes*, 1872, p. 30; 1874, p. 18; 1878, p. 35; Catholic Clergy, *Address . . . on President Grant's Indian Policy* (Portland, Oreg.: Catholic Sentinel Publishing, 1874), pp. 7, 14 (italics in text).

16. BIC, *Annual Report*, 1874, p. 147; CIA, *Annual Report*, 1875, pp. 22, 26-27.

17. *Independent*, August 12, 1875, p. 18.

18. EIC, Minutes, March 5, 1878.

19. *House Report* no. 167, 45th Cong., 3d sess.; *Senate Report* no. 693, 45th Cong., 3d sess., p. 8; *Congressional Record*, 44th Cong., 1st sess., p. 2682; 46th Cong., 2d sess., p. 2827; 3d sess., p. 530.

20. R. Dodge, *Our Wild Indians*, p. 94; *New York Tribune*, March 13, 21, 27, 1879.

21. J. Ayers, *Why the Indians Should Be Transferred* (n.p., 1879), pp. 4-7. The Peace Policy had forced Ayers's removal from office, and in 1870 the former agent asked Vincent Colyer to use the BIC's "powerful influence" to regain Ayers's old position for him. BIC:LR, Ayers to Colyer, March 21, 1870.

22. BIC, *Annual Report*, 1880, p. 105.

23. Oregon Conference, Methodist Church, *Minutes*, 1882, p. 48; the Teller-Reid correspondence is in the BIC, *Annual Report*, 1882, p. 52.

24. *Harper's Weekly*, February 18, 1871, October 24, 1874, December 25, 1876; *Independent*, December 16, 1873; *Old and New*, April 1871, pp. 445-46.

25. *Congregationalist*, April 1, 1869, p. 96; FHL:RG 2, Hallowell to Whipple, April 6, 1869.

26. AMA, *Annual Report*, 1881; one can trace the failing interest very markedly in the editorials of the *American Missionary*, 1870-82.

27. *Churchman*, June 19, 1875, p. 673; FHL:RG 2, Whipple to Hallowell, June 12, 1869.

28. Complete text of the debate is in the *Churchman*, October 30, 1880, pp. 498ff.

29. BIC, *Annual Report*, 1873, p. 208; BIC, *Journal*, 1873, p. 55; CIA, *Annual Report*, 1877, p. 175; AMA, Smith Papers, E. P. Smith to G. Whipple, December 8, 1870.

30. ABCFM:LR, S. Riggs to Treat, November 22, 1873; Riggs to Clark, June 22, 1877; March 29, 1879; T. Riggs to Clark, October 11, November 9, 1880; *Missionary Herald*, April 1877.

31. BIC, *Annual Report*, 1879, p. 113. For John Lowrie's political acumen, see Henry G. Waltmann, "John C. Lowrie and Presbyterian Indian

Administration, 1870-1882," *Journal of Presbyterian History* 34 (Summer 1976): 259-76.

32. Chief Joseph, "An Indian's View of Indian Affairs," *North American Review* 128 (April 1879): 432.

33. FHL:RG 2, S. Janney to Hallowell, December 16, 1869; January 8, 1870; Painter to Hallowell, February 7, 1870; J. Saunders to B. White, January 26, 1872; CIA, *Annual Report*, 1874, p. 224; Rocky Mt. Conf., Methodist Church, Journal, 1874, p. 85; Oregon Conf., Methodist Church, Minutes, 1872, p. 30.

34. FHL:RG 2, Hallowell to the Superintendent and Agents of the Northern Superintendency, June 12, 1869; Friends, *Joint Delegation*, p. 66; CIA, *Annual Report*, 1866; Ewing, *Chippewa Petition*, pp. 10-11; Rahill, *Catholic Indian Missions*, p. 45.

35. *Old and New*, 1873, pp. 238-39; CIA, *Annual Report*, 1869, pp. 340, 357-58, 376-77; BIC, *Annual Report*, 1874, p. 112; Friends Assoc. Exec. Comm., *Annual Report*, 1870; Friends, *Joint Delegation*, p. 27; *Spirit of Missions*, 1873, p. 18; U.S. Dept. of the Interior, *What the Government and the Churches Are Doing*, passim.

36. Friends, Assoc. Exec. Comm., *Minutes*, 1874, p. 7; CIA, *Annual Report*, 1875, pp. 278-79; WP, Petition of August 19, 1869; Rahill, *Catholic Indian Missions*, pp. 51-53, 99, 145.

37. DeSmet, *Life*, p. 1541; Eells, *Ten Years*, p. 163; CIA, *Annual Report*, 1874, p. 193; BIC, *Annual Report*, 1874, pp. 137-38; 1876, pp. 48, 90, 92.

38. PHS, Terry to Lowrie, May 12, 1880; CIA, *Annual Report*, 1873, p. 176; 1880, p. 113; BIC:LR, C. Hall to Brunot, January 20, 1872; Whitner, "Methodist Episcopal Church," pp. 123-25; Oregon Conf. of the Methodist Church, *Minutes*, 1880, p. 37; OIA, Inspector Reports, W. Vandever to CIA, June 4, 1875; [C. Ewing] *Official Construction of Grant's Indian Peace Policy* (Washington, 1876), pp. 2-6; Rahill, *Catholic Indian Missions*, pp. 145ff.

39. Wilbur claimed 10 percent of the Indians were Catholic, whereas Felix Brunot reported that only two hundred of the three thousand Yakima were Methodist. BIC, *Annual Report*, 1871, pp. 110-11, 285.

40. DeSmet, *Life and Letters*, p. 1135; CIA, *Annual Report*, 1870, pp. 21-22, 31-32; 1874; pp. 298, 314; BIC, *Annual Report*, 1871, p. 285; Whitner, "Methodist Episcopal Church," pp. 339ff.; Rahill, *Catholic Indian Missions*, p. 114. Milroy was a Methodist minister; Assistant Secretary of the Interior B. R. Cowen was also a Methodist. Whitner considers Wilbur a bigot who, like his church, viewed the Peace Policy as an alliance with the government to prevent the spread of Catholicism. See Whitner, "Grant's Peace Policy and the Yakima Reservation," *Pacific Northwest Quarterly* (October 1959), pp. 135-42. A. J. Splawn, who admired Wilbur as an ideal agent, admitted that Wilbur had

"little use for the Catholic red man, still less for the wild, blanket Indian who still clung to his ancient ceremony," *Ka-mi-akin*, p. 333.

41. WP, L. Stowe to Whipple, January 26, 1875; E. P. Smith to Whipple, August 25, 1875; W. K. Rogers to Whipple, April 3, 1877; OIA:LR, E. Whittlesey, Report on White Earth, 1875; BIC:LR, Whipple to Whittlesey, July 30, 1877; BIC, *Annual Report*, 1875, pp. 53-58; OIA, Inspector Reports, E. Kemble to J. Q. Smith, September 24, 1877; Kemble to E. A. Hayt, October 1, 1877.

42. Lawrence Murphy, *Frontier Crusader: W. F. M. Arny* (Tucson: University of Arizona Press, 1972), pp. 186-94, 283.

43. C. Ewing, *Petition . . . in behalf of the Pueblos*; BIC:LR, W. Arny to N. Pope, December 1, 1871; F. A. Walker to Arny, December 20, 1871; Arny to Walker, January 28, 1872; CIA, *Annual Report*, 1873, pp. 269, 278; SI:LR, G. Smith to Grant, February 3, 1876; Simpson Papers, J. Cole to Simpson, February 8, 1873; PHS, E. Dudley to E. Lewis, June 19, 1873; Lewis to Lowrie, July 21, August 7, 1873; PHS, Jackson Papers; J. Shields to Jackson, January 17, 1879; B. Thomas to Jackson, January 21, 1879. In 1875 a Catholic attempt to establish tax-supported sectarian schools in Arizona failed by one vote. A serious oversight in Rahill's work is a neglect of the Southwest, where he might have found valid reasons for Protestant mistrust of Catholics. Rahill instead concentrated on Oregon and the Dakotas, where Protestants appeared most bigoted.

44. OIA:LS, E. P. Smith to Monteith, May 24, 1873.

45. PHS, Ainslie to Lowrie, June 26, 1873; Monteith to Lowrie, July 2, 1873; A. L. Lindsley to Lowrie, September 10, 1873; see also Rahill, pp. 112, 131; Haines, *Nez Perce*, p. 204; W. Gray, *Moral and Religious Aspect*, p. 4.

46. PHS, Monteith to Lowrie, December 20, 1877.

47. OIA:LR, Delano to CIA, May 14, 1875; Red Cloud Commission, *Report*, pp. 692-93. See also Donald J. D'Elia, "The Argument Over Civilian or Military Indian Control, 1865-1880," *Historian* 24 (February 1962): 216, 221.

48. *House Report* no. 240, 44th Cong., 1st sess., pp. 2, 14, 22-25; *Congressional Record*, 44th Cong., 1st sess., pp. 2232-36, 2615, 2634, 2659.

49. "Our New Indian Policy," *Catholic World* 26 (October 1877): 90-108; *Congressional Record*, 45th Cong., 2d sess., p. 3208; 3d sess., p. 2404; *House Report* no. 167, 45th Cong., 3d sess.; *Senate Report* no. 693, 45th Cong., 3d sess., p. 8; *Senate Misc. Doc.* no. 53, 45th Cong., 3d sess., pp. 85, 242, 253.

50. *Friend's Intelligencer*, April 22, 1876, pp. 132-33; Howard L. Harrod, "The Blackfeet and the Divine Establishment," *Montana: The Magazine of*

Western History (Winter 1972), pp. 42-51; Harrod, *Mission Among the Black-feet*, chap. 6.

51. BIC, *Annual Report*, 1877, p. 62; 1878, p. 92; *House Report* no. 240, 44th Cong., 1st sess., p. 32. During their frequent visits to the White House, Sioux chiefs consistently requested priests. See Olson, *Red Cloud*, pp. 251-52, 260, 266-68.

52. Daniels Papers, Scrapbook clipping (c. 1877); EIC:LS, R. Rogers to Hare, June 11, December 29, 1877; Hyde, *Spotted Tail's Folk*, pp. 263, 276; Rahill, *Catholic Indian Missions*, pp. 247ff., 260ff.

53. *New York Tribune*, March 12, 13, 1879; *Independent*, March 27, 1879, p. 16; *Watchman*, April 24, 1879, p. 129.

54. ABCFM Transcripts, Newberry Library, J. B. Renville to S. B. Treat, February 6, 1871; BIC, *Annual Report*, 1874, p. 121; ABCFM:LR, A. Riggs to Treat, July 26, 1872; General Report of the Dakota Mission, 1877; ABCFM:LS, N. G. Clark to A. Riggs, June 13, 1877; CIA, *Annual Report*, 1876, p. 77; ABCFM, Dakota Mission MSS, vol. 5, Memorial to the Board, September 20, 1878; *Missionary Herald* 46 (November 1870): 383.

55. Expansion seemed urgent to the Riggses because Boston refused to send funds for the isolated Dakota schools "hemmed in [by] the Romanists on the one hand and the Episcopalians on the other." Clark to A. Riggs, March 19, 1879.

56. ABCFM:LR, A. Riggs to Clark, March 29, 1879; E. A. Hayt to A. Riggs, January 3, 1880. Renville officially represented the Dakota Missionary Society, a native organization; in practice there was little or no difference between it and the ABCFM missionaries.

57. ABCFM:LR, A. Riggs to Clark, January 19, February 11, 1880; R. E. Trowbridge to A. Riggs, May 27, 1880; A. Riggs to Schurz, February 11, 1880; ABCFM:LS, N. Clark to A. Riggs, March 4, 1880; PHS, J. Williamson to Lowrie, January 23, 1880.

58. ABCFM:LS, E. E. Strong to T. L. Riggs, June 18, 1880; Clark to A. Riggs, August 11, 1880; J. O. Means to A. Riggs, November 22, 1880; Clark to E. Whittlesey, December 22, 1880; Means to J. Ward, January 28, 1881; Report of the Dakota Mission, August 1880; ABCFM:LR, A. Riggs to Clark, June 11, 1880; ABCFM, Dakota MSS, vol. 5, Mark Hopkins to G. H. Atkinson, n.d.

59. C. L. Hall Scrapbook, p. 8; *Missionary Herald* 76 (September 1880): 343-46. Chap. 2 in Meyer, *Santee Sioux*, provides a general history of the Devil's Lake agency's stability and progress until the allotment period.

60. ABCFM:LS, Means to A. Riggs, January 27, 1881; BIC, *Annual Report*, 1881, pp. 81, 98-99, 109-13.

61. ABCFM:LR, E. Whittlesey to Means, January 20, 1881; ABCFM:LS, Means to Whittlesey, February 8, 1881.

62. RCA, T. M. Nichol to J. Ferris, March 2, 1881; ABCFM:LS, Means to A. Riggs, February 15, 1881. The new policy obviously did not answer Wilbur or Milroy's interpretation of the 1855 Yakima treaty, nor did it determine when a church was disruptive.

63. PHS, G. Wood to Lowrie, April 2, 1881. For the Roman Catholic role see Rahill, chap. 7, "A Victory for Religious Liberty."

64. ABCFM, Dakota MSS, vol. 5, H. Price to J. O. Means, September 15, 27, 1881.

65. Alice Fletcher, *Indian Education and Civilization* (Washington: Government Printing Office, 1888), passim.

66. Murphy, *Frontier Crusader*, pp. 219-22; Buntin, "Quaker Indian Agents," p. 218. For a description of the extent and success of Mormon Indian missions during the period, see Lamar, *Far Southwest*, pp. 322-23. On Grant's anti-Semitism, see McFeely, *Grant*, pp. 123-24.

67. Prucha, *Crisis*, pp. 193-96.

68. *Churchman*, September 22, 1877, p. 311; BIC, *Annual Report*, 1874, pp. 31, 105; 1876, pp. 45-46; CIA, *Annual Report*, 1871, pp. 271, 279-80; 1873, p. 319.

69. CIA, *Annual Report*, 1870, p. 37; 1880, pp. 57-58; BIC:LR, N. Cornoyer to BIC, April 2, 1872; Butler, *Indian Question*, p. 1; Otis, *Indian Question*, p. 96; Stanley Vestal, *New Sources of Indian History* (Norman: University of Oklahoma Press, 1934), pp. 288-89.

70. CIA, *Annual Report*, 1871, pp. 558-59; BIC, *Annual Report*, 1872, p. 160; Eells, *Ten Years at Skokomish*, pp. 47, 58, 83, 105.

71. CIA, *Annual Report*, 1874, p. 218; 1875, p. 293; 1877, p. 68; Howe, *Hare*, pp. 81-82, 214, 232; Daniels Papers, The Sacred Lodge.

72. E. S. Parker to Harriet Converse, October 4, 1887, quoted in A. C. Parker, *Parker*, p. 175. For Parker's extreme bitterness in his old age, see Armstrong, *Warrior in Two Camps*.

Chapter 10

1. *Independent*, August 12, 1875, p. 18.

2. *Nation*, July 13, 1876, p. 21; January 2, 1879, pp. 7-8; January 9, 1879, p. 22. See also Mardock, *Reformers*, pp. 132-39.

3. Pope, *Indian Question*, pp. 13-18, 29-30; Otis, *Indian Problem*, pp. 19-21; James Talbot, "The Indian Question," *United Service* 1 (January 1879): 141-52.

4. *Congressional Record*, 46th Cong., 3d sess., pp. 2224, 2250-51, 2405-6, 2486.

5. An American Citizen, *The Great American Empire; or Gen. Ulysses S. Grant, Emperor of North America* (St. Louis: W. S. Bryan, 1879).

6. Cudmore, *Grant and His Rings*, p. 14.

7. Sturgis, *Common Sense View of the Sioux War* (Cheyenne: Steam Book and Job Printing, 1877), p. 43; Sturgis, *The Ute War of 1879* (Cheyenne: Steam Book and Job Printing, 1879), pp. 4, 10, 17; E. S. Osgood, *The Day of the Cattleman* (Chicago: University of Chicago Press, 1957), pp. 78, 141–47; R. Dodge, *A Living Issue* (Washington: F. B. Mohun, 1882), p. 21; MacMahon, *Anglo-Saxon*, pp. 33–34.

8. *Senate Misc. Doc.* no. 53, 45th Cong., 3d sess., p. 31; WP, Sibley to Whipple, May 19, 1879; *American Missionary*, January 1879, pp. 20–21; Methodist Episcopal Church, *Journal of the General Conference*, 1880, p. 218; J. G. Shea, "What Right."

9. S. G. Arnold, "President Grant's Indian Policy," *Methodist Quarterly* 59 (July 1877): 429; *Friend's Intelligencer*, January 22, 1876; BIC:LS, Cree to Ferris, February 5, 1874; BIC:LR, E. Whittlesey to H. M. Dexton, n.d.; RCA, E. P. Smith to Ferris, January 30, 1875; BIC, *Annual Report*, 1874, p. 147.

10. The Belknap scandal is described in Marvin E. Kroeker, *Great Plains Command: William B. Hazen in the Frontier West* (Norman: University of Oklahoma Press, 1976), chaps. 7, 9, and McFeely, *Grant*, chap. 25. For the factors that led to the transfer of the OIA from the War Department to the Interior in 1849, see Trennert, *Alternative*, pp. 40–42.

11. Henry G. Waltmann, "The Interior Department, War Department, and Indian Policy, 1865–1887" (Ph.D. diss., University of Nebraska, 1962), points out the difficult administrative problems caused by dual control; he is also correct in concluding that many interests besides Indian policy were at stake during the great transfer debates between 1876 and 1879. Partisanship, sectionalism, racism, and patronage all reinforced the false dichotomy between army officers and humanitarians. For recent arguments that the military was much more sympathetic to the tribes than often believed, see John C. Ewers, "When Red and White Men Met," *Western Historical Quarterly* 2 (April 1971): 133–50. Leonard's "Red, White and Army Blue" is a good antidote to antimilitary stereotypes; it describes certain officers as sensitive, intelligent, and ambivalent about fighting Indians. Leonard's short essay is superior to Ellis's *Pope*, a clichéd protransfer book that glorifies the army as trying to save Indians from extermintion under a greedy and corrupt OIA. Also see d'Elia, "Argument Over Civilian or Military Indian Control." The best analysis and summary of the controversy is in Prucha, *Crisis*, chap. 3.

12. Major primary sources are in the San Carlos file, National Archives, and in the archives of the Reformed Church in America, New Brunswick, N.J. John Bret Harte's doctoral dissertation on San Carlos covers the Peace Policy period, and his article, "Struggle at San Carlos," describes the continuing civilian-military conflict after 1882.

13. Berthrong, *Cheyenne-Arapaho Ordeal,* pp. 5-19, 31-32.

14. Harold Umber, "Interdepartmental Conflict Between Fort Yates and Standing Rock: Problems of Indian Administration, 1870-1881," *North Dakota History* 39 (Summer 1972): 4-13; Olson, *Red Cloud,* chaps. 10, 12.

15. *House Report* no. 98, 42d Cong., 3d sess., pp. 16-17, 221, 237, 359.

16. EIC:LS, Rogers to Hare, March 20, 1876; WP, Brunot to Whipple, February 28, 1876; Sanborn to Whipple, April 23, 1876; Welsh to Whipple, May 13, 1876. Earlier in his testimony before the House committee, Welsh had said that army officers were intellectually superior but morally inferior to church agents. At that time he opposed transfer. *House Report* no. 240, 44th Cong., 1st sess., pp. 31-32; *House Report* no. 354, 44th Cong., 1st sess., pp. 218-21.

17. The vote was partisan, not sectional. Representatives from the West favored transfer, 28-14, compared with a 102-80 margin in the East and South, but Republicans voted against the bill, 66-14, and Democrats favored it, 112-25. The Democratic majority needed only one Republican or independent vote to pass the bill. The debate on H.R. 2677 is in the *Congressional Record,* 44th Cong., 1st sess., pp. 2229-40, 2428, 2463, 2575, 2614-19, 2625, 2630-31, 2659-64.

18. Ibid., pp. 3906, 3950; *Speech of Hon. John A. Logan of Illinois in the Senate of the United States, June 20, 1876* (Washington, 1876). Army supporters and opponents of the Peace Policy could make equally emotional charges against the OIA and the churches: "Agents, missionaries, traders . . . wax fat and grow rich while the government and Indians are plundered and cheated in the name of humanity, civilization and philanthropy" (Senator Richard Coke of Texas, *Congressional Record,* 45th Cong., 2d sess., p. 4236).

19. For the 1878 debate and the active church opposition to transfer see Mardock, *Reformers,* pp. 159-67.

20. Neither party platform in 1876 referred to Indian reform. Robert Mardock claims that the GOP planned to overhaul the Peace Policy, but he offers no evidence. Mardock's understanding of the actual state of the Policy during the Hayes administration is sketchy, often inaccurate, and based on unreliable secondary sources (Mardock, *Reformers,* pp. 150-58).

21. Rutherford B. Hayes, *Diary and Letters,* 5 vols. (Columbus: Ohio State Hist. Soc., 1924), 3:234-35, 488-89, 597; Richardson, *Messages* 7:475. Biographies of Hayes provide little accurate information about his Indian policy. Kenneth E. Davison, in *The Presidency of Rutherford B. Hayes* (Westport: Greenwood Press, 1972), and "President Hayes and the Reform of American Indian Policy," *Ohio History* 82 (Winter 1973): 205-14, offers only uncritical and superficial analyses of Hayes's Indian policy: Davison's work contains fundamental errors in fact, method, and interpretation.

22. BIC, Minutes, April 25, 1877; January 11, 1878; Hicksite Friends,

Annual Report, 1877; *Friends Intelligencer,* April 7, 1877, p. 102; WP, Brunot to Whipple, February 28, 1877; W. H. Lyon to Whipple, July 3, 1877.

23. U.S. Dept. of the Interior, *Report of the Board of Inquiry to Investigate Certain Charges . . . and Concerning Irregularities in Said Bureau* (Washington: Government Printing Office, 1878). Prucha, *Crisis,* pp. 97-98, is somewhat uncritical of Schurz. Prucha accepts the customary charges against the OIA and applauds Schurz's action to "bravely . . . clean out these Augean stables." But Schurz's "success" in eliminating corruption cannot be taken at face value or without pursuing the correctness of the charges and the actual conditions at the agencies, which Prucha neglects to do. The type of reports that Schurz accepted and that formed his initial reactions are always suspect in nineteenth-century Indian affairs—especially at the beginning of a new administration, when they appear with ritual frequency. A close study of any agency, such as Bret Harte's excellent work on San Carlos, will reveal endless counterclaims and massive confusion as to facts. The churches, according to Henry Fritz, felt that Schurz's motive was to entirely remove them from Indian affairs, but patronage pressure on the department forced the secretary to at least nominally support the Peace Policy. See Fritz, "The Board of Indian Commissioners and Ethnocentric Reform," p. 61.

24. For Schurz's view of Indian problems, see his *Annual Reports* and *Senate Report* no. 670, 46th Cong., 2d sess., pp. 373-74; also see *Senate Report* no. 693, 45th Cong., 3d sess., pp. xvi-xvii; BIC, *Annual Report,* 1879, p. 100; Schurz Papers, T. Cree to Schurz, December 17, 1879.

25. SI:LR, Ferris to Delano, August 5, 1874.

26. SI:LR, E. A. Hayt to Grant, January 20, 1877; PHS, Z. Chandler to Lowrie, January 16, 1877; WP, E. Whittlesey to Whipple, August 4, 1877; Schurz Papers, E. A. Hayt to Schurz, September 10, 1877; E. M. Kingsley to Schurz, September 11, 1877.

27. CIA, *Annual Report,* 1877, pp. 6-7; 1878, pp. iii-iv; BIC, *Annual Report,* 1879, p. 100; OIA, Inspector Reports, W. J. Pollock to Hayt, April 4, 1879; *Senate Misc. Doc.* no. 53, 45th Cong., 3d sess., pp. 321-25.

28. PHS, Baird to Lowrie, February 10, March 10, 1879.

29. PHS, Monteith to Lowrie, March 20, 1879; WP, E. A. Hayt to Whipple, August 15, 1879; *Congressional Record,* 45th Cong., 3d sess., p. 288; *Churchman,* October 5, 1878, p. 401. For Hayt's conflict with Dakota agents, see Olson, *Red Cloud,* chap. 13.

30. SI:LR, S. S. Cutting to W. Garvey, December 13, 1878; Morehouse to Hayt, August 6, 1879; Baptist Home Missionary Soc., *Annual Report,* 1878, p. 40; 1880, pp. 35-36; PHS, E. M. Kingsley to Lowrie, September 23, 1879; E. A. Hayt to Lowrie, February 5, 1879; B. Thomas to Lowrie, September 17, December 1, 1879; Sprague, *Massacre,* chap. 5. The best account of Hayt's campaign against church-nominated agents and of Schurz's subversion

of the Peace Policy is in Milner, "With Good Intentions." Milner makes a just evaluation of charges against Quaker agents Burgess, Griest, Searing, and Ely; he fully documents how Hayt's spy system worked at the Hicksite agencies; and he describes the politics that terminated the Northern Superintendency (pp. 233–66, 326–30, 396–411).

31. CIA, *Annual Report*, 1880, pp. 93, 128.

32. FHL:RG 2, F. Haines to Hallowell, May 5, 1870; J. Saunders to R. Roberts, June 9, 1873; Saunders to S. Janney, June 12, 19, 1873; FHL, Janney Papers, S. Janney to Elizabeth Janney, August 27, 1876; Haverford College, Hoag Collection, C. Beede to Hoag, January 17, 19, 1873.

33. SI:LR, Hayt to Schurz, February 4, 1878; Tatum, *Red Brothers*, pp. 202, 245–46, 261, 270, 283.

34. SI:LR, Hayt to Schurz, April 18, 1878.

35. WP, Francis [?] to Whipple, May 13, 1878; EIC:LS, Rogers to Hare, May 23, 1878.

36. EIC:LS, Rogers to Hare, April 16, 18, 1878.

37. BIC, *Annual Report*, 1879, pp. 82, 92, 118.

38. Superintendent Barclay White was retained in 1873 not because the eastern Friends sent memorials to Congress, but because an Omaha banker wanted to retain White's $60,000 account. Eastern Friends celebrated a victory but White wrote in his journal that they never knew why Congress had continued the superintendency. Barclay White Journal, 1:369.

39. FHL:RG 2, Saunders to M. Kent, May 23, 1876; B. White Journal, 1:368, 2:242–43, 3:52–54, 62, 145, 263–68; Hicksite Friends, *Minutes*, 1877; *Friends Intelligencer*, November 30, 1878, "Report of the Baltimore Yearly Meeting," pp. 650–51.

40. FHL:RG 2, R. Roberts, Aron Wright, B. White, and Stephen Hicks to Schurz, February 25, 1880; J. Mills to Cyrus Blackburn, October 16, 1881; SI:LR, J. Rhoads to H. Price, December 24, 1882.

41. FHL:RG 2, B. White to C. Blackburn, April 7, 1881; Levi Brown to Blackburn, May 1, 1881; Assoc. Exec. Comm., *Annual Report*, 1880, p. 1.

42. SI:LR, R. Rogers to Chandler, August 8, 1876; EIC:LS, Rogers to Hare, August 11, 1876; Rogers to Welsh, August 15, 21, 23, 1876; Rogers to J. Cleveland, August 23, November 22, 1876; EIC, Minutes, September 27, 1876.

43. EIC, Minutes, February 13, March 13, April 10, 1877; EIC:LS, Rogers to the Indian Office, April 16, 1877; Rogers to Welsh, March 15, 1877; Rogers to Hare, March 15, 1877. For an account of the Livingston scandal and the "Episcopal oligarchy" in Dakota, see Lamar, *Dakota Territory*, pp. 184–88. Livingston, elected to the Yankton school board during his trial, subsequently was acquitted despite a strong government case against him.

44. Schurz Papers, Welsh to Schurz, February 9, 1878; SI:LR, H. Dyer to

Schurz, May 22, 1878; EIC:LS, Dyer to Schurz, February 15, 1878; Rogers to Welsh, April 22, 1878; Rogers to Hare, April 23, May 15, 17, July 16, 1878.

45. ABCFM:LR, C. L. Hall to Clark, May 21, 1878, May 12, October 20, 1879; January 21, 22, March 23, 1880; Hall to A. Riggs, July 21, 1879; M. E. Strieby to N. G. Clark, April 10, 1880; Report of the Dakota Mission, 1879; ABCFM:LS, N. G. Clark to Hall, September 9, 1879.

46. EIC:LS, R. Rogers to Hare, November 13, 1878.

47. SI:LR, J. Irwin to Hayt, January 1, 1879; Irwin to Schurz, January 4, 1879.

48. EIC:LS, R. Rogers to Schurz, May 9, 1878; SI:LR, A. Twing to Hayt, March 24, 1879; January 13, 1880; various letters recommending C. Newell.

49. *Senate Misc. Doc.* no. 53, 45th Cong., 3d sess., p. 313; Domestic Correspondence, Protestant Episcopal Church, R. P. Goddard to Twing, May 27, 29, 1879; E. A. Hayt to Twing, August 7, October 9, 1879; January 20, 1880; Hayt to E. M. Kingsley, January 10, 1880; Rt. Rev. J. F. Spalding to Twing, April 8, May 31, June 12, 1879; H. Whipple to Twing, August 23, 1881; WP, Gilfillan to Whipple, March 6, 1876; March 21, 1877; August 24, 1879. C. A. Ruffee, *Report of the Condition of the Chippewas of Minnesota.*

50. WP, Daniels to Whipple, September 22, 1877.

51. *Congressional Record,* 44th Cong., 3d sess., pp. 320-23; 46th Cong., 2d sess., pp. 2396, 2484-87, 2823-28.

52. BIC, *Annual Report,* 1879, pp. 98-119.

53. Ibid., pp. 51-54, 93-96; BIC, Minutes, January 9, 1880.

54. *House Misc. Doc.* no. 167, 44th Cong., 1st sess., p. 23; RCA, E. P. Smith to Ferris, January 20, 1875; BIC, *Annual Report,* 1877, pp. 13-17.

55. Schurz Papers, C. Fisk to E. M. Kingsley, October 15, 1879; RCA, Schurz to Ferris, June 11, 1879; D. K. Osbourn to Ferris, December 1, 1879; Fisk to Ferris, December 24, 1879; January 5, February 14, 1880. BIC:LR, Fisk to BIC, November 5, 1879.

56. BIC, Minutes, January 8, February 5, 1880; *New York Tribune,* January 12, 29, 31, 1880.

57. Schurz Papers, Schurz to Garfield, January 28, 1881; BIC, *Annual Report,* 1881, pp. 84-88.

58. AMA, *Annual Report,* 1879, p. 7; BIC, *Annual Report,* 1882, pp. 37, 61; Presbyterian Board of Foreign Missions, *Annual Report,* 1883, p. 14.

59. D. E. Clark, *Samuel Jordan Kirkwood* (Iowa City: State Historical Society, 1917), p. 364; George F. Howe, *Chester A. Arthur: A Quarter-Century of Machine Politics* (New York: Unger Publishing, 1957), pp. 163, 212-13; Elmer Ellis, *Henry Moore Teller: Defender of the West* (Caldwell, Idaho: Caxton Printers, 1941). Teller was also a friend of Helen Hunt Jackson; he opposed severalty because he considered "the Anglo-Saxon idea of a

partition of the face of the earth [a] very doubtful question." His major Senate speeches on Indian policy are in the *Congressional Record*, 46th Cong., 2d sess., pp. 2059-60; 3d sess., pp. 780, 785. For a critical assessment of Teller as Secretary of the Interior see Hagan, *Indian Police*, pp. 47, 105.

60. 22 Stat. 70, May 17, 1882.

61. Methodists actually had been mustered out since the end of Grant's administration. Reid found nominal responsibility without actual control to be embarrassing and had tried to clarify matters in 1881 by warning Kirkwood that the Methodists must be granted the original 1870 conditions or they would withdraw. OIA:LR, Reid to S. J. Kirkwood, March 18, 1881.

Chapter 11

1. See Prucha, *Crisis*, pp. 145-61, for an accurate description of the civil religion of Indian reformers between 1880 and 1900. Prucha observes that three of the strongest commissioners of Indian affairs, 1867-93, were Protestant clergy (N. Taylor, E. P. Smith, and T. J. Morgan).

2. *Impressions of the Sioux Tribes*, quoted in Prucha, *Crisis*, p. 337. James Olson concluded that long before 1890 the patronage system stood as fully entrenched as it had been in 1868 and that it was one of the important factors leading to the Wounded Knee Massacre (*Red Cloud*, p. 325).

3. T. J. Morgan, *Indian Education* (n.p., n.d.), p. 10.

4. AMA, *Annual Report*, 1893, p. 34.

5. Ibid., 1888, p. 25. Wilcomb E. Washburn, *The Assault on Indian Tribalism: The General Allotment Law (Dawes Act) of 1887* (Philadelphia: J. B. Lippincott, 1975), is a brief introduction to the Dawes Act and the role of reformers in its passage. See Fritz, "Board of Indian Commissioners," for a description of the active political cooperation between the BIC, the churches and the reformers pushing for severalty. Otis, *The Dawes Act*, pp. 1-7, lists the important Peace Policy precedents. See also Prucha, *Crisis*, pp. 231-34, 244. A close look at the typical effects of allotment is in Donald J. Berthrong's "White Neighbors Come Among the Southern Cheyenne and Arapaho," *Kansas Quarterly* 3, no. 4 (Fall 1971): 105-15, and Burton M. Smith's "The Politics of Allotment: The Flathead Indian Reservation as a Test Case," *Pacific Northwest Quarterly* 70, no. 3 (July 1979): 131-40.

6. C. C. Painter, *Extravagance, Waste and Failure of Indian Education* (Philadelphia: Indian Rights Association, 1892), p. 18.

7. CIA, *Annual Report*, 1882, p. vi.

8. James Rhoads, *Our Next Duty to the Indians* (Philadelphia: Indian Rights Association, 1885), p. 5; Superintendent of Indian Education, *Annual Report*, 1887, p. 131.

9. Superintendent of Indian Education, *Annual Report*, 1886, pp. 96-97; 1887, pp. 98, 144.

10. Red Cloud Commission, *Report*, pp. 426-27, 712-14; EIC:LS, Hare to CIA, November 30, 1875; PHS, Jackson Papers, Kendall to Williams, July 30, 1878; ABCFM:LS, N. G. Clark to E. Whittlesey, March 19, 1879; Clark to C. Hall, May 24, 1879; Clark to Hayt, August 13, 1879.

11. *Baptist Home Mission Monthly* 14 (1892): 341; Baptist Home Missionary Society, *Annual Report*, 1879, p. 32; 1881, p. 34.

12. T. J. Morgan, *Roman Catholics and Indian Education* (Boston: American Citizens, 1893), passim. The best discussion of Morgan, his personality, programs, and powerful impact on Indian education is in chap. 10 of Prucha, *Crisis*. Prucha's *Americanizing the American Indian* contains seven of Morgan's essays.

13. Morgan, *Roman Catholics and Indian Education*, p. 25. See also H. J. Sievers, "The Catholic Indian School Issue and the Presidential Election of 1892," *Catholic Historical Review*, 1952, pp. 129-55. Contract funds were sharply reduced after 1896, although the controversy flared up again in 1904, when Bishop Hare and the Riggs family joined forces against the Catholics. In 1899 the Supreme Court ruled in *Bradford* v. *Roberts* (175 U.S. 291) that the government could purchase sectarian goods and services, and in 1908, in *Quick Bear* v. *Leupp* (210 U.S. 50), the Court reaffirmed the Bradford decision and added that use of Indian annuity funds involved no constitutional issue since the money belonged to the tribes, not the federal government. A few contract schools continued and were predominately Roman Catholic. Another controversy occurred in 1912, when the Indian Office ordered nuns to cease wearing religious garb; President William Howard Taft revoked that order. As I have observed in Chapter 9, these practices in Indian affairs made little impression on the contemporary theory of church-state relations in America. See Sanford H. Cobb's *Rise of Religious Liberty in America* (1902; reprinted. New York: Cooper Square Publishers, 1968); nowhere within its five hundred pages was there a single reference to native American religion, with missions receiving only a few passing comments. Isaac A. Cornelison, *Relation of Religion to Civil Government in the United States of America: A State Without a Church, But Not Without a Religion* (New York: G. P. Putnam's Sons, 1895), briefly mentioned the contract school system but contained nothing about Indian missions in four hundred pages.

14. Chief Joseph, "An Indian's View," p. 431.

15. BIC, *Annual Report*, 1876, pp. 7ff.

16. CIA, *Annual Report*, 1882, p. iv; H. Welsh, *The Indian Problem*, p. 27.

17. To take the most obvious example, the patronage system had begun forty years earlier under Andrew Jackson. See Satz, *American Indian Policy*,

chaps. 6-7. One of the best accounts of how the historical momentum in Indian affairs made quick reform impossible is Olson's *Red Cloud*. Problems with the Sioux began decades before the Peace Policy and continued long after it ended; the magnitude of physical violence changed following 1882 but not the corruption, human degradation, and suffering. The true success or failure of the Peace Policy can only be evaluated by assimilating dozens of well-researched, detailed tribal histories, most of which are not yet written. Until we have more books like those by Olson, Josephy, Milner, Unrau, Hagan, Meyer, Berthrong, and Harrod, the assessment of Grant's reform must remain incomplete.

18. William Unrau's discussion of the multiplicity of forces which destroyed the tribe is superb. In addition to poor agents, federal bungling, patronage, and the army, there was the weather; culture shock; the claims system; disease and starvation; squatters; and warfare with the Pawnees, Cheyennes, and Sioux. See chap. 6, *The Kansa Indians*, and *The End of Indian Kansas*, by the same author. John Unruh's complex study of the overland trails, *The Plains Across*, is also excellent for showing the diverse forms of interaction between tribes and emigrants. Unruh successfully establishes that no single group or factor was totally responsible for the growing hostility and violence between 1840 and 1860.

19. Meyer, *Santee Sioux*, chap. 12.

20. U.S. Superintendent of Indian Schools, *Annual Report*, 1887, p. 156.

21. BIC, *Annual Report*, 1877, pp. 12-13.

22. William Tecumseh Sherman, *Memoirs*, p. 437.

23. For sophisticated analyses of the influence of individualism in American political thought and action, see Garry Wills, *Nixon Agonistes: The Crisis of the Self-made Man* (Boston: Houghton Mifflin, 1970), and Doris Kearns, *Lyndon Johnson and the American Dream* (New York: Harper and Row, 1976).

24. Emmet John Hughes, *The Ordeal of Power* (New York: Atheneum Press, 1963), p. 160.

25. See Prucha, *Crisis*, chaps. 4 and 13 for a discussion of federal land policy during Grant's administration: "a conscious part of the peace policy worked toward the ultimate dispossession of the Indians," p. 110. A striking example was the forced removal of the Flathead Indians from the Bitterroot Valley in Montana, the result of an order from Grant. See Fahey, *The Flathead Indians*, pp. 161-65. H. Craig Miner's *The Corporation and the Indian: Tribal Sovereignty and Industrial Civilization in Indian Territory, 1865-1907* (Columbia: University of Missouri Press, 1976) is exceptional for the degree to which it reveals congressional, business, and OIA alliances and the growing corporate influences in the OIA during the 1870s and '80s. A typical

rationalization of plunder was C. J. Hillyer's *The Atlantic Pacific Railroad and the Indian Territory* (1871), discussed in Miner, pp. 78-81.

26. Photos of Grant between 1865 and 1875 reveal a change from a lean, hard, purposeful man in his prime to a squat, obese person whose awareness seems dulled. See Lawrence A. Frost, *U. S. Grant Album: A Pictorial Biography of Ulysses S. Grant* (Seattle: Superior Publishing, 1966). The most negative assessment of Grant's role in the Peace Policy is Waltmann's "Circumstantial Reformer." Waltmann, seeking to revise previous evaluations of the Policy, gives Grant credit for good intentions and little else. He was, according to Waltmann, a weak leader; he forced land cessions, violated treaties, tolerated corruption, and patronized the reformers. Waltmann's details on the presidency and the actual operation of the Peace Policy are superior to previous writers such as Henry Fritz, but in my view Waltmann is unduly harsh on Grant. Even harsher, however, was Ely S. Parker. Shortly after Grant's death Parker wrote that Grant as president had betrayed his old army friends, especially John Rawlins and Parker: "One great fault of his life was the abandonment of early best and truest friends, and the taking unto himself of false and strange gods who at last ruined him utterly. . . . Politics was not his forte and the love of filthy lucre floored him." Parker to John E. Smith, March 15, 1886, quoted in Armstrong, *Warrior in Two Camps,* p. 173. For a positive narrative of Grant's career and term of office, see Carpenter, *Grant.* The list of major literary figures who have written positively about Grant is impressive: Mark Twain, Hamlin Garland, Matthew Arnold, Gertrude Stein, Edmund Wilson.

27. Hughes, *Ordeal of Power,* pp. 43, 347, 360.

28. David Halberstam, *The Making of a Quagmire* (New York: Random House, 1965), pp. 222, 320.

29. Harrison, *Latest Studies on Indian Reservations,* p. 136.

30. Athearn, *William Tecumseh Sherman,* p. 307.

31. Edmund Burke, *Speeches and Letters on American Affairs* (London: J. M. Dent and Sons, 1942), "On Conciliation."

Bibliography

For seventy years after 1882 the Peace Policy fared almost as poorly from commentators and historians as it had previously at the hands of the politicians. In 1883 S. C. Armstrong of Hampton Institute denounced the Policy as a failure and condemned the combination of Church and State that it entailed. Armstrong declared that churches had appointed "decayed clergymen, hungry politicians, and the broken of every profession," making the title of Indian agent a term of reproach across the nation (*Indian Question*, pp. 7, 14). After 1890 the Society of Friends moralized that if Grant's reform had been honored, the massacre at Wounded Knee would not have occurred (*An Address*, 1890, p. 6). Others involved in Indian affairs seemed entirely unaware of the Peace Policy. William Barrows (*The Indian Side of the Indian Question*, 1887) argued that if only the United States government had imitated "the good times when Church and State were one in Massachusetts," the Indian problem would have been solved (pp. 21–22).

Participants in the Peace Policy also published memoirs and evaluations. Lawrie Tatum, though critical of the Policy, decided that the reform overall was a blessing for the Indians. Myron Eells felt that it had encouraged missions. Barclay White summarized Hicksite success with certain tribes and failure with others. (Tatum, *Red Brothers*, 1899; Eells, *History*, 1882; White, *Friends and the Indians*, 1886). Presbyterians admitted that the churches had made many errors but the denomination also concluded that there was a vast improvement in Indian agents and that the Indian Office could never return to its former level of corruption (BIC, *Annual Report*, 1883, p. 58).

Before the publication of Peter Rahill's book on the Roman Catholic church in 1953, scholarly studies of the Peace Policy were erroneous, sketchy, and inadequate. Elsie Rushmore's short doctoral thesis (1914) was a confused and poorly documented work, lacking discussion of the fundamental political questions raised by the Policy. An article in the *Mississippi Valley Historical Review* (Martha Edwards, "A Problem of Church and State in the 1870s," 1924), despite many factual errors, improved on Rushmore's interpretation. In 1951 Marshall D. Moody completed an uncritical master's thesis

315

on the Board of Indian Commissioners. His study included such mistakes as the assertion that William Welsh "had little influence" on the board; Moody added nothing new to Rushmore and Edwards. Robert Utley's article, "The Celebrated Peace Policy" (*North Dakota History*, 1953), marked another failure to understand the subject. Relying mainly on sources such as the *Nation*, Utley thought that the board appointed agents, accused E. P. Smith of "pious outrages" and "barefaced lies," and became confused by the Red Cloud controversy.

Other scholars who wrote in passing about the Peace Policy did little better. Mission historians G. E. E. Lindquist, George Hinman, and Augustus Beard produced undocumented, uncritical summaries. Rayner Kelsy's *Friends and the Indians* ignored Church-State problems and concluded that the Policy brought peace—"the effort was crowned with a fine success." Among works by secular historians of the American Indian, four books by George Hyde were only slightly helpful. Hyde assumed that all the churches were pacifistic and that "Christian meddlers . . . joyfully accepted" Grant's invitation in 1870. The "absurd and wicked" Policy, Hyde wrote, produced evil agents (*Red Cloud's Folk*, pp. 187–88, 197, 216; *Pawnees*, pp. 238, 269; *Sioux Chronicle*, pp. x, xi, 3, 146–49; *Spotted Tail's Folk*, pp. 167, 235). James Olson's excellent history of Red Cloud and the Sioux (1965) rendered obsolete everything written by Hyde. Another policy study, Loring Priest's *Uncle Sam's Stepchildren* (1942), piled cliché on cliché as Priest demonstrated no comprehension of nineteenth-century Church-State relations. Priest accused Protestants of lacking concern for the material well-being of Indians; he distorted source material to make agents and missionaries appear equally ridiculous. Other works that badly misrepresented the Peace Policy were H. J. Eckenrode's *Rutherford B. Hayes* and Elmer Ellis's *Henry Moore Teller*. Books by C. L. Sonnichson, Ruth Underhill, Francis Haines, Marshall Sprague, and Flora Seymour contained vague, undocumented generalizations about Grant's reform. Keith Murray's account, *The Modocs and Their War*, based its conclusions about the Policy on evidence limited to the Pacific Coast. One of the best early studies of Indian affairs in the 1870s is Robert Athearn's biography of Sherman, though Athearn oversimplified the Peace Policy as a purely eastern reform movement. Athearn's treatment of the Policy is much better than Richard Ellis's book, *General Pope and U.S. Indian Policy* (1970). Ellis, an army apologist highly critical of reformers, fell into many historiographical errors, e.g., judging the entire Peace Policy in terms of the Kiowa and Cheyenne agencies, stereotyping "bloodthirsty" Indians and "sentimental" Quakers, and overglorifying the army by turning plains warfare into melodrama.

Surveys of Indian and western history usually neglect the Peace Policy. For instance, Laurence Schmeckebier's study, *The Office of Indian Affairs*

(1927), devoted one paragraph to the Policy, describing it as "rather curious" (p. 54). Angie Debo's *History of the Indians of the United States* (1970) is a sympathetic general history of native Americans, yet her only reference to the Peace Policy is an undocumented footnote (pp. 172–73). John A. Hawgood, who won the Western History Prize for his *America's Western Frontiers: The Exploration and Settlement of the Trans-Mississippi West* (1967), did not mention Grant; he also utterly misunderstood the humanitarian movement of the 1870s and mistakenly gave Hayes and Schurz complete credit for initiating reform and seeking justice in Indian affairs.

Histories of Church-State relations written since 1953 marked a great improvement over anything done before, though it was not until 1976 that a thorough and fair overview of the Grant period in Indian affairs appeared. Peter Rahill, *Catholic Indian Missions and Grant's Peace Policy* (1955), Robert Whitner's dissertation, "The Methodist Episcopal Church and Grant's Peace Policy" (1959), Henry Fritz, *The Movement for Indian Assimilation* (1963), and R. Pierce Beaver, *Church, State, and the American Indians* (1966), all moved far beyond Rushmore, Edwards, and Priest. Rahill, however, relied too heavily on Priest's book for information about Protestants, and Fritz and Whitner too frequently were uncritical of their sources. Whitner generalized about the entire Policy in a limited study of the Methodists, while Fritz, despite his generally reliable observations, neglected to discuss the Parker and Hayt controversies fully, failed to document his conclusions about Welsh, E. P. Smith, and Saville, and tended to stereotype the West. Beaver's study was more sympathetic to the churches than any previous work and placed the Peace Policy in the context of mission history and American Church-State relations since 1600; it was based on printed sources. A solid analysis of public opinion about the Policy was Robert Mardock's *Reformers and the American Indian* (1971). When it moves beyond public reactions, however, Mardock's book should be used with caution; Mardock did not investigate Christian pacifism, religious motivations, church organization, or mission history. By far the best history of the period following the Civil War is Francis Paul Prucha's *American Indian Policy in Crisis: Christian Reformers and the Indian, 1865-1900* (1976). Prucha is one of the few writers bringing to his research an accurate, sympathetic understanding of the churches and of the religious motivation in humanitarian reformers. Prucha is especially good for seeing the continuity in Indian reform for the thirty-year period. His book is more extensive, detailed, and careful than any previous work about the entire Policy. Clyde A. Milner's dissertation, later published as *With Good Intentions: Quaker Work among the Pawnees, Otos, and Omahas in the 1870s* (1982), not only answers almost all questions about Hicksite involvement, but is a model study of the Policy's impact on tribal life; no other study is comparable for details on how the reform actually worked in the West.

Despite Prucha's accomplishment and Beaver's suggestive work, American church and mission histories have remained very weak when discussing Indians. Sidney Ahlstrom's *Religious History of the American People* (1972) makes poorly documented statements about Indians, contains only scattered references to missions, and says nothing about the Peace Policy. Books and articles by ethnohistorians such as Robert Berkhofer, Edward Spicer, Anthony Wallace, Grenville Goodwin, and Alvin Josephy have been consistently neglected by even the best American church historians—Robert Handy, Sidney Mead, Martin Marty, Robert Bellah. A notable exception is Howard Harrod's careful monograph, *Mission Among the Blackfeet* (1971), which combines psychology, ethnology, history, and theology in a skillful manner.

Many of the leaders in the Peace Policy—Hare, Brunot, Colyer, Whipple, Wilbur, Miles, Welsh, Delano, Schurz, Clum, and Hinman—merit critical biographical studies. A good model is William H. Armstrong's biography of Ely S. Parker, *Warrior in Two Camps* (1978), a reliable study sympathetic to Parker that places his years as commissioner of Indian affairs in the context of an exceptional career. Armstrong is presently writing a biography of E. P. Smith. William S. McFeely's *Grant: A Biography* (1981) comes closer to capturing Grant's entire life than any previous work; chapter 19 on the Peace Policy relies exclusively on secondary sources. Needing further study is the Hayes administration and the Peace Policy, a need that has been hindered rather than helped by Kenneth Davison's uncritical article, "President Hayes and the Reform of American Indian Policy," in *Ohio History* (1973). Although much has been written about Apache warfare, Indian life and mission affairs in the Southwest during this period deserve fuller attention than they have received. During the past ten years excellent southwestern tribal histories covering the Grant period have been written by Donald Berthrong, William Hagan, and John Bret Harte. On the other hand, D. C. Cole's 1977 article in the *Indian Historian* describing the Chiricahua Apache reservation demonstrates how thoroughly the Peace Policy can be misunderstood even at this late date.

Primary Sources

Manuscript Materials

Austin, Tex. Protestant Episcopal Church. Church Historical Society Archives. Episcopal Seminary of the Southwest.
　　Minutes of the Committee on Indian Agents, December 12, 1870 to February 25, 1871
　　Minutes of the Indian Commission, 1871–79
　　Letterbooks of the Indian Commission, 1873–79

Letterbooks of the Committee for Domestic Missions, 1879–82

Domestic correspondence of the Domestic and Foreign Missionary Society, 1879–80

Billings, Mont. Rocky Mountain College.

Journal of the Montana Annual Conference of the Methodist Episcopal Church, 1877–82

Journal of the Rocky Mountain Annual Conference of the Methodist Episcopal Church, 1872–76

Bismarck, North Dakota. North Dakota State Historical Society.

Charles Lemon Hall Journals, 1874–84, and Scrapbook

Cambridge, Mass. Houghton Library, Harvard University.

ABCFM Papers, Letters to Missionaries, 1854–57

Records of the Dakota Mission, 1871–82

Chicago, Ill. Newberry Library. Edward E. Ayer Collection.

Transcripts of Letters from ABCFM Indian Missionaries in Minnesota, Dakota, and Oregon, 1827–78

Manuscript no. 55c: C. H. Barstow letters from the Crow agency, 1879–91

Manuscript no. 61: Thomas B. Beall to Rufus Ingalls, July 12, 1870

Manuscript no. 149: George Catlin to Professor Harper, 1870

Manuscript files no. 343a, 343b: Benjamin Henry Grierson Papers, c. 1868–80

Manuscript file no. 676: Notes on Indian-white relations by Ely S. Parker, after 1882

Manuscript file no. 677: E. S. Parker to Harriet Converse, c. 1887

Manuscript file no. 684: Francis Parkman to Geo. R. Morse, Boston, August 28, 1877

Manuscript file no. 882: John Thayer to J. D. Cox, October 17, 1870

Manuscript file no. 907: Minutes of the Meetings of the Board of Indian Commissioners, 1869–1917; transcript

Chicago, Ill. University of Chicago Library. Special Collections.

Abel Bingham Correspondence, 1828–55

Haverford, Pa. Haverford College. Quaker Collection.

John B. Garret Collection

Enoch Hoag Letterbooks and Papers

Helena, Mont. Montana Historical Society.

W. W. Alderson, "Early Day Reminiscences," 1900; "A Talk to the Indians in Council at Fort Peck," January 24, 1874 (transcript)

Nashville, Tenn. Fish University. American Missionary Association Archives.

Edward P. Smith Papers, 1869–75

Miscellaneous Papers, 1870–80

New Brunswick, N.J. Gardner A. Sage Library, New Brunswick Theological Seminary. Reformed Church Archives.

Indian Agencies: Correspondence, 1870–81; Papers, 1868–79

New Orleans, La. Armistad Research Center.
  American Home Missionary Society Papers: Minnesota, 1862–64; Colo-
    rado, 1864–65
Olympia, Wash. Washington State Library.
  Correspondence of H. D. Gibson and Robert H. Milroy, 1874–80, Agency
    of Nisqually, Puyallup, and other Indian Tribes of Washington Territory
  Records of the Washington Superintendency of Indian Affairs, 1853–74;
    letters from agents and employees
  Records of the Washington Superintendency of Indian Affairs; miscella-
    neous
Philadelphia, Pa. Presbyterian Historical Society.
  American Indian Correspondence
  Sheldon Jackson Papers
Pierre, S.Dak. South Dakota State Historical Society.
  Mrs. Thomas L. Riggs, "The Work Among the Teton Sioux," 1903
Pullman, Wash. Washington State University Library.
  Henry Harmon Spalding Papers, 1869–74
  Lucullus V. McWhorter Papers, "Lieutenants Grant and Sheridan's Indian
    Wives," Typescript, file 1544
St. Paul, Minn. Minnesota Historical Society.
  Henry Benjamin Whipple Papers and Letterbooks, 1868–82
St. Paul, Minn. Mrs. Karen Daniels Petersen.
  Daniels Family Papers
Swarthmore, Pa. Swarthmore College. Friends Historical Library.
  Record Group 2: Philadelphia Yearly Meeting; Baltimore Yearly Meeting
  Journal of Barclay White
  Albert Green Papers
  Forbush Papers
  Samuel Janney Papers
  Thomas Lightfoot Papers
Washington, D.C. Library of Congress, Manuscripts Division.
  Ulysses S. Grant Papers, 1869–77
  John Philip Newman Papers, 1870–90
  Carl Schurz Papers, 1870–83
  Matthew Simpson Papers, 1868–75
Washington, D.C. U.S. National Archives.
  Record Group 48
    Secretary of the Interior, Appointments Division, 1869–82
  Record Group 75
    Board of Indian Commissioners: Letters Sent, 1869–82
    Board of Indian Commissioners: Letters Received, 1869–82
    Board of Indian Commissioners: Scrapbook

Data Book for the Civilization Fund, 1824-32

Office of Indian Affairs: Letters Sent, 1869-82

Office of Indian Affairs: Letters Received, 1869-82

Office of Indian Affairs: Inspectors' Reports, 1873-82

Office of Indian Affairs: Special Files no. 221, 247, 248, 269

Public Documents

American State Papers: Indian Affairs. 2 vols. Washington: Gales and Seaton, 1832-34.

Cohen, Felix S. *Handbook of Federal Indian Law.* 1942. Reprint. Albuquerque: University of New Mexico Press, 1971.

Hinman v. *Hare. Northeastern Reporter* (January 1887), pp. 41-58.

Journals of the Continental Congress: 1774-1789. 34 vols. Ed. Worthington C. Ford. Washington: Government Printing Office, 1904-37.

Kappler, Charles J., comp. *Indian Affairs: Laws and Treaties.* 2 vols. Washington: Government Printing Office, 1904.

New York Supreme Court. *Hinman* v. *Hare.* Vol. 356. 1884.

Red Cloud Commission. *Report of the Special Commission Appointed to Investigate the Affairs of the Red Cloud Indian Agency, July, 1875; together with the Testimony and Accompanying Documents.* Washington: Government Printing Office, 1875.

U.S. Board of Indian Commissioners. *Acts of Congress Relating to the Board of Indian Commissioners and By-Laws of the Board.* Washington: Government Printing Office, 1875.

——. *Annual Report.* 1869-83.

——. *Journal of the Second Annual Conference of the Board of Indian Commissioners with the Representatives of the Religious Societies Cooperating with the Government.* Washington: Government Printing Office, 1873.

——. *Minutes of the Board of Indian Commissioners.* Washington: H. Polkinhorn and Co., 1870.

U.S. Commissioner of Indian Affairs. *Annual Report of the Commissioner of Indian Affairs to the Secretary of the Interior.* 1869-83.

U.S. Congress. *Condition of the Indian Tribes: Report of the Joint Special Committee Appointed under Joint Resolution of March 3, 1865.* Washington: Government Printing Office, 1867.

——. *Report on the Conduct of the War: Massacre of Cheyenne Indians.* Washington: Government Printing Office, 1865.

U.S. Congressional Globe. 1869-73.

U.S. Congressional Record. 1873-83.

U.S. Department of the Interior. *Annual Report of the Secretary of the Interior.* 1869–82.

——. *Documents Relating to the Charges of Professor O. C. Marsh of Fraud and Mismanagement at the Red Cloud Agency.*

——. *Report of the Board of Inquiry Convened by Authority of Letter of the Secretary of the Interior of June 7, 1877, to Investigate Certain Charges Against S. A. Galpin, Chief Clerk of the Indian Bureau, and Concerning Irregularities in Said Bureau.* Washington: Government Printing Office, 1878.

——. *Report of the Commission Appointed by the Secretary of the Interior to Investigate Certain Charges Against Hon. E. P. Smith, the Commissioner of Indian Affairs.* Washington, 1874.

——. *Report of the Commission Appointed to Treat with the Sioux Indians for the Relinquishment of the Black Hills.* Washington: Government Printing Office, 1875.

——. *What the Government and the Churches are Doing for the Indians.* Washington: Government Printing Office, 1874.

U.S. House of Representatives. *Letters of Ely S. Parker and John Pope to General U. S. Grant.* Misc. Doc. no. 37. 39th Cong., 2d sess., 1867.

——. "Memorial of the Yearly Meeting of the Society of Friends, Relative to the Treatment of the Indians." Misc. Doc. no. 29. 40th Cong., 3d sess., 1868.

——. *Report of the Indian Peace Commissioners,* Exec. Doc. no. 97. 40th Cong., 2d sess., 1868.

——. *Affairs in the Indian Department.* Report no. 39. 41st Cong., 3d sess., 1873.

——. *Investigation of the Conduct of Indian Affairs.* Report no. 778. 43d Cong., 1st sess., 1874.

——. *Testimony Taken before the Committee on Indian Affairs Concerning the Management of the Indian Department.* Misc. Doc. no. 167. 44th Cong., 1st sess., 1876.

——. *Transfer of the Indian Bureau.* Report no. 240. 44th Cong., 1st sess., 1876.

——. *Reduction of Army Officers' Pay, Reorganization of the Army, and Transfer of the Indian Bureau.* Report no. 354. 44th Cong., 1st sess., 1876.

——. *Letter from the Secretary of the Treasury Transmitting Estimates of Appropriations Required for the Service of the fiscal year ending June 30, 1880.* Exec. Doc. no. 5. 45th Cong., 3d sess., 1878.

——. *Equal Rights to All Religious Denominations among Indians.* Report no. 167. 45th Cong., 3d sess., 1879.

——. *Transfer of the Bureau of Indian Affairs to the War Department.* Report no. 1393. 46th Cong., 2d sess., 1880.

U.S. Office of Indian Affairs. *Report upon the Condition and Management of Certain Indian Agencies in the Indian Territory, now under the Supervision of the Orthodox Friends.* Washington: Government Printing Office, 1877.

U.S. Senate. *Sand Creek Massacre.* Exec. Doc. no. 26. 39th Cong., 2d sess., 1867.

——. *Early Missionaries in Oregon.* Exec. Doc. no. 37. 41st Cong., 3d sess., 1870.

——. *Testimony taken by the Joint Committee Appointed to take into Consideration the Expediency of Transferring the Indian Bureau to the War Department.* Misc. Doc. no. 53. 45th Cong., 3d sess., 1879.

——. *Report of the Joint Committee Appointed to Consider the Expediency of Transferring the Indian Bureau to the War Department.* Report no. 693. 45th Cong., 3d sess., 1879.

——. *Letter from the Secretary of War . . . Communicating Information in Relation to the Escape of the Cheyenne Indians from Fort Robinson.* Misc. Doc. no. 64. 45th Cong., 3d sess., 1879.

——. *Removal of the Ponca Indians.* Report no. 670. 46th Cong., 2d sess., 1880.

U.S. Superintendent of Indian Schools. *Annual Report to the Secretary of the Interior.* 1882-87.

Reports

American Baptist Home Mission Society. *Annual Report.* 1869-84.

American Baptists. *Proceedings of the General Convention.* 1846-66.

American Board of Commissioners for Foreign Missions. *Annual Report.* 1869-83.

American Missionary Association. *Annual Report.* 1869-84.

American Unitarian Association. *Annual Report.* 1870-80.

Baptist Church. *Board of Foreign Missions. Minutes.* 1839-45.

——. *Proceedings of the General Convention.* 1814-45.

Methodist Episcopal Church. *Journal of the General Conference.* 1880, 1892.

——. *Minutes of the East Oregon and Washington Annual Conference.* 1874-76.

——. *Minutes of the Oregon Annual Conference.* 1855-83.

——. *Minutes of the Columbia River Conference.* 1877-84.

Presbyterian Church, U.S.A. *Annual Reports of the Board of Foreign Missions.* 1869-83.

Protestant Episcopal Church. *Authorized Reports of the Proceedings of the Congresses of the Protestant Episcopal Church.* 1874–82.
———. *Proceedings of the Board of Missions.* 1869–83.
Society of Friends, Orthodox. *Annual Report of the Associated Executive Committee on Indian Affairs.* 1870–83.
———. *Minutes of the Associated Executive Committee of Friends on Indian Affairs.* 1872–82.
———. *Minutes of the Indiana Yearly Meeting.* 1837–57.
———. *Minutes of the Western Yearly Meeting.* 1857–64.

Books, Tracts, and Sermons

"An American Citizen." *The Great American Empire: or, Gen. Ulysses S. Grant, Emperor of North America.* St. Louis: W. S. Bryan, Publisher, 1879.
Anderson, Rufus. *Foreign Missions, Their Relations and Claims.* New York: Charles Scribner and Co., 1869.
———. "The Theory of Missions to the Heathen." Sermon in Ware, Mass. 1845.
Armstrong, S. C. *The Indian Question.* Hampton, Va.: Normal School Press, 1883.
Arny, W. F. M. *Indian Agent in New Mexico: the Journal of Special Indian Agent W. F. M. Arny 1870.* Santa Fe: Stagecoach Press, 1967.
———. *Interesting Items Regarding New Mexico, Its Agriculture, Pastoral and Mineral Resources.* Santa Fe: Manderfield and Tucker, 1873.
Ayers, John. *Why the Indians Should Be Transferred to the War Department.* n.p., 1879.
Badeau, Adam. *Grant in Peace from Appomattox to Mount McGregor: A Personal Memoir.* Hartford: S. S. Scranton and Co., 1887.
Bartlett, S. C. *Historical Sketch of the Missions of the American Board among the North American Indians.* Boston: ABCFM, 1876.
Battey, Thomas C. *The Life and Adventures of a Quaker Among the Indians.* Boston: Lee and Shepard, 1875.
Beaver, R. Pierce, ed. *Pioneers in Mission: The Early Missionary Ordination Sermons, Charges, and Instructions.* Grand Rapids: Wm. B. Eerdman's Publishing, 1966.
———, ed. *To Advance the Gospel: Selections from the Writings of Rufus Anderson.* Grand Rapids: Wm. B. Eerdman's Publishing, 1967.
Blackbird, Andrew J. (Mac-ke-te-pe-nas-sy). *The Indian Problem From the Indian's Standpoint.* n.p., 1900.
Bland, T. A. *Life of Alfred B. Meacham.* Washington: T. A. and M. C. Bland, 1883.
Boston Merchant's Committee. *The Indian Question.* Boston: F. Wood, 1880.

Bourke, John G. *An Apache Campaign in the Sierra Madre*. 1885. Reprint. New York: Charles Scribner's Sons, 1958.

——. *On the Border with Crook*. New York: Charles Scribner's Sons, 1891.

Butler, E. *An Essay on "Our Indian Question."* New York: A. G. Sherwood and Co., 1882.

Catholic Clergy of the Province of Oregon [J. B. A. Brouillet]. *Address . . . to the Catholics of the United States on President Grant's Indian Policy in Its Bearing upon Catholic Interests at Large*. Portland, Oreg.: Catholic Sentinel Publication, 1874.

Catholic Indian Bureau. *Manual of Catholic Indian Missionary Associations*. Washington, [1875].

——. *Official Construction of President Grant's Indian Peace Policy*. Washington, [1876].

Catholic Young Men's National Union. *Catholic Grievances in Relation to the Administration of Indian Affairs*. Richmond: Catholic Visitor Print., 1882.

Child, Lydia Maria. *An Appeal for the Indians*. New York: Wm. P. Tomlinson [c. 1869].

Chipman, N. P. *Argument of N. P. Chipman on Behalf of Hon. E. S. Parker*. Washington: Powell, Ginck and Co., 1871.

Colyer, Vincent. *Peace with the Apaches of New Mexico and Arizona*. Washington: Government Printing Office, 1872.

Cornelison, Isaac A. *The Relation of Religion to Civil Government in the United States of America: A State Without Church, But Not Without a Religion*. New York: G. P. Putnam's Sons, 1895.

Cramer, M. J. *Ulysses S. Grant: Conversations and Unpublished Letters*. New York: Eaton and Mains, 1897.

Crocket, Columbus [H. Clay Pruess]. *Columbus Crocket to General Grant on the Indian Policy*. Washington: J. Bradley Adams, 1873.

Cross, Nelson. *The Modern Ulysses: His Political Record*. New York: J. S. Redfield, 1872.

Cudmore, Patrick. *President Grant and Political Rings: a Satire*. New York: P. J. Kenedy, 1878.

DeSmet, Pierre Jean. *Life, Letters and Travels of Father Pierre DeSmet, S. J., 1801-1873*. 4 vols. Ed. Hiram M. Chittenden and Alfred T. Richardson. New York: Francis P. Harper, 1905.

Dodge, Richard I. *Our Wild Indians: Thirty-three Years Personal Experience Among the Red Men of the Great West*. 1882. Reprint. New York: Archer House, 1959.

——. *A Living Issue*. Washington: Francis B. Mohun, 1882.

Eells, Myron. *Father Eells*. Boston: Congregational Sunday School and Publishing Society, 1894.

——. "The Hand of God in the History of the Pacific Coast." Address at Whitman College, 1888.

——. *History of Indian Missions on the Pacific Coast: Oregon, Washington, and Idaho.* Philadelphia: American Sunday-School Union, 1882.

——. *Justice to the Indian.* Congregational Association of Oregon and Washington, 1888.

——. *Ten Years of Missionary Work Among the Indians at Skokomish.* Boston: Congregational Sunday-School and Publishing Society, 1886.

Ewing, Charles. *Circular of the Catholic Commissioner for Indian Missions to the Catholics of the United States.* Baltimore: John Murphy and Co., 1874.

——. *Petition of the Catholic Church for the Agency of the Chippewas of Lake Superior.* Washington: Polkinhorn and Co., 1873.

——. *Petition of the Catholic Church in Behalf of the Pueblos and Other Indians of New Mexico.* Washington: S. and R. O. Polkinhorn, 1874.

Finerty, John F. *War-Path and Bivouac: the Conquest of the Sioux, a Narrative of Stirring Personal Experiences and Adventures in the Big Horn and Yellowstone Expedition of 1876.* Chicago: Donohue and Henneberry, 1890.

Finley, James B. *Life among the Indians.* Cincinnati: Curtis and Jennings, n.d.

Fletcher, Alice C. *Indian Education and Civilization.* Washington: Government Printing Office, 1888.

Goode, William H. *Outposts of Zion with Limnings of Mission Life.* Cincinnati: Poe and Hitchcock, 1863.

Grant, Ulysses S. *General Grant's Letters to a Friend.* Ed. James Grant Wilson. New York: T. Y. Crowell and Co., 1897.

——. *The Papers of Ulysses S. Grant, 1837–1863.* Ed. John Y. Simon. 8 vols. Carbondale: Southern Illinois University Press, 1967–.

——. *Personal Memoirs of U. S. Grant.* Ed. E. B. Long. 1882. Reprint. New York: Grosset and Dunlap, 1962.

——. *Speeches of General U. S. Grant, Republican Candidate for Eighteenth President of the United States.* Washington: Union Republican Congressional Executive Committee, 1868.

Gray, W. H. *The Indian Question!! The Civilizing Prospect.* n.p., 1878.

——. *The Moral and Religious Aspect of the Indian Question.* Astoria, Oreg.: Astorian Book and Job Printers, 1879.

Hare, William, and Hinman, Samuel. *Bishop Hare's "Rehearsal of Facts" in the Case of Samuel D. Hinman, with Mr. Hinman's Reply.* Printed by Friends of the [Santee] Mission, 1879.

Hay, C. C. *Letter to Hon. Edw. Pierrepont: Exposing Frauds of Indian Agency, at the Pai-Ute Reservation.* Denver: Rocky Mountain News Steam Printing House, 1875.

Hayes, Rutherford B. *Diary and Letters of Rutherford Birchard Hayes.* Ed.
Charles R. Williams. 5 vols. Columbus: Ohio State Archaeological and Historical Society, 1924.

Hibbetts, J. H. *The Indian Problem.* Topeka: Kansas Publishing House, 1877.

Hinman, Samuel D. *A Statement of Samuel D. Hinman, Presbyter and First
Missionary to the Dakotas.* Printed by Friends of the Mission, 1879.

Howard, O. O. *My Life and Experiences among Our Hostile Indians.* Hartford, Conn.: A. D. Worthington and Co., 1907.

Howe, M. A. DeWolfe. *Memorial of William Welsh: a Discourse Delivered in
St. Luke's Church . . . April 11, 1878.* Reading, Pa.: Owen Lavret, printer,
1878.

Hubbard, Jeremiah. *Forty Years among the Indians.* Miami, Okla.: Phelps
Printers, 1913.

Huntington, F. D. *Two Ways of Treating the Indian Problem.* New York: Indian Commission of the Protestant Episcopal Church, 1875.

Hurlbut, E. P. *A Secular View of Religion in the State.* Albany: Joel Munsell,
1870.

Jackson, Helen Hunt. *A Century of Dishonor: a Sketch of the United States
Government's Dealings with some of the Indian Tribes.* 1881. Reprint.
New York: Little Brown and Co., 1903.

Janney, Samuel M. *The Last of the Lenape and Other Poems.* Philadelphia:
Henry Perkins, 1839.

——. *Memoirs.* Philadelphia: Friends Book Association, 1890.

——. *The Separation of the Religious Society of Friends in America in 1827-
28.* Philadelphia: T. Ellwood Zell, [1868].

Ke-wa-ze-zhig. *An address delivered in Allston Hall, Boston, February 26th,
1861, before a Convention met to devise ways and means to Elevate and
Improve the Condition of the Indians in the United States.* Boston: Published by the author, 1861.

LaFlesche, Francis. *The Middle Five: Indian Schoolboys of the Omaha Tribe.*
1900. Reprint. Madison: University of Wisconsin Press, 1963.

Libby, Orin G., ed. *The Arikara Narrative of the Campaign Against the Hostile Dakotas.* Reprint. New York: AMS Press, 1977, from *North Dakota
Historical Collections,* no. 6, 1920.

Logan, John A. *Speech of Hon. John A. Logan of Illinois in the Senate of the
United States, June 20, 1876.* Washington, 1876.

Manypenny, George. *Our Indian Wards.* Cincinnati: Robert Clarke and Co.,
1880.

Marsh, O. C. *A Statement of Affairs at Red Cloud Agency made to the President of the United States.* n.p., 1875.

Marshall, J. T. *The Miles Expedition of 1874-1875: An Eyewitness Account
of the Red River War,* ed. Lonnie J. White. Austin: Encino Press, 1971.

MacMahon, Richard. *The Anglo-Saxon and the North American Indian*. Baltimore: Kelly, Piet, and Co., 1876.

McCoy, Isaac. *History of Baptist Indian Missions, embracing remarks on the Former and Present Conditions of the ABORIGINAL TRIBES: their Settlement within the Indian Territory, and their Future Prospects*. Washington: William M. Morrison, 1840.

——. *Remarks on the Practicability of Indian Reform*. Boston: Lincoln and Edmunds, 1827.

McKee, Thomas H., ed. *The National Conventions and Platforms of all Political Parties: 1789–1901*. Baltimore: Friedenwald, 1901.

McKenney, Thomas L. *Memoirs, Official and Personal*. 2 vols. New York: Paine and Burgess, 1846.

Meacham, A. B. *Wigwam and Warpath, or the Royal Chief in Chains*. Boston: John F. Dale and Co., 1875.

Miles, Nelson A. *Personal Recollections*. Chicago: Werner, 1896.

Morgan, Thomas J. *Roman Catholics and Indian Education*. Boston: American Citizen Co., 1893.

——. *Patriotic Citizenship*. New York: American Book, 1895.

Morse, Jedidiah. *A Report to the Secretary of War of the United States on Indian Affairs, comprising a Narrative of a Tour Performed in the Summer of 1820*. New Haven: Howe and Spalding, 1822.

Müller, Michael. *Public School Education*. New York: Sadlier and Co., 1873.

Neill, Edward D. *Effort and Failure to Civilize the Aborigines: Letter to N. G. Taylor*. Washington: Government Printing Office, 1868.

Nevin, Robert P. *Black-Robes, or Sketches of Missions in the Wilderness and on the Border*. Philadelphia: J. B. Lippincott and Co., 1872.

New York Indian Peace Commission. *A Thorough Digest of the Indian Question*. New York, 1876.

Newlin, James M. *Proposed Indian Policy*. [Philadelphia, 1881].

North, Luther. *Man of the Plains: Recollections of Luther North, 1856–1882*. Ed. Donald F. Danker. Lincoln: University of Nebraska Press, 1961.

Otis, Elwell S. *The Indian Question*. New York: Sheldon and Co., 1878.

Overton, B. F. *The Indians Opposed to the Transfer Bill: United Action of the Delegations of the Cherokees, Creek, Seminole, Chickasaw, and Choctaw Nations in Opposition to the Measure*. Washington: Gibson Brothers, 1878.

Owen, G. W. *The Indian Question*. n.p., 1881.

Pancoast, Henry. *Impressions of the Sioux Tribes in 1882 with some First Principles in the Indian Question*. Philadelphia: Franklin Printing House, 1883.

Parrish, Samuel. *Some Chapters in the History of the Friendly Association for*

Regaining and Preserving Peace with the Indians by Pacific Measures. Philadelphia: Friends Historical Association, 1877.

Pinart, Alphonse. *Journey to Arizona in 1876.* 1877. Reprint. Los Angeles: Zamorano Club, 1962.

Pond, S. W., Jr. *Two Volunteer Missionaries among the Dakotas or the Story of the Labors of Samuel W. and Gideon H. Pond.* Chicago: Congregational Sunday School and Publishing Society, 1893.

Pope, John. *The Indian Question.* [Cincinnati], 1878.

Pumphrey, Stanley. *Indian Civilization.* Philadelphia: Bible and Tract Distributing Society, 1877.

———. *Missionary Work in Connection with the Society of Friends.* Philadelphia, 1880.

Reid, John M. *Missions and Missionary Society of the Methodist Episcopal Church.* 2 vols. New York: Phillips and Hunt, 1879.

Representatives of Religious and Philanthropic Organizations (George Whipple, chairman). *Indians, Soldiers and Civilization.* New York: Dodge and Co., 1872.

Richardson, James D., ed. *A Compilation of the Messages and Papers of the Presidents: 1789-1902.* 10 vols. Bureau of National Literature and Art, 1904.

Richardson, Albert D. *Beyond the Mississippi: from the Great Plains to the Great Ocean; Life and Adventure on the Prairies, Mountains, and Pacific Coast.* Hartford, Conn.: American Publishing, 1869.

Riggs, Stephen. *Mary and I: Forty Years with the Sioux.* Chicago: W. G. Holmes, 1880.

———. *Tah-Koo Wah-Kan; or, the Gospel among the Dakotas.* Boston: Congregational Sabbath-School and Publishing Society, 1869.

Right-Hand Thunder. *The Indian and White Man or the Indian in Self-Defense.* Ed. D. W. Risher. Indianapolis: Carlon and Hollenbeck, 1880.

Ruffee, C. A. *Report of the Condition of the Chippewas of Minnesota.* St. Paul: Pioneer, 1875.

Schaff, Philip. *Church and State in the United States.* New York: G. P. Putnam's Sons, 1888.

Schurz, Carl. *Reminiscences of Carl Schurz with a Sketch of His Life and Public Services from 1869-1906 by Frederic Bancroft and William A. Dunning.* New York: McClure Co., 1908.

———. *Speeches, Correspondence and Political Papers.* 6 vols. Ed. Frederic Bancroft. New York: G. P. Putnam's Sons, 1913.

Seger, John H. *Early Days among the Cheyenne and Arapahoe Indians.* Ed. Stanley Vestal. Norman: University of Oklahoma Press, 1956.

Shea, John Gilmary. *History of the Catholic Missions among the Indian*

Tribes of the United States: 1529-1854. New York: E. Dunigan and Brother, 1855.

Sheridan, Philip H. *Record of Engagements with Hostile Indians Within the Military Division of the Missouri, from 1868 to 1882.* Washington: Government Printing Office, 1882.

Sherman, William T. *Home Letters of General Sherman.* Ed. M. A. DeWolfe Howe. New York: Charles Scribner's Sons, 1909.

———. *Memoirs.* 2 vols. New York: D. Appleton and Co., 1889.

Smith, Edward P. *Incidents of the United States Christian Commission.* Philadelphia: J. B. Lippincott and Co., 1869.

Society of Friends, Hicksite. *A Brief Sketch of the Efforts of the Philadelphia Yearly Meeting of the Religious Society of Friends to Promote the Civilization and Improvement of the Indians.* Philadelphia: Friends Book Store, 1866.

———. *An Address on Behalf of the Indians.* Philadelphia: Friends Book Store, 1891.

———. *Memorial of the Society of Friends in Regard to the Indians.* Baltimore: Rose and Co., [1867].

———. *Minutes of a Convention of Delegates . . . Having Charge of the Indians in the Northern Superintendency.* Philadelphia: Friends Book Association, 1877.

———. *Report of the Delegates Representing the Yearly Meetings of Philadelphia, New York, Baltimore, Indiana, Ohio, and Genesee on the Indian Concern, at Baltimore, tenth month, 1871.* New York: Published for the Yearly Meeting, 1871.

———. *Report of the Joint Delegation Appointed . . . to Visit the Indians under the Care of Friends in the Northern Superintendency.* Baltimore: J. Jones, 1869. Also reprinted in *Nebraska History* 54 (Summer 1973): 150-219.

———. Orthodox, Indiana Yearly Meeting. *Address to the People of the United States and to the Members of Congress in Particular.* Cincinnati: A Pugh, 1838.

———. Associated Executive Committee. *Need of Law on the Indian Reservations.* Philadelphia: Sherman and Co., 1878.

Stein, Bennett H. *Tough Trip Through Paradise, 1878-1879, by Andrew Garcia.* Boston: Houghton Mifflin, 1967.

Story, Nelson. *In the Matter of the Investigation into the Affairs at the Crow Agency and the Conduct of the Late Agent, Mr. Clapp, and Nelson Story.* n.p., 1877.

Strong, Josiah. *Our Country.* New York: Baker and Taylor, 1885.

Stuart, George H. *The Life of George H. Stuart.* Ed. Robert E. Thompson. Philadelphia: J. M. Stoddart and Co., 1890.

Sturgis, Thomas. *Common Sense View of the Sioux War, with True Method of Treatment, as Opposed to both the Exterminative and the Sentimental Policy.* Cheyenne: Leader Steam Book and Job Printing House, 1877.

———. *The Ute War of 1879.* Cheyenne: Leader Steam Book and Job Printing House, 1879.

Sumner, Charles. *Republicanism vs. Grantism: The Presidency a Trust; not a Plaything and Perquisite.* Washington: Rives and Bailey, 1872.

Tatum, Lawrie. *Our Red Brothers and the Peace Policy of President Ulysses S. Grant.* Philadelphia: John C. Winston and Co., 1899.

Thompson, Joseph P. *Church and State in the United States.* Boston: James H. Osgood and Co., 1873.

Tibbles, Thomas H. *Buckskin and Blanket Days.* 1905. Reprint. Garden City: Doubleday, 1957.

———. *Hidden Power: A Secret History of the Indian Ring, Its Operations, Intrigues, and Machinations, Revealing the Manner in Which it Controls Three Important Departments of the United States Government.* New York: G. W. Carlton and Co., 1881.

Tilton, Theodore. *Self-Condemned: Or, Grant's Platform bearing Witness against Grant's Administration.* New York: Golden Age Office, 1872.

United States Indian Commission. *A Specific Plan for the Treatment of the Indian Question.* New York, 1870.

Walker, Francis A. *The Indian Question.* Boston: James Osgood and Co., 1874.

Welsh, Herbert. *Four Weeks Among Some of the Sioux Tribes of Dakota and Nebraska, Together with a Brief Consideration of the Indian Problem.* Germantown, Pa.: 1882.

———. *The Indian Problem.* Philadelphia: H. F. McCann, 1882.

———. *The Indian Question Past and Present.* Philadelphia: Indian Rights Association, 1890.

———. *The Murrain of Spoils in the Indian Service.* New York: National Civil Service Report League, 1898.

Welsh, William. *Indian Office: Wrongs Doing and Reforms Needed.* Philadelphia, 1874.

———, ed. *Journal of the Rev. S. D. Hinman, Missionary to the Santee Sioux Indians; and Taopi, by Bishop Whipple.* Philadelphia: McCalla and Stavely, 1869.

———. *Sales of Indian Pine Timber.* Philadelphia, 1874.

———. *Sioux and Ponca Indians: Reports to the Missionary Organizations of the Protestant Episcopal Church and to the Secretary of the Interior, on Indian Civilization.* Philadelphia: McCalla and Stavely, 1870.

———. *Summing up of Evidence before a Committee of the House of Representatives Charged with the Investigation of Misconduct in the Indian Office.* Washington: H. Polkinhorn and Co., 1871.

——. *Supplementary Report of a Visit to Spotted Tail's Tribe of Brule Sioux Indian, the Yankton and Santee Sioux, Ponkas and the Chippewas of Minnesota, October, 1870.* Philadelphia: McCalla and Stavely, 1870.

——. *Women Helpers in the Church: Their Sayings and Doings.* Philadelphia: J. B. Lippincott and Co., 1872.

Whipple, Henry B. *Lights and Shadows of a Long Episcopate.* New York: Macmillan, 1900.

White, Barclay. *Friends and the Indians, Report . . . Exhibiting the Progress in Civilization of the Various Tribes of Indians Whilst under the Care of Friends as Agents.* Oxford, Pa.: Published for the Convention, 1886.

Wynkoop, Edward W. *Address Before the Indian Peace Commission of the Cooper Institute.* Philadelphia: A. C. Bryson, 1869.

Newspapers and Periodicals

Advance, 1873–76.

American Missionary, 1869–82.

Baptist Home Mission Monthly, 1877–82.

Baptist Quarterly, 1869–82.

Baptist Watchman, 1869–80.

Baptist Weekly, 1872–78.

Bismarck Tribune, 1873–77.

Butte Miner, 1876.

Churchman, 1875–81.

Congregationalist, 1869–73, 1879.

Friend's Intelligencer, 1869–82.

Harper's Monthly, 1867–1884.

Harper's Weekly, 1869–82.

Helena Weekly Herald, 1869–71.

Independent, 1869–70, 1875–82.

Methodist Magazine, 1818–42.

Missionary Herald, 1869–83.

Montanian, 1871.

Nation, 1869–82.

Old and New, 1870–75.

Religious Magazine and Monthly Review, 1869–73.

Spirit of Missions, 1869–83.

Union Dakotaian, 1871–75.

Unitarian Review, 1874–82.

Articles

"A Glance at the Indian Question." *Catholic World* 26 (November 1877): 195-203.

Abbott, Lyman. "Secular and Sectarian Schools." *Harper's Monthly* 40 (May 1870): 910-15.

Arnold, S. G. "President Grant's Indian Policy." *Methodist Quarterly* 59 (July 1877): 409-30.

Avery, J. B. "Chips from an Indian Workshop." *Overland Monthly* 11 (December 1873): 489-93.

Chever, Edward E. "The Indians of California." *American Naturalist* 4 (1870): 129-48.

Chief Joseph. "An Indian's View of Indian Affairs." *North American Review* 128 (1879): 412-33.

"F.J." "Is the United States Government a Nuisance To Be Abated?" *Catholic World* 34 (1881): 62-69.

Gilfillan, Joseph A. "Fruits of Christian Work Among the Chippewas." *The Church and the Indians,* 1873 pamphlet.

Godkin, E. L. "General Grant's Indian Policy." *Nation* 28 (January 9, 1879): 22.

——. "The Recent Change in the Indian Bureau." *Nation* 13 (August 17, 1871): 100-101.

Gulliver, John P. "The Romish War upon American Schools." *Congregational Review* 1 (1870): 172-85.

Hare, William. "Christian Schools Among the Indians." *The Church and the Indians,* 1874 pamphlet.

——. "Further Enlargement of the Work." *The Church and the Indians,* 1874 pamphlet.

Howland, Edward. "Our Indian Brothers." *Harper's Monthly* 56 (1878): 768-76.

Linn, J. M. "The Relation of the Church to the Indian Question." *Presbyterian Review* 1 (October 1880): 677-93.

Lossing, B. J. "Our Barbarian Brethren." *Harper's Monthly* 40 (May 1870): 793-811.

Lowrie, John C. "Our Indian Affairs." *Presbyterian Quarterly and Princeton Review* 3 (January 1874): 5-22.

"Management of the Indians." *National Quarterly Review* 40 (January 1880): 27-40.

Miles, Nelson. "The Indian Problem." *North American Review* 128 (1879): 304-14.

Milroy, R. H. "Our Indian Policy further Considered." *Presbyterian Quarterly and Princeton Review* 5 (October 1876): 624-28.

Nicholson, William. "A Tour of Indian Agencies in Kansas and the Indian Territory in 1870." *Kansas Historical Quarterly* 3, nos. 3-4 (August, November 1934): 289-326, 343-84.

"Our Indian Policy." *United Service* 6 (February 1882): 129-42.

"Our New Indian Policy and Religious Liberty." *Catholic World* 26 (October 1877): 90-108.

Patterson, Robert. "Our Indian Policy." *Overland Monthly* 11 (September 1873): 201-14.

Riggs, Thomas L. "Sunset to Sunset: A Lifetime with My Brothers, the Dakotas." *South Dakota Historical Collections* 29 (1958): 87-306.

Schurz, Carl. "Present Aspects of the Indian Problem." *North American Review* 133 (July 1881): 1-24.

Sellers, James L., ed. "Diary of Dr. Joseph A. Paxon, Physician to the Winnebago Indians, 1869-1870." *Nebraska History* 27, nos. 3-4 (July, October 1946): 143-204, 244-75.

Shea, John Gilmary. "What Right Has the Federal Government to Mismanage the Indians?" *American Catholic Quarterly Review* 6 (1881): 520-41.

Talbot, James J. "The Indian Question." *United Service* 1 (January 1879): 141-52.

Trowbridge, J. T. "The Indian Camp." *Harper's Monthly* 61 (April 1881): 748-49.

Victor, Frances F. "The Oregon Indians." *Overland Monthly* 7 (October, November 1871): 344-52, 425-53.

Whipple, Henry B. "Civilization and Christianization of the Ojibways in Minnesota." *Minnesota Historical Collections* 9 (April 1901): 129-42.

——. "Plea for the Red Man." *Missionary Paper* 24 (1863), pamphlet reprint.

——. "The Indian System." *North American Review* 99 (1864): 449-64.

Whittier, John Greenleaf. "Indian Civilization," in *The Prose Works of John Greenleaf Whittier*, 3:232-35. Boston: Houghton, Mifflin, 1904.

——. "The Indian Question." *Prose Works* 3 (1883): 238-40.

Williamson, Thomas. "The Indian Question." *Presbyterian Quarterly and Princeton Review*, 5 (October 1876): 608-24 [first published in the *North American Review*, April 1873].

Secondary Sources

Books and Dissertations

Abell, Aaron. *The Urban Impact on American Protestantism: 1865-1900.* Cambridge: Harvard University Press, 1943.

Armstrong, William H. *Warrior in Two Camps: Ely S. Parker, Union General and Seneca Chief.* Syracuse: Syracuse University Press, 1978.

Athearn, Robert G. *William Tecumseh Sherman and the Settlement of the West.* Norman: University of Oklahoma Press, 1956.

Ball, Eve. *In the Days of Victorio: Recollections of a Warm Springs Apache.* Tucson: University of Arizona Press, 1970.

Barclay, Wade C. *History of Methodist Missions.* 3 vols. New York: Board of Missions of the Methodist Church, 1949–57.

Barnard, Harry. *Rutherford B. Hayes and His America.* New York: Bobbs-Merrill, 1954.

Barton, Winifred W. *John P. Williamson: A Brother to the Sioux.* Chicago: Fleming H. Revell, 1919.

Bass, Althea. *The Arapaho Way: A Memoir of an Indian Boyhood.* New York: Clarkson N. Potter, 1966.

Beard, Augustus F. *A Crusade of Brotherhood: A History of the American Missionary Association.* Boston: Pilgrim Press, 1909.

Beaver, R. Pierce. *Church, State, and the American Indians.* St. Louis: Concordia Publishing House, 1966.

———. *Ecumenical Beginnings in Protestant World Mission: A History of Comity.* New York: Thomas Nelson and Sons, 1962.

Benjamin, Philip S. *The Philadelphia Quakers in the Industrial Age: 1865–1920.* Philadelphia: Temple University Press, 1976.

Berkhofer, Robert F., Jr. *Salvation and the Savage: An Analysis of Protestant Missions and American Indian Response: 1787–1862.* Lexington: University of Kentucky Press, 1965.

———. *The White Man's Indian: Images of the American Indian from Columbus to the Present.* New York: Alfred A. Knopf, 1978.

Berthrong, Donald J. *The Cheyenne and Arapaho Ordeal: Reservation and Agency Life in the Indian Territory, 1875–1907.* Norman: University of Oklahoma Press, 1976.

———. *The Southern Cheyennes.* Norman: University of Oklahoma Press, 1963.

Bowden, Henry Warner. *American Indians and Christian Missions: Studies in Cultural Conflict.* Chicago: University of Chicago Press, 1981.

Bret Harte, John. "The San Carlos Indian Reservation, 1872–1886: An Administrative History." Ph.D. diss., University of Arizona, Tucson, 1972.

Brimlow, George F. *The Bannock Indian War of 1878.* Caldwell, Idaho: Caxton Printers, 1938.

Brown, Arthur Judson. *One Hundred Years: A History of the Foreign Missionary Work of the Presbyterian Church in the U.S.A.* New York: Fleming H. Revell, 1936.

Carpenter, John A. *Sword and Olive Branch: Oliver Otis Howard.* Pittsburgh: Pittsburgh University Press, 1964.

———. *Ulysses S. Grant.* New York: Twayne Publishers, 1970.

Catton, Bruce. *U.S. Grant and the American Military Tradition.* New York: Universal Library, 1954.

Clark, Dan Elbert. *Samuel Jordan Kirkwood.* Iowa City: State Historical Society, 1917.

Clark, Robert C. *The Life of Matthew Simpson.* New York: Macmillan, 1956.

Clum, Woodworth. *Apache Agent: the Story of John P. Clum.* Boston: Houghton Mifflin, 1936.

Craig, Reginald S. *The Fighting Parson: The Biography of Colonel John M. Chivington.* Los Angeles: Westernlore Press, 1959.

Current Richard N. *Pine Logs and Politics: A Life of Philetus Sawyer, 1816–1900.* Madison: State Historical Society of Wisconsin, 1950.

Danziger, Edmund J., Jr. *Indians and Bureaucrats: Administering the Reservation Policy During the Civil War.* Urbana: University of Illinois Press, 1974.

Davison, Kenneth E. *The Presidency of Rutherford B. Hayes.* Westport, Conn.: Greenwood Press, 1972.

Drury, Clifford. *Henry Harmon Spalding.* Caldwell, Idaho: Caxton Printers, 1936.

———. *Presbyterian Panorama: One Hundred and Fifty Years of National Missions History.* Philadelphia: Board of Christian Education, Presbyterian Church, U.S.A., 1952.

Eastman, Elaine G. *Pratt: the Red Man's Moses.* Norman: University of Oklahoma Press, 1935.

Eckenrode, H. J. *Rutherford B. Hayes: Statesman of Reunion.* New York: Dodd, Mead and Co., 1930.

Ege, Robert S. *Strike Them Hard.* Bellevue, Nebr.: Old Army Press, 1970.

Elliott, Errol T. *Quakers on the American Frontier.* Richmond, Ind.: Friends' United Press, 1969.

Ellis, Elmer. *Henry Moore Teller: Defender of the West.* Caldwell, Idaho: Caxton Printers, 1941.

Ellis, Richard N. *General Pope and U.S. Indian Policy.* Albuquerque: University of New Mexico Press, 1970.

Emmitt, Robert. *The Last War Trail: The Utes and the Settlement of Colorado.* Norman: University of Oklahoma Press, 1954.

Fahey, John. *The Flathead Indians.* Norman: University of Oklahoma Press, 1974.

Fries, Robert F. *Empire in Pine: The Story of Lumbering in Wisconsin, 1830–1890.* Madison: State Historical Society of Wisconsin, 1951.

Fritz, Henry E. *The Movement for Indian Assimilation, 1860–1890.* Philadelphia: University of Pennsylvania Press, 1963.

Frost, Lawrence A. *U. S. Grant Album: A Pictorial Biography of Ulysses S. Grant.* Seattle: Superior Publishing, 1966.

Garland, Hamlin. *Ulysses S. Grant: His Life and Character.* New York: Doubleday and McClure, 1898.

Garretson, Margaret Ann. "The Yakima Indians: 1855-1935. Background and Analysis of the Rejection of the Indian Reorganization Act." M.A. Thesis, 1968, University of Washington.

Goldhurst, Richard. *Many Are the Hearts: the Agony and the Triumph of Ulysses S. Grant.* New York: Reader's Digest Press, 1975.

Goodwin, Grenville. *Western Apache Raiding and Warfare*, Keith H. Basso, ed. Tucson: University of Arizona Press, 1971.

Goodykoontz, Colin B. *Home Missions on the American Frontier.* Caldwell, Idaho: Caxton Printers, 1939.

Grant, Ulysses S., III. *Ulysses S. Grant: Warrior and Statesman.* New York: William Morrow and Co., 1969.

Hagan, William T. *Indian Police and Judges: Experiments in Acculturation and Controls.* New Haven: Yale University Press, 1966.

——. *United States-Comanche Relations: The Reservation Years.* New Haven: Yale University Press, 1976.

Handy, Robert T. *A Christian America: Protestant Hopes and Historical Realities.* New York: Oxford University Press, 1971.

Harmon, George D. *Sixty Years of Indian Affairs: Political, Economic, and Diplomatic, 1789-1850.* Chapel Hill: University of North Carolina Press, 1941.

Harrod, Howard L. *Mission Among the Blackfeet.* Norman: University of Oklahoma Press, 1971.

Hebard, Grace R., and Brininstool, E. A. *The Bozeman Trail: Historical Accounts of the Blazing of the Overland Routes into the Northwest, and the Fights with Red Cloud's Warriors.* Cleveland: Arthur H. Clark, 1922.

Helland, Maurice. *There Were Giants: The Life of James H. Wilbur.* Yakima: Shields Bag and Printing, 1980.

Hesseltine, William B. *Ulysses S. Grant: Politician.* New York: Ungar Publishing, 1957.

Hinman, George W. *The American Indian and Christian Missions.* New York: Fleming H. Revell, 1933.

Hoig, Stan. *The Sand Creek Massacre.* Norman: University of Oklahoma Press, 1961.

Howe, M. A. DeWolfe. *The Life and Labors of Bishop Hare.* New York: Sturgis and Walton, 1913.

Howe, Mark DeWolfe. *The Garden and the Wilderness: Religion and Government in American Constitutional History.* Chicago: University of Chicago Press, 1965.

Hudson, Winthrop. *American Protestantism.* Chicago: University of Chicago Press, 1961.

Hyde, George E. *Pawnee Indians.* Denver: University of Denver Press, 1951.

———. *Red Cloud's Folk: A History of the Oglala Sioux Indians.* Norman: University of Oklahoma Press, 1937.

———. *A Sioux Chronicle.* Norman: University of Oklahoma Press, 1956.

———. *Spotted Tail's Folk: A History of the Brule Sioux.* Norman: University of Oklahoma Press, 1961.

Jones, Douglas C. *The Treaty of Medicine Lodge: The Story of the Great Treaty Council as Told by Eyewitnesses.* Norman: University of Oklahoma Press, 1966.

Josephson, Matthew. *The Politicos: 1865-1896.* New York: Harcourt, Brace, and Co., 1938.

Josephy, Alvin M. *The Nez Perce Indians and the Opening of the Northwest.* New Haven: Yale University Press, 1965.

Keiser, Albert. *Lutheran Mission Work among the American Indians.* Minneapolis: Augsburg Publishing House, 1922.

Kelsey, Rayner W. *Friends and the Indians: 1655-1917.* Philadelphia: Executive Committee of Friends, 1917.

Knight, Oliver H. *Following the Indian Wars: the Story of the Newspaper Correspondents Among the Indian Campaigners.* Norman: University of Oklahoma Press, 1960.

Kroeker, Marvin E. *Great Plains Command: William B. Hazen in the Frontier West.* Norman: University of Oklahoma Press, 1976.

Lamar, Howard R. *Dakota Territory, 1861-1889: A Study of Frontier Politics.* New Haven: Yale University Press, 1956.

———. *The Far Southwest, 1846-1912: A Territorial History.* New Haven: Yale University Press, 1966.

Lewis, Lloyd. *Captain Sam Grant.* Boston: Little, Brown and Co., 1950.

Lindquist, G. E. E. *The Red Man in the United States: An Intimate Study of the Social, Economic and Religious Life of the American Indian.* New York: George H. Doran, 1923.

Long, Clarence D. *Wages and Earnings in the United States: 1860-1890.* Princeton: Princeton University Press, 1960.

Mardock, Robert Winston. *The Reformers and the American Indian.* Columbia: University of Missouri Press, 1971.

May, Henry. *Protestant Churches and Industrial America.* New York: Harper and Brothers, 1949.

McFeely, William S. *Grant: A Biography.* New York: W. W. Norton and Co., 1981.

McLoughlin, William G., ed. *The American Evangelicals, 1800-1900: An Anthology.* New York: Harper and Row, 1968.

——. *Revivals, Awakening and Reform: An Essay on Religion and Social Change in America.* Chicago: University of Chicago Press, 1978.

McNitt, Frank. *The Indian Traders.* Norman: University of Oklahoma Press, 1962.

Mead, Sidney E. *The Lively Experiment.* New York: Harper and Row, 1963.

——. *The Old Religion in the Brave New World.* Berkeley: University of California Press, 1977.

Meyer, Roy W. *History of the Santee Sioux: United States Indian Policy on Trial.* Lincoln: University of Nebraska Press, 1967.

Milner, Clyde A. "With Good Intentions: Quaker Work and Indian Survival; the Nebraska Case, 1869-1882." Ph.D. diss., Yale University, 1979.

Miner, H. Craig. *The Corporation and the Indian: Tribal Sovereignty and Industrial Civilization in Indian Territory, 1865-1907.* Columbia: University of Missouri Press, 1976.

Moody, Marshall Dwight. "A History of the Board of Indian Commissioners and Its Relations to the Administration of Indian Affairs, 1869-1900." M.A. thesis, American University [1951].

Moorhead, James H. *American Apocalypse: Yankee Protestants and the Civil War, 1860-1869.* New Haven: Yale University Press, 1978.

Murphy, Lawrence R. *Frontier Crusader: W. F. M. Arny.* Tucson: University of Arizona Press, 1972.

Nevins, Allan. *The Emergence of Modern America: 1865-1878.* New York: Macmillan, 1939.

——. *Hamilton Fish: the Inner History of the Grant Administration.* 2 vols. New York: Ungar Publishing, 1957.

Nye, Wilbur S. *Carbine and Lance: The Story of Old Fort Sill.* 3d ed. Norman: University of Oklahoma Press, 1969.

Ogle, Ralph H. *Federal Control of the Western Apaches, 1848-1886.* Albuquerque: University of New Mexico Press, 1940.

Olson, James C. *Red Cloud and the Sioux Problem.* Lincoln: University of Nebraska Press, 1965.

Otis, D. S. *The Dawes Act and the Allotment of Indian Lands.* 1934. Reprint. Norman: University of Oklahoma Press, 1973.

Parker, Arthur C. *The Life of General Ely S. Parker: Last Grand Sachem of the Iroquois and General Grant's Military Secretary.* Buffalo: Buffalo Historical Society, 1919.

Pitkin, Thomas M. *The Captain Departs: Ulysses S. Grant's Last Campaign.* Carbondale: Southern Illinois University Press, 1973.

Priest, Loring B. *Uncle Sam's Stepchildren: The Reformation of the United States Indian Policy, 1865-1887.* New Brunswick: Rutgers University Press, 1942.

Protestant Episcopal Church, Board of Missions. *A Handbook of the Church's*

Mission to the Indians. Hartford, Conn.: Church Missions Publishing Co., 1913.

Prucha, Francis Paul. *American Indian Policy in Crisis: Christian Reformers and the Indian, 1865-1900.* Norman: University of Oklahoma Press, 1976.

——. *American Indian Policy in the Formative Years.* Cambridge: Harvard University Press, 1962.

——. *Americanizing the American Indian: Writings by the "Friends of the Indian," 1880-1900.* Cambridge: Harvard University Press, 1973.

——. *The Churches and the Indian Schools, 1888-1912.* Lincoln: University of Nebraska Press, 1979.

——. *Indian Peace Medals in American History.* Madison: State Historical Society of Wisconsin, 1971.

Rahill, Peter J. *The Catholic Indian Missions and Grant's Peace Policy: 1870-1884.* Washington: Catholic University Press, 1953.

Rister, Carl C. *Baptist Missions Among the American Indians.* Atlanta: Home Mission Board of the Southern Baptist Convention, 1944.

Robbins, Webster S. "The Administration and Educational Policies of the United States Federal Government with Regard to the North American Indian Tribes of Nebraska from 1870 to 1970." Ed.D. diss., University of Nebraska, Lincoln, 1976.

Rushmore, Elsie M. *The Indian Policy During Grant's Administrations.* Jamaica, N.Y.: Marion Press, 1914.

Satz, Ronald N. *American Indian Policy in the Jacksonian Era.* Lincoln: University of Nebraska Press, 1975.

Schafer, Joseph. *Carl Schurz: Militant Liberal.* Evansville, Wis.: Antes Press, 1930.

Schmeckebier, Laurence F. *The Office of Indian Affairs: Its History and Organization.* Baltimore: Johns Hopkins Press, 1927.

Schultz, George A. *An Indian Canaan: Isaac McCoy and the Vision of an Indian State.* Norman: University of Oklahoma Press, 1972.

Seymour, Flora Warren. *Indian Agents of the Old Frontier.* New York: Appleton-Century, 1941.

Simon, John Y., ed. *General Grant By Matthew Arnold with a Rejoinder by Mark Twain.* Carbondale: Southern Illinois University Press, 1966.

Sizer, Sandra. *Gospel Hymns and Social Religion: The Rhetoric of Nineteenth Century Revivalism.* Philadelphia: Temple University Press, 1978.

Slattery, Charles Lewis. *Felix Reville Brunot.* New York:Longmans, Green, and Co., 1901.

Slotkin, Richard. *Regeneration Through Violence: The Mythology of the American Frontier, 1600-1860.* Middletown, Conn.: Wesleyan University Press, 1973.

Sonnichsen, C. L. *The Mescalero Apaches.* Norman: University of Oklahoma Press, 1958.

Spence, Clark C. *Territorial Politics and Government in Montana, 1864-1889.* Urbana: University of Illinois Press, 1975.

Splawn, Andrew Jackson. *Ka-mi-akin: Last Hero of the Yakimas.* Portland, Oregon: Binfords and Mort, 1944.

Sprague, Marshall. *Massacre: The Tragedy at White River.* Boston: Little, Brown and Co., 1957.

Stokes, Anson Phelps. *Church and State in the United States.* 3 vols. New York: Harper and Brothers, 1950.

Strong, William E. *The Story of the American Board: An Account of the First Hundred Years of the American Board of Commissioners for Foreign Missions.* Boston: Pilgrim Press, 1910.

Thompson, Gerald. *The Army and the Navajo.* Tucson: University of Arizona Press, 1976.

Trennert, Robert A., Jr. *Alternative to Extinction: Federal Indian Policy and the Beginnings of the Reservation System, 1846-51.* Philadelphia: Temple University Press, 1975.

Turner, Katherine. *Red Men Calling on the Great White Father.* Norman: University of Oklahoma Press, 1951.

Underhill, Ruth. *The Navajos.* Norman: University of Oklahoma Press, 1956.

Unrau, William E. *The Kansa Indians: A History of the Wind People, 1673-1873.* Norman: University of Oklahoma Press, 1971.

Unrau, William E., and Miner, H. Craig. *The End of Indian Kansas, 1854-1871.* Lawrence: Regents Press of Kansas, 1977.

Unruh, John D., Jr. *The Plains Across: The Overland Emigrants and the Trans-Mississippi West, 1840-60.* Urbana: University of Illinois Press, 1979.

Utley, Robert M. *Frontier Regulars: The United States Army and the Indian, 1866-1891.* New York: Macmillan, 1973.

——. *Frontiersmen in Blue: the United States Army and the Indian, 1848-1865.* New York: Macmillan, 1967.

——. *Last Days of the Sioux Nation.* New Haven: Yale University Press, 1963.

Viola, Herman J. *Thomas L. McKenney: Architect of America's Early Indian Policy, 1816-1830.* Chicago: Swallow Press, 1974.

Waltmann, Henry G. "The Interior Department, War Department, and Indian Policy, 1865-1887." Ph.D. diss., University of Nebraska, 1962.

Washburn, Wilcomb E. *The Assault on Indian Tribalism: The General Allotment Law (Dawes Act) of 1887.* Philadelphia: J. B. Lippincott, 1975.

Weisberger, Bernard A. *They Gathered at the River.* Boston: Little, Brown and Co., 1958.

White, Leonard. *The Republican Era: 1869-1901.* New York: Macmillan, 1958.

Whitner, Robert L. "The Methodist Episcopal Church and Grant's Peace Policy: A Study of the Methodist Agencies, 1870-1882." Ph.D. diss., University of Minnesota, 1959.

Woodward, C. Vann. *Reunion and Reaction*. Garden City: Doubleday Anchor Books, 1956.

Articles

Abel, Annie H. "Proposals for an Indian State, 1778-1878." American Historical Association, *Annual Report* 1 (1907): 87-104.

Allen, Virginia R. "Agency Physicians to the Southern Plains Indians, 1868-1900." *Bulletin of the History of Medicine* 49 (Fall 1975): 318-30.

——. "The White Man's Road: The Physical and Psychological Impact of Relocation on the Southern Plains Indians." *Journal of the History of Medicine and Allied Sciences* 30 (April 1975): 148-63.

Anderson, Grant K. "Samuel D. Hinman and the Opening of the Black Hills." *Nebraska History* 60 (Winter 1979): 520-42.

Beaver, R. Pierce. "American Missionary Motivation Before the Revolution." *Church History* 31 (June 1962): 216-26.

——. "Church, State, and the Indians: Indian Missions in the New Nation." *Journal of Church and State* 4 (May 1962): 11-30.

Berthrong, Donald J. "Cattlemen on the Cheyenne-Arapaho Reservation, 1883-1885." *Arizona and the West* 13 (Spring 1971): 5-32.

——. "White Neighbors Come Among the Southern Cheyenne and Arapaho." *Kansas Quarterly* 3 (Fall 1971): 105-15.

Bret Harte, John. "Conflict at San Carlos: The Military-Civilian Struggle for Control, 1882-1885." *Arizona and the West* 15 (Spring 1973): 27-44.

——. "The Strange Case of Joseph C. Tiffany: Indian Agent in Disgrace." *Journal of Arizona History* 16 (Winter 1975): 383-404.

Brown, Lawrence L. "The Episcopal Church in the Arid West, 1865-1875: A Study in Adaptability." *Historical Magazine of the Protestant Episcopal Church* 30 (1961): 142-71.

Buntin, Martha. "The Quaker Indian Agents of the Kiowa, Comanche, and Wichita Indian Reservations." *Chronicles of Oklahoma* 10 (June 1932): 204-18.

Castile, George P. "Edwin Eells, U.S. Indian Agent, 1871-1895." *Pacific Northwest Quarterly* 72 (April 1981): 61-68.

Cole, D. C. "Reorganization, Consolidation, and the Expropriation of the Chiricahua Apache Reservation." *Indian Historian* 10 (Spring 1977): 3-7.

Cutler, Lee. "Lawrie Tatum and the Kiowa Agency, 1869-1873." *Arizona and the West* 13 (Autumn 1971): 221-44.

Davison, Kenneth E. "President Hayes and the Reform of American Indian Policy." *Ohio History* 82 (Winter/Spring 1973): 205-14.

D'Elia, Donald J. "The Argument Over Civilian or Military Indian Control, 1865-1880." *Historian* 24 (February 1962): 207-25.

Edwards, Martha L. "A Problem of Church and State in the 1870s." *Mississippi Valley Historical Review* 11 (June 1924), 37-53.

Ellis, Richard N. "The Humanitarian Generals." *Western Historical Quarterly* 3 (April 1972): 169-78.

——. "The Humanitarian Soldiers." *Journal of Arizona History* 10 (Summer 1969): 53-66.

Fritz, Henry E. "The Board of Indian Commissioners and Ethnocentric Reform, 1878-1893," in Smith, Jane F., and Kvasnicka, Robert M., eds., *Indian Relations: A Persistent Paradox*, pp. 57-77. Washington, D.C.: Howard University Press, 1976.

——. "The Making of Grant's 'Peace Policy.'" *Chronicles of Oklahoma* 37 (Winter 1959): 411-32.

Gates, Charles M. "The Lac Qui Parle Indian Mission." *Minnesota History* 16 (June 1935): 133-51.

Goodwin, Gerald J. "Christianity, Civilization, and the Savage: the Anglican Mission to the American Indian." *Historical Magazine of the Protestant Episcopal Church* 42 (June 1973): 93-110.

Green, Norma Kidd. "The Presbyterian Mission to the Omaha Indian Tribe." *Nebraska History* 48 (Autumn 1967): 267-88.

Hagan, William T. "Indian Policy After the Civil War: The Reservation Experience," in *American Indian Policy*. Indianapolis: Indiana Historical Society, 1971.

Harrod, Howard L. "The Blackfeet and the Divine Establishment." *Montana the Magazine of Western History* (Winter 1972), pp. 42-51.

Hayter, Earl W. "The Ponca Removal." *North Dakota Historical Quarterly* 6 (1932): 262-75.

Hilliard, Sam B. "Indian Land Cessions West of the Mississippi." *Journal of the West* 10 (July 1971): 493-510.

Holmes, Kenneth L. "Bishop Daniel Sylvester Tuttle in the West." *Historical Magazine of the Protestant Episcopal Church* 23 (1954): 54-64.

Illick, Joseph E. "'Some of Our Best Indians are Friends . . .': Quaker Attitudes and Actions Toward Western Indians During the Grant Administration." *Western Historical Quarterly* 2 (July 1971): 283-94.

Kelsey, Harry. "The Doolittle Report of 1867." *Arizona and the West* 17 (Summer 1975): 107-20.

King, James T. "'A Better Way': General George Crook and the Ponca Indians." *Nebraska History* 50 (Fall 1969): 239-56.

Kirby, James E. "Matthew Simpson and the Mission of America." *Church History* 36 (September 1967): 299-307.

Kurland, Philip. "Of Church and State and the Supreme Court." *University of Chicago Law Review* 29 (January 1961): 1-96.

Leitman, Spencer L. "The Revival of an Image: Grant and the 1880 Republican Nominating Campaign." *Bulletin: Missouri Historical Society* 30 (April 1974): 196-204.

Leonard, Thomas C. "Red White and the Army Blue: Empathy and Anger in the American West." *American Quarterly* 26 (May 1974): 176-90.

LeVan, Sandra W. "The Quaker Agents at Darlington." *Chronicles of Oklahoma* 51 (Spring 1973): 92-99.

Lewitt, Robert T. "Indian Missions and Anti-Slavery Sentiment: A Conflict of Evangelical and Humanitarian Ideals." *Mississippi Valley Historical Review* 50 (June 1963): 39-55.

Littlefield, D. F., Jr., and Underhill, L. E. "Timber Depredations and Cherokee Legislation, 1869-1881." *Journal of Forest History* 18 (April 1974): 4-13.

Mardock, Robert W. "Alfred H. Love, Indian Peace Policy, and the Universal Peace Union." *Kansas Quarterly* 3 (Fall 1971): 64-71.

Mattingly, Arthur H. "The Great Plains Peace Commission of 1867." *Journal of the West* 15 (July 1976): 23-37.

Mead, Sidney E. "The American People: Their Space, Time, and Religion." *Journal of Religion* 34 (September 1954): 244-55.

——. "American Protestantism Since the Civil War: From Denominationalism to Americanism." *Journal of Religion* 36 (January 1956): 1-16.

——. "American Protestantism Since the Civil War: From Americanism to Christianity." *Journal of Religion* 36 (April 1956): 67-89.

——. "Church and State in the United States." *Religion in Life* 20 (1950): 36-46.

——. "Denominationalism: The Shape of Protestantism in America." *Church History* 23 (1954): 291-321.

——. "From Coercion to Persuasion: Another Look at the Rise of Religious Liberty and the Emergence of Denominationalism." *Church History* 25 (1956): 317-37.

——. "The 'Nation with the Soul of a Church.'" *Church History* 36 (September 1967): 262-83.

——. "Neither Church Nor State: Reflections on James Madison's 'Line of Separation.'" *Journal of Church and State* 10 (Autumn 1968): 349-63.

——. "Thomas Jefferson's 'Fair Experiment'—Religious Freedom." *Religion in Life* 23 (1953-54): 566-79.

Paige, John C. "Wichita Indian Agents, 1857-1869." *Journal of the West* 12 (July 1973): 403-13.

Parker, Watson. "The Majors and the Miners: The Role of the U.S. Army in the Black Hills Gold Rush." *Journal of the West* 9 (January 1972): 99–113.

Pfaller, Louis. "The Forging of an Indian Agent." *North Dakota History* 34 (Winter 1967): 62–76.

Powers, Ramon. "Why the Northern Cheyenne Left Indian Territory in 1878: A Cultural Analysis." *Kansas Quarterly* 3 (Fall 1971): 72–81.

Prucha, Francis Paul. "American Indian Policy in the 1840s: Visions of Reform," in Clark, John G., ed., *The Frontier Challenge: Responses to the Trans-Mississippi West*. Lawrence: University Press of Kansas, 1971.

——. "Thomas L. McKenney and the New York Indian Board." *Mississippi Valley Historical Review* 48 (March 1962): 635–55.

Ripich, Carol A. "Joseph W. Wham and the Red Cloud Agency, 1871." *Arizona and the West* 12 (Winter 1970): 325–38.

Sizer, Sandra S. "Politics and Apolitical Religion: The Great Urban Revivals of the Late Nineteenth Century." *Church History* 48 (March 1979): 81–98.

Steele, Aubrey L. "The Beginning of Quaker Administration of Indian Affairs in Oklahoma." *Chronicles of Oklahoma* 17 (December 1939): 364–92.

Sterling, Everett W. "Bishop Henry B. Whipple: Indian Agent Extraordinary." *Historical Magazine of the Protestant Episcopal Church* 26 (1957): 239–47.

——. "Moses Adams: A Missionary as Indian Agent." *Minnesota History* 35 (December 1956): 167–77.

Teaford, Jon C. "Toward a Christian Nation: Religion, Law and Justice Strong." *Journal of Presbyterian History* 54 (Winter 1976): 422–37.

Trennert, Robert A., Jr. "A Grand Failure: The Centennial Indian Exhibition of 1876." *Prologue* 6 (Summer 1974): 118–29.

Umber, Harold. "Interdepartmental Conflict Between Fort Yates and Standing Rock: Problems of Indian Administration, 1870–1881." *North Dakota History* 39 (Summer 1972): 4–13f.

Unrau, William. "The Civilian as Indian Agent: Villain or Victim?" *Western Historical Quarterly* 3 (October 1972): 405–20.

——. "Indian Agent vs. the Army." *Kansas Historical Quarterly* 30 (Summer 1964): 129–52.

Utley, Robert M. "The Celebrated Peace Policy of General Grant." *North Dakota History* 20 (1953): 121–42.

Waltmann, Henry G. "Circumstantial Reformer: President Grant and the Indian Problem." *Arizona and the West* 13 (Winter 1971): 323–42.

——. "John C. Lowrie and Presbyterian Indian Administration, 1870–1882." *Journal of Presbyterian History* 54 (Summer 1976): 259–76.

——. "Presbyterian and Reformed Participation in the Indian 'Peace Policy' of the 1870s." Conference Group for Social and Administrative History, *Transactions* 5 (1974): 8–25.

Weber, Francis J. "Grant's Peace Policy: A Catholic Dissenter." *Montana the Magazine of Western History* (Winter 1969): 56–93.

White, Lonnie J. "Indian Raids on the Kansas Frontier, 1869." *Kansas Historical Quarterly* 38 (Winter 1972): 369–88.

Whitehead, Margaret. "Christianity, A Matter of Choice." *Pacific Northwest Quarterly* 72 (July 1981): 98–106.

Whitner, Robert L. "Grant's Indian Peace Policy on the Yakima Reservation, 1870–1882." *Pacific Northwest Quarterly* 50 (October 1959): 135–42.

Woodruff, K. Brent. "The Episcopal Mission to the Dakotas: 1860–1898." *South Dakota Historical Collections* 38 (1934): 554–603.

Index